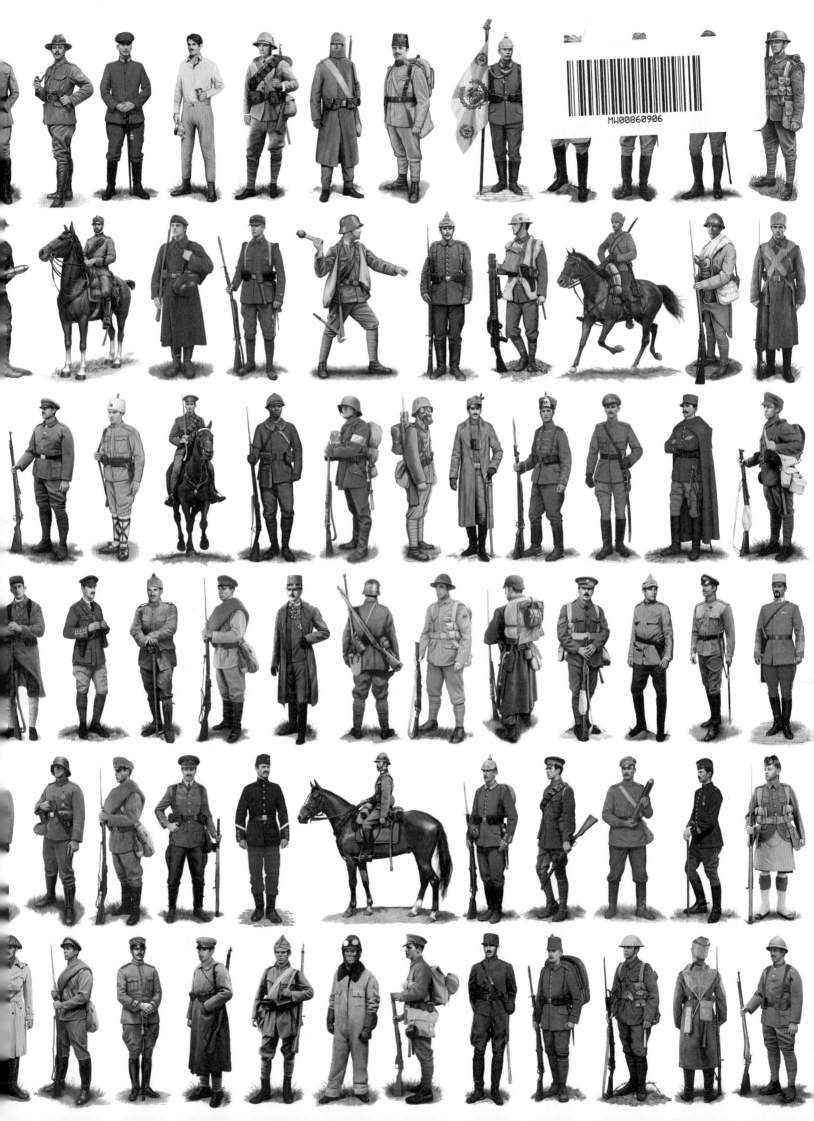

AN ILLUSTRATED ENCYCLOPEDIA OF
UNIFORMS OF WORLD WAR I

AN ILLUSTRATED ENCYCLOPEDIA OF
UNIFORMS OF WORLD WAR I

A expert guide to the uniforms of Britain, France, Russia, America, Germany and Austria-Hungary, with additional detail on the armies of Portugal, Belgium, Italy, Serbia, the Ottomans, Japan and more

JONATHAN NORTH • CONSULTANT: JEREMY BLACK MBE

LORENZ BOOKS

This edition is published by Lorenz Books
an imprint of Anness Publishing Ltd, Blaby Road,
Wigston, Leicestershire, LE18 4SE
Email: info@anness.com

www.lorenzbooks.com; www.annesspublishing.com

If you like the images in this book and would like to investigate
using them for publishing, promotions or advertising, please visit
our website www.practicalpictures.com for more information.

UK distributor: Book Trade Services; tel. 0116 2759086; fax 0116 2759090;
uksales@booktradeservices.com; exportsales@booktradeservices.com
North American distributor: National Book Network;
tel. 301 459 3366; fax 301 429 5746; www.nbnbooks.com
Australian distributor: Pan Macmillan Australia;
tel. 1300 135 113; fax 1300 135 103; customer.service@macmillan.com.au
New Zealand distributor: David Bateman Ltd;
tel. (09) 415 7664; fax (09) 415 8892

Publisher: Joanna Lorenz
Editorial Director: Helen Sudell,
Executive Editor: Joanne Rippin
Illustrations: Peter Bull Studio, Tom Croft, Jim Mitchell, Carlo Molinari,
Simon Smith, Sailesh Thakrar, Matthew Vince.
Designer: Nigel Partridge
Production Controller: Mai Ling Collyer

ETHICAL TRADING POLICY
Because of our ongoing ecological investment programme, you, as our
customer, can have the pleasure and reassurance of knowing that a tree is
being cultivated on your behalf to naturally replace the materials used to
make the book you are holding. For further information about this scheme,
go to www.annesspublishing.com/trees.

PUBLISHER'S NOTE
Although the advice and information in this book are believed to be accurate
and true at the time of going to press, neither the authors nor the publisher
can accept any legal responsibility or liability for any errors or omissions that
may have been made.

Frontispiece: A group of British soldiers about to board the train at Victoria
Station, London, on their way to the front line, 1915.

CONTENTS

INTRODUCTION 6
THE POLITICAL ARENA OF 1914 8
THE WAR'S ORIGINS 10
THE WORLD REACTS 12
THE GLOBAL VIEW 14
MANPOWER AND CONSCRIPTION 16
WEAPONS AND NEW TECHNOLOGY 20
UNIFORMS 22
THE CAMPAIGNS 24
AFTERMATH AND PEACE 34

GREAT BRITAIN 36
THE BRITISH ARMY 38
GENERALS AND STAFF 42
GUARDS 44
THE WESTERN FRONT 46
INFANTRY: OTHER THEATRES 56
CAVALRY 60
YEOMANRY 64
AVIATION 67
ARTILLERY 68
TECHNICAL TROOPS 70
TROOPS FROM CANADA AND NEWFOUNDLAND 72
TROOPS FROM AUSTRALIA AND NEW ZEALAND 74
AFRICAN TROOPS 76
THE INDIAN ARMY 78

FRANCE 80
THE FRENCH ARMY IN 1914 82
WARTIME DEVELOPMENTS 84
GENERALS AND STAFF 86

INFANTRY	88
CHASSEURS AND MOUNTAIN TROOPS	98
FOREIGN TROOPS	102
COLONIAL TROOPS	104
CAVALRY	108
ARTILLERY	112
TECHNICAL TROOPS	114
FLYING TROOPS	116

RUSSIA	**118**
THE RUSSIAN EMPIRE IN 1914	120
THE RUSSIAN ARMY	122
GENERALS AND STAFF	126
IMPERIAL GUARD	128
ELITE INFANTRY	130
INFANTRY	132
CAVALRY	142
COSSACKS AND NATIVE CAVALRY	144
ARTILLERY	146
TECHNICAL TROOPS	148
THE RUSSIAN CIVIL WAR: RED ARMIES	150
THE RUSSIAN CIVIL WAR: WHITE ARMIES	152

AMERICA AND OTHER ALLIES	**156**
THE USA ENTERS THE WAR	158
ALLIED ARMIES	160
US INFANTRY	162
US MARINES	166
US TECHNICAL TROOPS	168
PORTUGAL	170
BELGIUM	172

ITALY	176
SERBIA AND MONTENEGRO	180
ROMANIA	182
GREECE	184
JAPAN	186

GERMANY	**188**
A MILITARY STATE	190
PRUSSIA AND THE GERMAN STATES	192
WARTIME DEVELOPMENTS	194
GENERALS AND STAFF	196
GUARDS	198
INFANTRY	200
COLONIAL UNIFORMS	208
JÄGERS AND MOUNTAIN TROOPS	210
STORMTROOPERS	212
LANDWEHR	214
CAVALRY	216
ARTILLERY	220
TECHNICAL TROOPS	222

AUSTRIA-HUNGARY AND GERMANY'S OTHER ALLIES	**224**
THE HAPSBURG MONARCHY	226
AUSTRO-HUNGARIAN GENERALS AND STAFF	228
AUSTRO-HUNGARIAN INFANTRY	229
AUSTRO-HUNGARIAN CAVALRY	236
AUSTRO-HUNGARIAN LANDWEHR AND HONVÉD	238
AUSTRO-HUNGARIAN TECHNICAL TROOPS	240
THE OTTOMAN EMPIRE	242
BULGARIA	246

GLOSSARY	248
INDEX	251

INTRODUCTION

The war that started in 1914 was a dreadful blunder of unquantifiable proportions. It began following a series of political, military and diplomatic miscalculations and, arguably, ended in tragedy for those countries and individuals who were dragged into it. And it was a tragedy. What other word can be used to describe a series of events, which meant that, in 1919, there were 208,641 widows (out of a population of 2,426,187 women) in the small country of Bulgaria, or that France would lose 73 per cent of its mobilized men?

This was a war that bankrupted the victors and utterly destroyed the economies of the vanquished; pain

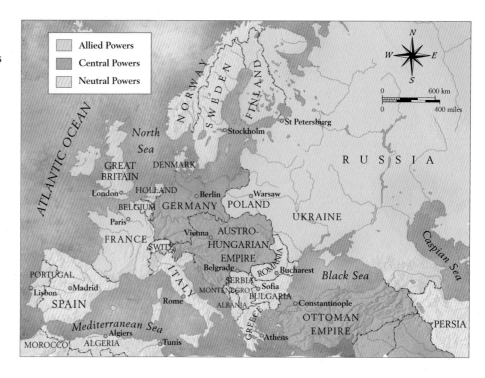

▲ In 1914, Europe's patchwork of rival powers coalesced into three sections: the Allies, the Central Powers, and the neutral countries.

augmented by a punitive peace. It was a conflict that disrupted the slowly evolving democratic systems and ushered in the age of the dictator, unleashing forces that could not be controlled by politicians. It also saw a series of campaigns of attrition, and massive battles that scarred the face of Europe, blighted European culture and made pre-war Europe seem like a golden age.

Edwardian Europe was not, of course, golden. For most people, particularly those on the margins of society, life was short and unpleasant. That fact has eluded the popular conception, which is to view Europe in 1914 as vibrant, progressive and opulently dressed.

When it comes to the subject of this particular study, the uniforms worn by the armies involved, the contrast between pre-war Europe and 1919 could not be more apparent. Many of the soldiers of 1900 were clothed in dark blues, reds, greens and whites. Those of 1919 dressed in khaki. This was an evolutionary process, designed to save lives and made more urgent by quickly developing battle technology.

▼ Army uniforms changed radically between 1853 and 1915: left, French Captain, 2nd Lancers 1853; middle, British Captain 2nd Hussars, 1858; right, German Sergeant, 17th Infantry Regiment (4th Westphalian), 1915.

Technical and Uniform Advances

Around 1910 most armies were adopting neutral colours in order to protect their soldiers from the ever-increasing weight of firepower available to Europe's military. It was a very sensible process and those who did not adapt paid a high price in lives lost: the fittest and the most highly trained were often killed first. Uniform was a key component in the attempt to negate the power exerted over the battlefield by weapons like the Maxim machine gun, France's 75mm gun or a Mauser fitted with an optical sight.

How bright, conspicuous uniforms were swapped for browns and greens, how badges of rank became subtle rather than flamboyant, and how protective equipment was adapted for the demands of modern warfare is a fascinating subject of study. One small example would be the use of divisional or brigade insignia. A series of signs and badges was developed by most armies once it became clear that denying intelligence to the enemy was of paramount importance. Use of insignia was supposed to confuse the enemy, and it has not made the historian's task any easier.

Inclusions and Exclusions

The book's focus on the armies of Europe and their colonies and dominions, plus those of Japan and the United States, has led to the exclusion of some fascinating units. One omission is the Brazilians (a medical detachment was sent to France in 1918), whose uniforms initially heralded French influence but then changed to a light brown uniform similar in style to the Portuguese. Others are the Senussi, who waged war on the Italians in Libya and troubled the British in Egypt; the uniforms worn by those states becoming independent in the Caucasus in 1918 and 1919 (Georgia, Armenia and Azerbaijan); and those adopted by Siam or the Chinese officers sent as observers to the Western Front. Persian uniforms deserve a book on their own, its armed forces including both Cossacks and European gendarmes;

Limitations of space have also meant that very few pages of this study have been devoted to naval warfare and uniforms, even when naval units were fighting on land. That is not to downplay the role of such units as Germany's Seebatallione or the 63rd (Royal Naval) Division. The war at sea was vital. The blockade of Germany prevented receipt of supplies, restricted the import of food and had a staggering effect on morale. Germany's submarine warfare, which brought the US into the war, and the shipping of troops also had massive implications for the way the war was fought.

▼ *German forces (shown in red) gathered to punch their way through to Paris and, much as they had done in 1870, end the war with one shattering blow. French forces (blue), supported by the British Expeditionary Force and the Belgian Army, positioned themselves to block the most likely routes to the capital.*

The book has been able, however, to give the reader a sense of the variety and complexity of uniforms worn during the conflict. While uniform regulations offer a guide, and contemporary photographs and descriptions give a reflection of the realities of war, it would not be too far-fetched to state that no two soldiers of this first world war looked the same. This inexhaustible supply of subjects and sources is what makes studying the military costume of this war so fascinating. This book serves as an exploration of a vast area of study which, despite the domineering presence of khaki and field grey, is also a very colourful subject.

'The Central Powers' is used throughout as a commonplace to denote Germany, Austria-Hungary, the Ottoman empire and Bulgaria; 'the Allies' refers to the numerous nations arranged against them.

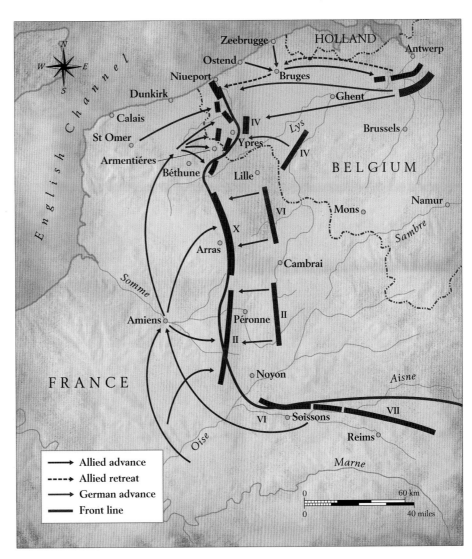

→	Allied advance
---→	Allied retreat
→	German advance
▬	Front line

THE POLITICAL ARENA OF 1914

In some ways, Europe was a flourishing continent in 1914. Its population of 467 million enjoyed more prosperity, improving health and political freedoms unimagined by their forebears. Women and the working classes were both beginning to flex their political muscles, and the old aristocratic ruling elite and status quo were being challenged. Populations were growing, which led to pressure in towns and cities, and also led to emigration from some of Europe's harsher peripheries (Scandinavia, southern Italy, Scotland) to the United States and South America. However, although conditions in many areas were improving, for many life was still short and uncomfortable.

Wealth, whether generated by industrialization, increased purchasing power or money flowing in from colonies, had a crucial impact on politics and daily life. For those lucky enough to have it, it opened up a world of possibilities from travel to

▼ *A corps of female drummers at a Votes for Women Exhibition in London, 13 May 1909. Women's emancipation was one of the new political movements of the early 1900s.*

fine art. For those marginalized by the wealth of others, it caused political agitation. Socialism, aiming to reduce inequalities, was on the rise in most countries and was a significant force in Germany, Italy and Russia. Politics was, however, still generally controlled by a narrow elite.

Great Britain
Enjoying a unique position as ruler of the world's largest empire (one fifth of the world's territory), Great Britain would grow still more by 1919. The island's population of 46 million was steadily rising, while those of Canada, Australia, and New Zealand were also predicted to show modest gains. The population of India was also on the increase, perhaps to 330 million by 1920. India was very much dependent on Britain, while Canada had achieved a measure of independent action in 1867, Australia in 1901, New Zealand in 1907 and South Africa in 1910.

Germany
Universally recognized as being Europe's most powerful state at the beginning of the 1900s, Germany had a thriving economy and a growing population (68 million in 1914). It stretched from Alsace and Lorraine all the way to what is now northern Poland and ran along the Baltic coast as far as modern Lithuania. It governed some minor colonies in the Pacific as well as more substantial African territory. Ruled by a kaiser (or emperor), and dominated by a Prussian political upper class, the Germans had waged successful short wars against France, Denmark and Austria-Hungary in order to unite.

Germany's Social Democrats may have been popular agitators for reform of an oppressive political system at the time, and were the largest party in parliament after 1912. The levers of power were, however, very much controlled by conservative forces.

▲ *Kaiser Wilhelm of Germany, pictured here in the foreground, with his personal entourage, sometime during 1914.*

France
Europe's most important republic, France had a population of 39.7 million and, since the humiliation of defeat by Prussia in 1870, had been an enthusiastic collector of colonies (which by 1914 included Algeria, Morocco and large parts of central and western Africa). Periodically, calls for revenge and to take back Alsace and Lorraine, annexed by Germany, made their presence felt particularly when Raymond Poincaré became president. Poincaré was from Lorraine, and recovery of lost land and prestige was the cornerstone of his policies. To the northeast, France was bordered by a fragile Belgium inhabited by French and Flemish speakers.

Italy and Portugal
Only united under the House of Savoy in the 1860s, Italy had a population of 35.3 million in 1914 but was divided between the thriving industrialized north, and a south where abject poverty tormented a largely illiterate population. Politically, the government enjoyed little popular support but occasionally stirred patriotic feeling by waging war for colonies (Abyssinia,

Libya, the Dodecanese islands), intriguing against France or defending Austria-Hungary's Italian-speaking minority. Portugal was in a similar position. Despite owning a vast empire, the majority of the population lived in poverty, misgoverned by a narrow elite of landowners.

The Austro-Hungarian Empire

This patchwork of ethnic minorities was Germany's principal ally in Europe. It was territorially impressive, including modern-day Slovakia, Czech Republic, Austria, Hungary, Croatia, Slovenia, Bosnia, southern Poland as well as most of modern Romania, but politically backward. It was known as the Dual Monarchy as the emperor of Austria was also king of Hungary. This divided the empire in two as the Hungarians had an autonomous government in Budapest, which ruled most of the empire's eastern territories (including Transylvania, a territory containing many Romanians who wanted to join the independent state of Romania on the eastern border). The empire had a joint army and a common foreign policy.

Russia

The Russian empire was physically even more impressive than the Austro-Hungarian territories. Russia's European population stood at 148.2 million people and the country's economy was expanding rapidly: steel production increased by 1000 per cent between 1880 and 1914.

Politically, Russia was an autocracy, dominated by the czar, a figure of hate for Europe's liberals as well as the increasingly angry socialists and violent anarchists in Russia's urban wastelands. The revolutionary unrest following defeat by Japan (1904–05) had led to some political reform and the establishment of the Duma, a poor substitute for a parliament.

Real power remained in the hands of the czar and a close circle of advisers. In addition to present-day Russia, the empire included Belarus, Ukraine, the eastern half of Poland, modern-day Moldova, Finland and the Baltic States. In the Caucasus and Asia it had absorbed vast territories but still squabbled with China, Persia and the Ottomans and British over borders.

▼ *Ottoman Army officer uniforms of 1895.*

▲ *Czar Nicholas II of Russia, and his wife, Alexandra, walk to the Duma, 1906.*

The Ottoman Empire

Ottoman decline had accelerated sharply between 1911 and 1913. Italy had defeated the European territories of the empire in North Africa and seized some islands in the Aegean. Serbia, Bulgaria and Greece had defeated the Ottomans in the Balkans and reduced the empire to a rump around the bustling city of Constantinople. Disaster, as so often before, pushed the Ottoman government slowly towards reform. The government itself was largely bankrupt, as most of the country's wealth had been handed over to European powers (France owned 62 per cent of the empire's foreign debt), but it turned to German advisers for technical expertise, and British ones for naval reform, in an attempt to modernize. The Ottomans maintained their control over most of the Middle East, including modern Iraq, much of Syria, Lebanon, Israel and Saudi Arabia. During the war, the empire was run by three pashas; Mehmed Talat, Ismail Enver and Ahmed Djemal.

Of those who gained from Ottoman defeat, Greece and Serbia were notable winners, while Bulgaria lost out to these Balkan rivals in the Second Balkan War. Serbia absorbed Kosovo and much of Macedonia, and became a formidable regional power and a threat to another tottering institution, the Austro-Hungarian empire.

THE WAR'S ORIGINS

As Archduke Franz Ferdinand lay bleeding to death in the back of a Gräf and Stift limousine, war was inevitable, but many assumed that when it came it would be a localized conflict. The nature of European politics meant that when war did break out, however, it quickly became general, sucking antagonists into a massive conflict of unprecedented proportions. The origins of that conflict can be traced back over the centuries and, although the war could have come sooner, by 1914 there was willingness, across Europe, to use war as a way of continuing diplomacy.

Political Pressures

The Europe of 1914 was no stranger to crisis but a major war had been avoided for decades. After the forces unleashed by the French Revolution had been defeated, Europe's Great Powers (Britain, Austria, Russia and Prussia), agreed to impose and keep the peace. This partnership could not last, however, and gave way to the new pressures that were exerted upon it by the unification of Germany and the waning of the Ottoman empire.

▼ *A French satirical print showing the Triple Alliance of Germany, Austria and Italy, published in* Le Petit Journal, *June 1896.*

▲ *The Congress of Berlin (1878) was held in order to halt Russian expansion into the Ottoman empire and to bolster that ailing power.*

Prussia had played a key role in the defeat of Napoleon, gaining territory and dictating terms to lesser states. The defeat of Austria-Hungary in 1866 sealed Prussia's status, and unification was given added lustre by the defeat of France and the seizure of Alsace-Lorraine in the Franco-Prussian War. Germany claimed the status of a great power, acquiring colonies and enjoying rapid economic growth.

An alliance with Austria-Hungary in 1879 formed a new bloc in central Europe and, three years later, Italy joined the alliance, creating the so-called Triple Alliance. The policies of Otto von Bismarck, Chancellor of Germany from 1871 to 1890, were assertive, ensuring Germany's voice was heard and its concerns treated as legitimate. His diplomatic skill meant that he largely operated in a restrained manner but, nevertheless, for Germany's neighbours the growth and ambitions of the new power were unsettling. France and Russia signed a military convention in 1892 and sealed this with a closer alliance in 1894. Britain, alarmed by German policies, especially its colonial ambitions, and naval expansion, entered into alliance with France in 1904 and with Russia in 1907. It did so, in part, to ensure that it was at peace with its colonial rival,

France, and with its imperial rival in much of Asia, Russia. As rivalries continued, and efforts to break alliances only led to a strengthening of resolve, the network of friendly powers became much more than guarantees of security. In many cases parties were now ready to act not only in self defence, but in defence of an alliance partner. When matters became strained beyond diplomacy, such a situation could only lead to hostile escalation.

The Balkan Problem

Ottoman territory in Europe had been shrinking steadily throughout the 19th century with Romania, Greece and Serbia emerging from Ottoman control. In the 1870s, in a more dramatic series of events, Serbia expanded at Ottoman expense, Bulgaria emerged as an autonomous territory and Austria-Hungary occupied Bosnia and Herzegovina.

The Great Powers intervened, and set new boundaries at the Congress of Berlin in 1878. But the situation remained tense until 1908, when a

▲ *Archduke Franz Ferdinand and his wife Sophie one hour before they would be killed by Gavrilo Princip as they drove through the streets of Sarajevo.*

group of reformers seized control of the Ottoman government, and Austria-Hungary scandalized Europe by opportunistically annexing Bosnia that October. Russia was outraged, Serbia mobilized and German warnings forced a Russia weakened by the turmoil of 1905 into accepting the situation. The Ottomans were then further weakened by a war with Italy in 1911 and defeat at the hands of the Balkan powers in the First Balkan War, a victory which enlarged Serbia and helped it recover from the humiliation of 1908.

The Austro-Hungarians smarted at this reversal of fortune and partially mobilized along the Serbian border in 1912 in order to 'protect' Bosnia (and added to the tension by announcing emergency rule there in May 1913). Russia countered with its own partial mobilization in Poland, and the situation was only defused by strenuous diplomatic efforts in which the Austro-Hungarians were mollified by the creation of an independent Albania blocking Serbian expansion to the Adriatic. The Germans supported their ally, insisting on the withdrawal of Serb troops from Albanian territory.

For decision-makers in Vienna, and those who supported them in Berlin, it was clear that the situation in the

Balkans could be managed by force, that there was little reason to grant concessions to Slavs in the Austro-Hungarian empire (a policy advocated by Archduke Franz Ferdinand, heir to the imperial throne), and that, while Russia was dominated by Germany, Austria-Hungary could dictate terms. Russia was itself faced by a loss of influence in the region – Bulgaria was sullenly pro-Austrian, while the Ottomans turned to Germany to reinvigorate their defeated armed forces. Only Serbia remained pro-Russian, although there was no formal treaty between the two powers.

The Spark and the Powder Keg

That was the tense and complex political situation in June 1914 when Franz Ferdinand visited Sarajevo, the administrative capital of Bosnia and

Herzegovina, on a state visit. A radical group opposed to Austrian rule, known as Young Bosnia, had been plotting an assassination since Emperor Franz Josef's visit to Bosnia in 1909. A bomb had targeted the military governor in 1910, and in January 1914 plans were being made to kill Franz Ferdinand in Paris. News that the archduke would attend military manoeuvres that summer and visit Sarajevo on 28 June (a key Serbian national day) sent the plotters into fevered activity.

Working closely with the Black Hand organization, a secret Serbian faction, Young Bosnia members, some of whom had been training in Serbia, conceived a plot in which a series of attempts would be made on the archduke's life. In the event, after a series of near misses, one of the Young Bosnia activists, Gavrilo Princip, was presented with the ideal opportunity when the archduke's car reversed past him while trying to get back on the main road.

The assassin killed the archduke's Czech wife, Sophie, instantly, with a shot to the stomach, while the second shot hit the archduke himself in the jugular. Archduke Franz Ferdinand was unconscious by the time he reached hospital and died from blood loss shortly afterwards.

▼ *The assassin who shot Archduke Franz Ferdinand and his wife, Gavrilo Princip, was arrested after the shooting. Here he is dragged into police headquarters in Sarajevo.*

THE WORLD REACTS

Many in the Austro-Hungarian government saw the assassination as an opportunity to settle scores with Serbia, a state which might one day presume to break up the Hapsburgs multinational but fragile empire. That such a localized conflict might drag in Russia, startled by decreasing influence in the Balkans, was a known risk, but it was assumed that German support would offset this. The first step, it was decided, was to punish Serbia for the act of some Bosnian renegades.

Vienna's first priority was to confirm German support, and this was unconditionally given by Berlin by 6 July. An ultimatum, designed to be unacceptable, was then issued to Serbia on 25 July. The Serbs went so far as to almost accept the conditions, only rejecting the clause that Austrian officials take part in an official enquiry into the assassination. Their reply was handed over to the Austrian ambassador on the same day; he declared it unacceptable and promptly left Belgrade. The Serbs evacuated their capital, mobilized their army and prepared for hostilities, which began the next day.

▼ Serbian volunteers joined up to prevent Austro-Hungarian aggression. Here, some time during 1914, a group of them arrive at the War Bureau to enlist.

▲ King Peter of Serbia faced an impossible situation in August 1914.

Germany's Dilemma

In Germany, the government was divided between those who wanted to seize the moment and wage war with a resurgent Russia, and those who balked at what the consequences might be. Austria-Hungary's declaration of war on Serbia was overshadowed by Russia's reaction. This time it was apparent that Russia would stand by the Serbs; Russia's ambassador in Vienna had made a friendly but firm declaration on 22 July that Russia would not suffer Serbia's dignity being compromised. Austria's ultimatum, however, made it clear that it would push ahead regardless; Russia sought the diplomatic intervention of the Great Powers, and counselled Serbia 'to offer no resistance'.

Russia's Reaction

The recall of soldiers to barracks on 26 July was Russia's first response. A partial mobilization, something the Russians had not planned for, but which seemed an appropriate warning to Austria, was next decided on, even though only 13 corps were ordered up (while plans called for 16 corps in any war with Austria) and then only in the Kiev, Odessa, Kazan and Moscow districts (but not Warsaw, which bordered Austrian territory). The Russians sent telegram 1539 on 28 July, declaring a partial mobilization.

Germany warned against this, saying that a continuation of military preparations would lead to war. The nervous czar reminded the kaiser in a telegram on 31 July that even full mobilization did not necessarily mean war. Generals in every capital, however, knowing that in the age of the offensive, the first to strike held all the advantages, hectored the politicians. Then the Austrians bombarded Belgrade. Russia's generals urged the czar to order full mobilization; he dithered, but placards eventually went up all over Russia on 31 July. Germany declared war on Russia the next day.

Germany knew that it had to be a double-fronted war. All its plans were built around the fact that if Russia and Germany went to war, then France would be involved too. Indeed, France was the more dangerous opponent. France had been supportive of Russia, and Chief of the French General Staff, Joseph Joffre, even reminded the Russians that the alliance required full mobilization and an offensive into East Prussia. Had the Russians hoped that the existence of a Franco-Russian alliance might intimidate Germany, they were wrong. The Germans were

▲ *A troop of Cossacks prepare to ride westwards in 1914.*

aiming at defeating France first before turning eastwards. Russia's speedy mobilization triggered a fast German response: Berlin demanded that France remain neutral. No assurances were received, and with French mobilization beginning on 1 August, Germany declared war on the French on 3 August and prepared to invade.

Great Britain's Crisis

Germany's chosen invasion route was through Belgium, a state whose neutrality had been protected by a treaty of 1839, even though France, Britain and Germany had all contemplated infringing those rights in the event of war. Germany was the first

▼ *A patriotic postcard from 1915 entitled 'United against barbarism' depicts a French and an English soldier side by side.*

actually to do so, and following an ultimatum of 2 August, German troops crossed the frontier on the morning of 4 August 1914.

Great Britain had initially hoped for a diplomatic solution to the situation, and was bitterly disappointed that Germany had been unable to halt or moderate Austro-Hungarian actions. In any case, obligated to France and Russia, and nervous that a German success against either would guarantee German domination of Europe, the British government of Asquith was prepared to enter the war before the Belgian border was breached, but were not sure that such a move would prove popular with the electorate. Belgium under threat solved everything, however, it united public opinion and provided a cause; on 4 August Britain was also at war with Germany.

▼ *Londoners present flowers to British troops heading for the Western Front in 1916.*

Acceleration

The race to get armies on to trains began, and the push to induce the non-aligned into the conflict also continued apace. The Ottomans, smarting at defeat in 1913, and grateful to Germany for military assistance and loans, allied themselves with Germany in November 1914. Italy, nominally allied to the Central Powers, was at first neutral but was tempted by the Allies with promises of Austro-Hungarian territory (whereas the Central Powers could offer very little) and entered the war in 1915. Bulgaria followed the opposite path, siding with the Central Powers in 1915 in order to be revenged on Serbia.

The war cannot be said to have started by accident. Cold calculations were at work, just as much for the smaller powers as for the Great Powers. That these calculations were, in reality, an outrageous form of gambling would only be revealed in hindsight.

THE GLOBAL VIEW

It was inevitable that the European powers would export the 1914 conflict beyond the frontiers of the continent. Their international activity and colonial commitments ensured that they would fight each other in Africa, in Asia and on the high seas.

War Beyond Europe

Naturally, this range of activity led to independent powers retaliating against threats, or creating opportunities to benefit from the wider conflict. The United States declared war on Germany to retaliate against unrestricted submarine warfare. Japan was more aggressive, being involved in the conquest of German territory in the Pacific and the German concession at Tsingtao, besieged and conquered in 1914. Japan, indeed, would be a great beneficiary of the war; at the cost of relatively few casualties it acquired a useful foothold in China, new markets and, following the Russian Revolution, a presence in Siberia that would last until 1923.

Colonial Involvement

Exporting the war also meant that Europe's colonies would be involved in campaigns. The Allies and the Central Powers sought to divert their enemies from other theatres or acquire new territory at the expense of their foes. Thus, German colonies in Africa found themselves in the front line, while the Kaiser's possessions in the Pacific were soon forced to surrender in the face of overwhelming odds.

European powers also exploited manpower from colonies and territories. Many units raised from African and Asian personnel fought in Europe, others were despatched to fight in campaigns in Africa or the Middle East, or to serve in garrisons on newly conquered territories. Troops from Senegal served in France's armies on the Western Front and in the Balkans, at Gallipoli and in Africa. This was not a first, France's African subjects had fought the Prussians in 1870, but now the larger scale, and conscription, led to social unrest in West Africa.

▲ *A balloon observer, prepares to make an ascent over Mesopotamian territory.*

▼ *French colonial infantry, probably Algerian, inspect equipment that has been captured from German forces during the Battle of the Marne of September 1914.*

Recruitment was not restricted to volunteers for the armed forces; many colonial civilians, particularly Africans, worked as carriers. Some were conscripted, some volunteered. In the course of the war Britain employed more than a million such labourers. Conditions were harsh and disease killed and crippled many thousands.

Finance, Trade and Self-determination

Europe's colonies and dominions also provided financial support (India granted Britain £100 million outright in 1918, for example) and material goods (from food to boot leather). Nor did the peoples of Africa and Asia go economically untouched by the conflict, because local economies were often tied up in the global economy. Economic hardship brought about by the onset of war in 1914 was quickly felt in West Africa, while South America suffered from disruption to imports and the supply of skilled labour. A shortage of shipping meant that vital trade was marginalized in favour of the needs of war which, in turn, led to a fall in revenue from customs duties. A run on currencies affected prices in India and the Middle East, and a lack of gold and silver led to India buying in American silver. Some economies benefited from such a situation; US industry began penetrating new markets, while Japan was remarkably effective as an economic power in China and India, and even sold arms to Russia.

As the war continued, such trade hardships were augmented by an increased financial burden on colonies and dependencies, together with greater pressure to supply soldiers or labourers. India was forced to introduce local taxation. Certain foods were scarce (such as salt and, sporadically, grain) either because of the demand to export, poor harvests or the lack of the means to distribute effectively. Populations concentrated in towns, particularly in India, suffered from shortages and rampant inflation. Similar financial hardship led to revolution in Russia, while in India it

▲ *The war at sea was predominantly the struggle against German submarines, and to keep the sea lanes open for vital food and supplies for Europe.*

caused a series of strikes and widespread looting. Such hardships forced imperial governments to grant concessions such as constitutional reform in India in 1919. In India, war had radicalized public opinion and, to a certain degree, nurtured a nascent nationalism. A similar process could be observed in Canada and Australia where participation in a European

▼ *Indian soldiers formed a part of the British Expeditionary Force in France in 1914.*

conflict turned many against being dictated to from Europe, but also forged a stronger sense of national identity. Even in Africa, where society was less cohesive, similar results could be seen.

France encouraged recruits from Algeria by granting the colony financial and political concessions and special exemptions that remained in force after the war. The withdrawal of European workers and administrators meant that some posts were made available for native populations. But political concessions, akin to those granted to Indians, were not made in British Africa and, even in French territories, were largely restricted to North African colonies.

Neutral States

Aside from belligerents making demands on their possessions, the war would also have an impact on neutrals. The Netherlands experienced hardship due to food shortages and the pressures brought about by an influx of refugees. A similar situation prevailed in Scandinavia. Added to this, neutral countries sustained a great number of casualties among their merchant navies. The war had a greedy and global grasp, and its impact, like that of no other European war, shook a world far away from the confines of Flanders, the mountains of Italy or the plains of Poland.

MANPOWER AND CONSCRIPTION

With such a huge conflict zone, involving several countries, borders and terrains, manpower was almost immediately the most pressing concern of every nation involved in the war.

Whether in peacetime or during times of war, national service was a fact of life in 1914 for the majority of European males. Britain was an exception, relying on a professional force of volunteers. What the British Army had in quality, however, it lacked in quantity (prompting Bismarck to quip that if it invaded Germany he would send the police to arrest it) and, as casualties mounted, Britain too was forced to rely on conscription.

Exemptions

Nations in arms may have been the ideal in 1914, but in reality there were so many exemptions that conscription tended to target certain groups.

Conscripts were referred to as the class or cohort of a particular year. Peacetime service was followed by obligatory service in some kind of reserve followed by service in a

▼ A Russian war poster urges civilians to buy war bonds; 'All for the war, all for Victory'.

territorial unit. In wartime reservists would be called back into the ranks or, additionally, men could be called up early, so that the class of 1916 could be called to the colours in 1915.

As the scale of the war increased, and the numbers of men in combat mounted, Europe's governments were forced to reduce exemptions while, at the same time, requiring more and more labourers for the industries supporting the war effort. The population was therefore squeezed at both ends, often with unfortunate results. Austria-Hungary, for example, would be forced to field a regiment (number 104) whose personnel consisted of men with eye infections, while Britain sent the medically unfit 2/10 Royal Scots to northern Russia in 1918 to fight the Bolsheviks.

Conscription in Russia

In 1912 Russia's system conformed to a pattern of three bands, with peacetime conscripts, aged 21, serving for three years with liability then to serve in the reserves and the territorial militias. Obligation to serve was weakened by numerous exemptions: only sons, for example, and the educated, who served a shorter term in the ranks. Certain religious minorities and ethnic groups were also excused service.

Initial conscription led to many workers badly needed in munitions factories being conscripted, and then released. The Army, which was short of manpower, had low physical standards, leading to large numbers falling sick in 1914. Casualties were also so high that Russia mortgaged its future by calling up cohorts earlier than anticipated, sending the wounded back to the front, and decimating rural communities. This led to friction and, eventually, revolution. Paradoxically Russia did well out of foreign volunteers, raising two divisions of Serbs, a Romanian Volunteer Corps and, most famously, the Czech Legion.

▲ Two German Army officers paste up mobilization posters in Berlin, Germany, on 1 August 1914.

French Reserves

Unlike Russia, France entered the war with fewer exemptions and some 80 per cent of males aged between 18 and 46 would be serving with the armed forces by 1915. This hit French society hard and the government was forced to explore alternatives such as colonial conscripts and Chinese labourers. France also benefited from the arrival of foreign volunteers: Italians joined the Foreign Legion as did Peruvians, Czechs and Poles.

French colonies provided large numbers of military personnel. Conscription had been introduced into many colonies in 1912 and was extended to others in 1914. In Africa enforcement was poor, with local authorities making up numbers by press ganging the sick or troublesome. The bulk of the conscripts served in the colonial army and received lower pay, could not become officers and received a smaller pension following discharge. Nevertheless, they were fed familiar food and French authorities took the

▲ *The warrior knight was a common image in 1914, as shown in this German poster.*

▲ *Germany asks support for its submarine fleet with 'Give to the U-boat collection'.*

trouble to winter colonial units in warmer climes. Concessions were also made so that, by 1917, distinguished service led to French citizenship.

Italy's Soldiers

As a comparatively young and fragile state, only really united in 1870, Italy had a fragmented population, and politicians saw conscription as a way of making the country's subjects feel Italian. However, as the north was heavily industrialized, the burden of conscription fell predominantly on the rural south. Italy opted for neutrality in 1914, something that was actually in accordance with its agreements as part of the Triple Alliance.

Militarily, Italy was indeed unprepared, and social unrest, headed by the Socialist Party, which organized a national protest against war in February 1915, worried the ruling classes to such an extent that, in March 1915, when the country declared war it was only on Austria-Hungary. Even then the lack of a clear war aim meant that a high proportion of Italians failed to respond to the call to arms (some of these were absent, working abroad). On the day war was declared, Italy fielded 14 Army Corps and the majority of its troops were available for

service in Europe, while a strong presence of 43,000 men was maintained in recently acquired Libya. By July Italy had 31,037 officers and 1,059,042 troops under arms.

The German System

Germany, for all that it was seen as a militaristic state, had wrestled with conscription laws since the 1870s. The Army's peacetime strength had stagnated at around 500,000 even as late as 1904; conservatives were unwilling to expand further because they did not want to dilute the officer class, while moderates felt it would prove unpopular. In 1912 reforms were put in place to increase the Army to 750,000, but only 53 per cent of those eligible for service actually served.

German conscripts joined the army aged 20 and were then liable to serve until they were 45. The system was flexible and relatively fair: the very young and the old were kept in reserve. Compared to the Russian system, there were fewer exemptions and Germany actually mobilized slightly more men than Russia and a much higher proportion of its population. Conscripts were supported by a large number of volunteers joining the Army in the first months of war, with

perhaps some 300,000 flocking to the colours. Some of these had travelled great distances out of a sense of duty: the 26th Dragoons included two volunteers from Jerusalem and one from Argentina. By the first month of the war, Germany had 2.9 million men under arms and by 1918 some 7 million. This was achieved by calling in the exempt, the young and the unfit.

The Empires

Austria-Hungary had a relatively lax system of recruitment when war broke out. Its economy meant that it had to keep its army small, and less than 1 per cent of the population were serving in 1914. Military service was unpopular and, in certain sectors, deeply resented whether it was in the Imperial Army, Landwehr units from Austrian territory or Honvéd units from the Kingdom of Hungary. The nature of the empire resulted in the majority of officers being of German origin (although there were two Chinese in 1914). Even in non-German units, rank and file were recruited across multinational subject peoples.

The Ottoman Empire was the most severely challenged of the larger powers. Its population of 23 million

▼ *New recruits to the Austro-Hungarian Army. The extravagantly decorated hats and garlands denote their newly enlisted status.*

could not provide as many troops as those of the European Great Powers. Endemic corruption, stagnation and a lack of resources meant that mobilization was an incredibly complex operation – an operation exacerbated by the fact that the army would have to serve on four or five fronts simultaneously. It was a situation made worse by the loss, in 1912 and 1913, of most of the empire's more wealthy European territories.

The reformist government that came to power in 1908, best, although loosely, known as the Young Turks, attempted to put in place fundamental reforms. In 1909, for example, they sacked a huge number of elderly generals and promoted from younger officers. They also made it clear that compulsory conscription, regardless of religion, was to be enforced. The laws regarding conscription for the Muslim majority were also tightened, the population of Constantinople being, for the first time, obliged to undergo military service. Even so some reports stated that only 75 per cent of those obliged to serve actually made it to the colours. Wartime mobilization made it possible for the Ottomans to field some 800,000 men, a small number considering Gallipoli alone led to 300,000 casualties. By March 1918, the

Ottomans had only around 200,000 men under arms, a situation made worse by severe levels of desertion.

The Ottoman regular army preferred to recruit Kurds into gendarme units, and some escaped the obligation of serving in the army through corruption and bribery. Yet numbers of Jewish and Christian minorities served the Ottoman rulers, fighting alongside the vast majority of illiterate peasant soldiers recruited from the Ottoman heartlands of eastern Anatolia.

Britain's Volunteers

Great Britain was the exception to the Great Power rule. Ministers were aware of the demands of modern, global warfare and that those demands would require manpower, but Britain relied on a system of voluntary enlistment. It had a regular army, backed up by a small reserve and part-time Territorial troops, who made no commitment to serve abroad. Britain's regular army was supposed to meet the initial challenge and was boosted by a surge of volunteers: 175,000 volunteered in the first week of September 1914 alone. The volunteers were, as in Germany, mostly middle

▲ *A British Army poster attracts recruits by showing the new technology available*

class. However, by the winter of 1915, it was apparent that Britain's role in the war could only be maintained or expanded by compulsory service in one form or another. A Military Service Act in January 1916 conscripted single men and childless widowers in England, Scotland and Wales between 18 and 41. This was expanded to include married men in May 1916. By 1918 just under five million men were under arms. Of these half were volunteers and half were conscripts.

The contribution of the British Isles was supplemented by manpower from the overseas empire. Some 2.8 million men from the empire would fight in the war, half of them coming from India. Australia deployed 416,000 volunteers in the Australian Imperial Force, but resisted conscription. New Zealand introduced conscription in the summer of 1916 (exempting Maoris), but South Africa preferred to rely on volunteers. In Canada conscription was introduced in May 1917, and met with widespread hostility. However, most of the 365,000 Canadians who served were volunteers. Indian regiments were recruited predominantly from the Punjab and Nepal, and concentrated in units of the same ethnic group.

▼ *Recruits gather in response to Lord Derby's recruiting campaign in Southwark, London.*

▲ *An American poster urges recruits to remember the sinking of the* Lusitania.

Smaller States

The majority of smaller European states followed the standard pattern. Bulgaria, which mobilized the greatest proportion of its population, adopted the Russian system. Every male, except those who had forfeited their rights, was liable. Those who were unfit could pay to be exempt, while non-Christians could pay a tax of 500 Francs to avoid conscription. Recruits generally joined the colours in February, although in wartime recruitment was automatic following a man's eighteenth birthday. Military service, of one kind or another, continued until men reached the age of 46.

America's Policy

The United States was different again, having a small peacetime army of just 100,000 strong in early 1917 and one singularly unprepared for war outside the USA. In May 1917 the Selective Service Act, a kind of conscription for those between 21 and 30, came into force. Some 24 million men would register and 2.8 million men were actually drafted. Some bodies remained all-volunteer units, such as the Marine Corps. The US President, Woodrow Wilson, had advanced this

form of enlistment as being the most democratic, and the draft, as it was called, did indeed mean that large numbers of men from ethnic minorities and recent immigrants found themselves in uniform.

It is still argued whether or not draft boards accepted African-American volunteers so that white Americans could stay at home. Whether nor not this was the case, the Army leadership certainly preferred to concentrate black recruits into pioneer regiments or into specific black units (such as the 369th). Segregation was so rigorously applied that the black troops were actually loaned to the French and were largely equipped and fed by America's allies. Native American Indians were, on the other hand, fully assimilated, despite many of them not being US citizens (it was not until 1924 that citizenship was conferred on all American Indians).

In America, and in the other countries involved in the war, the constant need for manpower led to the armies of 1914 and, more so, of 1918, welcoming volunteers of all kinds, drawing indiscriminatingly from all sections of society. Conscription, the tool of democracy and autocracy alike, meant that by 1918 the healthy and enthusiastic would be fighting

▲ *Uncle Sam calls 'Don't Wait for the Draft' in an American recruitment poster.*

alongside the unfit and reluctant. This situation was mirrored in the factories and fields. Such was the pressing need for manpower that it seemed that entire nations were serving the war.

▼ *Canada objected to conscription from Britain, but many individuals volunteered to fight, as this huge crowd outside Toronto Town Hall shows.*

WEAPONS AND NEW TECHNOLOGY

The industrialization of the 19th century, and the advent of new technologies, made a lasting impression on the battlefield. New technology, produced on a large scale, changed the face of warfare forever.

Heavy Artillery
Some 67 per cent of all casualties in World War I were inflicted by artillery. It would dominate the battlefield, shape the terrain and make a lasting (and terrible) impression on all the infantrymen involved in the war.

By the close of the 19th century armies were already overhauling their artillery. A major change came in 1896 when the French introduced the 75mm field gun. It had an ingenious hydraulic system, which absorbed recoil, it was quick to load and could fire around 20 rounds (of shrapnel) a minute. Germany deployed some extremely heavy pieces, such as 420mm howitzers, with a range of six miles that were useful when the war began to stagnate, along with 305mm mortars, useful for trench warfare.

The intensity of artillery use increased during the war. The barrage before the Somme offensive on 1 July 1916 saw the British use 1,431 guns firing 1.7 million shells in seven days.

▲ One of Germany's railway guns, which were mounted on, transported by and fired from specially designed railway wagons.

Infantry Weapons
Breech-loading rifles made an appearance in the 1840s and enabled infantry to load quickly, and from a prone position. From this the magazine rifle quickly developed and, by the time of the Boer War, most armies could boast relatively effective, rapid-fire rifles. The Boers had German Mausers, and the British used Lee

▼ French troops in 1915 use one of the earliest forms of gas masks.

Enfields. The Mauser could be loaded with a clip of five rounds, an advantage that led to the British adopting the improved Short Model Lee Enfield (SMLE) in 1902. The SMLE was a manually operated, rotating bolt action magazine-fed rifle, with the magazine containing 10 rounds in two five-round clips. Such weapons were capable of rapid fire, but only in the hands of a highly trained professional. Most conscripts could probably achieve ten rounds per minute.

The advent of lighter semi-automatic weapons later in the war meant that even hurriedly trained troops could rely on a sustained rate of fire with the adoption of the light machine gun in 1915.

Machine Guns and Grenades
Heavy machine guns had developed in the 1850s, and the appearance of the Gatling gun in 1862 marked a new phase in warfare. Although this gun required hand cranking, it began a technological race that soon led to the production of the Maxim machine gun in 1884. The Germans were quick to adopt a weapon based on the Maxim in 1901, developing it in 1908 (the Maschinengewehr 08). The British took up the idea later, developing the Vickers Mark I in 1912. The French had the Hotchkiss, which could fire 600 rounds per minute or, in sustained fire, 450 rounds per minute. This was a devastating contribution to warfare.

Trench warfare called for weapons that had been reserved for siege warfare. First among these was the hand grenade. Hand grenades had been used in the Russo-Japanese War, and in 1913 the German Army adopted the round Kugelhandgranate. Stick grenades were also developed as were smaller, portable bombs (the 'egg' grenade of 1917). Grenade throwers and trench mortars added to the type of firepower that could be brought to bear on the opponent's trench.

Gas

The French police had teargas grenades, but it was the Germans who first used 'asphyxiating or deleterious gasses' in warfare (all too quickly followed by the indignant Allies). Gas shells were fired against the Russians in early 1915 but with little result; the Germans then released gas from 5,700 cylinders on 22 April 1915 near Ypres. It caused panic but the Germans did not take advantage of the confusion to achieve a breakthrough. From then on, however, gas, and the means to fight it, became a permanent feature on most fronts. Some 30 different substances were selected as being the most effective, from tear gas to asphyxiates (phosgene and chlorine) to the horrific mustard gas used in 1917. After the war, gas would be used against the Bolsheviks in Russia and against rebellious tribes in Egypt and Iraq.

Land Transportation

In 1897 the Austro-Hungarian Army's purchase of a Daimler lorry quietly started a revolution in military mobility. Although railways wrought fundamental changes in the way troops were mobilized and transported, road vehicles would increasingly play a vital role in moving supplies and dragging

▲ *A German observational balloon, in Poland.*

artillery (and then, with the creation of the armoured car and later the tank, in creating mobile firepower). They were also useful for the staff, both for staff cars and motorbike despatch carriers.

Bulgaria could organize a fleet of 150 military vehicles in 1913, while the entire Ottoman empire contained fewer than 300 motor vehicles. Most trucks were usually commandeered from civilians in 1914 (Parisian taxis ferried troops to the Marne in 1914) but, slowly, distinct branches of service were equipped with vehicles and required to maintain them.

Flight

Petrol engines also enabled the construction of machines that could propel themselves into the air. Balloons had been used in the 1790s for observation purposes (and they would feature heavily in the same role between 1914 and 1918). Airships began to make an appearance in the late 1890s, with the first Zeppelin taking to the air in 1900.

Other flying machines quickly surpassed this leviathan of the air in speed and manoeuvrability (if not in the ability to remain in the skies for an extended period). On 25 July 1909 the French aviator Louis Blériot had successfully crossed the English Channel for the first time. Just two years later the Italians were dropping bombs over Ottoman forces in Libya, and air raids made an appearance in the Balkan Wars. The Germans watched with interest and, making use of skills that had been developed in the manufacture of airship engines, turned to the creation of aeroplanes. Britain was more hesitant, but formed an air battalion in 1911.

As the war began, light aircraft used for reconnaissance evolved into observation aircraft or fighters. Heavier aircraft, for longer range bombing duties, would follow.

▼ *The taxis of the Marne, outside the Ecole Militaire. In 1914 French authorities dispatched some 600 cabs to ferry 6,000 reserve infantry troops to the front before the First Battle of the Marne.*

THE UNIFORMS

World War I is still seen as the birth of the modern era when it comes to uniforms. In fact, most armies had switched to what we might call something resembling today's military dress well before 1914, and those that had delayed (France, Belgium and Austria-Hungary) quickly found the resources to catch up in late 1914.

The Limits of Colour

As far back as the Seven Years War (1756–63) German light infantry (jägers) had shown a preference for dark green uniforms with black leather equipment. European troops serving in hot climates also made use of practical white, buff or brown. In battlefields that were shrouded in thick smoke and with troops using highly inaccurate weapons, camouflage was never really an issue. Indeed it was vital that a general could recognize and control his own troops from a distance. This led to brightly clothed lines and columns of infantry criss-crossing European battlefields. Even Napoleonic armies, however, famous for their resplendent colours, covered

▼ *The Battle of Isandlwana, 22 January 1879, during the Zulu War, where British soldiers were still wearing their red coats.*

their bright reds and blues with grey or brown greatcoats to protect uniforms manufactured from cloth and dyed with natural colours that soon faded.

Troops in the American Civil War (1861–65) were more restrained, partly due to the cost of equipping hastily raised mass armies, but those of the Franco-Prussian War (1870–71)were again brightly uniformed. This immediately led to high casualties; in August 1870 at the Battle of Gravelotte, firepower decimated the closed ranks of Prussian Guards as they advanced at St Privat, resulting in 20,163 casualties. By the end of the war, the Germans knew they had to offer as small a target as possible and that bright colours were an unwelcome distraction.

Modification

British experience in the Boer War (1899–1902), combined with pressure from officers who had served in India, led to the universal introduction of khaki in 1908. Other countries followed suit or used local cloth that could reduce visibility (the Bulgarians used brown). Of the vast conscript armies, the Germans adopted field grey in 1910, Russia adopted a light green after defeat against Japan in 1904–05. The French toyed with a greenish

▲ *Not all uniforms worn by the British were khaki, as shown here in these uniforms in India at the start of the war.*

brown cloth in 1911, but the experiment did not receive official sanction and the French Army went into battle in the summer of 1914 in blue and red. Conservatives defended the move, suggesting that camouflage was cowardly and that, as French tactics revolved around letting the enemy see and be intimidated by bayonet attacks, bright colours served a purpose. It proved a costly experiment.

Maintaining Regulations

The uniforms worn by men going into battle were not strictly uniform, and quickly became even less so. Each army had dress regulations, detailed codes for various functions (full dress, campaign dress), but these were not always adhered to in the field. For example, British regulations required brown ankle boots for service dress, but black boots were very common. Modifications were made by individual soldiers, as can be seen in contemporary photographs, or as are detailed in memoirs and letters, sometimes with the sanction of officers, sometimes without.

Supplying quickly raised armies posed problems for all commissariat departments, and it was frequently the case that soldiers being sent to the front had to make use of outdated uniform items and individual

▲ *This photograph of a British soldier eating his dinner, taken some time in 1917, shows how uniforms were adapted to the dreadful conditions of life in the trenches.*

equipment. Some German Landwehr units were sent westwards in 1914 sporting dark blue tunics. This situation was more pronounced when it came to leather equipment (which was usually long-lasting) and a variety of belts, cartridge pouches and knapsacks were taken into battle. Replacement items arrived sporadically, if at all, and most units ended up with a mixture of items.

Some armies relied on captured material, having insufficient resources of their own. The Bulgarians made use of German equipment captured from the Ottomans in the Balkan Wars (and later supplemented directly from their German ally's stocks). The Serbian Army, after 1916, was almost completely re-equipped by the French. White units in the Russian Civil War could be seen wearing British or French uniforms.

A few armies were so short of items that they made use of civilian items, particularly boots, and paid conscripts to retain whatever footwear they were wearing on arrival at the barracks. Even throughout the war, soldiers wore items sent from home. Troops in the trenches wore gloves, balaclavas and sheepskin jackets to keep warm. Officers, who purchased their uniforms privately, showed even greater variety in overcoats, waterproofs and even the exact cut and colour of their uniforms.

New items of equipment, such as helmets, were introduced at certain dates but not always issued on time or universally. For example, photographs of French infantry regiments marching to the front in the autumn of 1915 show the troops wearing a mixture of helmets and caps. British troops initially wore helmets in the trenches only, leaving these items behind for their replacements when they were finally relieved.

Uniforms themselves were often manufactured to different standards. Most cloth was dyed synthetically in 1914, but natural dyes were sometimes used when demand was too great or supplies of synthetic components too short. The mass-produced cloth was supposed to follow a colour standard, but this was difficult to achieve as so many different factories and mills were at work, and variation in colours was normal. Natural dyes were particularly prone to bleaching or being washed out but even synthetic dyes faded, and French horizon blue in particular quickly faded to a light grey.

Evolution in the Field

Uniforms evolved during the course of the conflict. Conditions at the front made modifications to uniforms essential. Officers quickly found it prudent to disguise their rank as much as possible to prevent themselves from being targeted. Some wore other ranks' dress with a minimum of insignia.

▲ *A group of British officers, including winner of the Victoria Cross, Lieutenant Walter Lorrain Brodie (first left), shows how army uniforms were meant to look.*

Helmets, which might glisten in the sun and attract attention, were painted matt or worn with a cloth cover. Experience in the trenches led to improvements in footwear and waterproofing (woollen greatcoats were incredibly heavy in wet weather), while colourful facings were reduced to strips of cloth or subtle piping.

The soldier of 1918 was very different from the soldier who had marched out in the summer of 1914, not least in the way he was dressed.

▼ *In an artist's interpretation of the combined French and British forces, entitled 'Blue and Khaki', French troops cover the evacuation of British wounded.*

THE CAMPAIGNS

As Europe's diplomats and politicians threatened each other with war in July 1914, hostilities actually began between Serbia and an Austria-Hungary keen for revenge. Fighting also occurred in Africa. These first skirmishes suffered from poor communication between allies, and different interpretations of early promises of support, but still were a definite opening of hostilities. What follows in the next few pages is a brief summary of the major campaigns of World War I.

War on Serbia 1914

Austrian gunboats on the Danube, together with on-shore batteries, bombarded the Serbian capital on 29 July, but, due to a series of inept blunders, the actual offensive was delayed as troops were first shifted from facing Russia and then sent back into Hapsburg Poland. At last, on 12 August, the Austrians launched their offensive under General Oskar Potiorek, who had been travelling in Franz Ferdinand's car on that fateful day. This initial attack was driven back within two weeks.

The Serbs and Montenegrins staged a relatively weak thrust into Bosnia but were themselves forced back. Then Potiorek, with more determination than competence, tried an offensive again that autumn and managed to seize Belgrade on 2 December. A determined Serbian counterattack retook the capital on 15 December, and, despite heavy losses, the Serbs celebrated the expulsion of the Austrians from Serbian territory.

▲ *A Serbian woman accompanies her husband as he leaves for the front in the summer of 1914.*

Germany and France 1914

The Germans too had resolved on a knock-out blow: to destroy the French – who were conveniently massing along German borders – before Russia could open its own offensive on the Eastern Front. France was not prepared to sit and wait, however, and launched an offensive into Alsace and Lorraine; this was unsuccessful, as troops briefly entered Mulhouse but fell back with heavy casualties as bayonet charges were launched against machine guns.

Attention soon switched northwards to Flanders. The Schlieffen Plan, Germany's overall strategic plan for a war on two fronts, had predicted victory within 40 days. With this in mind the Germans raced through Belgium, taking the fortress of Liège, and Brussels but outstripping their supplies. They then found themselves embroiled in a series of bitter encounter battles. This included the Battle of Mons, which began on 22 August, where the Germans and the newly arrived British Expeditionary Force (BEF) succeeded in bloodying each other. However, on 25 August, the French began a co-ordinated retreat.

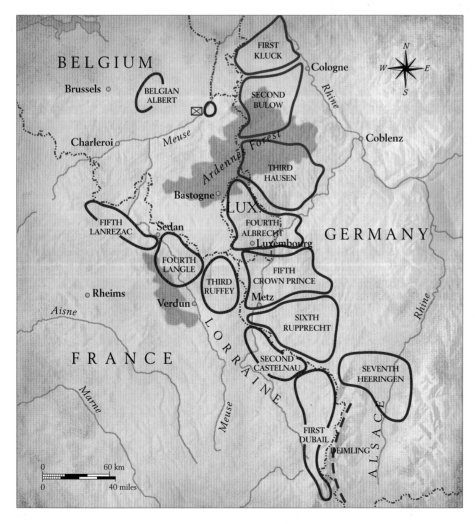

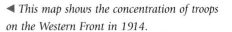

◄ *This map shows the concentration of troops on the Western Front in 1914.*

Despite German pressure, the withdrawal was orderly, although the government abandoned Paris for Bordeaux. The Germans, close on the heels of the French and British, sensed victory, even sending two corps eastwards to confront the Russians. In a determined push General Helmuth von Moltke's Germans marched for Paris and reached the river Marne, east of the capital. They were unable to get beyond the river, however, as the desperate French attacks first held them and then forced a retreat to the Aisne river.

The German retreat was closely followed by the Allies whose attempt to outflank the Germans, led to a race to the coast and the German capture of the Belgian cities of Ostend and Zeebrugge. An attempt to push aside the BEF led to a prolonged battle of attrition, known as the First Battle of Ypres, and 80,000 German casualties, many of them young volunteers. After this failure the Germans began to dig and with the onset of cold, rainy weather, offensives gave way to trenches. Although their push to Paris had failed they retained a hold on France's most industrial region and, with the fall of the city of Antwerp, conquered Belgium. There would be no quick victory in the west.

Eastern Fronts 1914
In the east, Russia remained true to its promises to the French and launched an offensive into East Prussia against the Germans. In addition the Russian overall commander, Grand Duke Nicholas (uncle of the czar), sent four armies against the Austro-Hungarians in Galicia (the Austro-Hungarian share of Poland). In the north, progress was reasonable for the first two weeks as the Russians benefited from German mistakes and inflicted a defeat on the elderly General von Prittwitz. This led to the replacement of the German commander by Paul von Hindenburg and Erich Ludendorff, and they built on plans for a counter-attack.

The Germans enjoyed the luxury of being able to intercept uncoded messages, and the Russian focus was distracted by divisions between their army commanders. The Germans drew the Russian 2nd Army further into Prussia and managed to encircle it by 28 August. The Russians were caught in a trap and defeated at the Battle of Tannenberg, with the 2nd Army being destroyed and the 1st reeling back into Russian Poland.

The Germans attempted to push on as far as Warsaw but overstretched themselves and fell back; this did, however, relieve pressure on the Austro-Hungarians. With Russian attention focused on attacking the Germans, the Austro-Hungarians had seized the opportunity to invade Russian Poland. Poorly organized and ineffectively supplied, the invasion came to nothing and troops were quickly redeployed to oppose a Russian offensive, which in the event overran much of Austrian Galicia.

Austro-Hungarian casualties were heavy (around 350,000) and only the German attacks in Poland limited Russian success. Recognition of this fact was confirmed when Paul von Hindenburg was made commander in the east (assuming responsibility for Austro-Hungarian forces as well as German). So it was that 1914 closed, in the west as well as in the east, with armies digging in for a long, harsh winter.

▲ *German General Von Hindenburg stands centre, in front of his staff, to his left is General Erich Ludendorff.*

Overseas 1914
Elsewhere the Ottoman empire shuffled into the war at the end of October, closing the Dardanelles but suffering a resounding defeat in the Caucasus against Russian armies that were well led and ably supported by the mountainous terrain. Britain landed troops in Mesopotamia (Iraq) and occupied Basra in the south.

Allied attempts to seize German colonies abroad met with mixed success. Japan, declaring war on Germany on 23 August, besieged the German enclave at Tsingtao in China (it fell in November) and hastily took possession of the Marshall, Caroline and Mariana islands in the Pacific. New Zealand occupied Samoa. Colonies in Africa were more extensive and harder to overrun; Togoland surrendered in 1914 but resistance continued in south-west Africa until 1915 and in Cameroon until early 1916. In East Africa the German commander, Paul von Lettow-Vorbeck, staged a determined guerrilla campaign in the difficult terrain. He continued to be a thorn in the flesh for the British, Belgians and Portuguese until his surrender, on 25 November 1918.

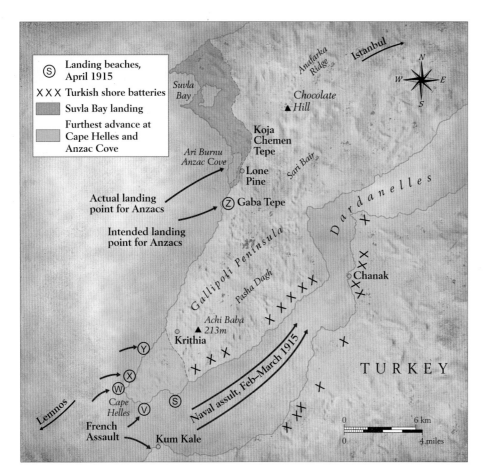

Map legend:
- Ⓢ Landing beaches, April 1915
- X X X Turkish shore batteries
- Suvla Bay landing
- Furthest advance at Cape Helles and Anzac Cove

Suvla Bay

Anafarka Ridge

Istanbul

Chocolate ▲ Hill

Koja Chemen Tepe

Ari Burnu Anzac Cove

Lone Pine

Sari Bair

Dardanelles

Actual landing point for Anzacs

Ⓩ Gaba Tepe

Intended landing point for Anzacs

Gallipoli Peninsula

Pasha Dagh

Chanak

Achi Baba ▲ 213m

Krithia

Ⓨ

Ⓧ

Ⓦ

Cape Helles

Lemnos

Ⓥ

Ⓢ

Naval assault, Feb–March 1915

TURKEY

French Assault

Kum Kale

0   6 km

0   4 miles

The Dardanelles

The entry into the war of the Ottoman empire made it a strategic necessity to do something to contain the Central Powers and support Russia. The strategy of forcing the Dardanelles and bombarding Constantinople was an old one, but it was revived in late 1914, and by early 1915 preparations were in hand to send an Allied fleet into the straits. The scheme was abandoned after serious losses of ships on an Ottoman minefield. A vital lull followed before a hastily concentrated Allied landing force was sent in, with British troops and the Australia and New Zealand Army Corps (Anzac) on the Gallipoli Peninsula, and French troops on the shore of Asia Minor. On 25 April the Allies waded ashore on six different beachheads but failed to advance quickly enough, and were stopped by an Ottoman defence that was masterminded by a German. Despite attacking for nearly a year, the troops suffered heavily and were eventually extricated with more skill than had been demonstrated during their landing.

▲ *Allied amphibious operations at Gallipoli were designed to secure the Dardanelles and knock the Ottomans out of the war. A stout defence, and Allied confusion, led to the defeat of the offensive.*

The Ottomans also achieved an unexpected victory in Mesopotamia against an Anglo-Indian force that had pushed northwards from Basra under General Townshend. He reached Kut and made some onward progress before falling back on that town. There he and his force were besieged, as the Ottomans beat off a series of attempts to relieve the place.

The Ottomans were less successful in the Caucasus, a defeat that sparked terrible reprisals against the empire's Armenian population, and in their attempt to launch an offensive into Egypt. There Ahmed Djemal, one of the empire's three governing pashas, tried to launch a surprise attack on the Suez Canal, but it was beaten off and he was forced to retreat. However, victory at Gallipoli seems to have outshone these disasters. It even persuaded Bulgaria into joining the Central Powers in October 1915.

The Bulgarians attacked the Serbs from the east while the Germans and the Austro-Hungarians attacked from the north and west. Such a blow helped knock Serbia out of the war by December and allowed the Central Powers to create a secure link between Austria-Hungary and the Ottomans. That winter many Serbs fled through hostile Albania, and some 140,000 were evacuated to Corfu by early 1916.

An expedition sent to Salonika, chiefly composed of French and British troops but later joined by Italian, Serb, Russian and Greek forces, was wrong footed by an initial Greek declaration of neutrality and found itself isolated.

▼ *Allied troops arrive in Salonika in 1916.*

Russian Defeats 1915

Russia had watched developments with concern. Gallipoli had been a costly failure and the success of the Central Powers in the Balkans was a great setback for a country aiming to dominate the Dardanelles. All this was overshadowed, however, by the Russian loss of much of Poland in the summer. Initial Russian success against the Austro-Hungarians (capturing 120,000 men at Przemysl) was quickly overshadowed by failed attempts to break through the Carpathians and a German offensive that culminated in success at the city of Tarnow in south-east Poland.

Lemberg (now Lviv in western Ukraine) was taken by the Germans in June, and in August, Warsaw itself fell, having been softened up by bomb-dropping Zeppelins that July, and the Russians fell back in considerable disorder. Kovno (now Kaunas in Lithuania), and Brest-Litovsk (now in Belarus) both fell, while Vilnius (now in Lithuania) followed in September. Only the exertions of Grand Duke Nicholas, German exhaustion and Austro-Hungarian confusion allowed the Russians time to recover, establishing 1,000 miles of defensive lines from the Baltic to the Black Sea and rapidly replacing casualties. That autumn, following questionable

▼ *A German aviator manually drops a small bomb from a Kogenluft 909 fighter aircraft.*

▲ *British artillerymen struggle in the mud in the wasteland that was Flanders, 1916.*

advice, the czar himself assumed the position of commander-in-chief, sending Grand Duke Nicholas off to the Caucasus.

Italian Action 1915

Hapsburg attention had been distracted by Italy's entry into the war on 23 May 1915. Such a move had been suspected but, nevertheless, was a blow to the Austro-Hungarians who, at that time, found themselves fighting a war on three fronts. They were saved from disaster because the Italian Army was fighting its own war with the Italian political system and was not yet ready to take to the field. Indeed, such had been the confusion that the general staff and commander-in-chief, Luigi Cadorna, were half expecting war against France before the politicians (hoping to gain Dalmatia) renounced the Triple Alliance and began war against the Hapsburgs. A series of costly offensives along the Isonzo river resulted, and the fighting stagnated to a brutal stalemate in harsh, mountainous terrain.

The Western Front

The landscape on the Western Front had been turned into a wasteland. By the end of that first, terrible winter, trenches dominated the scene. Both sides mounted limited offensives that winter, but, with the French and British not yet co-ordinating properly, and the Germans distracted by Russia, there were few gains. The Belgians were reduced to defending the banks of the Yser river while German occupation of the rest of Belgium began to bite.

The French, focused on winning back their industrial regions, launched an unimaginative attack in the region of Champagne, throwing 300,000 men and 2,000 guns into action to little avail. The British also tried to break the German lines at the village of Neuve Chapelle. Attacks and counter-attacks (including the German use of gas) took place in Flanders, around Ypres. The British and Canadians suffered 65,000 casualties for little gain. More offensives followed that summer and continued into the autumn. The British attacked around Loos and the French in Artois, again suffering heavy casualties. Sir Douglas Haig replaced Sir John French as British commander-in-chief in December, signalling that a renewed effort would be made to break the German lines in 1916.

Verdun and the Somme 1916

The Chantilly conference of late 1915 had instilled in the Allies the belief that a more thorough co-ordination of offensives would strain the Central Powers beyond breaking point. But it was the Germans who struck first.

With Russia recovering from severe losses, and unlikely to take the offensive, the Germans shifted their attention westwards. Chief of General Staff Erich Falkenhayn, supported by his kaiser, fixed on the idea of bleeding the French dry by attacking their salient at Verdun. It was a heavily fortified area (and had been since the days of Vauban) but the Germans pushed on regardless. Fort Douaumont fell at the end of February but from then on the struggle degenerated into one of sheer attrition. French commander Philippe Pétain, given overall command of the defence, was shrewd enough to rotate divisions in and out of the firing line but, even so, the strain was enormous. By June the French had almost broken, but by then Germany could not afford to maintain the attack, and by August, with Falkenhayn relieved of his command

▼ *French troops use large stones and rocks to dislodge German soldiers from hillside positions in 1916.*

and replaced by Hindenburg and Ludendorff, the Germans went back on to the defensive.

Both sides counted the cost: the French had lost nearly half a million men, the Germans at least 370,000. Little territory ultimately changed hands and neither side came close to making a breakthrough. Joseph Joffre, now a French marshal, finished the year by allowing an extraordinary attack, conceived by the artilleryman Robert Nivelle and carried out by General Mangin (the Butcher). Four divisions, launched the attack, supported by four more, but ground to a halt in the appalling weather.

German attention had been distracted by a joint Anglo-French offensive farther north. The British had husbanded their shell supply before letting loose a massive bombardment and assaulting the German positions in the chalky soil north of the Somme. Although effective in places, the artillery failed to destroy German defences or defeat German morale (the Germans were using bunkers deep underground). The attack began early on 1 July, and by the close of the day, the British had lost 60,000 men. Most fell to machine guns (often given unmissable targets by men carrying heavy kit advancing in line formation)

▲ *French General Franchet d'Esperey, left, Italian Chief of Staff General Luigi Cadorna, middle, and the commander-in-chief of French armies on the Western Front, General Joseph Joffre, right, in 1916.*

or effective artillery support. Regiments suffered appalling casualties: the Royal Newfoundland Regiment lost 684 out of 752, the Accrington Pals were virtually destroyed. With the French still locked in the life or death struggle at Verdun, pressure was put upon General Haig to press on. So it was that the fighting continued that July, with the South Africans distinguishing themselves at Delville Wood, and on into September, when tanks were deployed for the first time, with mixed results. Beaumont Hamel, an objective on 1 July, was finally taken in November, but on the 19th, Haig decided that, with bad weather setting in enough was enough, and brought the Battle of the Somme to an end.

Russian Victories 1916

The Germans at Verdun had perhaps been distracted even more by troubling news from the east. Russia had recovered and, worse, had launched its own offensive, motivated by the promises made at Chantilly. Although delayed by supply problems, four Russian armies under the competent and intelligent General Brusilov began an extraordinary offensive on 4 June. Although conceived as a secondary attack, it managed to obliterate the

4th Austro-Hungarian Army of Archduke Joseph Ferdinand, and captured Luck (or Lutsk) on 7 June. Brusilov was only stopped by the arrival of Austro-Hungarian reserves who, together with German divisions, rushed over to bolster the line.

Brusilov himself found it impossible to bring up sufficient reserves to exploit his initial success and, by August, both sides were reduced to warily watching each other. Russia had inflicted a massive defeat on the Hapsburgs, capturing 200,000 prisoners and winning much territory, but success came at an enormous price – nearly one million Russian casualties. The Austro-Hungarians were reduced to acting as a junior partner to the Germans, the Germans themselves feeling that they were being 'shackled to a corpse'. However, the offensive did lead to Romania joining the Allies.

The Romanians successfully invaded Hungarian territory in late August but found themselves assailed by German-led offensives, which included Ottoman troops, and Bulgarian

▼ The most effective Russian offensive of the war was masterminded by General Brusilov. It mauled the Austro-Hungarians, who were saved by German intervention, and gave a much-needed boost to the Russian war effort.

intervention from the south. Despite Russian assistance the Romanian army was very quickly driven back, and Bucharest fell in December. The Romanians took up desperate positions in the east of their country, but much oil and grain fell into German hands and helped alleviate the effects the Allied naval blockade was having on German industry and the German home front.

The Russian offensive had also relieved pressure on Italy, where the Austro-Hungarian Army had been exerting considerable force, and allowed the Italians to prepare a counterattack. The Allies were also able

▲ Mounted British soldiers and their native guides in Mesopotamia, 1916.

to push forward at Salonika, where French General Maurice Sarrail made some progress against a stubborn German-Bulgarian defence, despite inter-Allied squabbling.

The Middle East 1916
The Ottoman success of 1915 was crowned by the Allied evacuation of Gallipoli in early 1916, followed by General Townshend's surrender at the town of Kut, in April 1916, where the survivors were dragged off to endure imprisonment after having survived flies, starvation and the constant failed promise of relief. The war at this point did not go entirely the Ottoman way, however. Hussein, head of the Hashemite clan, maintained pressure on the Ottomans by lifting the standard of revolt (supported by British gold) in the Hejaz. The Arabs captured Mecca and Jedda and, with support from a strange collection of military advisers (including T.E. Lawrence), mercenaries, and turncoat Ottoman forces, marched on Syria.

Russian success in the Caucasus also increased the pressure on the Ottomans (Trebizond, on the Black Sea, fell that April), as did a defeat in Sinai against the British. This was the overture to a more impressive British offensive in Egypt, which would be launched under General Archibald Murray in early 1917.

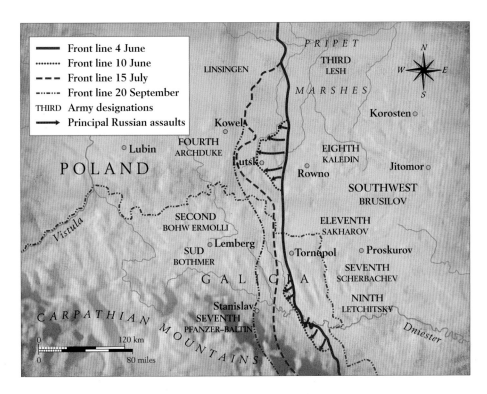

Front line 4 June
Front line 10 June
Front line 15 July
Front line 20 September
THIRD Army designations
Principal Russian assaults

PRIPET

THIRD
LESH

LINSINGEN

MARSHES

Korosten

Kowel

FOURTH
ARCHDUKE

Lubin

EIGHTH
KALEDIN

POLAND

Lutsk

Jitomor

Rowno

SOUTHWEST
BRUSILOV

SECOND
BOHW ERMOLLI

ELEVENTH
SAKHAROV

SUD
BOTHMER

Lemberg

Proskurov

Tornopol

GALICIA

SEVENTH
SCHERBACHEV

NINTH
LETCHITSKY

CARPATHIAN MOUNTAINS

Stanislav
SEVENTH
PFANZER-BALTIN

Dniester

Vistula

0   120 km
0   80 miles

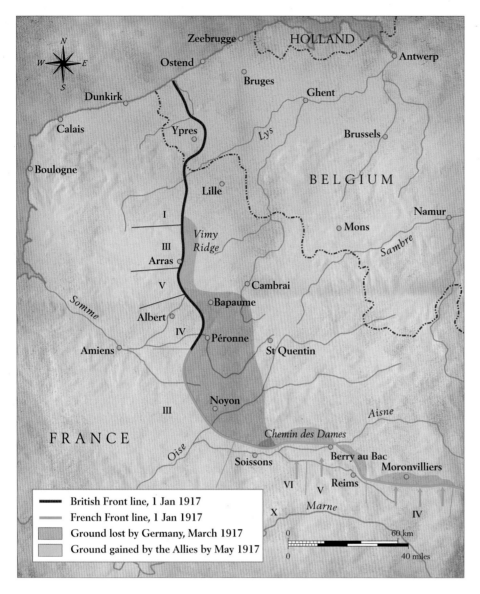

British Front line, 1 Jan 1917
French Front line, 1 Jan 1917
Ground lost by Germany, March 1917
Ground gained by the Allies by May 1917

The Allies Attack 1917

To strengthen their hand in the west the Germans withdrew some 24km (15 miles) to specially prepared defensive positions, on what was known as the Hindenburg Line. That spring the Allies set in motion a series of large-scale offensives. In northern France the British attacked at Arras that April and the Canadians captured Vimy Ridge at considerable cost. Further south, Nivelle, now France's chief of staff, attacked in Champagne, hoping that German losses at Verdun had sufficiently weakened his foe. Using creeping barrages and, true to his artillery background, massive firepower, Nivelle could nevertheless make little headway against a resolute German defence. Casualties were enormous (some 120,000 men), especially on the Chemin des Dames

▲ *The Nivelle offensives, and those launched in support, were costly attempts to break the German line by the French.*

▼ *German troops travel the famous Chemin des Dames, from Soissons to Craonne, on their way to the Aisne battlefields, 1917.*

ridge. Added to the recent strain of Verdun, such costly warfare led to a series of mutinies in the French Army. That May, entire regiments refused to march into the firing line. By June, 54 divisions were involved. It was Pétain who restored some order, promising generous leave, improved conditions, and an end to pointless offensives.

Pétain knew that he could now afford to wait. The United States, with all its resources of men and material, had declared war on Germany that April. Exasperated by repeated German submarine attacks and machinations in Mexico, President Woodrow Wilson brought America on to the Allied side and was prepared to despatch a small, but properly trained and well equipped expeditionary force to Europe.

In the meantime, the Allies continued their policy of grab and hold. Nivelle had failed but in July Haig began his own offensive around the Ypres salient. Mud and German efficiency rendered the attacks extremely costly, although the British pushed as far as the Belgian village of Passchendale, near Roulers, that November. Greater success was achieved at Cambrai, where the massed use of tanks paid off, but exploitation of the victory was poor and a chance to really break the German line was lost.

Other Theatres 1917

In the Balkans the Allies at Salonika had failed in their attempts to break the German/Bulgarian defences and that theatre too had degenerated into

▲ *A patrol of the North Lancashires march into the ruins of Cambrai, November 1917.*

trench warfare. The Italians achieved more in Albania, exerting pressure on the Austro-Hungarians and linking up with the Allies, who had left Salonika and were now pushing into Macedonia. The Allies could take heart from a Greek declaration of war on the Central Powers, after months of chaos and in-fighting, but Allied progress was sharply reined in by the stubbornness of the Bulgarians, and heavy casualties suffered during night attacks around Lake Doiran.

Other armies too were making costly mistakes. Italy continued to attack along the Isonzo river and, despite huge losses, forced the Austro-Hungarians to appeal to the Germans for support. This was effectively given

▼ *Members of the Russian Red Guard firing from an armoured car in Moscow during the early days of the Revolution, 1917.*

when the Germans, making use of tactics learned on the Eastern Front, infiltrated and turned the Italian positions and devastated Commander-in-Chief Cadorna's armies at the Battle of Caporetto between 24 October and 19 November. The Italians fell back, and were on the brink of collapse. Large numbers deserted and only draconian measures (including the decimation of mutinous regiments) restored order.

Russian Revolution 1917

France and Italy may have suffered from mutinies, but it was in Russia that the greatest social upheaval occurred. The Germans had encroached on the Baltic territories in 1917 and had stabilized the front after General Brusilov's offensive. The strain on Russian society was being felt. Strikes in urban centres became more frequent and widespread. Troops brought in to restore order refused to disperse civilians and then, especially in St Petersburg, went over to join the strikers, as did sailors from the Kronstadt naval base.

The czar abdicated, fearing that his family, and his dynasty, were in danger; he was right. A provisional government, later led by Alexander Kerensky, took over. Despite popular pressure, and increased agitation, the government remained in the war. Kerensky, who imagined himself as something of a Bonaparte, even launched an offensive that summer; with disastrous results. Thousands of soldiers took to the roads, heading for

▲ *General Allenby enters Jerusalem on foot through the Jaffa Gate, December 1917.*

home. An opportunistic group of Bolsheviks, led by Vladimir Lenin, took advantage of the government's lack of popular support and German advances into Latvia and Estonia, and seized the levers of power on 7 November. The Reds, as they were soon known, began to negotiate peace with Germany on 26 November, a peace that would eventually be signed at Brest Litovsk.

German terms were harsh; the Central Powers made a determined land grab into the Ukraine and also managed to knock Romania out of the war. Russia began to disintegrate, and the Baltic States declared independence, as did most nationalities on the peripheries of the Russian empire. The Germans, sucked into pacifying the Ukraine, managed to haul off quantities of grain but failed to share the proceeds with the Austro-Hungarians and Bulgarians.

The Fall of Jerusalem 1917

The British offensive from Egypt into Palestine showed considerable imagination and made extensive use of gas (firing 2,500 chlorine shells into Gaza). General Allenby, who replaced General Murray, made great use of cavalry and harassed the Ottoman troops and their German technical supports all the way through the Holy Land, and Jerusalem fell that December. Earlier in the year, Baghdad had fallen to the Anglo-Indians pushing up once again from Basra.

Germany's Gamble 1918

The Central Powers now had the potential to switch all their resources westwards, and defeat an exhausted France and a despairing Britain, perhaps before the American presence began to make itself felt.

The Allies, having agreed to co-ordinate politically and militarily (a Supreme War Council was established), expected a German offensive that spring. They would not be disappointed. Having brought divisions over from the Russian front (not without loss – there were many desertions) the Germans were in a position to attack with a force that had increased from 150 divisions in November 1917 to 192 by March. A major part of these divisions were gathered in northern France, around Cambrai and St Quentin, and they made preparations for an advance using assault tactics honed in experience in the west or used against the Russians at Riga.

The assault began on 21 March at around 10.00 am, the infantry came forward, often preceded by stormtroopers. Their assault was a great success, capturing 21,000 British troops

▼ *General John Pershing, the American commander in Europe, steps off the boat in France with the first American soldiers.*

▲ *A French poster encouraging its citizens to support the war: 'They Shall not Pass! Twice I have stood fast and conquered on the Marne, my brother civilian. A deceptive "peace offensive" will attack you in your turn; like me you must stand firm and conquer. Be strong and shrewd – beware of Boche hypocrisy.'*

and inflicting heavy casualties, but the Germans lacked the ability to exploit their victory, mounting a series of disparate offensives. The Allied nerve held. By April the impetus had gone and Germany had suffered huge losses.

The troops were called upon to make a final push in Champagne, but the French – under General, soon to be Marshal, Foch – gallantly counter-attacked and the Germans went back on the defensive. The French took the initiative, sending French and American troops against the Argonne sector in September and October while the British and Belgians attacked in the Ypres sector. Germany began to recognize the inevitable.

Defeat of the Central Powers 1918

Impetus for peace came from another front entirely. The Allies in Macedonia, under French General Louis Franchet d'Esperey, launched an assault on the Germans and Bulgarians on 14 September. It had been preceded by a heavy bombardment and the massive use of gas, which the Bulgarians were

poorly equipped to face, and the offensive was a complete success. French cavalry swept northwards into Macedonia and Serbia while the Bulgarians were pursued towards Sofia. Two weeks later Bulgaria appealed for an armistice.

The Ottomans were also now in dire straits. Britain had succeeded in securing the cities of Baghdad and Mosul, and the most severe fighting was now in Palestine. Here, General Allenby took the offensive in the cooler autumn, severely defeating the Ottomans at Megiddo, and forcing a way into Damascus in early October.

The Austro-Hungarians fared little better. Unsettled by food shortages and strikes, they had mounted a tentative assault in Italy, but this had failed and, by the autumn, the Italians were increasingly aggressive. The Italians finished the process off with a successful offensive in October, crossing the Piave river and reaching the town of Vittorio in the Veneto.

Armistice 1918

Germany was next. Unrelenting Allied pressure in the West, and the loss of all its allies, forced Germany to the negotiating table. Unrest in Germany, particularly among naval crews, in cities and in the east, led to mutinies and coups. The kaiser abdicated and fled to the Netherlands. An armistice was concluded so that hostilities would cease at 11.00 on 11 November and Germany could at last surrender.

The war continued, however. In the Caucasus, British and Indian troops had tried to fill the vacuum left by Russia's collapse and find allies willing to continue the war against Germany. They made enemies of the Bolsheviks and of the Turks, fighting over Baku, Azerbaijan's largest port, and the oil fields that autumn.

Britain also intervened in Central Asia, sending troops across the Russian border and supplying arms and finance to local leaders; the Tashkent Union received two million roubles in August 1918. Money and arms went to the Don Cossacks when they showed signs of resisting Bolsheviks unwilling to

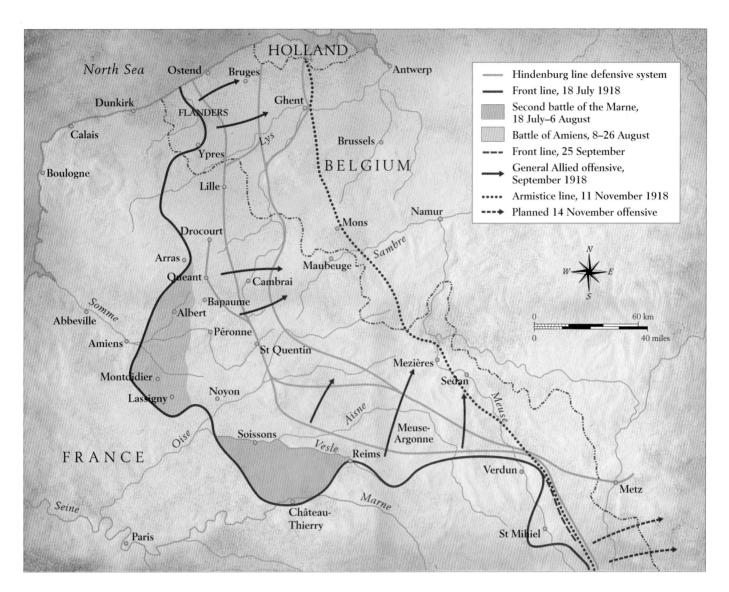

Legend:

— Hindenburg line defensive system
— Front line, 18 July 1918
▨ Second battle of the Marne, 18 July–6 August
▨ Battle of Amiens, 8–26 August
--- Front line, 25 September
→ General Allied offensive, September 1918
•••• Armistice line, 11 November 1918
-→ Planned 14 November offensive

fight Germans, and continued to do so after the armistice with Germany, in order to defeat the Red menace. The British government's Russia Committee even urged the Japanese to advance to the Urals and the Cossacks into the Ukraine hoping that, hemmed into northern Russia, the Bolsheviks would be starved into submission.

It was not to be. The Russian Civil War spread and soon sucked in some 100,000 foreign soldiers from 14 different countries. There were Americans in Siberia and Murmansk, Greeks in the Ukraine, British in Archangel, on the Russian coast, and the Japanese even stayed in Siberia until 1923.

In eastern Europe, the newly independent states fought wars of their own: there was civil war in Finland; Romania fought Hungary; Poland attacked the Ukraine and, then,

following an unwise Polish offensive, the Poles took on the Russian Bolsheviks in 1919. In the wake of the world war came the long, protracted settling of accounts.

▲ *Operations in the summer and autumn of 1918 concluded with the November armistice.*

▼ *The crowd celebrating the armistice at the end of the war outside Buckingham Palace.*

AFTERMATH AND PEACE

The first dramatic change after the armistice was the disintegration of Austria-Hungary. Hungary broke away and turned Bolshevik that winter. The Czechs and Slovaks formed their own state crafted from Bohemia, Moravia, Slovakia and Ruthenia, and the southern Slavs (Yugoslavs) united around Serbia to form a Yugoslav kingdom. Meanwhile, Romania occupied Transylvania. The Italians seized what territory they could and fell into dispute with Yugoslavia as to who should own the Adriatic port of Fiume. Poland was also detached, created from territories that had been ruled by Germany, Austria and Russia.

The Treaty of Versailles

These events were already taking place by the time the peace delegates arrived in Paris. Victorious heads of state, including President Woodrow Wilson, who arrived in Paris in January 1919, gathered to preside over the Allied peace terms. Wilson wanted to set up a League of Nations to impose international order, and hoped that his Fourteen Points would allow for a just

▼ *The wounded being treated in a derelict bombed-out church in northern France, 1918.*

settlement. But these ideals could not last in the face of demands made by victors who had endured such a hard war and had been promised so much. Italy, for example, had been promised Dalmatia and much of the Ottoman empire in order to get it into the war. Germany, beset by internal strife and revolution – Bavaria briefly had a Soviet government – sent a delegation to hear the terms. There was to be no negotiation. Alsace and Lorraine were returned to France, Upper Silesia and most of the Prussian coast went to

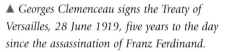

▲ *Georges Clemenceau signs the Treaty of Versailles, 28 June 1919, five years to the day since the assassination of Franz Ferdinand.*

Poland. Belgium received a thin strip of land around Malmédy and even neutral Denmark came away with a piece of Schleswig Holstein. Germany's industrial heartland in the Saar and along the Rhine was to be occupied and all of Germany's colonies were handed out to the victors. The Army was to be reduced to 100,000 men, and the modern technology of warfare (submarines, aircraft, tanks, heavy artillery) was to be denied to the new German Republic. Worse, Germany was to pay for the war and heavy reparations were to be made to France, Britain and Belgium; although it was quickly realized that Germany would be either too strong to pay them, or too weak to afford them.

Germany was also informed that it had to sign the guilt clause, admitting that it bore responsibility for starting the war. The Germans protested, but signed on 28 June 1919.

Austria, now stripped of most of its territories was not allowed to join Germany but was established as a republic with a small army and a large debt. Hungary could only be dealt with

Estimated Military Casualties

	Mobilized	Dead	Wounded
Germany	11,000,000	1,808,500	4,216,058
Russia	12,000,000	1,700,000	4,950,000
France	8,410,000	1,385,000	4,266,000
Austria-Hungary	7,800,000	1,200,000	3,620,000
Great Britain	8,904,467	908,371	2,090,212
Italy	5,615,000	460,000	947,000
Romania	750,000	335,706	120,000
Ottoman	2,850,000	325,000	400,000
US	4,355,000	126,000	234,300
Bulgaria	1,200,000	87,500	152,390
Serbia	707,300	45,000	133,148
Belgium	267,000	13,716	44,686
Portugal	100,000	13,000	18 400
Greece	230,000	8,365	21,000
Montenegro	50,000	3,000	10,000
Japan	800,000	1,300	907

after the defeat of the Reds, and the Allies only made a cruel peace with the shattered country at Trianon in June 1920. The last of the peace treaties was with the Ottomans in August 1920, but it was soon overtaken by events as Greece and Turkey went to war, and an accord was only finally reached in 1923. That left Russia, and the consequences of the Russian Civil War made themselves felt, unrestrained by any peace treaty.

Despite the coming of peace, or at least its imposition, Europe was exhausted and bankrupt. A serious influenza epidemic (known as Spanish flu) had made terrible inroads among the sick and vulnerable. Blockades and destruction of crops kept thousands on the verge of starvation and political instability set countless refugees on to the roads.

Casualties
The true cost of the war will never be known. It is estimated that more than 40 million people died, but the exact number of wartime casualties can never be fixed with absolute certainty. Those countries that kept good records, which have survived, allow a reasonably accurate calculation to emerge. For others, estimates are the only possible method, especially when other factors, such as Spanish flu, had

an impact on the overall figure. For the Ottoman and Russian empires, which moved from world war into civil wars and clashes with intervening powers, we can only rely on generalizations.

Commemoration
Armistice Day on 11 November was regarded as a national holiday of remembrance across much of Europe

and the United States. In Britain a two-minute silence was called for on the first anniversary of the armistice in 1919. France followed a similar tradition. In the 1920s, Germany and Bulgaria held days of national mourning on All Souls Day. Other countries commemorated days of national importance like Anzac Day.

Commemoration of the fallen was an essential part of giving meaning to their deaths. Relatively early on, war graves were given official sanction and cemeteries were tended and recorded at national level for Allied dead on the Western Front. Memorials, along with the Cenotaph and the Tomb of the Unknown Warrior, served as focal points for national grief.

The concept of the 'unknown soldier' was a significant development. France placed the body of an unidentified soldier beneath the Arc de Triomphe in November 1919, just as the body of a British soldier was laid to rest in London's Westminster Abbey. Germany did the same in Berlin, in 1931, as did Australia in 1993.

▼ *The territories of Europe were radically changed after the war ended in 1919.*

GREAT BRITAIN

Britain had traditionally relied on a combination of the Royal Navy and Continental allies to keep enemies at bay. In 1914, with a modest land army and some trained but underfunded reserves, Britain had to face the demands of a modern war on a large scale. Concerns that there might be an invasion of the British Isles were raised by the threat of German naval activity in the North Sea, and few troops were available for service overseas when war came in August 1914. An initial expeditionary force (the British Expeditionary Force, or BEF) was sent to France, but this only consisted of four infantry divisions and five brigades of cavalry. The numerical limitations imposed on Britain's military planners would partially give way with the arrival of thousands of troops from the British empire and, eventually, with the introduction of conscription. This meant that towards the end of the conflict Britain was able to wage war on multiple fronts, with 3.5 million men under arms in November 1918, 1.5 million of whom were stationed in France.

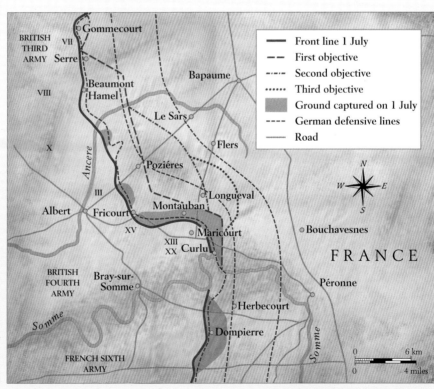

▲ *The Third Battle of Ypres, popularly known as Passchendale, was an Allied offensive fought in muddy conditions in the autumn of 1917.*

◀ *This photograph of British troops in the trenches of the Western Front at nightfall is undated, but the steel helmets show it was taken during the second half of the war.*

THE BRITISH ARMY

Great Britain began the war with a small professional army, but it was soon evident that numbers would play the most significant part in this rapidly expanding conflict. Measures were hastily adopted to swell the ranks of Britain's military.

The Regulars

Britain's regulars had served the country well throughout the 19th century. They had provided garrisons for forts and cities across the globe, made up numbers for punitive expeditions and imperial conquests, and even fought a set-piece war with Russia in the Crimea. But, as Germany began to upset the balance of power in Europe, and Europe's conscript armies grew ever larger, military planners

▼ *General Viscount Kitchener at Army Headquarters, Pretoria, South Africa, at the end of the Boer War, 19 July 1902.*

▲ *Field Marshal Douglas Haig reviewing Canadian troops, a vital component in Britain's efforts to win on the Western Front.*

looked for ways to increase the size of the Army with new recruitment policies. One problem was that recruits were just not coming forward to join the Army and maintain it at even its limited pre-war size.

Although Britain's demographic outlook was better than that of France, a very large number of young men had emigrated (mostly to Canada, but also to Australia). This removed potential recruits, and also created job vacancies at home (filled by the unskilled and unemployed, two key sources for recruits). The Army needed around 35,000 recruits a year to maintain its strength in 1908, but it could only recruit some 30,000. In May 1914 the Army establishment had a shortage of 11,000 men.

There were also shortages of officers of every rank. These had traditionally been drawn from military families, the gentry, graduates and public school leavers. Few came from professional families. Yet, even these traditional sources of supply were being diverted to commercial or government jobs, many of them in the colonies.

Auxiliaries

Britain had long maintained a militia, and volunteer units had been assembled in great numbers during the Napoleonic invasion scares. It was evident that something had to be done now, with new invasion fears and the very real possibility of large-scale conflict. If an expeditionary force was sent to France (62,000 men had been sent to South Africa to deal with the Boers, so it was obvious many more would be required for a European war), the homeland would be stripped bare and left vulnerable. A Special Reserve (supposed to be 75,000 men) was formed in the summer of 1907, and this would provide drafts for replacements for regulars sent abroad. These measures were inadequate but were supplemented by the formation of Territorial units from April 1908, some of which were attached to regular units, some of which were uniquely Territorial. By June there were 144,620 officers and men in infantry, cavalry, artillery and engineering units, mostly directly descended from volunteer militia and yeomanry (cavalry militia) units. They were volunteers who signed up for a four-year term, and who could volunteer for service abroad upon mobilization (the so-called Imperial Service obligation).

Despite initial enthusiasm, the Territorial force had similar problems in finding sufficient recruits and was dwindling from its established strength by 1912. In addition, only 1,090 officers and 17,788 men had taken the Imperial Service obligation by September 1913.

The limitations imposed by such a system were apparent in August 1914. Leading military planners, including Sir Douglas Haig (a career soldier commanding much of the British Expeditionary Force – BEF) and Horatio Kitchener (a popular hero of the wars in Sudan who became Secretary of State for War on 5 August 1914), predicted a long struggle and insisted that only a sudden increase in the Army's size would allow it to make the necessary commitment.

Kitchener, an experienced officer whose opinions carried considerable weight, viewed the possible use of Territorials as unrealistic and set about expanding the regulars. On 7 August an appeal went out for 'an addition of 100,000 men to His Majesty's Regular Army'. Those between ages 19 and 30 were asked to volunteer for three years or the duration of the conflict, and most of these would be formed into a battalion for each infantry regiment. These were called Service Battalions. A standard regiment, such as the Royal Berkshire Regiment, had two Regular battalions (1st and 2nd), the 3rd Battalion was part of the Reserve, the 4th was a Territorial battalion and the 5th was a Service Battalion.

▲ *This dashing image in an early recruiting poster was soon to be superseded by the harsh realities of modern artillery-based warfare.*

▼ *British soldiers camping on the quay at Rouen, 1914, on arrival in France.*

▲ *Demonstrators protesting in London against the Military Service Act of 1916, which brought in full conscription for the first time in British military history.*

Volunteers

War triggered a wave of patriotic feeling and a surge in the number of recruits. These volunteers were to be directed into the Regulars or into the Territorials. The initial process was beset by problems but, eventually, a system emerged.

The number of volunteers was high in August 1914. Between 4 and 8 August some 8,193 volunteers were enrolled, most of whom had crowded into London's overwhelmed recruiting stations. The retreat from Mons in late August 1914 actually boosted recruitment, and it peaked around the end of August and the first week of September (patriotic factors counted, but numbers were also swollen by an increase in unemployment).

Meanwhile, Territorial units were also experiencing an upsurge in numbers. But the response of Territorials to the Imperial Service obligation, which made an individual liable for service overseas, was relatively poor, most units being split between 50 per cent who volunteered for overseas service and 50 per cent who kept to their original terms. Some 318 battalions would serve abroad.

Additional calls were made for more men, the Reserve was brought up to strength and casualties were replaced, and authority was also granted to regional bodies to raise battalions of local men with local connections. These recruits were gathered into so-called Pals battalions, which were locally raised service battalions incorporated into existing regiments. The Hull Commercials, for example, formed the 10th Battalion East Yorkshire Regiment. Artillery was raised this way too.

That summer and autumn, new battalions (whether Pals or not) were added to the line, organized around cadres drawn from Regulars, and the First New Army began to emerge. Between 4 August and 12 September, 478,893 men had joined the Army.

Conscription

These volunteers were not a constantly renewable resource. Heavy casualties throughout 1915 caused a rethink. Some restrictions on service were eased, for example Bantam battalions (men under the required height) were raised. Pressure was building for compulsory service, with Winston Churchill, for one, pushing hard for conscription. A national register was brought in that revealed there was just over five million men of eligible age not in the armed forces, and that 2.1 million of these were unmarried.

A Military Service Bill was introduced in January 1916 and was passed with a large majority, becoming law that March. Initially the number of exemptions was very high, with the

▼ *Recruitment was a pressing concern throughout the war. This march in London in 1916 was led by Lance Corporal Dwyer, the youngest soldier at that time to have been awarded the Victoria Cross.*

▲ *The 1st Canadian Expeditionary Force pose for a photograph on Salisbury Plain, where they were quartered in November 1914.*

authorities being concerned about public opinion, and large numbers failed to respond to the summons (of 193,891 initially called up by the Act, 57,416 failed to appear). A second Bill was introduced in May, now ordering married men to be called up, coming into effect on 25 May (except in Ireland, where there was concern that there might be a backlash).

At around the same time, with Britain's military leaders emphasizing the massive shortage of recruits and the need for an offensive, those Territorials whose period of service was about to expire now found that they were to be retained for the duration of the war. Britain therefore joined the rest of the Continental powers as a conscript nation in March 1916.

The situation in the empire was more complicated. Australia and South Africa would despatch a considerable number of volunteers to fight, but they resisted conscription. New Zealand introduced conscription in the summer of 1916. The situation in Canada was more complicated. Conscription was finally introduced in May 1917, although it met with resistance and did not result in many recruits; many Canadian volunteers but few conscripts were sent to the front. Indian Army units continued to rely on local levies, although labourers were conscripted as they were in Africa.

Shortages of manpower continued, particularly among officers and those required for the new branches of military science. It took years to train sound engineers, for example. Nevertheless, Britain's armed forces largely obtained the manpower and found the necessary supplies for its own men as well as those of its allies. Romania, for example, would be largely re-equipped by Britain in 1918, and in the course of the war, Russia would receive thousands of tons of military supplies – much of which ended up in the hands of the counter revolutionaries in 1918 and 1919.

There was some resistance to the introduction of compulsory military service, but, on the whole, it failed to act in an organized or concerted manner. Only the Independent Labour Party and the No-Conscription Fellowship spoke out against the imposition of conscription. Powerful forces, from the National Service League to the government and military pressed for its introduction.

▼ *The health and vigour of British recruits was a serious concern in 1914.*

GENERALS AND STAFF

British generals wore a variety of uniforms but most of those serving at or near the front during the course of the war would be dressed in officers' service dress. Even so, when in the field, generals allowed themselves to stray from absolute adhesion to regulations, as did the men serving in the trenches. General officers consisted of field marshals, generals, lieutenant generals, major generals and brigadier generals.

Jackets and Breeches

Officers of all kinds wore privately tailored uniforms and so there was inevitably some variation in cut and in shades of regulation colour.

The jacket was usually that adopted in 1914 and was officially of 'drab mixture serge'. It was single breasted, with an open collar and narrow lapels. The jacket closed with four buttons and had two breast pockets and two skirt pockets. Highlanders wore a different cut of jacket. It was supposed to be worn with a drab (olive green) shirt but all shades of shirts could be seen, from light green to dark brown.

The shirt was to be worn with a drab or green tie or cravat, and was usually pinned across the shirt collars.

General officers were distinguished primarily by scarlet tabs on the collar. These were known as gorget patches and carried variations of metallic braiding. Field marshals, generals, lieutenant generals, major generals and brigadiers all had gold oak leaves.

Rank was also shown on the shoulder straps of the jacket. Field marshals had crossed batons, wreath and crown, generals had crossed sabre and baton below a pip and crown, lieutenant generals had the same but without the pip, major generals had the same but replaced the crown by a pip and brigadiers just had the crossed sabre and baton.

Cord breeches were popular with general officers and these were mostly tied or buttoned at the knee and worn with boots or gaiters. Breeches generally had reinforced inners, but trousers were also worn.

Headgear

General officers wore peaked service caps with leather chinstraps, scarlet bands and badges reflecting the man's rank. These were mostly worn stiff, but stiffeners could be removed for a baggier look. On more formal occasions caps with two rows of gold

◄ **BRIGADIER GENERAL, 1915** *This officer wears a standard uniform for his rank, complete with riding breeches and boots, with spurs attached. The brassard worn on his right arm denotes that he is serving at an Army Corps Headquarters.*

► **LIEUTENANT GENERAL, 1917** *This figure wears a privately purchased helmet with a cap badge soldered to the front. He carries a map case slung over his right shoulder.*

▲ FIELD MARSHAL, 1917 *This field marshal's cap badge includes a lion, and his rank is also shown on his shoulder straps and the oak leaves on his gorget patches.*

braid on the peak were worn. Field marshals wore badges as per the shoulder straps but with a lion, all other generals the same but with a crossed sabre and baton rather than crossed batons.

When helmets were introduced, a number of generals continued to wear badges on the front of their headgear. There are some examples of privately purchased French Adrian helmets with such badges attached, worn from mid-1915. Some other privately purchased helmets were also worn by generals but such helmets were later prohibited and regulation helmets worn instead (the Brodie helmet was patented in August 1915 but took some time to make it to the front). Helmets were sometimes worn, and these were covered in cloth with the badge stencilled on in black.

Accoutrements

Generals usually wore Sam Browne belts (with or without the shoulder belt), and carried pistols, binoculars and map cases. According to personal taste, a walking stick, swagger stick or canes of various kinds were inevitable additions. Moustaches were actually obligatory for officers, generals included, at this time.

Staff Officers

Officers attached to the staff also wore the scarlet gorget patch. Those with the rank of general had gold chain braid (gimp), colonels on the staff had red silk gimp. Administrative officers wore blue patches with crimson gimp and intelligence officers wore green patches. Staff officers generally had scarlet cap bands.

Staff officers, from assistant military secretaries to aides-de-camp and inspectors, were authorized to wear the staff forage cap, with peak embroidered or plain according to rank, and with a cover of drab material, fitted so as to show the scarlet band, badge and peak.

Brassards

Cloth arm bands, or brassards, worn on the right arm distinguished officers on divisional or brigade staff or undertaking staff duties, although they were only supposed to be worn at headquarters.

Those attached to general headquarters wore a brassard with red above blue with a black crown above and the following letters in red below: 'MS' (for military staff), 'A' (for Adjutant General), 'Q' (for Quartermaster General). Divisional staff wore red bands (with 'CD' for cavalry or a stencilled gun for artillery), brigade staff wore blue bands (with 'CB' for cavalry). Many of the divisional bands later bore divisional insignia. Tank Corps officers attached to the staff had green, red and brown brassards with a tank badge in white. Staff cars would have flags or pennants attached in the same design.

▼ STAFF CAPTAIN, 1917 *This staff officer wears a fluted helmet, which looked like it should give extra strength but was non-regulation. He also wears a brassard on his right arm, denoting that he was serving at an Army Corps Headquarters.*

GUARDS

The Guards were the elite of Britain's Regular Army and consisted of infantry and cavalry regiments, plus some supporting troops. In 1914 there were four regiments of Guard infantry, known as Foot Guards (the Grenadier Guards, Coldstream Guards, Scots Guards and Irish Guards); a fifth, the Welsh Guards, was added in 1915. There were three regiments of Household Cavalry (men from these also formed a battalion as infantry, the Household Battalion). The Guards Machine Gun Regiment was added in 1918.

◀ PRIVATE, GRENADIER GUARDS, 4TH BATTALION, 1917 *The Guards wore cloth shoulder titles, something quite rare among the line units, and, in the case of the Grenadier Guards and Scots Guards, this was red with white lettering.*

Guard Infantry

British Guard infantry regiments were of ancient lineage and, much like their Continental counterparts (at least in Russia and Prussia), conserved some of their time-honoured traditions. They were, however, generally armed and equipped like the line infantry. Being Guards, however, meant that they did preserve some key differences.

Guard infantry wore drab service uniforms of a style adopted in 1902. The tunic was single breasted with falling collar and had four large pockets fastened by buttons. The tunic itself was fastened with four yellow metal buttons. Shoulders were reinforced with extra cloth and plain shoulder straps were worn by Guard infantrymen (officers wore rank insignia on the shoulder of their jackets or transferred the insignia if they wore other ranks' tunics). Guards wore cloth shoulder titles at the end of the shoulder strap, unlike the regular line infantry regiments, who largely ceased to wear cloth titles in November 1907 and used various forms of brass lettering instead. The Grenadier Guards and Scots Guards (2nd Battalion with an additional thistle) had red cloth square-ended patches with titles sewn

on in white, a style they seem to have retained throughout the war, and the Irish white on green. The Welsh had white on a drab base, the Coldstream Guards did without. Gilded metal shoulder titles do seem to have been worn on some occasions, as were slip-on titles, introduced in 1916.

Trousers were also in drab serge and could be worn with either a belt or braces. Puttees were worn, even by officers (although senior officers were mounted and wore breeches and boots), as were ankle boots ('ammunition boots'), and these were either blackened or in brown leather.

The service cap, introduced in 1905, was usually worn with stiffened crown, a drab peak and a leather chinstrap attached to the cap by two small regimental buttons (the chinstrap was usually left above the peak rather than worn under the chin). Cap badges varied from regiment to regiment.

Buttons usually replicated the badge, although the Irish had a harp and crown device. The Machine Gun Regiment was formed in 1918; before that date, machine gun companies were formed with a Guards star as the cap badge, crossed machine gun barrels on the collar and MG patches with roman numerals indicating the company on the sleeve. Guard units indicated their battalion with Roman numerals (Arabic numerals for the 2nd Grenadiers) in red, blue (Scots) or green (Irish) worn below the shoulder patch.

Guard Infantry Cap Badges

Grenadier Guards	Bursting grenade
Coldstream Guards	Star of the Order of the Garter
Scots Guards	Star of the Order of the Thistle
Irish Guards	Star of the Order of St Patrick (with shamrock)
Welsh Guards (1915)	A leek
Household Battalion	Cypher in an oval with crown
Machine Gun Regiment (1918)	Cypher of George V on scroll over crossed machine gun barrels

Cavalry Regiment Cap Badges

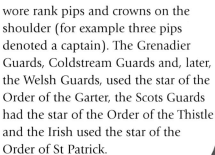

1st Life Guards	Cypher with First Life Guards and crown
2nd Life Guards	Cypher with Second Life Guards and crown
Royal Horse Guards	Cypher with Royal Horse Guards and crown
Household Cavalry (cyclist companies)	Cypher within garter, below crown

The Household Battalion was disbanded in February 1918, with all personnel returning to their orignal parent units. Britain also had line cavalry regiments, confusingly titled as Dragoon Guards, which are detailed in the cavalry section.

When the Brodie helmet was introduced, it was often worn with a cover. The 1st Scots Guards had a patch of Stewart tartan and the 2nd had dicing, other units using regimental badges in stencils or patches. Units serving in the Guards Division had the distinctive open eye insignia.

Although officers were supposed to wear cuff rank distinctions, the Guards were exceptions here too. Officers wore rank pips and crowns on the shoulder (for example three pips denoted a captain). The Grenadier Guards, Coldstream Guards and, later, the Welsh Guards, used the star of the Order of the Garter, the Scots Guards had the star of the Order of the Thistle and the Irish used the star of the Order of St Patrick.

Guard Cavalry

Cavalry generally wore a uniform similar in cut to that worn by the Guard infantry but with breeches, boots and ammunition bandoliers. They also wore white or light brown lanyards.

Troops served in France in a Composite Regiment in 1914, but this was dissolved later that year. The seven regiments of Dragoon Guards are detailed in the cavalry section.

In May 1918 the 1st and 2nd Life Guards and the Royal Horse Guards became the first three battalions of the Guards Machine Gun Regiment. A fourth battalion, drawn from the machine gun companies, was also formed with a fifth in reserve.

◄ PRIVATE, SCOTS GUARDS, 2ND BATTALION, 1917 *The additional thistle below the shoulder title denoted the 2nd Battalion. When the helmet was not worn, this unit wore a peaked cap rather than the Glengarry.*

► TROOPER, 1ST LIFE GUARDS, 1914 *This trooper wears a relatively simple uniform but rides a superior mount. His sword is the 1908 pattern cavalry sword with its handsome nickel-plated hilt.*

THE WESTERN FRONT

Britain's small Regular Army was rapidly expanded in 1914 and subsequent years. Few new regiments were formed, but existing units were enlarged by battalions of volunteers and Territorial battalions.

British infantry were traditionally formed into line infantry units (which also included light infantry regiments) and uniforms were largely standardized for such regiments. Exceptions were the fusilier regiments, Highland regiments, Scottish regiments and rifle regiments. Here there were some major distinctions in full dress, and some notable variations in service dress. Within the Highland regiments themselves, of course, there were marked differences in uniform.

Originally intended for home defence should the Regulars be sent abroad, the Territorial force was an important source of manpower. Infantry battalions were generally formed in support of a parent regiment. The Guards had no Territorial battalions, nor did any of the Irish regiments. A few Territorial infantry regiments existed, set apart from the Regular line infantry, but, on the whole, a regiment could expect to have two battalions of Regulars, a battalion of the Reserve with perhaps the 4th and 5th Battalion composed of Territorials.

Uniforms revolved around khaki, a colour worn by British troops serving in India and elsewhere, but which only gained universal acceptance during the last of the Boer Wars.

The 1902 Model Tunic

British infantrymen wore the khaki field service tunic (1902 Model), although Highlanders wore a different version and troops serving in Africa and the Middle East (and, to some extent, hot climates closer to home) wore adapted uniforms. Most units sent to France in 1914 and 1915 followed a reasonably standard code of dress. Tunics had a falling collar (fastened with hooks and eyes), reinforced shoulders and shoulder straps (attached with a regimental button and bearing a metallic shoulder title). There were generally four generous pockets, usually with flaps and closed with buttons, and stamped with the infantryman's number on the inside. The tunic was fastened by regimental buttons, each regiment having a distinctive design. The King's

◄ SERGEANT, THE QUEEN'S (ROYAL WEST SURREY REGIMENT), 1ST BATTALION, 1914 *This experienced NCO has wrapped his rifle in waterproofed canvas to protect the mechanism.*

► PRIVATE, ROYAL SUSSEX REGIMENT, 1914 *The shoulder title for the men of this regiment bore the insignia 'Royal Sussex' and the cap badge was a star and feather.*

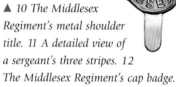

▲ NCOs' Rank Chevrons, 1914
1 Regimental sergeant major.
2 Regimental quartermaster sergeant.
3 Bandmaster.
4 Sergeant drummer.
5 Company sergeant major.
6 Company quartermaster sergeant.
7 Sergeant.
8 Corporal.
9 Lance corporal.

▲ 10 The Middlesex Regiment's metal shoulder title. 11 A detailed view of a sergeant's three stripes. 12 The Middlesex Regiment's cap badge.

◄ Regimental Quartermaster Sergeant, Middlesex Regiment, 1915 *This senior NCO wears the four inverted stripes of his rank on the lower sleeve.*

Royal Rifle Corps, Rifle Brigade and the Royal Irish Rifles had black buttons. The collar was generally unadorned on active service, although on formal occasions a badge (resembling the cap badge) was worn on both collars.

Officer's Distinctions

Infantry officers wore a jacket of the type that was adopted in 1914 and was officially of 'drab mixture serge', that is marginally greener than that worn by the enlisted men and NCOs. As most officers' jackets were privately tailored in any case, there were great variations in colour. The jacket was

▼ *A kit inspection for a Highland regiment of the British Army fighting on the Western Front, 1916.*

◀ **CAPTAIN, WEST YORKSHIRE REGIMENT, 1914** *Officers adapted their dress to front-line conditions relatively quickly. This captain has the worsted lace rank insignia at the cuff, but has adopted the enlisted man's rifle.*

▶ **CAPTAIN, NORTHUMBERLAND FUSILIERS, 5TH BATTALION, 1915** *This officer has gone even further in his use of other ranks' equipment. His lapel badges show the fusiliers' traditional bursting grenade.*

running around the cuff. These chevrons were of worsted lace and braid. Second lieutenants and lieutenants had one row, captains had two rows, majors three rows with braiding between, lieutenant colonels three rows of lace and four of braiding and colonels four of lace and five of braiding. Regimental badges were worn on each of the jacket's collars (where the collar meets the lapel). NCOs wore chevrons (mostly points down) on the upper or lower sleeve, depending upon specific rank.

Shirts and Leg Wear

Underneath the tunics both enlisted men and NCOs wore shirts. Most of these were grey-blue flannel, closed by three buttons and with a button on each cuff. The shirt was collarless, which meant that most troops experienced uncomfortable rubbing from their tunic collars. In hot climates the shirt could be worn without the tunic.

single breasted, with an open collar and narrow lapels. The jacket was to be worn with a drab shirt but, again, all shades of shirts could be seen from light green to khaki. The shirt was to be worn with a drab or green tie or cravat, and most officers pinned the tie back across the shirt collars. The jacket closed with five regimental buttons and had two breast pockets and two skirt pockets. Rank insignia was to be worn at the cuff (although not by the King's Royal Rifle Corps), which had three-pointed flaps edged with chevron lace. Within the flap, pips and crowns designated rank, as did chevrons

Trousers were made of the same design and could be worn with a waist belt or with braces (buttons were fitted at the waist for this purpose, more buttons being added in 1915). The trousers were fastened with five buttons at the fly and were worn straight. Drivers, or those assigned to cycling units, wore breeches in cord. Many officers wore breeches; a number because they were expected to ride, but others out of preference because they found them more comfortable. Cord breeches were also deemed to be a more fashionable garment than the straight-cut trouser.

Troops wore puttees, long strips of khaki cloth bound around the lower leg, and these, for the infantry, were wound anticlockwise from the boot up to the knee. Putting them on was comparatively simple, although some tried to imitate the French custom of criss-crossing the cloth. Vast numbers were required during the war, some 35 million pairs being ordered.

Footwear

Ankle boots (either brown or blackened) were worn by infantrymen and these were made from Indian

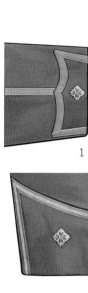

1 2 3 4 5 6

leather and had studded soles (studs being concentrated at the tip and on the heel). Officers had the option of wearing tall (butcher) boots, or ankle boots and puttees or ankle boots and Stohwasser leggings.

Headgear

Most troops wore a service dress cap (1905 Model) on active duty. It was a khaki peaked cap with black oilskin lining (which made the head sweaty) and had simple stiffening to produce a rounded effect (this was often

◀ CAPTAIN, KINGS ROYAL RIFLE CORPS, 1915 *This unit was unusual in that it had black buttons and a blackened cap badge. The buttons bore the bugle and crown motif.*

▼ LANTERN USED IN THE TRENCHES *Lanterns were used for signalling, as were flares and flags, but they were also issued to troops mining and excavating dugouts. Civilian items predominated.*

▲ RANK INSIGNIA *Top row: British line regiments, bottom row: Scottish Highland and Lowland regiments. 1 Second lieutenant. 2 Lieutenant. 3 Captain. 4 Major. 5 Lieutenant colonel. 6 Colonel.*

removed, giving the cap a squashed appearance). The cap had a brown leather chinstrap held in place by two small regimental buttons (as used on the shoulder straps). The regimental cap badge was pinned to the front of the cap and was the key distinguishing feature from regiment to regiment.

▼ *Bernard Law Montgomery, a captain on the staff, in France 1917. Relatively unknown then, he would become 'Monty', 1st Viscount Montgomery of Alamein in World War II.*

Infantry Cap Badges

Regiments	Badge	Regiments	Badge
(by army precedence, Scottish separate)		(by army precedence, Scottish separate)	
Queen's (Royal West Surrey)	Paschal Lamb and scroll	South Lancashire	Sphinx and Prince of Wales plume
Buffs (East Kent)	Dragon in silver and scroll		
King's Own (Royal Lancaster)	Lion in silver with title	The Welsh	Prince of Wales plume and scroll
Northumberland Fusiliers	Grenade with St George and dragon within	Oxford & Bucks Light Infantry	Bugle with strings
Royal Warwickshire	Antelope in silver with scroll	Essex	Castle and key with sphinx in oak wreath
Royal Fusiliers	Grenade with Order of the Garter within	Nottinghamshire and Derbyshire	Maltese cross beneath crown
King's (Liverpool)	White horse in silver and scroll	Loyal North Lancashire	Royal crest and rose with scroll
Norfolk	Figure of Britannia with tablet	Northamptonshire	Castle and key within wreath
Lincolnshire	Sphinx over Egypt with scroll	Royal Berkshire	Dragon of China with scroll
Devonshire	Castle within eight-pointed star	Royal West Kent	White horse of Kent with scrolls
Suffolk	Castle and key in a circle, below a crown	King's (Yorkshire Light Infantry)	French horn with white rose
Somersetshire Light Infantry	Bugle and crown with scroll		
West Yorkshire	White horse in silver with scroll	King's Own (Shropshire Light Infantry)	Bugle, strings and KSLI
East Yorkshire	Rose in laurel wreath on eight-pointed star	Middlesex	Prince of Wales plume within wreath
Bedfordshire	Maltese cross on eight-pointed star	King's Royal Rifle Corps	Maltese cross and crown, circle within and bugle within
Leicestershire	Tiger with two scrolls	Wiltshire	Cross with plate and cypher, with scroll
Royal Irish Regiment	Harp, crown and scroll		
Yorkshire	Alexandra's cypher, coronet, scroll and rose	Manchester	Manchester arms over scroll
Lancashire Fusiliers	Grenade with sphinx and Egypt within	North Staffordshire	Staffordshire knot, Prince of Wales plume
Cheshire	Star with acorn and leaves, scroll	York and Lancaster	Tiger and scroll within wreath with rose
Royal Welsh Fusiliers	Grenade with P of W plume within circle	Durham Light Infantry	Bugle, strings, crown and DLI
		Royal Irish Rifles	Harp and crown with scroll
South Wales Borderers	Sphinx within laurel wreath	Royal Irish Fusiliers	Grenade with harp and P of W plume within
Royal Inniskilling Fusiliers	Grenade with castle within		
Gloucestershire	Sphinx and two laurel leaves	Connaught Rangers	Harp and crown above scroll
Worcestershire	Lion and scroll within eight-pointed star	Leinster (Royal Canadians)	Prince of Wales plumes above scroll
East Lancashire	Sphinx and wreath below crown	Royal Munster Fusiliers	Grenade with tiger within
East Surrey	Shield within eight-pointed star	Royal Dublin Fusiliers	Grenade with tiger and elephant within
Duke of Cornwall's Light Infantry	Bugle below P of W coronet		
		Rifle Brigade	Maltese cross within wreath below crown
Duke of Wellington's (West Riding)	Crest of the Duke of Wellington		
Border	Maltese cross and lion on star below crown	**Territorial regiments**	
		Honourable Artillery Company	Grenade with HAC within
Royal Sussex	Star and feather with Garter within the star	Monmouthshire	Welsh dragon with scroll
Hampshire	Eight-pointed star and crown	Cambridgeshire	Castle with scroll
South Staffordshire	Staffordshire knot below crown, with scroll	London Regiment	Varied per battalion, most were variations on grenade
Dorsetshire	Castle, key and sphinx within wreath	Hertfordshire	Stag and scroll below crown
		Herefordshire	Lion with scroll

It was generally of yellow metal, the rifles having blackened metal. Distinctive badges are shown on the table, left, (a very few Pals battalions were issued their own badges).

In late 1914 many troops opted for the cap, winter service dress, or 'gorblimey', with its neck flaps and comfortable padding. The popularity of the cap waned in 1916, when balaclavas began to be worn under the steel helmet.

The officers' trench cap also had flaps which could fold down and protect the head in bad weather. Waterproof cloth covers added extra protection if needed.

Highland Regiments

Those regiments which traditionally wore a kilt wore a kind of service tunic or jacket with rounded ends. This Highland Pattern tunic had been introduced in 1902 and, apart from the cut, resembled the ordinary tunic. Highland officers wore pointed, gauntlet-style cuffs with pips and crowns below the lace and braiding denoting rank.

▼ **PRIVATE, EAST YORKSHIRE REGIMENT, 2ND BATTALION, 1915** *A front view with the gorblimey. This drab wool cap had flaps which were tied beneath the chin, making a chinstrap obsolete.*

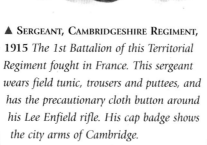

▲ **SERGEANT, CAMBRIDGESHIRE REGIMENT, 1915** *The 1st Battalion of this Territorial Regiment fought in France. This sergeant wears field tunic, trousers and puttees, and has the precautionary cloth button around his Lee Enfield rifle. His cap badge shows the city arms of Cambridge.*

◄ **PRIVATE, ALEXANDRA, PRINCESS OF WALES'S OWN YORKSHIRE REGIMENT (GREEN HOWARDS), 1915** *This private wears the cap, winter service dress, affectionately known by the troops themselves as the 'gorblimey', but unpopular with officers because it looked so scruffy and shapeless.*

Several Highland regiments wore a dark blue Glengarry (dark green for the Cameronians) with ribbons and a cap badge. The Seaforths, Gordons and the Argyll and Sutherland Highlanders had a dark blue (dark green for Light Infantry) woollen Glengarry (a cap worn tilted on the head) with ribbons, a strip of tartan dicing and regimental badge (shown on the table, right).

While all the above regiments wore the Highland Pattern tunic, the Highlanders generally wore kilts (although only two battalions of the Highland Light Infantry did so) and, with few exceptions, the other Scottish regiments wore trousers, trews or breeches.

Highlander and Lowland Cap Badges

Regiment	Cap Badge
Black Watch	Star of the Order of the Thistle with oval below cross
Seaforth Highlanders	Stag's head, coronet and scroll
Gordon Highlanders	Huntly crest within ivy wreath
Cameron Highlanders	St Andrew and cross within wreath
Argyll & Sutherland	Cypher, boar's head, cat within circle, within thistle wreath
Highland Light Infantry	Horn and HLI within star of the Order of the Thistle

The following Lowland regiments also wore the Glengarry:

Royal Scots	Thistle within circle within star of the Order of the Thistle
Royal Scots Fusiliers	Grenade, royal arms within
Kings Own Scottish Borderers	Circle and crest within thistle wreath
Cameronians (Scottish Rifles)	Mullet and bugle within thistle wreath

Kilts came in regimental tartans and on active service were generally worn with a khaki apron (with pocket) to protect the kilt and to reduce visibility. Black Watch tartan was worn by the Black Watch and Argyll and Sutherland Highlanders, Mackenzie tartan by the Seaforths (5th Battalion wore Sutherland) and the 6th and 9th battalions of the HLI, the Gordons wore Gordon and the Camerons wore Cameron tartan. The 9th Battalion of the Royal Scots wore kilts (Hunting Stuart), the rest wore khaki trousers, khaki breeches or trews in that tartan. A few Territorial battalions dressed in Scottish or Highland dress. The Tyneside Scottish had Glengarrys as did the 10th Battalion of the Liverpool Regiment (in Forbes kilts) and the 14th Battalion of the London Regiment (London Scottish). Hose and gaiters were worn with kilts, even spats were sometimes seen. These were very impractical, gaiters were uncomfortable

◄ LIEUTENANT, KING'S OWN SCOTTISH BORDERERS, 1915 *This lieutenant wears a privately tailored jacket made from superior cloth. He also wears trews with, incongruously, puttees.*

► PRIVATE, SEAFORTH HIGHLANDERS, 2ND BATTALION, 1915 *Highland cut or standard service jackets were modified in the field to give that distinctive cut-away front. This figure wears the impractical spats.*

and unsuitable for trench warfare and were quickly replaced by boots and short puttees. A flash of coloured cloth attached to the garter, was used to hold up the hose.

Territorial Regiments

Few Territorial infantry regiments were actually raised but Territorial battalions were added to existing regiments. Troops serving in these regiments wore regulation service dress, as did officers. Officers added a metallic 'T' below the badge worn on the collar/lapel of their jacket, while infantrymen usually had a 'T' added to their shoulder titles. This was usually placed above the battalion number which, in turn, was above the short regimental name. As usual, there were exceptions. The London Scottish simply wore London Scottish titles and some units showed a preference for cloth shoulder titles in red with white lettering (perhaps in imitation of the Guards). Scrolls on regimental badges were sometimes left blank, or adjusted to show the battle honours won by any volunteer elements attached to the regiment. Those men who had volunteered for overseas service wore a white metal badge on the right breast, bearing the words 'Imperial Service' beneath an imperial crown.

Some infantry battalions sought to distinguish themselves with other insignia. Those attached to fusilier or light infantry regiments, for example, used grenade or hunting horn badges on their shoulder straps to set themselves apart from other Territorials.

Infantry Equipment

If uniforms showed some variation, the vast majority of infantrymen wore a standard set of equipment. This consisted chiefly of the 1908 pattern web equipment. This was an extremely novel, and very flexible system which marked

▶ **INFANTRY KIT, 1918** *1 Canteen. 2 Small Box Respirator gas mask. 3 Entrenching tool head. 4 Entrenching tool shaft. 5 Wire cutters in pouch.*

British troops apart from their Continental allies and enemies, still reliant on the less practical and uncomfortable leather belts and pouches. The web equipment was manufactured from durable cotton and had been the subject of repeated testing between 1899 and 1906. A Mills-Burrowes prototype had been produced in 1906 and the equipment was adopted in early 1908. Troops carried different kinds of equipment for different duties. In battle order equipment was kept to a minimum – British troops were unencumbered by bulky equipment and 'could run like hares', as one German officer noted.

The waist belt came in three sizes and braces could be fitted to it when no cartridge pouches were worn (i.e. by soldiers issued with pistols). The buckle was simple and made of brass. Bayonets were suspended from the belt by means of frogging, which

also secured the bayonet and stopped it from falling out on the run, and the cover of the entrenching tool could be strapped to the bayonet cover. Cartridge pouches were fixed to either side of the belt buckle. There were now five on each side, allowing 150 rounds to be carried (in clips). Modifications were made in October 1914 as the pouches were found to open too easily, causing the loss of ammunition. Water bottles were also suspended from the

▼ **PRIVATE, LANCASHIRE FUSILIERS, 5TH BATTALION, 1918** *The Lancashire Fusiliers had the traditional fusiliers' bursting grenade on their shoulder straps with 'LF' below.*

belt as was a haversack. This contained first aid dressings, a few rations, documents and personal effects. A larger pack could also be worn, and if this was the case the haversack would be worn to one side (usually the left) and the pack would be worn on the back with suspension belts over the shoulder. The pack contained a change of clothes and boots, a greatcoat and personal effects. The steel helmet was often strapped to the back of the pack.

Most British infantrymen were issued with the Short Magazine Lee Enfield rifle, a bolt-action rifle of noted reliability. Experienced troops covered the breech on the march with a canvas cloth or handkerchief.

Local Variations

All the above seems to suggest a neatly uniformed army dressed according to regulations, one in which every officer adhered to the directive that 'The hair of the head will be kept short. The chin and under lip will be shaved, but not the upper lip. Whiskers, if worn, will be of moderate length.' But the expansion of the army in 1914 led to serious supply problems. Desperate measures were called for. Some 500,000 suits of blue serge were purchased that autumn, and the same

▼ *French and British soldiers in the trenches on the Western Front share cigarettes, 1916.*

number of civilian greatcoats, to supply uniform dress for the influx of volunteers. A further 900,000 greatcoats were ordered from North America. Men in Kitchener's New Armies (the plethora of new battalions formed from volunteers) used armbands to distinguish officers and NCOs from the rank and file. Items were privately purchased, especially for Pals battalions (the 11th Battalion Welsh Regiment had brown uniforms, that of the Border Regiment initially had grey), and obsolete items made a reappearance. Hasty purchasing often meant shoddy equipment: shoes and belts were especially poor. Much of this equipment was used in France. Leather belts and ammunition pouches could be seen, as could privately purchased overcoats.

Field Adaptations

The onset of trench warfare in the autumn of 1914, and the start of cold, wet weather, had an impact on British military dress. The service cap, which was fine in good weather, was often replaced by the famous gorblimey cap. This had a soft visor and unstiffened crown and had a flap which could be let down to cover the neck and ears. It was popular with the troops but was not deemed to be smart. The cap was worn without a chinstrap. Subsequent soft caps were

▲ PRIVATE, MANCHESTER REGIMENT, 1917
This Lewis gunner wears a specialist's badge on his lower left sleeve and also has a fleece jacket to keep him warm in the last winter of the war.

introduced in 1917. Scottish regiments mostly retained the Glengarry, although the round Balmoral bonnet was also worn and the more practical tam-o'-shanter became more popular. Footwear was now almost universally puttees and ankle boots. Officers were starting to attempt to make themselves less conspicuous, something which ultimately led to rank distinctions moving from the cuff to the shoulder.

Various fur jackets, jerkins and overcoats were used to supplement or replace standard or civilian greatcoats. Fingerless gloves, cap comforters and thigh boots or gum boots were also issued or purchased for use in the trenches. Gas masks obviously played an important part in any infantryman's kit after 1915. Various types were in use, but by the end of the war the 'small box respirator' was easily the most common, worn on the front and slung around the man's neck.

Protective Headgear
The most significant change in the profile of the British infantryman came with the introduction of the helmet. France had introduced a steel helmet in mid-1915 and Germany was working on the problem at the same time. Metal discs worn under the cap were tried, as were some French helmets and privately manufactured round hats. A kind of helmet designed by John Brodie was patented in the summer of 1915. Type A was made of steel; subsequent modifications led to it being made from manganese steel. Helmets were issued sparingly in the autumn of 1915, with troops instructed to reserve them for whoever was serving in the front-line trenches. The new helmets arrived en masse in early 1916 and modifications (leading to the manufacture of the Mark I, with its blunt rim, double liner and khaki finish) led to the near universal issuing of the well-known helmet. Badges were sometimes attached, or were stencilled on to the helmet cover. Divisional insignia was often painted on.

Wound Stripes
Vertical bars in braid were introduced as wound stripes in 1916, chevrons for overseas service not coming into use until early 1918. These latter were to be worn above the right cuff, and they were generally blue (red was worn for service before 1915). Scouts could wear green bands on their sleeves, signallers might have yellow. Proficiency badges could also be worn (crossed rifles on the left sleeve for marksmen, a red grenade on the right sleeve for a

bomber). Good conduct badges and battle badges also added to the ornamentation, but the most colourful aspect of the infantryman's uniform was going to be devices or insignia on his service dress tunic and helmet.

Infantry Battle Insignia
Various means of seeking to identify troops by additions to their uniforms had been experimented with in 1914 and 1915. Assault troops had tried armbands or squares of cloth pinned to the backs of their uniforms. The Australians took a lead in promoting more complicated signs and, by 1916, divisional or brigade insignia was becoming common.

Some divisions introduced signs to be worn by all troops in the division, others for those relegated to rear area duties. Some divisions elected to differentiate between brigades, others by regiment or battalion. Some regiments added their own insignia or combined battalion identification insignia with divisional insignia (various geometrical shapes in different colours denoting a particular battalion), and others just used regimental insignia (as in the 2nd Division). The Guards had an open eye device; the 1st Division had the signal code for 1; the 3rd used yellow devices on the sleeve; the 4th had a ram's head; the 6th a circle; the 7th had dots (coloured for each brigade); the 9th later adopted a thistle; the 12th had a spade on a circle; the 16th had a shamrock; the 18th had 'ATN' in a disc; the 19th had a butterfly; the 20th had a black cross on a white disc; the 21st had distinctive signs in red; the 22nd had a horseshoe; the 29th had a red triangle; the 30th had a Derby crest; the 31st adopted a white and red rose in 1917; the 33rd showed two dice with the number three displayed; the 34th a chessboard; the 35th had seven fives forming a cogged wheel; the 37th used a horseshoe; the 38th had a Welsh dragon; the 40th had a white diamond on a bantam. Regular divisions serving in Macedonia added coloured strips to the end of their shoulder straps: the 10th had green,

the 22nd had black, the 26th had blue, the 27th yellow, the 28th had red. Divisions composed of Territorials also had distinctive badges: the 49th had a white rose, for example, the 51st had 'HD' (Highland Division) and the 62nd a pelican. The 47th had the ingenious idea of using the symbols from a deck of cards for battalions. The 1st Brigade had yellow aces, spades, clubs and diamonds, the 2nd had green and those in the 3rd had red.

▼ CORPORAL, NORTH STAFFORDSHIRE REGIMENT, 1918 *Shorts were not regulation issue, but were often just cut down versions of drab trousers. This veteran has tilted his helmet forward to wear the chinstrap behind the head.*

INFANTRY: OTHER THEATRES

Although Britain's main effort was focused on the Western Front, British troops were despatched to various theatres where standard service issue was simply unsuitable as clothing.

Adaptations for Warmer Climates

British troops in the Mediterranean, in Macedonia, Mesopotamia and Palestine, Africa and India wore uniforms designed to make life more bearable for the scalding days and chilly nights which dominated warfare in such climates. Of course, such distinctions could not always be made in the chaos of war. Troops serving at Gallipoli wore a mixture of items from Western Front-style uniforms (such as the service cap) and khaki drill uniform, depending on the provenance of the unit involved.

This was also true of troops serving in Macedonia and in Italy, where the Brodie helmet was as common as the tropical version (the Brodie was not worn at Gallipoli; it was introduced too late to be issued to troops at the Dardanelles). For example, the South Staffordshire Regiment wore Brodie helmets in Italy, simply painting on a Staffordshire knot by way of insignia. Other examples abound.

Troops of the London Regiment, serving in Macedonia (following the landings at Salonika) wore drab service tunics with khaki drill shorts. This was probably because much of the fighting was in the mountains, where temperatures could rise and fall without much warning.

Jackets and Leg Wear

British troops sent to fight in hot climates wore a khaki drill uniform. This was primarily composed of a cotton jacket and trousers (although shorts, cut below the knee, were often worn). The fabric was lighter and more comfortable in hot weather, and the colour was a light, sand colour, deemed more appropriate for the terrain of Egypt or India.

The jacket had falling collars, was fastened with five regimental buttons, had pockets with rectangular flaps (earlier versions had had pointed flaps) and, usually, had pointed cuffs. Officers had jackets similar in cut to those worn on the Western Front, although shirts were usually khaki or beige with ties of a similar hue. Rank distinctions were worn at the shoulder, rather than at the cuffs, which were, as for the other ranks' cuffs, pointed.

Some officers in Africa wore bush shirts, a compromise between a jacket and a shirt. Many soldiers opted to wear their collarless grey-blue or sand-coloured flannel shirt (most commonly known as the greyback) rather than the jacket and rolled the sleeves back; equipment was worn over the shirt. Locally tailored khaki shirts with breast pockets were also worn in Africa and the Middle East. Greatcoats were generally not worn, although various coats and raincoats were pressed into service.

▲ SERGEANT, THE LONDON REGIMENT, 1/19TH BATTALION (ST PANCRAS), 1917 *The simplified service dress jacket (or utility jacket), without buttons on the pocket flaps, is being worn with upturned collar in the chill of a desert morning.*

◀ *British personnel are moved up to the Palestine front on board the trucks of an open-topped narrow-gauge goods train.*

Trousers were long and worn with puttees and (brown) ankle boots. Officers wore breeches or trousers with boots or leggings. Puttees were usually sand coloured but drab or even green items could be seen. Puttees were also worn with the long shorts common in the British Army, even though this looked odd and also exposed the knees to insect bites and, in Africa, bush thorns. The 6th Battalion of the Highland Light Infantry served at Gallipoli in kilts (with khaki aprons). This produced a singular looking uniform: tropical helmet, flannel or khaki shirt, kilt with apron, hose and gaiters or puttees and boots.

▲ *Personnel in Mesopotamia with a camel, from an album compiled by Lt Kindom who was associated with the 134th Coy Machine Gun Corps and the 7th Meerut Division.*

Headgear

The most distinctive feature of British troops serving in hot climates was the Wolseley helmet. This sun helmet, named after Garnet Wolseley, the great Victorian soldier who had campaigned in Egypt and the Sudan, had come into use during the last of the Boer Wars, and it was generally known as a topi (and it should not be referred to as a pith helmet).

The helmet itself was made of cork and was covered in khaki cloth. It had a peak which ran all the way around the helmet, protecting most of the head from the sun. A band ran around the base of the helmet's crown, and this was known as a pagri. It was mostly khaki, although the white full dress version had white bands (except for the Northumberland Fusiliers who

◀ **PRIVATE, HIGHLAND LIGHT INFANTRY, 1/6TH BATTALION, 1915** *This is something of a composite uniform – a flannel shirt worn with a kilt and puttees. The more traditional shoes and gaiters have been discarded.*

▶ **CAPTAIN, THE LONDON REGIMENT 2/15TH BATTALION, BULGARIA, 1916** *This officer wears the symbol of the 60th Division, a bee, stitched to his signals brassard. He wears a civilian raincoat.*

had red and white, and the Duke of Cornwall's Light Infantry who had red). The chinstrap was of brown leather. Ventilation was provided by means of a zinc button on the top of the helmet.

Troops sent into northern Russia in 1917 and 1918 wore fur caps and boots as well as canvas greatcoats lined with sheepskin. This uniform was supposedly designed by Ernest Shackleton. Smocks with hoods and padded trousers were also worn. Troops in Siberia wore a mixture of British equipment, Canadian clothing and Russian hats. The Russian Relief Force wore a Polar star insignia.

The dress regulations of 1911 made it clear that 'no badges, plumes, hackles or ornaments of any description are to be worn with the khaki helmet', but this was widely ignored. Some other kinds of tropical helmets, such as the flatter peaked Bombay bowler, were also used, as were privately purchased items. Peaked caps made of khaki drill were also worn by some officers, often with the addition of neck flaps. Later in the war, perhaps imitating Australian or Boer fashions, slouch hats became increasingly popular. These were often worn with one of the brims turned up and pinned with some kind of insignia.

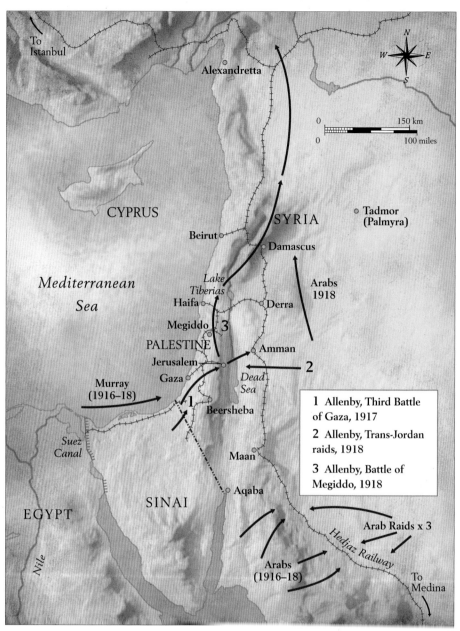

◄ **PRIVATE, SEAFORTH HIGHLANDERS, 1ST BATTALION, 1915** *The private's Glengarry cap was made from dark blue wool reinforced with a strip of leather along the base. It was decorated with tartan 'dicing' plus a cap badge and, on occasion, a hackle.*

▲ *Operations in Palestine safeguarded the Suez Canal from Ottoman attempts to cut this vital supply line from India to Europe. The 1917 campaign here would culminate in the Allied seizure of Jerusalem, and in 1918 the British pressed on to invade Syria.*

Most soldiers and officers found the Wolseley to be comfortable and relatively practical. Further protection for the neck was often provided by an additional khaki cloth neck flap.

When most troops in Europe were adding flashes or patches to their uniforms and helmets, those far from the Western Front were following suit. Coloured strips of cloth known as flashes were being added to the side of the tropical helmet, as were some coloured bands and badges. Patches were also being added to the khaki drill jacket.

Flashes

Helmet flashes seem to have been designed by unit commanders, there being no authorized system of issuing such insignia. Officers of the Kent Cyclist Battalion, based in India, for example, adapted their regimental badge and fixed a rearing white horse

◄ PRIVATE, LANCASHIRE FUSILIERS, 5TH BATTALION, 1915 *A bandolier worn over the chest allowed this infantryman to carry extra ammunition and made up for difficult supply conditions.*

► PRIVATE, PRINCE ALBERT'S 1/4TH BATTALION (SOMERSET LIGHT INFANTRY), MESOPOTAMIA, 1918 *This private wears a four-button grey ordinary shirt that was manufactured without a collar, and made from flannel material. By the end of the war some 200 million yards of flannel had been used for manufacturing army shirts alone.*

flashes according to the particular battalion. The 1st Battalion of the Sussex Regiment had Royal Sussex in white on a red triangle; the 4th Battalion had a rectangle in light blue with a dark blue stripe; the 5th Battalion had orange and blue rectangles piped in grey. The Welsh Fusiliers had rectangles divided into green and white. The Hampshires had variations on squares vertically or diagonally bisected. The Essex Regiment had its 4th Battalion with a circle divided into red on one side and black on the other; the 5th had the same but for a triangle; the 6th had an oblong and the 7th had a square. The 31st Division preferred divisional flashes, with the 1st Brigade having a square with white over red, the 2nd having a square diagonally split between white (above) and red (below), while the 3rd had a square split red over white. Such flashes were generally worn on both sides of the helmet. The 42nd Division had its patches on the khaki drill uniform: diamonds in red, green and yellow with the battalion number superimposed. The 54th (involved in the campaign in Palestine) had coloured patches according to regiment.

Standard infantry equipment was worn, although troops serving in India, or sent from there, might have used older Slade Wallace belts and leather ammunition pouches or the 1914 pattern leather equipment issued in such quantities to Territorial or New

above the word 'Invicta' on to a black diamond patch and wore this over the pagri. It also used locally manufactured shoulder titles. The 6th Battalion of the Highland Light Infantry adopted a flash of Mackenzie tartan for its Wolseley helmets. The Norfolk Regiment took its original facing colours (yellow) and wore an oblong in that colour with a central black stripe. The Suffolk Regiment, however, took its regimental badge (a castle) and wore that as a helmet flash. Some regiments went further. The Royal Sussex and the Hampshires varied their

Army units. This was due to economy as well as to the distance from home. Bandoliers were popular in Africa, and items of local manufacture were also used. Most officers wore Sam Browne belts, carried binoculars and a cane or swagger stick and made use of a Smith and Wesson or Webley revolver, usually carried in a brown holster (Colt pistols were much less common). Gas protectors were issued to troops at Gallipoli (it was feared the Ottomans would use gas shells), and gas masks were naturally issued to troops in Palestine, Italy and Macedonia.

CAVALRY

British line cavalry was divided into dragoon guards, dragoons, lancers and hussars. By 1914 traditional differences in dress had all but ceased, and they were largely uniformed in service dress.

Cavalry Organization

In addition to the seven regiments of dragoon guards (deemed to be elite troops), Britain could field 21

▼ TROOPER, 13TH HUSSARS, 1914 *Cavalry troopers, and mounted artillery, wore a lanyard at the left shoulder, seen here. It was attached to a tool, worn in the breast pocket, to pick and clean horses' hooves.*

regiments of regular cavalry. These were numbered sequentially but, for historic reasons, were divided into dragoons, hussars and lancers. Dragoons had originally been mounted infantry, but were regarded as standard line cavalry in 1914 (Britain did not have heavy line cavalry as such). Hussars had originally been tasked with skirmishing and scouting and, at least initially, retained that role. Lancers too, were viewed as light cavalry, but they at least retained the distinction of being armed with that fearsome, if difficult to master, weapon, the lance. They were used by the BEF in France and Belgium to flank advances, scout and seize prisoners for information.

▼ REGIMENTAL SERGEANT MAJOR, 5TH (ROYAL IRISH) LANCERS, 1915 *Cavalry had traditionally carried carbines, but in the British Army these were replaced by the SMLE rifle in 1902 – seen here in its holster.*

Service Dress

Cavalry service dress uniforms had been thoroughly reformed before the war began in 1914. Cavalrymen would find themselves dressed in drab tunics from 1902 of a pattern similar to that worn by the regular infantry and with gilded buttons (hussars had domed buttons, other regiments had insignia and regimental badges, as appropriate). Again regimental distinctions were relegated to the shoulder titles (variations on the regimental name) and to the cap badge.

For full dress, smaller collar badges were worn on the tunic collar (these were reduced versions of the cap badge) and officers wore collar insignia on the lapel/collar of their service jacket and rank insignia at the cuffs. This gradually died out, as rank insignia moved to the shoulder, but examples of cuff insignia could be found throughout the war and, indeed, on in to the 1920s.

Khaki drill tunics and jackets were worn in hotter climates as were khaki drill trousers (rather than breeches). Busbies, czapkas and helmets were to be left in the barracks. The cavalry were now to wear the standard drab service cap for active duty in western Europe. This had a chinstrap of brown leather, which was supposed to be worn down when on duty (and not worn above the peak of the cap). The cap had a metal badge on the front carrying various designs, as shown in the table overleaf.

Troops serving in the Middle East, Macedonia, the Mediterranean, India, Africa and Italy often used the Wolseley tropical helmet. Brodie helmets came into near universal use from 1916. Regimental badges were stencilled on to these, sometimes metal badges were riveted on.

Leg Wear

Mounted troops wore breeches (universal pattern), many officers opting for Bedford cord, which was supposed to be very hardwearing, or pantaloons with buckskin strapping (reinforcement) at the knee and at the seat of the garment. Breeches with puttees were worn by many rank and file. For mounted troops, puttees started below the knee and on the left leg went anticlockwise, clockwise on the right. The puttee was supposed to finish in a V-shape on the outside of the leg. Ankle boots were worn. Officers wore cavalry boots, although puttees or Stohwasser leggings were often used. Jack spurs made of steel were worn, although an exception was made for troops travelling on board ships.

► TROOPER, 12TH (PRINCE OF WALES ROYAL) LANCERS, 1914 *Lancers, as well as some hussars, carried lances, swords and rifles. This lancer has unfurled his pennon, traditionally attached to the end of the lance to scare oncoming (enemy) horses. Using a lance required great skill and those proficient in the arm would wear a small crossed lances badge in worsted material on their lower left sleeve. The best man in each regiment wore this badge with a small crown above it.*

Cavalry Cap Badges

Regiment	Cap Badge
1st (King's) Dragoon Guards	Austrian eagle with scroll*
2nd Dragoon Guards	The word 'Bays' in a laurel beneath a crown
3rd (Prince of Wales's) Dragoon Guards	Prince of Wales plume with coronet
4th (Royal Irish) Dragoon Guards	Star of the Order of St Patrick, with scroll
5th (Princess Charlotte's) Dragoon Guards	Circle with motto around white horse, beneath crown
6th Dragoon Guards (Carabiniers)	Order of the Garter on crossed carbines, beneath a crown
7th (Princess Royal's) Dragoon Guards	A lion issuing from a coronet, with scroll
1st (Royal) Dragoons	Royal crest with scroll below
2nd (Royal Scots Greys) Dragoons	Eagle over the word 'Waterloo', with scroll
3rd (King's Own) Hussars	White horse in silver
4th (Queen's Own) Hussars	Circle above laurel below a crown
5th (Royal Irish) Lancers	5 in silver within circle on crossed lances
6th (Inniskilling) Dragoons	Inniskilling castle in silver over a scroll
7th (Queen's Own) Hussars	The letters QO in a circle, below a crown
8th (Royal Irish) Hussars	Silver harp below gilt crown, with scroll
9th (Queen's Royal) Lancers	9 in silver on crossed lances, below crown
10th (Prince of Wales's Own Royal) Hussars	Prince of Wales plume (silver), gilt coronet
11th (Prince Albert's Own) Hussars	Prince Consort's crest
12th (Prince of Wales's) Lancers	Prince of Wales's plumes on crossed lances with XII
13th Hussars	Circle and XIII within wreath below crown
14th (King's) Hussars	Black Prussian eagle**
15th (The King's) Hussars	Garter with XV KH with scroll
16th (The Queen's) Lancers	16 in silver on crossed lances with crown and scroll
17th (Duke of Cambridge's Own) Lancers	Death's head with motto 'OR GLORY'
18th (Queen Mary's Own) Hussars	XVIII within a ring on laurel, below crown
19th (Queen Alexandra's Own Royal) Hussars	Dannebrog and A, below coronet
20th Hussars	xHx below a crown
21st (Empress of India) Lancers	Imperial cypher and XXI on crossed lances

*Replaced with a star and crown in 1915.

** This was discarded in 1915 and replaced by a royal crest and scroll bearing 14th King's Hussars.

▼ TROOPER, 20TH HUSSARS, 1915
A bandolier, containing 90 rounds, was commonly worn by cavalry troopers, or slung around the horse's neck. The chinstrap, which can be seen just above the peak on this smart example of a service dress cap, was required to be worn when the trooper was mounted.

Accoutrements

Various capes and waterproofs were issued to the men. Officers had privately purchased items or drab greatcoats. These greatcoats would have branch of service piping on the shoulder straps. For cavalry this piping was in yellow, rank badges being in gilt metal. Cavalry carried different equipment from the infantry. The most significant item was the bandolier containing ammunition. These 1903 pattern leather bandoliers had originally been issued to infantry and naval troops, but web equipment displaced them and they were assigned to the cavalry. Each bandolier consisted of a wide leather strap, worn over the shoulder, with nine cartridge pouches. Each cavalryman therefore had 90 rounds, although two bandoliers could be worn or an extra one slung around the horse's neck. All mounted troops wore a cord lanyard, at the end of which was attached a tool for scraping horse hooves that was kept in the top pocket.

Officers wore Sam Browne belts with two braces (although normally just one was used), revolver holster, ammunition pouch and frogging with a brown leather holster. Most troops wore a haversack, slung around the shoulder, and a leather waist belt with canteen attached.

Additional equipment was carried on the horse: bags with personal effects, blankets, feed bags and forage, leather horseshoe cases with nail pockets and a rifle (held in a leather boot). British cavalrymen used the Short Magazine Lee-Enfield (SMLE) Mark I rifle; carbines were not deemed necessary. The cavalryman usually carried a 1908 cavalry pattern sword, officers wore loose sword knots with the Sam Browne belt. Saddlebags and dispatch bags were optional, but were often used by officers in the field. Bayonets and entrenching tools began to be used later in the war. Lancers

▶ CAPTAIN, 2ND DRAGOONS (ROYAL SCOTS GREYS), 1916 *Perhaps by virtue of this officer being assigned to remount duties, he has managed to procure a grey horse, a colour traditionally favoured by this regiment.*

carried 1909 pattern bamboo lances with pennons of red over white. Gas masks were issued for man and horse.

Insignia

Cavalry also began to adopt colourful insignia as the war continued. The 3rd Cavalry Division was the only cavalry division known to have worn its own distinctive divisional insignia. They elected to wear the three horseshoes. The 2nd Division may have used two horseshoes, the 1st a white rectangle bisected by a red line. Individual regiments made much use of particular insignia. The 17th Lancers wore its Death's Head insignia on sleeves and helmets; the 3rd Hussars used their white horse on sleeve patches and helmets.

Service stripes, wound stripes and good conduct stripes were also worn. Farriers wore a horseshoe emblem on the upper right sleeve, instructors wore a white spur. Crossed swords on the lower left sleeve denoted an expert swordsman, crossed lances for expert lancers. Signallers had crossed flags on the left cuff.

Horse Furniture

Saddles were usually of the 1912 universal pattern. This was made out of hogskin with white wool padding below. Bits were of steel and bridles were in bridle leather with brass fittings and buckles. Stirrups were of nickel or steel. Horses themselves were often branded with a regimental mark. This followed the pattern of 21L (21st Lancers) or 14H (14th Hussars), for example. Tails were no longer docked.

YEOMANRY

The cavalry of the Territorial force were termed yeomanry, and many of these regiments had their origins in the militias raised during the Napoleonic invasion scares. They were volunteers originally intended for home defence. As the war progressed, many found themselves sent abroad to serve in the Middle East and France.

After the Napoleonic Wars yeomanry cavalry were retained to act as police to control social unrest. In 1908 the yeomanry had been combined with the Volunteer Force to form the Territorial Force. The mounted militia became the Special Reserve Cavalry at the same time. All these troops were trained to fight as mounted infantry, and the

designations of lancers and hussars were used just to reflect traditions and historic roles. In 1914 there were some 57 regiments of yeomanry. They were raised by County Associations, and most had titles based on their recruiting areas, but they were not attached to regular cavalry regiments in the same way that the Territorial force's infantry raised battalions for existing regiments. The table opposite shows the units that were raised and served during the war (units had first line, second line and third line designations, ie 1/1st Welsh Horse, 2/1st Welsh Horse, 3/1st Welsh Horse), and they wore various cap badges.

Uniform Distinctions

Yeomanry regiments were dressed in the style adopted by the regular cavalry. Imperial Service badges were common in the early years of the war. Yeomanry regiments had metal shoulder titles with the short forms of their regimental names (sometimes with a 'T' over a 'Y' over the regimental name), and they wore caps with regimental badges. The Welsh Horse had distinctive shoulder titles with the regimental name on a solid bar of curved metal. Some units had cloth titles, including the Shropshire Yeomanry who had white lettering on red cloth. This was worn in addition to the metal titles on the shoulder strap.

Yeomanry regiments did serve abroad – the Derbyshire Yeomanry were at Gallipoli, for example – but many of those mounted units which remained in Great Britain had their mounts taken away to resupply units sent overseas. Those deprived of their horses were often issued with bicycles instead.

Many yeomanry regiments became cyclists in 1916; the 74th Division was largely composed of dismounted Yeomanry personnel. However, a Yeomanry Mounted Division did serve in Palestine in 1917. Troops in the Middle East wore tropical helmets and khaki drill. They wore flashes in their helmets but little by way of divisional insignia was worn. Flashes and distinctions in the Middle East include

◀ **TROOPER, EAST YORKSHIRE YEOMANRY, 1917** *Horses were often loaded with additional equipment. This one carries an extra bandolier and two blankets: one rolled behind the saddle for the rider and one underneath the saddle for the horse, which provided extra support and leg protection.*

Yeomanry Cap Badges

Regiment	Type	Cap Badge
In army precedence order		
Wiltshire	Hussars	Prince of Wales's plumes
Warwickshire	Hussars	Bear and ragged staff
Yorkshire	Hussars	Rose with Prince of Wales's plumes
Sherwood Rangers	Hussars	Bugle horn and strings
Staffordshire	Hussars	Staffordshire knot with crown
Shropshire	Dragoons	Shield in circle beneath crown
Ayrshire	Hussars	Lion's head in wreath, scroll below
Cheshire	Hussars	Prince of Wales's plumes with scroll
Queen's Own Yorkshire	Dragoons	Rose below crown, blackened
Leicestershire	Hussars	LY in a wreath, below a crown
North Somerset	Dragoons	Ten-pointed star below crown
Duke of Lancaster's Own	Dragoons	Rose in a wreath, with scrolls and coronet
Lanarkshire	Lancers	Double-headed eagle
Northumberland	Hussars	Castle within circle beneath crown
South Nottinghamshire	Hussars	Oak leaf and acorn
Denbighshire	Hussars	Prince of Wales's plumes with scroll
Westmoreland & Cumberland	Hussars	Heather in a circle below a crown
Pembrokeshire	Hussars	Prince of Wales's plumes, motto (Fishguard)
Royal East Kent	Mounted Rifles	White horse of Kent in Garter, below crown
Hampshire	Carabiniers	Rose in an oval, crossed carbines, crown
Buckinghamshire	Hussars	Swan within circle, crown above
Derbyshire	Dragoons	Scrolls within a wreath, crown above
Dorsetshire	Hussars	QODY beneath crown
Gloucestershire	Hussars	Portcullis with chains below coronet
Hertfordshire	Dragoons	Hart on a ford
Berkshire	Dragoons	White horse on scroll
Middlesex	Hussars	Eight-pointed star with cypher
Royal 1st Devonshire	Hussars	Royal crest
Royal Devon	Horse	Lord Rolle's crest in circle below royal crest
Suffolk	Hussars	Castle and 1793 within scroll
Royal North Devonshire	Hussars	NDH below crown
Worcestershire	Hussars	Pear blossom in a wreath, crown above
West Kent	Hussars	White horse and scroll with Invicta
West Somerset	Hussars	Wyvern within circle, scroll below
Oxfordshire	Hussars	Queen Adelaide's cypher and crown
Montgomeryshire	Dragoons	Welsh dragon above WY
Lothians and Border	Horse	Bushel
Glasgow	Dragoons	Crest of Scotland and thistles
Lancashire Hussars	Hussars	Rose of Lancashire
Surrey	Lancers	Lord Middleton's crest
Fifeshire and Forfarshire	Dragoons	Thane of Fife badge
Norfolk	Dragoons	Royal cypher
Sussex	Dragoons	Six martlets on a shield, crown above
Glamorganshire	Dragoons	Prince of Wales's plumes above scroll
Welsh Horse	Lancers	Leek between W and H
Lincolnshire	Lancers	Lincoln arms in wreath below crown
City of London (Roughriders)	Lancers	City of London arms below crown
Westminster	Dragoons	Westminster arms above scroll ▶

▲ **Lieutenant, Oxfordshire Yeomanry, 1914** *This lieutenant wears standard service dress with two pips on his cuffs. The cap badge is Queen Adelaide's cypher below a crown and above a bugle. The British cavalry used trumpets when in barracks but in the field switched to bugles. These were initially used for signalling, calling a halt to a charge, for example, and there are examples of them being used in 1914. A trumpeter or bugler held an appointment, rather than a rank, but they were considered senior to privates.*

the following (all first line units):
COUNTY OF LONDON YEOMANRY: yellow square with black and green edging, tipped point.
GLOUCESTERSHIRE YEOMANRY: blue and gold blue ribbons worn on the khaki pagri.

Regiment	Type	Cap Badge
3rd London Sharpshooters	Hussars	3 in a circle on crossed rifles, crown above
Bedfordshire	Lancers	Eagle and castle below crown
Essex	Dragoons	Shield in circle bearing Decus et tutamen
Northamptonshire	Dragoons	Hanoverian horse
East Riding of Yorkshire	Lancers	Fox above scroll
The Lovat Scouts	Horse	Stag's head within circle
Scottish Horse	Horse	St Andrew's cross in oval and wreath, below crown

Special Reserve Cavalry

North Irish Horse		Irish harp below crown, scroll below
South Irish Horse		Shamrock bearing SIH
King Edward's Horse		Laurel and oak wreath with shield, royal crest above
2nd King Edward's Horse		Laurel and oak wreath, scroll above and below, crown above

LINCOLNSHIRE YEOMANRY: Lincoln green square bisected with a white stripe.
BERKSHIRE YEOMANRY: blue diamond bisected by a yellow stripe with a red stripe on each side.
STAFFORDSHIRE YEOMANRY: a diamond split into three bands of red, white and blue.
1ST SCOTTISH HORSE: the regimental badge was on a triangle of Atholl tartan worn on the left side of the helmet only.
CITY OF LONDON (ROUGHRIDERS): a diamond quartered into blue top and bottom, and purple left and right.

◄ TROOPER, WESTMINSTER DRAGOONS, 1915
The desert called for practical uniforms. The non-regulation string blinkers on the horse kept flies away. Note the fork and spoon tucked handily into the rider's puttees. The saddle is the 1912 universal type, and the amount of extra equipment carried shows that the trooper expects to be out in the field for some considerable time. The rifle is stored in a leather bucket and a sword and bayonet are also being carried.

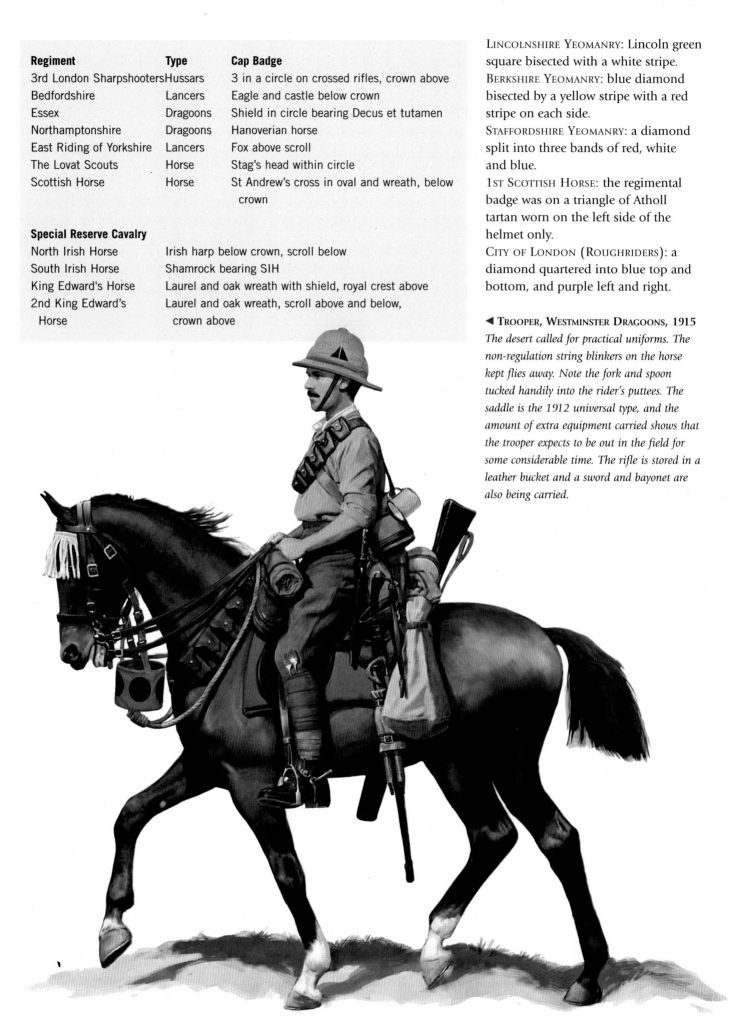

AVIATION

In April 1912 the Royal Flying Corps obtained its Royal Warrant and by 1913 a distinctive uniform was emerging. In 1912 a khaki serge tunic was introduced (known as the 'maternity tunic') with a plastron front, buttoned on the right with concealed RFC buttons. Cloth shoulder titles were worn on each shoulder.

Officers wore a jacket with a stiffer collar which often had collar badges in gilt metal. Wings were introduced in February 1913 and generally worn on the left breast. Observers wore their own winged badge on their tunics.

RFC personnel were issued with a peakless side cap (known as an Austrian cap) and this bore the RFC badge in gilt metal or in bronze on the left front. Service caps were also worn by ground crew or by officers. Officer cadets wore the cap with a white band.

Ground crew generally wore breeches with puttees and ankle boots.

Officers had breeches or pantaloons with boots or leggings (or aviator's boots, laced all the way up the front). RFC pilots and ground crew operating in hot climates wore khaki drill along with slouch hats or Wolseley tropical helmets. Shorts or breeches with puttees were usually worn. Officers generally wore Sam Browne belts with one strap. All ranks carried pistols, either in holsters attached to webbing equipment or on the Sam Browne.

▼ OBSERVER, ROYAL FLYING CORPS, 1915
The maternity tunic was made from twill with a silk lining and was a distinctive component of the RFC uniform.

▼ LIEUTENANT, PILOT, ROYAL FLYING CORPS, 1914 *The tunic has an officer's pip at the shoulder but no button on the shoulder strap. Officers wore pilot's wings on the left breast.*

▼ PILOT, ROYAL FLYING CORPS, 1917 *Pilots in the Middle East wore cotton jacket and riding breeches. The flying helmet here is privately purchased.*

ARTILLERY

Britain began the war with artillery that was soon seen as deficient in many respects. The huge scale of the war made enormous demands on Britain's artillery, and initial problems were only overcome by late 1916.

The main weapon of Britain's field artillery throughout the war was the 18-pounder field gun, though a 13-pounder also saw much use. These had a relatively limited range (and with the shrapnel shells available in the early part of the war made a poor impression on German defences). Larger guns included the 60-pounder being used by the BEF in 1914. Artillery also made use of howitzers for higher-angle fire. The 4.5-inch was the lightest and most common of the standard types but numbers of heavier 6-inch and 9.2-inch types were introduced as the war progressed.

Personnel was provided by the Royal Regiment of Artillery. The Royal Field Artillery manned the batteries of 18-pounders and howitzers, the Royal Garrison Artillery manned the heavy batteries and mobile batteries were the charge of the Royal Horse Artillery.

Royal Field Artillery

Personnel of the Royal Field Artillery wore service dress in 1914. This consisted of the drab tunic with gilt, and dome buttons bearing the device of a gun and crown. Gunners and NCOs wore a shoulder strap with the initials 'RFA'. Officers wore jackets with rank shown at the cuff and with a lapel/collar badge of a bursting grenade above a scroll bearing the motto 'UBIQUE' (everywhere). Khaki drill jackets and tunics were worn in hotter climates, but gunners often just wore the blue-grey flannel shirt.

Gunners wore trousers with braces or belts, only those serving as drivers wearing breeches with puttees or leggings and ankle boots with spurs

▶ BOMBARDIER, ROYAL HORSE ARTILLERY, ATTACHED TO THE 2ND CAVALRY DIVISION, 1918 *When in shirt sleeves, only the insignia on this figure's helmet denotes the man's formation. His tunic would bear the standard RHA shoulder title.*

◀ 4.5-INCH HOWITZER *This gun entered service in 1909. Throughout the war some 3,000 were manufactured, including 600 that were sent to supply Russia in 1916.*

(mounted drivers also wore lanyards). Officers tended to wear breeches of the universal pattern with brown cavalry boots or brown leather leggings.

Equipment was as for the infantry, officers wearing Sam Browne belts. Swords, if worn, were half-basket types with a slightly curved blade. These were quickly obsolete, some officers electing to carry daggers or bayonets in addition to their pistols. Caps bore a bronze badge with a gun between two scrolls bearing 'UBIQUE'. on the upper scroll, and 'QUO FAS ET GLORIA DUCUNT' (where duty and glory lead) on the lower, all beneath a crown.

▼ GUNNER, ROYAL FIELD ARTILLERY, 9TH DIVISION, 1916 *This figure's divisional symbols are more distinctive than the simple 'RFA' worn on the shoulder strap.*

Royal Garrison Artillery

Before the war much of the British Army's heavy artillery resided in garrisons and forts. The Royal Garrison Artillery took to the field in 1914, however, serving some enormous guns, and providing much needed range and weight on the battlefield.

The Royal Garrison Artillery were dressed as for the Field Artillery but with 'RGA' as a shoulder title. There were no other discernible differences, although according to regulations RGA officers were supposed to wear knickerbocker breeches and puttees rather than cord breeches and leather leggings. As many officers of the RFA wore puttees, it was largely a theoretical distinction.

Royal Horse Artillery

Horse artillery traditionally served lighter pieces and were attached to cavalry divisions and brigades. Increased mobility meant that they could be brought up quickly to clear away obstinate enemy positions, or to plug dangerous gaps. The Royal Horse Artillery manned lighter pieces and generally took on the same appearance as the cavalry.

Uniforms reflected those of the cavalry. Shoulder titles bore the initials 'RHA' and the cap badge and officers' collar/lapel badge was as for the Royal Field Artillery. Gunners wore lanyards and breeches with leggings or puttees and boots with spurs. Officers wore breeches, Stohwasser leggings and brown boots. Horse furniture was as for the cavalry.

Other Artillery Units

There were also Territorial artillery units. The most famous of these was the Honourable Artillery Company, which raised two batteries of horse artillery. These had 'HAC' shoulder titles with an 'A' or 'B' above to signify a particular battery. The company's bursting grenade badge also bore HAC on the ball of the grenade.

Territorial Horse, Field and Garrison Artillery also existed. This last was often used to man coastal defences. They wore shoulder

▲ DRIVER, ROYAL FIELD ARTILLERY, 1914 *This driver wears very sturdy and high riding boots to protect his knees when riding pillion. Horses were still the most effective way of moving guns around; no reliable mechanical system was put in place before 1918.*

titles with a 'T' above 'RHA', 'RFA' and 'RGA' respectively, and sometimes bore a divisional number below. Their cap badges were the same as those of the regulars, but with a spray of laurel replacing the motto.

In addition, Britain also had the Royal Malta Artillery – whose cap badge was a circle with 'Royal Malta Artillery' below a crown – and the Bermuda Militia Artillery, who wore a badge as for the RGA but with the addition of an 'M'.

TECHNICAL TROOPS

As with most armies, there was a steady growth in the technical services of the British Army as the war continued. The difficulties of breaking through formidable enemy defences, or constructing similar defences called for technical expertise of many different kinds.

Machine Gun Corps

Infantry did operate Lewis guns and other weapons, and personnel assigned to these duties wore an 'LG', 'HG' (Hotchkiss Gunner) or 'MG' in a wreath on the lower arm. However, by 1915 there was a Machine Gun Corps composed of companies assigned to particular brigades. They wore standard infantry dress, substituting pistols with rifles and cartridge pouches, with 'MGC' shoulder titles (above an 'I' for those assigned to the infantry) and a cap badge of crossed machine gun barrels under a crown – a device also worn on the officer's collar and later stencilled on to the front of the Brodie helmet or its cover. Crossed machine gun barrels were worn on collars for full dress.

When the helmet was introduced, it usually bore 'MG' in a diamond on the side of the helmet. Colours varied according to division. Sleeve patches with this device were also worn. Territorial machine gunners wore a 'T' above their shoulder titles.

▶ DESPATCH
RIDER, ROYAL
ENGINEERS,
1916 *This rider
carries a wicker
cage for carrier
pigeons, and wears a
brassard showing
that he is attached to
the 57th Division.*

Tank Corps

From an experimental section of the Machine Gun Corps in 1916, it would take a year for the Tank Corps to become an independent entity. However, it would eventually have 26 numbered battalions by 1918. Initially, tank crews wore the crossed machine gun cap badge (officers having the same on their collars) and 'MGC' shoulder titles or 'HMGC' (Heavy Section Machine Gun Corps).

When the Tank Corps received its Royal Warrant in the summer of 1917 a new badge came into use. This had a tank insignia within a wreath, below a crown and with 'Tank Corps' on a scroll. Shoulder titles bore the simple 'TC' and were usually a plain cloth patch placed below the strap (this was because the Tank Corps had coloured patches on the ends of their shoulder straps to denote specific battalions). Overalls were generally worn inside the tank, along with visors, face

masks and leather caps. Puttees were generally not worn.

Cloth patches or tallies on the shoulder strap were as follows (for each battalion): 1st red; 2nd yellow; 3rd green; 4th light blue; 5th red over light blue; 6th red over yellow; 7th red over green; 8th red over blue; 9th red over brown; 10th red over white; 11th red over black; 12th red over purple; 13th green over black; 14th green over purple; 15th green over yellow; 16th black, yellow, black; 17th green over white; 18th green over blue; 19th red, white, red; 20th red, yellow, red; 21st red, black, red; 22nd red, green, red; 23rd red, blue, red; 24th green, yellow, green; 25th green, black, green; 26th green, white, green. White tank badges were also worn on the sleeve by those who had been through the tank training course.

Royal Engineers

These technical troops were crucial in the kind of warfare that dominated the battlefields of the war. Royal Engineers on mounted duty wore uniforms very similar to the cavalry but with 'RE' shoulder titles. Their cap and collar badges consisted of the garter in a laurel wreath below a crown and with 'Royal Engineers' on a scroll below. Troops serving on foot wore infantry uniforms but with these badges.

▼ CAPTAIN, ROYAL ENGINEERS, 1916 *This captain wears a soft cap, with wire removed, but otherwise conforms to regulations. The engineers were initially sent to France in field companies and signal companies. One signal and two field companies were part of each infantry division in 1914.*

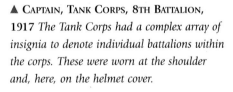

▲ CAPTAIN, TANK CORPS, 8TH BATTALION, 1917 *The Tank Corps had a complex array of insignia to denote individual battalions within the corps. These were worn at the shoulder and, here, on the helmet cover.*

Other Technical Service Distinctions

The Army Service Corps (ASC) wore shoulder titles with 'ASC' and bronze cap badges consisting of an eight-pointed star below a crown. Mounted officers wore universal pattern breeches, dismounted officers wore knickerbocker pattern breeches. Drivers usually wore overalls and leather caps and overcoats. The Ordnance

▲ CORPORAL, ROYAL ENGINEERS, 1914 *This junior NCO wears a uniform almost identical to that worn by his infantry counterparts. Only his shoulder titles ('RE') show that he is from a technical branch. Also, unusually, the engineers had the rank of 2nd Corporal, the equivalent of a bombardier in the artillery, and a slightly more junior NCO to the corporal in the infantry.*

Corps wore badges with three guns and three roundshot within a shield and above a scroll bearing 'Army Ordnance Corps'.

Officers belonging to the Army Motor Reserve wore infantry uniforms but with a badge with that title within a circle and below a crown.

TROOPS FROM CANADA AND NEWFOUNDLAND

Canada contributed large numbers of troops to the war effort, and suffered accordingly, particularly at the Somme.

Canadian Expeditionary Force

Canada had relied on militias for home defence and its permanent army was very small. When war was declared, the Canadians began to concentrate volunteers into battalions. These battalions would eventually number more than 250 and had titles denoting the region which had raised them. These were supplemented by the

Royal Canadian Regiment and Princess Patricia's Canadian Light Infantry – a force raised at private expense. Some of the battalions carried historical titles, such as the Cape Breton Highlanders (185th) or the Toronto Light Infantry (201st). American volunteers were concentrated in the 97th Battalion of the CEF.

Canadians in Europe

The 1st Division was sent to England and arrived in France in February 1915. Infantrymen wore drab service tunics (1903 pattern) with seven buttons and pointed cuffs. It had a standing collar with Canadian badges on either side (some units had distinctive badges, others made use of a numeral beneath a 'C') and pointed cuffs. Buttons bore 'Canada' and a badge, or some units had their own style of button manufactured. The first arrivals had blue-piped shoulder straps (red for artillery, green for rifle regiments) but subsequent arrivals had standard drab versions, usually with a Canada shoulder title in brass (a few units, including Princess Patricia's Canadian Light Infantry, had cloth titles with short regimental names embroidered on in white cloth). Officers wore twill jackets of a cut similar to that worn by their British counterparts but with Canada badges and pointed cuffs (rank insignia was

quite often on the shoulder strap rather than at the cuff). Regiments dressed in Highland-style uniforms had Highland cut-away jackets with five buttons and kilts (although kilts were discontinued in 1918), usually worn with aprons. Tartans had initially been complicated, but a simplified version was being worn by 1916. Officers either wore kilts or trews. Headgear consisted of a stiffened

◄ LIEUTENANT, PRINCESS PATRICIA'S CANADIAN LIGHT INFANTRY, 1915 *With a uniform very much like that worn by his British counterparts, this Canadian has darkened brass collar badges and rank insignia at the cuff.*

► PRIVATE, PRINCESS PATRICIA'S CANADIAN LIGHT INFANTRY, 1918 *The Canadian service jacket had seven buttons and a stiffer collar but was comparatively rare by 1918. This private has managed to preserve his original tunic with its cloth shoulder titles.*

service dress cap with appropriate badge. A softer version was common in 1916, the year the Brodie helmet was also issued. Highland regiments had Glengarrys, then Balmorals, before the helmet came into use.

Greatcoats were either of the British pattern or the seven-button Canadian pattern with a stiff collar. By 1917 British tunics were also being issued to Canadian troops.

Equipment had initially consisted of 1899 pattern leather equipment, but this was largely (although not entirely) replaced by web equipment before departure for France. Those arriving later were sometimes issued with modified Oliver pattern leather equipment. Infantry carried the Ross rifle, a very unpopular make due to its ability to jam.

The Canadian Machine Gun Corps had a badge of crossed machine gun barrels below a crown on a maple leaf.

Cavalry had initially worn yellow-piped shoulder straps but were quickly brought into line and issued uniforms very similar to British cavalry uniforms.

As with the British Army, divisional or coloured unit insignia became very common among the Canadians. A systematic approach was adopted in 1916 based on geometric shapes. The 1st Division had red rectangles, the 2nd blue, the 3rd light blue and the 4th grass green. The 5th Division wore maroon but did not actually serve outside England. Different shapes (circle, half circle, triangle and square) denoted a battalion and these were coloured according to which brigade the battalion served in (green, red or blue). Officers of the 2nd Division had 'CII' sewn to their jacket patches quite early on, gold maple leaf insignia was being worn by those of the 4th Division.

Canadian cavalry in Europe served in the British 3rd Cavalry division and wore the three horseshoe badge of that division.

Newfoundland Regiment

This regiment wore British infantry uniform but with the addition of a Newfoundland badge on the cap and 'NFLA' on the shoulder title. They were sent to Gallipoli in 1915 in khaki uniforms and tropical helmets but returned to Europe in time for the Somme, suffering heavily. It was granted the title Royal in 1917.

◀ TROOPER, FORT GARRY HORSE, 1918
Canada had three regiments of cavalry. The other two regiments to serve in Europe were differentiated by their insignia. Lord Strathcona's Horse, had a diamond insignia with red over green. The Royal Canadian Dragoons had a complex square patch of red over blue over yellow over blue over red. A cavalry machine gun squadron supported these three regiments in the Cavalry Brigade.

TROOPS FROM AUSTRALIA AND NEW ZEALAND

Australia and New Zealand contingents serving at Gallipoli won lasting fame, but Anzacs – as the Australian and New Zealand Army Corps were known – also fought on the Western Front. Australian mounted units also fought in Palestine and Syria.

Australian Imperial Force

The AIF was composed of volunteers and managed to raise some 60 battalions for service overseas. Most of these were recruited from specific states and were grouped into five brigades. Cavalry was supplied by regiments of light horse.

Australian infantry wore khaki twill tunics with five buttons and four exterior pockets. It was a greener colour than that worn by British troops. It had a sunburst badge (bearing 'Australian Imperial Force') on each collar as well as on the service cap or pinning back the brim of the slouch hat. The shoulder straps bore the battalion number in metal above 'INF' with below that 'Australia' in a curved shoulder title. The service cap was the same as that issued to the British infantry, the slouch hat (or bush hat) was greenish-brown with a khaki hat band. The badge was usually worn on the left-hand side. Brodie helmets were issued from 1916.

Troops serving in Murmansk in 1919 were issued with fur caps. Australians wore baggier trousers than their British counterparts, and these were generally in the same colour as the tunic (it would fade to blue-grey after exposure to the sun). Equipment was generally made of leather (and was known as 1908 pattern equipment). British webbing equipment was also used but was in short supply. Armament was as for the British.

The Australians were quick to adopt patches denoting divisions and units to be worn on the sleeve. Divisions were denoted by coloured patches: the 1st Division had a rectangle, the 2nd Division a diamond, the 3rd Division an oval and the 4th Division a circle. The 5th had a triangle. These patches were coloured according to the brigade, with the first brigade wearing green, the second wearing red and the third light blue (one brigade in the 5th Division had yellow). Individual battalions then wore a colour patch split into two. It was the shape of their respective division with the lower part in the brigade colour and black for the first battalion of the brigade, purple for the second, brown for the third and white for the fourth. There were some exceptions, but this generally allowed for quick recognition of a battalion. Troops who had served at Gallipoli were later allowed to have an 'A' added to their patch. Machine gunners wore crossed machine gun barrels beneath it.

◀ TROOPER, 1ST AUSTRALIAN LIGHT HORSE, 1917 *A regimental insignia of a rectangle, split diagonally with blue over white was worn on the upper left sleeve.*

Australian Light Horse

Australia fielded 15 regiments of light horse. These were dressed in khaki tunics with rising sun badges, breeches and puttees with boots or leather leggings. Many served in Palestine in shirt-sleeve order. The tunic had the Australia badge on each shoulder strap as well as a coloured unit patch on the top of each sleeve. This corresponded to a scheme in which the brigade colour was shared with a unit colour on a geometrical shape. A number of light horse regiments adopted unofficial badges in the course of the war. The Imperial Camel Corps chose a camel on a rising sun. The light horse wore bandoliers with ammunition pouches and, rarely, emu plumes in the centre of a slouch hat.

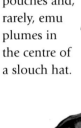

New Zealand

Infantry from New Zealand went to war in the famous lemon-squeezer hat with khaki band and red coloured pagri. It bore a regimental badge on the front, which was also sometimes worn on the tunic collars.

Tunics largely conformed to the type worn by the Australians (khaki drill in hot weather), but were browner, and bore 'NZR' for rifle regiments. Buttons had four stars and bore 'New Zealand Forces'. Mounted rifles (some of whom fought as infantry at Gallipoli) had a green pagri on their hat band and the shoulder title 'NZMR'. Cord breeches and leather bandoliers were worn. Artillery had a dark blue band with red pagri running along the centre and 'NZFA' as shoulder titles.

▲ **SERGEANT, NEW ZEALAND, 17TH RUAHINE REGIMENT, 1915** *This NCO's hat has a green khaki band around it with, on top, a thinner red band. The star within a wreath hat badge is clipped behind the bands.*

◄ **PRIVATE, AUSTRALIAN IMPERIAL FORCE, 23RD BATTALION, 1915** *Australian troops wore the sunburst badge on their caps and collars. This individual has a field cap, but the slouch hat was more popular among Australians.*

► **TROOPER, NEW ZEALAND, 4TH WAIKATO MOUNTED RIFLES, 1915** *According to New Zealand regulations, the hat was supposed to be worn brim horizontal, crown dented with a crease running from front to rear.*

AFRICAN TROOPS

As expected, the war did spread beyond Europe and into the colonies, including Africa; but Africans also came to Europe to fight. South Africa sent a brigade northwards in 1915 as well as providing troops for the subjugation of German colonies in Africa. A number of African regiments, with predominantly European officers, were also formed for local defence and to counter German colonial units.

South African Infantry

A number of white South African battalions were raised for overseas service in the autumn of 1915. The expeditionary force eventually assembled consisted of: 1st South African Infantry Regiment (Cape of Good Hope Regiment); 2nd South African Infantry Regiment (Natal and Orange Free State Regiment); 3rd South African Infantry Regiment (Transvaal and Rhodesia Regiment); 4th South African Regiment (South African Scottish Regiment)

Those sent to Europe were largely uniformed and equipped as for their British counterparts (khaki cotton drill in Egypt, drab serge on the Western Front, although the cap badge was the distinctive springbok head within a circle and shoulder titles had 'SAI' (South African Infantry) on the right and the Afrikaans' equivalent 'ZAI' (Zuid Afrikaansche Infanterie) on the left. The circle bore 'UNITY IS STRENGTH' and the Afrikaans translation 'EENDRACHT MAKKT MACHT'. The 4th Regiment had a distinctive Highland-style uniform complete with Glengarry, cut-away tunic and kilt (Atholl Murray tartan) with

◀ PRIVATE, 2ND SOUTH AFRICAN INFANTRY BATTALION, 1915 *The South African infantry wore shoulder titles with 'SAI' on the right and 'ZAI' on the left. The cap badge bore the message 'UNITY IS STRENGTH'.*

▶ PRIVATE, 9TH SOUTH AFRICAN BATTALION, 1915 *Coloured insignia worn on the band of the cork helmet indicate the man's unit and formation as his shirt is devoid of shoulder titles. He wears webbing equipment but the older Slade Wallace equipment was issued to some units due to shortages. This older equipment proved uncomfortable and unpopular.*

apron. Officers wore jackets in a cut similar to their English or Scottish counterparts in the British Army.

South African troops serving in theatres other than the Western Front tended to wear tropical helmets, khaki drill (or khaki shirts) and shorts. Puttees were worn with brown or black ankle boots. The helmet usually had the springbok badge pinned to the front while a coloured

flash designated a particular unit. The 5th Regiment had a diamond split into green on the left and white on the right; the 6th Regiment had blue and gold; the 7th white and red; the 8th crimson and gold; the 9th (the Sportsmen battalion) green above gold; the 10th a white cross on a blue diamond; the 11th a triangle divided into black and yellow; and the 12th a red and gold diamond. Some units had their own regimental (or battalion) flashes or patches. Equipment in Africa was usually kept to a minimum due to the possibility of heat exhaustion.

South African Cavalry

The cavalry consisted of mounted rifle regiments. There were some 12 regiments in all. They wore khaki drill tunics and jackets, or khaki shirts, tropical helmets, slouch hats or locally manufactured brimmed hats with band. The springbok badge was pinned to the front and the Mounted Rifles wore shoulder titles bearing the initials 'SAH' on the right and 'ZAR' on the left. Regimental numerals were often worn above such titles. Regiments appear to have worn flashes in their helmets, the main colour being yellow squares with the addition of a regimental colour. The 5th had such a square with a green stripe running across it horizontally. A number of volunteer units operated in civilian clothes but with bandoliers and equipment of South African or British manufacture.

Artillery wore badges bearing 'UBIQUE' (Everywhere) and 'South Africa' and exploding grenade badges were worn on the collar. Shoulder titles were 'SAFA' for the field artillery.

Kenya and Uganda

The most distinctive regiment serving in Africa was the King's African Rifles, largely recruited in Kenya and Uganda. Rank and file were black Africans called 'askaris', while most officers were seconded from British Army regiments. Troops initially wore a red fez but this was either covered or a cylindrical cap with neck flap was worn instead. Officers wore tropical helmets.

▲ SOUTH AFRICAN INFANTRY KIT, 1914
1 A nine-pouch bandolier which could contain 90 rounds. It had closed pockets, to prevent the two clips of ammunition from falling out, and was made of robust leather. 2 A five-pouch bandolier which could accommodate 50 rounds and was often worn by mounted personnel. Issued in 1903. 3 A canteen.

Headgear bore a black square with 'KAR' in green for the 1st Battalion, the 2nd Battalion had dark blue, the 3rd had a white Arabic '3' on a red diamond and the 4th had an Arabic '4' on a green diamond.

Another three battalions were raised. Officers wore khaki jackets and shorts, other ranks had khaki tunics or shirts and shorts. Puttees and boots were worn, but some natives went barefoot.

▶ LIEUTENANT, 1ST BATTALION KING'S AFRICAN RIFLES, 1914 *Although many officers favoured the cork sun helmet worn here, a soft khaki fez with neck flap was also popular. This lieutenant carries a swagger stick – a cane originally carried by infantry officers to dress the line when units were on parade or lined up for action.*

Other African Units

The Royal West African Frontier Force, later known as the Nigeria Regiment, had officers attired in bush shirts and khaki breeches but without badges. The regiment was an amalgamtion of the Northern Nigeria Regiment and the Southern Nigeria Regiment, and it served in west and east Africa.

Various other regiments or native contingents served in Africa, such as the East Africa Mounted Rifles or Southern Rhodesia Volunteers, who wore round hats, bush shirts and breeches or shorts. Bandoliers or leather equipment predominated.

THE INDIAN ARMY

As well as sending troops to Europe, the Indian Army provided manpower for the war against the Ottoman empire in Mesopotamia (Iraq), in Arabia and in Africa. In total some 1.3 million men would serve in the ranks.

The majority of officers in the Indian Army were European. The troops themselves were volunteers drawn from what the British termed the warlike peoples – Sikhs and Punjabis. Regiments of Gurkhas were also formed, some serving overseas.

Organization

The Indian Army had been overhauled in the late 1890s, as an attempt was made to create a more unified force. Even so, the situation was complex. Infantry units numbered from 1 to 130

(12 were vacant) and these bore a regimental numeral plus a historic title or a regional title. There were also ten Gurkha regiments from Nepal. Regiments could include men from just one caste or religion, although other regiments had separate companies of different classes. This led to some variation in head dress even within regiments.

Uniform Distinctions

Infantry uniforms consisted of trousers, khaki puttees and a khaki turban (this varied in style from a round Sikh turban to a more conical version in use by Muslim troops) and, for Muslim troops a red kulla cap around which the turban was based. The khaki drill tunic had skirts and patch pockets.

▲ PRIVATE, 90TH PUNJAB REGIMENT, 1916
Indian Army regiments wore different styles of turban even within the same regiment. Sikh turbans worn by officers and other ranks were also of different styles.

Shoulder titles bore regimental numerals along with shortened regimental names or initials, for instance the 29th Punjabis had '29P'.

European officers wore either turbans (with chinstraps) or, more likely, the tropical helmet with khaki pagri and, perhaps, the addition of a

Indian Cavalry Regiments

Number	Name	Number	Name
1st	(Duke of York's Own) Bengal Lancers (Skinner's Horse)	18th	(King George's Own) Tiwana Lancers
2nd	Bengal Lancers (Gardner's Horse)	19th	Bengal Lancers (Fane's Horse)
3rd	Bengal Cavalry [also known as Skinner's Horse]	20th	Deccan Horse
4th	Bengal Lancers	21th	(Prince Albert Victor's Own) Punjab Cavalry (Frontier Force)
5th	Cavalry	22th	Sam Browne's Cavalry (Frontier Force)
6th	Prince of Wales's Bengal Cavalry	23th	Cavalry (Frontier Force)
7th	Hariana Lancers	25th	(Frontier Force) 26th Prince of Wales's Own Light Cavalry
8th	Lancers		
9th	Bengal Lancers (Hodson's Horse)	27th	Light Cavalry
10th	(Duke of Cambridge's Own) Bengal Lancers (also known as Hodson's Horse)	28th	Light Cavalry
		29th	Lancers (Deccan Horse)
		30th	Lancers (Gordon's Horse)
11th	(Prince of Wales's Own) Bengal Lancers (Probyn's Horse)	31th	Duke of Connaught's Own Lancers
12th	Cavalry	32th	Lancers
13th	Duke of Connaught's Bengal Lancers (Watson's Horse)	33th	Queen's Own Light Cavalry
14th	Bengal Lancers (Murray's Jat Horse)	34th	Prince Albert Victor's Own Poona Horse
15th	Bengal Lancers (Cureton's Multanis)	35th	Scinde Horse
		36th	Jacob's Horse
16th	Bengal Lancers	37th	Lancers (Baluchi Horse)
17th	Bengal Lancers	38th	Central India Horse
		39th	Central India Horse.

regimental badge. Turbans had coloured elements, even within the same regiment, to reflect the status of a wearer. The Indian Army was notoriously loath to spend money, and leather was cheap in India. Most troops were therefore issued with the 1903 pattern bandolier. Officers had Sam Browne belts, khaki or drab jackets and breeches with boots. Indian officers (Viceroy's Commissioned Officers) wore the same but usually elected to wear turbans. Some Brodie helmets were issued, but these were comparatively rare in Indian regiments.

Gurkhas wore slouch hats (left brim turned up) with khaki and green cloth band (known as a puggaree), short khaki jackets (shoulder titles bore

▶ PRIVATE, DECCAN HORSE, 1916 *The regiment wore a regimental badge pinned to the turban or, later in the war, stencilled to the helmet.*

'1G' for the 1st Regiment etc), shorts and puttees. The 39th Garhwal Rifles adopted this style of dress and, like the Gurkhas, were clean shaven.

Indian Cavalry

There were 38 regiments of cavalry in 1914 (number 24 was disbanded in 1885) with historic or regional titles. Uniforms resembled the infantry with a long tunic for the men and jackets for the officers. Those on the Western Front wore drab tunics and jackets and

◀ SERGEANT, 29TH PUNJAB REGIMENT, 1915 *This NCO wears the shoulder title '29P 'and rank insignia on the lower sleeve.*

steel helmets. Shoulder titles on shoulder straps were numeric with regimental short names, lancers tended to have chain mail ornamentation in place of shoulder titles. Breeches were worn, as were bandoliers. Turbans again varied according to the wearer. Muslim troops had a white kulla, with the turban wrapped around it. Sikhs had a round turban. Officers had tropical helmets or turbans, and Sam Browne belts. Saddles were as for the British Army. Most of the cavalry wore turbans and tropical helmets (with badges) for officers, or service caps with badges, and carried lances and the SMLE or long Lee Enfield.

FRANCE

The Third Republic of France presided over an age of great prosperity, when French trade and colonial expansion blossomed, but such success barely disguised a yearning for revenge for what the German empire had done to France in 1870. By 1912 the dominant powers in French politics were advocating an end to colonial expansion and were focusing on what to do to restore the French frontier as it had stood in 1869. Alliances had been forged with this end in mind, and France worked closely with its main ally, Russia, to contain Germany and threaten the Reich from the west and east, as well as isolate it from the sea and its own newly acquired colonies. This plan ultimately bore fruit but, for at least the first half of the war, France bore the strain at Verdun, on the Western Front. Although France would emerge on the winning side, the war bankrupted the nation and swept away the nation's youth. It was a high price to pay for victory.

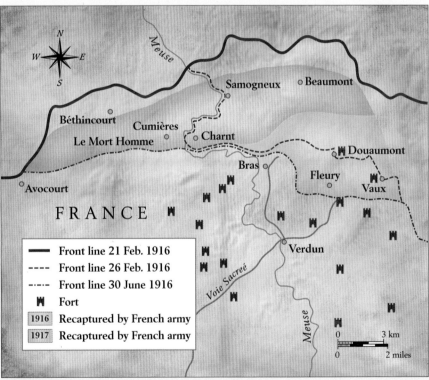

▲ *The Battle of Verdun in 1916 was an epic struggle which, for many, summed up the war. Huge efforts were made to capture insignificant positions, casualties were at catastrophic levels on both sides and little territory exchanged hands.*

◄ *French infantry march in to occupy Essen in 1918. Essen, home of the Krupp Works, was part of Germany's industrial heartland. The French would occupy it, and strip it of much industrial infrastructure, for 11 years.*

THE FRENCH ARMY IN 1914

France had just cause to go to war in August 1914. The country was fighting an invader, moreover an invader that had inflicted a humiliating defeat upon it in 1870, and was still occupying French territory (the disputed territory of Alsace and Lorraine). There was a very real danger in the minds of many, that France's population of 39 million would be overwhelmed by 65 million Germans, and the French people turned out en masse to do their patriotic duty.

The Government and the Military

The majority of French men who were signed up served in the army and, consequently, in the infantry. Conscription had been extended in 1912 and the French system allowed for few exemptions. So it was that 80 per cent of males aged between 18 and 46 had been called up by early 1915. It was a national effort that placed considerable strain on all levels of French society, but the German attack, at least for the time being, united what

▼ *The first casualties of war arrive at Rheims station. In the autumn of 1914 many of the injured suffered wounds to the head – a spur to the development of an affordable helmet.*

had been a fragmented country. The army had suffered through a series of unfortunate scandals and as a politically conservative body had not emerged as a modern force in spite of experience in colonial warfare.

The Army had been rebuilt following the disaster of the Franco-Prussian War. Its officer corps was, however, largely divorced from France's republican political elite. Politicians had long attempted to republicanize the military, trying to increase the power and influence of the Minister of War over the army. A compromise was eventually devised, and reforms after 1911 set in place. The post of Chief of the General Staff was created to establish some sense of unity, and offered to Joseph Joffre, whose experience was largely gained in the colonies. By 1914, as tension with Germany increased, the French Government started to give the military a freer hand.

Strategy and Tactics

French military planners and politicians did agree on one thing; the necessity to launch an offensive. The French knew that the Germans would come through Belgium but deemed it

▲ *Joseph Jacques Césaire Joffre had been a lieutenant at the time of the Franco-Prussian War. In 1911 he was Chief of the General Staff and in late 1916 he was created a marshal of France.*

essential to launch an offensive of their own into Alsace Lorraine. Experience in the Russo-Japanese and Balkan wars had found that defensive positions were more vital than ever, but political necessity, combined with a poor understanding of defensive capabilities, ensured that France would launch wave after wave of infantrymen during the summer of 1914. French generals were optimistic that élan was enough to break into Germany and meet the Russians in Berlin.

This strategy and the tactics used conspired to create conditions for a military disaster. Guidelines issued in April 1914 emphasized the importance of bayonet attacks led by officers; even if the enemy were attacking, French troops were ordered to advance to meet them. The effects of such a foolhardy tactic were soon felt. Losses (dead, missing and captured) in August and September 1914 averaged 164,500 per month, the majority in the infantry.

▲ *Morroccan drivers transport supplies to the front. The French made widespread use of North African personnel as labourers, drivers and logistical staff. Some were also drafted into distinctive units such as the tirailleurs.*

Officers and Men

France's strength lay in its infantry. It boasted 173 regiments of infantry, most of three battalions, in 1914 and each one of these had a related reserve regiment (numbered 201 to 373). There were also 31 battalions of light infantry (chasseurs). In addition there were 152 regiments of territorial militia, tasked with auxiliary duties. Front line troops therefore numbered some 1,100 battalions of infantry, a formidable-looking force.

Moreover, France could call upon its overseas possessions to augment its troops. Frenchmen living overseas, indigenous troops and colonial subjects were called up and began arriving towards the end of August. There were sharpshooters (tirailleurs) from Algeria, Tunisia and Morocco; zouaves, made up of French citizens from North Africa; troops of the Foreign Legion and penal battalions (the Infanterie Légère d'Afrique). In addition there were colonial troops (administered by its own department), and these included 12 regiments of colonial infantry (recruited within France) and Senagalese, Madagascan, Indochinese and Annamite battalions (all usually defined as tirailleurs). These were originally intended for local defence duties but they were increasingly sucked into the conflict.

France, like most European armies, lacked officers, with 800 vacancies for lieutenants just before the war. The artillery did not have enough trained officers and enrolment in the officer-training colleges was down. Military surgeons were rarer still.

Equipment and Supplies

Such a mobilization of manpower also caused considerable problems for the Intendance, the service tasked with supplying French troops, and there was an immediate lack of uniforms and equipment. Footwear was so rare that conscripts were paid to retain their civilian boots.

The standard rifle of the French Army, the Lebel, was effective but the army could only lay its hands on 2.6 million such weapons. Some troops were issued the 1907 Berthier rifle (lighter and shorter) but, given that initial losses of rifles were very high, the Army faced a considerable problem right from the early days of the war. Problems were particularly pronounced in the artillery. There was a severe shortage of heavy field artillery in 1914, and although the Army's 75mm guns were effective, they suffered from poor range and a steadily increasing shortage of shells (something which began to bite in late 1914). Such guns were increasingly useless when the Germans developed tactics involving defence in depth. The French government embarked on an energetic attempt to boost production of heavy guns and shells in 1915, at considerable cost.

Uniforms

French uniforms were also under review as the war began. The majority of the infantry wore bright red trousers, first introduced in 1829 and modified in 1887. The infantryman's headgear also dated from the 1880s: a kepi, ill suited for modern warfare but comfortable and cheap to mass-produce in only three sizes. He wore a greatcoat first issued in the 1870s, which disguised the fact that tunics were rare in the French Army. Most of the leather equipment had been designed in the 1880s and early 1900s.

When it came to modernizing, French policy-makers had acted with lethargy, despite Germany adopting field grey and Britain khaki. In July 1914, horizon blue had been selected as a more effective colour for a campaign uniform. This shade of blue was a mix of white, dark blue and light blue wool and, after being judged effective by the Intendance, greatcoats gradually began to be issued in August 1914, with a tunic following in December of that year.

The French Army, the Allies' most powerful force on the Western Front, had embarked on a very steep learning curve at considerable cost; nevertheless, there were remarkable achievements.

▼ *A popular, and reassuring, representation of French infantry from a magazine cover. The reality of trench warfare was very different.*

WARTIME DEVELOPMENTS

Heavy casualties made a sudden, devastating impression on the armed forces. The heaviest casualties were suffered by the infantry (22.9 per cent of effectives were killed in the infantry, only 7.6 per cent in the cavalry). Young cadres were called up early; wounded men were quickly returned to the ranks. Those seeking to avoid conscription were rigorously hunted down by the gendarmes. But still the number of effectives went into decline.

Looking for Solutions

One remedy was to call up more and more colonial subjects. Indeed, by the end of the war, there were 57 North African battalions and 47 battalions from Africa and Asia at the Front. Something like 13 per cent of infantry effectives were colonial subjects by the time of the armistice.

Even so, the reduction in effectives had an impact on the average infantry battalion; companies were reduced from 250 men to 200, for example. However, in order to increase the

▼ *This poster hopes to persuade people to subscribe to (purchase) national bonds, and contribute financially towards final victory.*

▲ *Tunisians at a mosque in 1915 await call-up instructions. Many found themselves in indigenous units. French nationals in Tunisia would normally be recruited in to the zouaves.*

efficiency of the battalion, the high command made a determined effort to increase firepower. A section of grenadiers was formed in each company to throw hand grenades, and half a section of bombardiers were also formed to operate trench mortars and grenade-throwers. The number of machine guns was also increased from six per regiment in 1914 to 16 per regiment in 1915. Battalions were also eventually equipped with a 37mm field gun for fire support.

Although 40 per cent of French coalfields would be lost to the Germans (when they overran north-east France) and France would suffer a 58 per cent loss in steel production, attempts were made to overcome the shortage of heavy field artillery – with an emphasis on weight – France would even field 400mm railway guns. A lack of shells was also overcome in 1915 and this had an immediate impact on tactics. Barrages could now last for whole days rather than for a few hours. France, now locked in trench warfare, was quick to adapt to new conditions.

Initial problems led to intensive training of all recruits. Defensive tactics were modified, although French

positions were never as redoubtable as German defences (and French trenches were deemed sloppy by friend and foe alike). Trench raids, targeted-assaults and limited offensives were mounted after some costly failures in 1915. France developed the concept of the creeping barrage, responding to concerns by the infantry that preliminary barrages had not always reduced German positions.

The desire to maximize the impact of new and improving technology associated with tanks, gas and air power also came to the fore. General Robert Nivelle's disastrous and costly offensives of 1917 reinforced the message that French generals should stick to attrition, prepare to meet the German onslaught following Russia's descent into chaos and preserve as many troops as possible for ultimate victory. That way France could be present at the peace table and capable of preventing the tribute of victory from slipping through its fingers.

Preserving Lives

If strategy and tactics underwent convulsions, so did daily life for the soldier. Trench warfare necessitated new behaviour (such as putting a cork into the rifle muzzle and wrapping oilcloth around the bolt – to keep it dry), new training, new levels of tolerance (for the weather and for food – rations of beef were termed 'monkey' by French troops) and, inevitably, new levels of patience.

Uniform Reforms

The other significant development for the ordinary soldier was in matters of uniform. Although it is true that in 1914 French infantry charged into battle dressed in blue and red, the French Army had experimented with duller colours before the war in the light of experience gained from observing the Balkan Wars, and changes implemented by friendly and rival powers.

It soon became apparent that the headgear issued to the troops was unsatisfactory. The frequency of head injuries in the first months of the war had been relatively normal and the soldiers' caps (kepi), which were light and comfortable in warm, wet or cold

weather, were deemed sufficient. But as soon as deadlock set in at the front, and the troops began to dig in, large numbers of troops succumbed to head injuries from artillery projectiles or hand grenades. Many of these wounds proved fatal. By late 1914 and in early

▼ *A mobile field kitchen, pictured behind the front. Note the wooden barracks, which probably denotes a rest station several miles from the trenches.*

▲ *A relaxed crew load a 120mm French heavy artillery gun with a shell in 1915. The undamaged trees show that this permanent battery is positioned well behind the lines.*

1915, in certain sectors of the front, some 70 per cent of wounds were to the head. The Army introduced a round metal bowl in March 1915 that would be worn under the cap; it proved difficult to wear and made the head very sweaty, but even so the number of head wounds declined.

Experiments on head protection continued, and a number of prototypes were produced. The easiest one to manufacture was deemed to be the Adrian helmet and this was quickly put into production. The Adrian was well received but the semi-matt blue colour it was painted in at the factories made it too visible. Instructions were issued to cover it with a brown helmet cover, but this fell into disuse when cloth fragments were found to be infecting wounds. It was painted matt instead, and by 1917 head wounds were down to 11 per cent of injuries.

Perhaps still more could have been done. Equipment was heavy and the French soldier was burdened with an 85lb (39kg) pack to carry backwards and forwards to the trenches. Even so, France's army had succeeded in transforming into a thoroughly modern force in just five years.

GENERALS AND STAFF

General officers commanded brigades, divisions, corps, armies and army groups. The most senior position was marshal. French generals were dressed in a relatively simple style and retained a practical look throughout the war.

Marshals and Generals

In 1914 the majority of French generals wore a tunic that had been introduced in 1906. It was black and bore rank insignia in the form of stars on tabs on the shoulder and at the tunic cuffs.

General officers who had served in the French cavalry, or commanded cavalry units, preferred to wear a cavalry dolman. This was black and had black braid across the chest and on the sleeve. A blue or white cravat or neckerchief was worn beneath the standing collar. There were no marshals in 1914, but the rank was reintroduced in 1916.

Generals wore an M1882 sword, with golden sword knot, a black or brown sword belt, a pistol holster with a case for carrying maps and a binocular case, along with a black or brown waist belt. Sam Browne belts became increasingly popular. All generals wore bright red trousers, which after 1883 had a black stripe, cavalry officers sometimes elected to have a Hungarian knot.

◀ MARSHAL, 1918 *There were three French marshals by 1918 – Joffre, Pétain and Foch. All three wore a uniform similar to that of a general commanding a corps, seen here. The kepi, however, had distinctive and additional oak leaf decoration. Interestingly, General Gallieni was also made a marshal – but posthumously in 1921, well after his death in 1916.*

▲ *The Allied commanders, including all three French marshals, gather at Strasbourg in 1919, to celebrate the liberation of Alsace-Lorraine. From left to right, Marshal Joffre, Marshal Foch, General Wygand, Sir Douglas Haig, General Pershing and Marshal Pétain.*

Riding boots were the expected footwear, as generals were supposed to be mounted, although officers often switched to wearing brown or black ankle boots with puttees or leather gaiters as the war wore on. The kepi was the Saumur model, higher in the crown with a black leather visor (edged subtly in gold), black band and bright red crown. A gold Hungarian knot was worn on the top of the crown.

Rank was shown in the form of bands of oak leaves, a row of gold embroidery on the black band, and vertical stripes of braid on the red crown. There was a gilded chinstrap. Cavalry generals sometimes opted to wear a helmet. Greatcoats, capes or an elegant overcoat (issued in 1913 and worn with insignia on the fold-down collar and cuffs) were worn in cold weather. Initially these were in dark blue, but horizon blue was used from 1915. Gloves were also worn, mostly

◀ **Officer on Divisional Staff, 1916** *Staff officers had insignia on the collar and a silk brassard denoting the division they were attached to. As with most armies of the period, officers wore privately-tailored uniforms that were made to measure and were usually of superior cloth. It usually led to a departure from the regulation attire.*

Rank Distinctions

In 1914, a general of brigade wore two stars on the cuff and a wide band of oak leaves on the kepi. Generals of division wore three silver stars and two narrow bands of oak leaves. Corps commanders had four stars, while army commanders had five (plus an extra thread of silver embroidery on the kepi) and those commanding army groups had six stars. Marshals wore seven stars with three rows of oak leaves on the kepi. With the introduction of the horizon blue kepi and helmet, the stars were used on the front of the headgear.

Staff Officers

These officers frequently wore the uniform of their branch of service, modifying and adjusting according to the evolution of the relevant items of dress. When horizon blue uniforms were introduced, for example, piping was according to branch of service, with infantry officers having yellow stripes, the cavalry dark blue and the artillery scarlet.

Various uniform modifications were used to specifically denote a staff function. The regimental number, which would have been worn on the tunic's standing collar, was replaced with a gold wire or metal winged thunderbolt device. To further distinguish staff officers, silk brassards trimmed with gold were worn in the field. Officers on the general staff or those sent on service by the Ministry

of War had a horizontal tricolor, those on the staff of army groups or armies had white and red horizontal stripes; all had golden winged thunderbolts as an emblem.

Divisional staff had red brassards and brigade staff wore dark blue. Officers serving on divisional or brigade staff had a grenade above the divisional or brigade number; cavalry divisions and brigades replaced the grenade with an eight-pointed star and had the brigade number in roman numerals. Those on the engineering staff wore a helmeted cuirass.

brown leather (commonly called dog-skin). Decorations were worn at the throat or on the breast of the tunic or, later, were worn as bars (red for the Legion of Honour) on the left breast.

In late 1914, horizon blue began to make an impact, although the black and red kepi was often retained even when the tunic was horizon blue. The red trousers were discarded in favour of horizon blue with a dark blue stripe. Rank distinctions were retained on the cuff, service stripes were eventually worn on the sleeve and stars denoting rank were worn on the horizon blue kepi. This practice was retained when the Adrian helmet was introduced.

▶ **General of Division, August 1914** *This general wears a dolman with Brandenburg knots in black and olive, although a simpler unadorned tunic was also commonly worn. There were 117 such generals in 1912 and the rank was only supposed to be held by those who were aged less than 65.*

INFANTRY

France had traditionally dressed its infantry in blue and red, and the infantry went to war in 1914 resembling their compatriots of 1870.

Patriotic Uniforms

In 1902 an experimental grey-green colour had been tested and before the war the 106th Infantry Regiment provoked much interest in Paris by parading in a trial version, complete with helmet. It was not a great success among the military, however, and when war

broke out in the summer of 1914, French infantrymen went to the front dressed in blue coats and bright red trousers. Some officers declared that to have changed the uniform on the eve of war would have been a mark of cowardice or, at the very least, an indication that France was intimidated. A new uniform was in development, but the delay resulted in tragedy, quickly followed by hasty measures to implement a new uniform in the autumn of 1914.

Officers of 1914

In September 1913 infantry officers had been instructed to adapt their profile to resemble that of their men. French officers wore a dark blue tunic with upper and lower pockets on either side (adopted in 1913 and made obligatory in April 1914, replacing a black version from 1893). There was a standing collar, with rounded edges, bearing the regimental number in gold. Rank insignia were worn on the cuffs. Silk scarves, or white or blue neckerchiefs were often worn under the collar to stop chaffing.

Bright red trousers were worn with black 45mm-wide piping down the sides. Ankle boots were worn with leather gaiters or dark puttees, although boots with spurs were an option (captains and lieutenants commanding a company might ride).

Headgear consisted of the kepi, either the fuller Saumur version, or a lower, stiffer version (known as a polo), which had a leather peak, edged in gold, a black band bearing the

◄ CAPTAIN 2ND INFANTRY REGIMENT, 1914
The 1914 campaign uniform was comfortable and easy to wear. The red-topped kepi was covered with a blue cover. Off duty, a fatigue cap with red piping was worn. Officers usually wore white shirts (flannel in winter, cotton in summer) under the tunic; the rougher blue shirt (known as a bourgeron) was confined to other ranks.

▲ *An infantryman in 1915. He has buttoned back his greatcoat for marching. This was originally done to show off the red trousers.*

regimental number in gold and a red crown. Stripes of gold lace above the black band denoted rank, as did vertical stripes at the front sides and rear of the kepi. The top of the crown had gold lace in the form a Hungarian knot. The chinstrap was gilded leather. After 1913 a dark blue cover was worn on the kepi on campaign, sometimes being pushed to the top of the kepi to display the regimental number, and a black side cap (or bonnet de police) was worn off duty.

Waist belts were predominantly of black leather, with belts holding a binocular case (binoculars were obligatory for officers). Most officers were armed with a sword (most often the M1845) in a brown leather scabbard and hanging from the M1882 sword belt. Revolvers (the M1892 was the most common) were worn with holsters and a leather pouch containing additional ammunition. A blackened leather map case was often worn on the sword belt on the right hip. A whistle had been introduced in 1896, to ease communication. Some officers went into battle with canes or walking sticks. From 1890, personal effects were carried in a satchel but some officers made use of knapsacks as worn by other ranks.

Greatcoats were worn in winter (some officers electing to wear that of the other ranks, which was double breasted, and worn with belts and equipment on the outside; officers replaced the ordinary buttons with golden buttons). An overcoat,

▼ **LIEUTENANT 22ND INFANTRY REGIMENT, AUTUMN 1914** *The distinctive French infantryman's greatcoat was often worn by officers in cold weather, although a 1913 model light coat was also common. Regulations issued in December 1914 unsuccessfully sought to impose some clarity on officers' coats and greatcoats.*

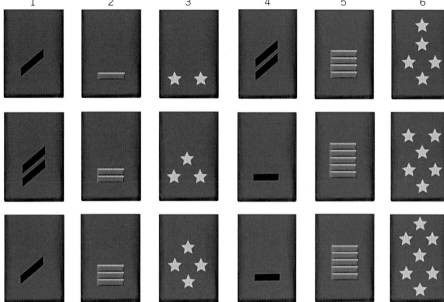

▲ **RANK INSIGNIA, INFANTRY, 1916** *From top to bottom: 1 Soldier, first class, Corporal, Sergeant. 2 Second lieutenant, Lieutenant, Captain. 3 General of brigade, General of division, Corps commander. 4 Sergeant, Adjutant, Chief adjutant. 5 Major, Lieutenant-colonel, Colonel. 6 Army commander, Army group commander, Marshal.*

introduced in 1913, was popular. It was of dark blue cloth, had two side pockets, stretched down to below the knee and closed with six gold buttons. Capes, similar to those worn by mounted troops, were also permitted. All these coats bore rank insignia at the sleeve and the overcoat had regimental numerals on each (falling) collar. Brown leather gloves had replaced white ones in 1881.

Rank Insignia

Second lieutenants wore one gold stripe at the sleeve and a single stripe above the band of the kepi. Lieutenants wore two and captains three (with an extra stripe on the vertical lace on the kepi), while battalion commanders wore four, lieutenant-colonels wore five and colonels six.

▶ **SERGEANT 105TH REGIMENT, 1914** *This NCO wears a 1914 tunic with an 1845 model belt, with plaque, and this was the oldest item of equipment in use by the French in 1914.*

Rank and File Uniform

Most French infantrymen would go into battle dressed in a greatcoat, regardless of the weather. The M1877 greatcoat was dark blue (a shade known officially as blue, iron-grey) and was worn with all belts and

▼ PRIVATE, 19TH INFANTRY REGIMENT, 1914
The 1893 model knapsack was heavy, uncomfortable and loaded with additional equipment and, like the 1905 cartridge pouches, was made from blackened leather. The 1905 pouches were an improved version of the 1888 model, but the weak leather fastening still had an unfortunate habit of snapping and spilling the cartridges.

equipment on the outside. The coat was double breasted, with six buttons (bearing a flaming grenade) on each side, and two pockets. The front skirts of the coat could be buttoned back for ease of movement, a popular option in wet weather when the garment became heavy and caked in mud. The greatcoat had an uncomfortable standing collar bearing collar patches in red with blue regimental numerals. A blue or white neckerchief was worn beneath the collar. The coat had shoulder straps, rolled shoulder straps being introduced in 1913 to support the rifle sling and equipment straps.

There was a tunic (the 'vareuse', known colloquially as the short-arse) but it was not popular and not very common. The 1867 model and 1897 model were similar, differing only in the number of buttons (nine as opposed to seven). It had a collar like that of the greatcoat.

French infantrymen famously wore baggy red trousers (mostly the M1867, modified in 1887 and 1893) with a rear half-belt for adjustment. Many French troops wore overtrousers in a more subdued colour, or replaced them with brown or black corduroy. Ankle boots were generally worn, with puttees or gaiters. Such boots ('brodequins') dating from 1893 were common and were modified in 1916 by rivets in the sole. There was a general shortage of footwear and endless variation.

Soldiers wore the comfortable kepi with a leather peak and chinstrap, dark blue band and red crown. There was a thin blue vertical line at the front, sides and rear of the crown and the regimental number (in blue) was sewn on the front. A cover was often worn, dyed to resemble the colour of the greatcoat. A waterproofed version also became available in 1913.

Rank insignia consisted of stripes on each sleeve, near the cuff. A private (first class) wore one red stripe, a corporal two, a sergeant one metallic (slightly thicker) stripe and a sergeant-major, two. Sappers wore the traditional badge of crossed axes

▲ PRIVATE, 58TH TERRITORIAL REGIMENT, 1914 *The 1913 tunic was a relatively rare sight as it was usually concealed by the ubiquitous 1877 greatcoat. France was short of two million sets of uniforms in 1914, and so territorial units, which were figuratively at the end of the queue, were often dressed and equipped with obsolete items. This tunic is of civilian manufacture, as the 1870 and 1914 models did not have concealed buttons.*

(surmounted by an exploding grenade) in red on the upper left sleeve. Most NCOs wore the 1897 model tunic.

Reserve infantry wore the same uniform, but territorial units used white regimental numerals on the cap and on the greatcoat's collar.

Equipment and Weapons

Equipment was heavy; it averaged 29kg (64lb), uncomfortable, and difficult for the individual soldier to put on. The M1893 knapsack was of black leather (around a wooden frame) and black leather strapping. Inside it the soldier stored cleaning equipment, shaving kit, clean linen and – for territorial units only – a nightcap. Certain soldiers were tasked with carrying a cooking pot or coffee mill. Various kinds of haversack or bread bags were hung beneath it, while spare sheets or a blanket, surmounted by a mess tin, were placed on top.

An entrenching tool was also carried, usually on the left of the pack. The water (more likely, wine) canteen held a litre of liquid and had a distinctive design; by 1915 it was being replaced by a 2-litre version.

The soldier's belt was likely to be the M1873, with brass plaque, rather than the 1903 Model with buckle. Black cartridge pouches, either of the 1888 or 1905 models, were worn on either side of the belt. The bayonet hung on leather frogging suspended from the waist belt. The most common rifle was the Lebel (1893 model) and it could be carried at the shoulder by means of a brown leather strap.

◀ **PRIVATE, 13TH INFANTRY REGIMENT, 1914** *This uniform was worn by reinforcements heading to the front in the winter of 1914. The simplified greatcoat was manufactured from English cloth.*

▶ **PRIVATE, 112TH INFANTRY REGIMENT, 1915** *The transitional uniform of late 1914 and early 1915 also included a modified single-breasted greatcoat and looser trousers.*

▼ *Three French infantrymen on the Western Front, 1915. They wear newly issued caps without regimental numerals and with flat tops to prevent the rain from collecting.*

Uniform Reforms

Red trousers were quickly covered with blue overalls (intended for use with puttees) to make the wearer less visible. In 1915 a simplified greatcoat also began to be issued to troops moving up to the front. It was single breasted with painted buttons and appeared in all shades of blue from one similar to the older pattern to horizon blue. The falling collar was more comfortable and bore the regimental numeral in blue on yellow collar patches (issued in December 1914). Much of the cloth came from Britain, and the colour (medium blue) was known as English blue.

In February 1915 a metallic skull cap was also developed for wear beneath the kepi. It was a stop-gap measure (only 700,000 were ordered), designed to protect troops from head wounds, but it proved extremely unpopular, being difficult to secure and making the head very sweaty.

In response to the German adoption of gas cylinders and then gas shells in the spring of 1915, the first anti-gas compresses came into use. The C1 compress was carried in a waterproof envelope that was hung around the neck. It was sometimes worn with goggles or protective glasses (610,000 were delivered to the depots in the summer of 1915). A hood was also issued, but it inhibited the wearer's vision and was soon dropped; a protective mask (Tampon T) was then issued in October 1915 and was used until mid-1916. The use of protective equipment led to a decline in beards and moustaches; facial hair got in the way when soldiers were scrambling to

▼ PRIVATE, 95TH INFANTRY REGIMENT, 1916 (FRONT VIEW) *In December 1914 brown leather cartridge pouches and belts were introduced as these were quicker to manufacture than the previous versions.*

▲ PRIVATE OF INFANTRY KIT, 1915–16
1 *This 1915 flask, was based on the 1877 model and had two openings, one wider than the other.* 2 *Private's haversack of 1916 with spare boots and tent canvas. It contained everything from a spare pair of socks (new ones were issued each month) to a first-aid kit. Cooking utensils were shared out among members of the platoon.*

▼ PRIVATE, 96TH INFANTRY REGIMENT, 1916 (REAR VIEW) *This shows the canvas backpack which was manufactured in large numbers from 1914. It is crowned by the mess tin, tilted to allow firing from the prone position.*

▲ *A French artilleryman, wearing an early tampon P2 gas mask, adjusts the aim of a 75mm gun, sometime in 1915.*

put on their masks. Equipment was still heavy and cumbersome, and now frequently augmented by additional items such as grenades or gas masks.

Horizon Blue

Although experiments with grey-green had proved a failure in 1911, work continued on finding an acceptable and neutral colour. A mix of red, blue and white was attempted, although red dyes were more difficult to guarantee in sufficient quantity. Once red was taken out of the equation, a light blue resulted and this was quickly branded horizon blue. Production of horizon blue cloth had begun in the summer of 1914 and it began to make a tardy appearance that autumn. However, it was only in the spring of 1915 that the cloth was issued in sufficient quantities to transform the appearance of most French soldiers. Production was so urgent that a variety of colours resulted, most of which could be called light blue or steel blue.

Kepis and greatcoats were priorities but, from the late summer of 1915, tunics were also issued, this time with aluminium buttons and with the regimental number on blue cloth on the collar. Trousers were also issued with yellow piping for the infantry. Fatigue caps (bonnets de police) and berets were also issued in the new blue cloth.

Buttons were now made from artificial materials, painted alloy or cheap aluminium. Most metals were now needed for munitions. The majority continued to bear the flaming grenade symbol.

The kepi was now simplified and no longer showed the unit's number on the front. The greatcoat did bear the regimental number; initially it was blue on yellow with blue piping to the rear of the numeral, although blue on red squares of cloth also made an appearance. Soon blue numerals on a lighter patch of blue became the standard way to identify a unit.

Rank insignia was also adjusted. Instead of bright red stripes, dark blue bars were used at the base of the sleeve near the cuff. This was to make the NCOs, of which France had a shortage, less conspicuous.

The Adrian Helmet

A most significant development in 1915 was the issue of the Adrian helmet. General Joseph Joffre had seen that the metal skull cap was unsuitable and had ordered production of a new helmet as soon as possible. In February 1915, he was urging that a design by George Scott be put into production, and some thousands were produced before production ceased at the end of September 1915. The Scott helmet was too expensive, and there would be delays in manufacture, so a simpler design by August Louis Adrian, an officer of the commissariat, was commissioned instead.

▶ PRIVATE, 115TH INFANTRY REGIMENT, 1917
This figure is carrying full assault order, which included an ARS (Appareil Respiratoire Spécial) gas mask. He also carries a rolled blanket and tent canvas for extra protection before and during trench fighting. The blanket roll also helped protect the vital organs from stab wounds.

A prototype was tested in April 1915 and production began in May. Some 1,600,000 helmets with a flaming grenade were being produced for the infantry, and these were delivered to the depots by June and issued from then on. By December a total of 3,125,000 helmets had been delivered.

The helmet was often issued to colonial troops too, painted a semi-matt blue, which reflected the light – and provided a target for the enemy. This was later changed to a matt colour, and the helmets were also often covered in mud for extra camouflage.

Soldiers of 1917

The mixture of uniform styles worn in 1915 (photographs show the kepi and the helmet being worn by troops heading to the front) began to give way to a much more consistent appearance in 1916 and this lasted until the end of the war. Infantry were wearing the Adrian helmet with flaming grenade badge (stamped 'RF' for République Française), usually covered by a beige cover attached by cords beneath the visor and neck guard. When this cover was discarded, various matt colours from horizon blue to very dark grey were used in the field.

▶ PRIVATE, 43RD INFANTRY REGIMENT, ASSAULT ORDER, 1917 *This man wears a tunic and an M2 gas mask. The canister for the mask was usually of light blue or grey metal and was hung for easy access below the belt. This canister was problematic – it had been designed for an earlier mask and the M2 had to be folded to be put back in. This often led to the mask tearing and becoming useless. A new mask, the ARS, was issued in 1917 but was not common before 1918.*

A tunic, of a cut first adopted in 1914, was commonly worn, and this was fastened with five metallic buttons painted grey-blue. A white linen tunic was sometimes worn in the summer, or when the soldier was off duty. In cold weather the horizon blue tunic was worn beneath the greatcoat. The greatcoat followed the pattern adopted in 1915 and the trousers, increasingly without the stipulated yellow piping, were now in horizon blue. Scarves or neckerchiefs, mostly in light blue or mid-blue cotton, were worn around the neck as they were in 1914. Puttees in horizon blue were common, and ankle boots (usually of the 1912 pattern) were preferred, as they were the most comfortable footwear for trench warfare. Some modifications to the boots were made in 1916 and 1917, rivets being hammered into the sole to stop slippage and strengthen the boot.

Uniform Distinctions

In July 1916 a coloured disc was introduced, and this was supposed to be worn on the collar of the tunic and the collar of the greatcoat. It identified the wearer's

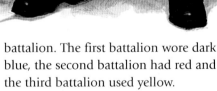

◀ CORPORAL, 35TH INFANTRY REGIMENT, 1918 *Rank is indicated by two small diagonal lines on the lower cuff. The trousers bore yellow piping from 1915 onwards but in wet weather it faded to beige or white, as here. There were three sizes of puttee in use in the French Army during the war – a 2.6 metre version, a 2.75 metre version and a 2.2 metre version. All three were held in place below the knee by a band of cloth in the same colour, although officers sometimes had a leather strap for this purpose.*

battalion. The first battalion wore dark blue, the second battalion had red and the third battalion used yellow.

Chevrons, to indicate length of service, were worn on the left sleeve of the greatcoat from April 1916. One chevron indicated a year of service, and an additional chevron indicated a further period of six months (five chevrons totalling three years).

Brassards could also be worn in the field. The most common was that worn by stretcher bearers and this was frequently a dark blue or white Maltese cross. Drivers often wore a brassard bearing the regimental number.

Those detached on liaison duties wore a brassard marked with an 'L'. White armbands were sometimes worn by soldiers participating in an assault, or white rectangles were worn on the back of the greatcoat or tunic.

Identity plaques on a chain were worn from 1917, replacing a previous version adopted in 1899. This bore a name and number and, on the reverse, the day, month and year the soldier entered military service.

On 10 January 1917 new collar patches began to be issued to the infantry. The new patches were in a lozenge shape and fixed to the ends of the greatcoat

collar. The regimental numeral was still displayed in blue and there were two rows of piping above the numeral. The battalion coloured discs were worn at the very points of the collar. These discs proved very unpopular and so are rarely seen being worn in contemporary photographs.

Added to these distinctions, brassards or specific insignia could be worn to denote specialists or particular functions. The red crossed axes for sappers had now become dark blue. Marksmen were awarded a hunting horn, worn as a blue cloth badge (gold for those who excelled) on the left sleeve. Signallers wore a blue five-pointed star with lightning bolts, a distinction also given to telephone operators in September 1916. Grenadiers wore a blue flaming grenade (for officers commanding grenadiers this was usually of gold thread), while those assigned to operate machine guns wore crossed cannon barrels (or a light machine gun beneath a flaming grenade). Gunners operating 37mm regimental guns wore a wheeled cannon badge from August 1916. Cyclists had a cycle badge, musicians wore a lyre badge (and also a red, white and blue bar on the lower left sleeve) and armourers wore crossed rifles with a grenade. Scouts sometimes wore a blue five-pointed star.

Wound Stripes

A wound stripe was devised as a mark of honour to be worn by Allied soldiers who had been wounded in combat. It was typically worn on the left forearm of the uniform or jacket.

◀ SERGEANT, 22ND INFANTRY REGIMENT, 1918 *This NCO has two wound stripes on his upper arm. These had been introduced in 1916. He has a revolver and a pocket lantern attached to his belt.*

▶ LIEUTENANT, 82ND INFANTRY REGIMENT, 1918 *The seven-button tunic was often made from gabardine cloth and usually had straight pocket flaps. This tailored version has pointed flaps on the four pockets and the tunic also had interior pockets.*

In France, the wound bar or 'Insigne des blessés militaires', was awarded, beginning in 1916. It was worn on the right sleeve following return to service. The wound bar was blue and 8mm wide. Officers often made use of thinner chevrons in metallic thread for their wound and service stripes, but some preferred the less conspicuous blue.

From April 1916 it became possible for soldiers of a distinguished regiment to wear a lanyard around the neck. The colour varied, for example in the colours of the Legion of Honour (red) or the Military Cross (red and green, interwoven).

▲ LIEUTENANT, 35TH INFANTRY REGIMENT, 1918 *This tunic is another variation on the regulation 1913 tunic and came into service in 1916. It has a 45mm high collar and buttons which could either be metallic or leather. This officer has a map case slung over his shoulder (these became progressively smaller as trench warfare began and positional maps shrank) and also carries an 1892 revolver (an item which remained in service until 1935) in a leather holster, an item affectionately nicknamed 'a ham',*

▲ *A French team, with a Hotchkiss gun, in their trenches at the Western Front in 1915.*

Assault Order

French troops were still lumbering backwards and forwards from the trenches carrying full equipment. Such a practice was impractical when troops were ordered to assault enemy positions. New cartridge pouches were issued in 1916, and by 1917 equipment was increasingly issued in natural unblackened leather.

A new gas mask, the M2, was also issued and this was kept in a blue metallic box worn hung beneath the cartridge pouch. Officers continued to carry a small first, aid kit. Knapsacks were being left in the rear trenches, and attacking infantry went forward dressed in their Adrian helmet, tunic, trousers, puttees and boots. Kit was kept to a minimum and usually consisted of a rolled blanket (worn across the chest in the Russian manner), one or two 2-litre canteens (containing wine and water), a bread bag and a gas mask container (the ARS came in a new cylindrical model, resembling the German version, and it began to be used in the early months of 1918). Most men also carried a camping lantern and an entrenching tool (either a spade, a pick or an axe). Empty sand

▲ SERGEANT, 4TH INFANTRY REGIMENT, IN THE TRENCHES, 1918 *The greatcoat issued to French troops was not particularly waterproof and, as often happened, this figure wears a cape fashioned out of tent canvas in order to stay dry while on trench duty. This NCO has his regimental number sewn on to his greatcoat collar. By this late stage of the war, these numerals were supposed to be set within lozenges at the tip of the greatcoat collar, but this was not always adhered to and photographs show numerous variations.*

bags or grenade bags could also be carried. Most infantry were armed with the Berthier or Lebel rifles, trench knives (of various designs) and even maces. Grenades were also carried, either clipped to the belt or in grenade bags slung over the shoulder.

Variations

The standard Adrian helmet could be fitted with a visor designed by Jean Dunand, but this was relatively rare. Helmets could also be fitted with suspended chainmail to protect the face, but this also

proved unpopular, as it added to the weight of the helmet. Body armour was less common (but captured German items were put to use), although a padded vest was being used in 1915. It proved too uncomfortable.

In really foul weather various civilian oilcloths were worn but troops could also be seen wrapped in their tents. Troops also made use of civilian scarves and gloves, and wrapped the firing mechanism of their rifles in oilcloth or handkerchiefs. Drivers wore fur coats in winter and also made use of fur mittens and waterproofed overalls. Clogs were very popular.

Soldiers were issued with white (which began life as a very light beige)

◄ CAPTAIN, 175TH INFANTRY REGIMENT, GALLIPOLI, 1915 *This officer wears a tunic with concealed buttons, as well as a tropical helmet first produced in 1886. He has a covered notebook attached to his belt as well as a leather map case. In his breast pocket he would keep a whistle, which he would have been expected to purchase privately. A leather strap enabled the wearer to strap the whistle chain to the tunic pocket's button. Although there were some 40,000 Frenchmen at Gallipoli, there were only two infantry regiments (the 175th and 176th), the rest of the expeditionary force being made up of elements of the Foreign Legion, zouaves and colonial regiments. These troops were later diverted to Salonika.*

overalls in snowy weather, a measure first introduced for foot soldiers in 1911. These were rather basic, fastened with zinc buttons and provided some camouflage. This was an effect improved upon when the helmet was also painted white.

Troops sent to theatres beyond Europe (French infantry regiments operated at Gallipoli, Salonika and Macedonia and in Palestine) generally wore a tunic (in horizon blue) with horizon blue or white trousers. Officers sometimes elected to wear a tropical helmet (first issued in 1886), rather than the Adrian helmet, and this resembled the British pith helmet. It was usually in light brown or beige and for line infantry units it was generally worn without any specific insignia. This helmet provided poor protection but was light and comfortable, and did protect the head and neck from the sun. Although horizon blue was stipulated for all troops from metropolitan France, as of February 1915 troops serving in hot climates could also be issued with a light (linen) khaki tunic and trousers.

▼ *French troops onboard a troop ship heading for Gallipoli in 1915. A French expeditionary force, largely composed of troops garrisoned in North Africa, was scraped together and sent against Ottoman positions on Cape Helles. They suffered 15,000 casualties.*

CHASSEURS AND MOUNTAIN TROOPS

France's light infantry (the chasseurs à pied and chasseurs alpins) wore distinctive uniform in the early years of the war and saw themselves as something of an elite force. The mountain troops in particular had tremendously high morale.

Foot Chasseurs

France's chasseurs were formed into battalions rather than regiments. There were 31 battalions in 1914, and 19 of these were foot chasseurs (chasseurs à pied) and 12 were alpine chasseurs (chasseurs alpins). There were also reserve battalions, making for a grand total of 62 battalions. Nine new battalions were formed in 1915, and some alpine chasseurs would find themselves grouped into the so-called Blue Division (the 47th Division).

Unlike the line infantry, France's light infantrymen did without red and restricted themselves to a uniform which was dark blue with yellow facings, with equipment being issued in black leather. It was a relatively practical uniform and officers tended to dress very much like their men, including the use of puttees rather than riding boots and greatcoats rather than tunics (except in the alpine chasseurs, where everyone wore a tunic). The kepi was the same as that worn by the infantry but was dark blue with yellow piping around the crown and the battalion number in yellow. The collar of the greatcoat and the officers' tunics also bore the battalion number. Puttees (2.6m long and 120mm wide) and ankle boots were preferred.

The chasseurs wore buttons bearing a traditional hunting horn rather than the flaming grenade. They also carried more equipment and more ammunition (120 rounds) than the average line infantryman.

Foot chasseurs had their kepi replaced with a simpler version without yellow piping. Horizon blue greatcoats were issued in 1915, although the darker trousers were retained. Experiments were made with various shades of blue, but the alpine chasseurs, at least, were keen to preserve their traditional dark blue. Pressure to force these troops to switch to a lighter blue met with little success in the winter of 1914, and existing stocks of dark blue uniforms were sufficient to keep the troops in a darker shade.

Gradual Evolution

In November 1915 green replaced yellow as the colour for the battalion numeral and for the piping on the trousers. It was also used to indicate rank for NCOs; the different ranks following the practice of the line infantry regiments. By this time a dark blue Adrian helmet (with a hunting horn and the letters 'RF', rather than a grenade) was also being worn. The alpine chasseurs were again resistant to change and preferred to make use of their distinctive beret as much as possible. Even so, some 100,000 helmets bearing the hunting horn

◄ CORPORAL, 5TH BATTALION CHASSEURS À PIED, 1914 *This chasseur NCO wears a double-breasted greatcoat with hunting horn buttons. His dark blue trousers with yellow piping differentiated him from his line infantry counterparts. Swords, a traditional symbol of rank, were seen in the field in 1914 but were increasingly left at the depots as trench warfare began.*

▼ *Cycle units were established in the 1900s. By 1905 – the date of this poster – the concept of using them for scouting and reconnaissance was well established.*

▲ SCOUT, 7TH BATTALION CHASSEURS À PIED, 1914 *This chasseur carries a heavy load even without the bicycle – most of his personal effects are stored in a canvas bag, or 'musette'. This was largely filled with the daily ration of food, and invariably, tobacco. The folding bicycle was first produced by a Captain Gérard and saw service in the French and Belgian armies in early 1914, before trench warfare brought such mobility to a halt.*

device of the chasseurs were delivered to the depots in June 1915.

By early 1916, most chasseurs found themselves dressed in a much lighter blue, distinguished only by having a hunting horn on the helmet, green hunting horns on the tip of each greatcoat collar (along with the battalion numeral) and hunting horns on the buttons of the greatcoat and tunic. The tunic itself was issued with five buttons. Most of the foot chasseurs resembled line infantrymen (although a few opted to wear the beret of their mountain-climbing colleagues).

War had ensured that the distinctions, so long cherished by the chasseurs, were now reduced to a minimum.

Alpine Chasseurs

France had raised and trained mountain troops in the 1880s to guard a sensitive frontier with the newly united Italy. In the war that began in 1914, such troops saw action in the Vosges mountains and in the initial attack on the Germans in Alsace.

Uniform Distinctions

The alpine chasseurs differed from the foot chasseurs in some significant details. They tended to wear a tunic (the vareuse-dolman) adopted in 1891, as it was less cumbersome than the greatcoat. The tunic had the battalion number in yellow at the points of the falling collar. These numerals were in white for territorial units.

The tunic was fastened with seven small buttons, made from white metal, and had two pockets at the bottom of the front. It had slits in the side, to ease climbing. Cuffs were folded back. A dark blue woollen sash was also worn.

Rank insignia was worn on the sleeve, that of the sergeant being placed slightly higher than that of the corporal. Other insignia was similar to that worn by the line infantry. Crossed cannons denoted machine gunners (some battalions had a Hotchkiss machine gun section, mules being used to transport the gun and spare ammunition) and, from 1912, a hunting horn denoted a marksmanship qualification. Officers tended to wear a tunic of the same cut as that of their men, but in finer cloth and in two versions: a lighter cloth for summer, and a heavier cloth for winter.

The alpine chasseurs also wore a dark blue beret (after 1902 it could be worn with a white cover during hot weather or on long marches) with a yellow or golden hunting horn insignia on the right-hand side. It was first adopted in 1889 but was then modified in 1896.

▼ CAPTAIN, 3RD BATTALION CHASSEURS À PIED, 1914 *This officer wears a neat fatigue cap, or 'bonnet de police', which is complete with hunting horn, rank insignia and yellow piping. There were simpler versions worn, and they were issued in various different shapes and colours.*

Trousers were dark blue (a shade that was created by mixing 95 per cent blue wool with 5 per cent white wool) with yellow piping and could be covered with white overalls. The cut of the trouser was relatively narrow in 1914 but, from then on, a baggier trouser began to be worn, it was gathered at the knees and calves and looser on the thigh. Although piping was supposed to be worn it was often left off.

Instead of a greatcoat, these mountain troops tended to wear a hooded coat first issued in 1892. It was fastened by four uniform buttons and two hooks and had rank insignia on the sleeve (in yellow or silver).

▲ *French Alpine troops, nicknamed 'the blue devils' by their German foes, study a 37mm mountain gun.*

Equipment

The alpine chasseurs carried a brown leather pack that was supposed to be better suited for mountain warfare. The coat was rolled up and placed on top of the pack; in place of an entrenching tool many chasseurs carried a mountain stick and, when operating in the mountains, a coil of rope. In 1892 it had been ordered that cartridges were no longer to be placed in the knapsack and, instead, were to be carried at the waist in black leather cartridge pouches. Most chasseurs had three such cartridge

▲ **SERGEANT, 12TH BATTALION OF CHASSEURS ALPINS, 1914** *The dark blue woollen beret worn by the alpine chasseurs bore a yellow hunting horn insignia on the right, an emblem which would, by 1916, be repeated on this NCO's collar.*

▶ **FRENCH WEAPONS, 1917**
1 A Hotchkiss machine gun with an adjustable tripod stand. These versatile weapons were prone to overheating.
2 A French flare gun, of a revised model issued in 1917, with a range of 60 metres (66 yards).

pouches (although sergeants were allowed to have just two), mostly of the M1888 pattern. Officers were armed with a revolver and a sword, as were drummers and buglers. Few chasseurs carried camping equipment but most did carry a canteen, cooking pot, and mess tin. These items were often of aluminium, as these had been sent for the alpine chasseurs to test in the 1890s. Haversacks and bread bags were also worn.

▼ CHASSEUR FROM A SKI COMPANY 1916
Ski companies served in the Vosges mountain and were drawn from alpine battalions. The white beret cover and white overtrousers were standard issue for those troops too.

Bicycle and Ski Companies

The chasseurs provided bicycle companies, which were assigned to cavalry divisions. These were equipped with folding bicycles and artillery carbines. Ski companies were also formed after trials in 1903. Volunteers were called for in the winter of 1914 to counter German skiers in the Vosges and these acted initially as scouts but then as more formal companies.

These companies wore a special yellow insignia (silver for officers), introduced in 1916, showing a pair of skis. Many variations existed before a standardized insignia came into force in the 1920s. In the winter these ski troops wore their white beret cover, white overalls and a specially designed white tunic which was very baggy and could be buttoned at the cuffs. Specialist insignia included thunderbolts for telegraph operators and signalmen, a silver hunting horn

▲ CHASSEUR, 7TH BATTALION OF CHASSEURS ALPINS, 1916 *Alpine troops wore a hunting horn badge on their Adrian helmets and carried a curve-handled Alpine stick and a folded, hooded cloak under a tent canvas.*

for marksmen, crossed swords for master swordsmen, two crossed gun barrels beneath a bursting grenade for machine gun operators, a harp for musicians and a crossed pick and spade for chasseurs who carried tools. The two groups of mountain cyclists formed in 1912 wore a bicycle motif on their sleeve.

FOREIGN TROOPS

The demands and fortunes of war meant that France would make use of foreign nationals in its armies in a variety of ways.

The Foreign Legion

There had been a long tradition of employing foreign volunteers in French armies, from the Swiss regiments of the Bourbons to the Polish troops of Napoleon. A foreign legion, of very mixed nationality, was formed in the 1830s. In 1914 battalions on detached service were gathered into so-called March Regiments (composed of battalions from different parent regiments). Personnel was augmented by a wave of foreign volunteers (principally Italians).

Uniform Distinctions

The legionaries were armed and equipped in a style similar to the line infantry but wore distinctive buttons (bearing the words 'Légion Etrangère'), and they also had the right to wear white cotton trousers, a blue waistband or sash. This colourful uniform was quickly modified. Khaki trousers and tunics were issued in late 1914, although the greatcoat was increasingly horizon blue. The colour of the cloth varied from yellowish brown to a darker brown (most frequently imported from Britain). By 1916 the legion's officers and men had been issued with khaki greatcoats bearing a green grenade and piping on the collar. The style of these collar patches followed that of the line infantry.

The Adrian helmet was worn with a grenade badge and was initially blue but quickly painted light brown once the khaki greatcoats began to be worn. The distinctive blue waistband was largely only worn on ceremonial occasions. At around the same time the men of the Legion's March

◀ PRIVATE, 1ST MARCH REGIMENT, FRENCH FOREIGN LEGION, 1916 *The blue waist band was worn by zouaves and the Foreign Legion and was supposed to provide extra back support during long marches in areas difficult to resupply.*

▶ PRIVATE, CZECH LEGION, 1918 *The Adrian helmet issued to Czech troops bore a badge that included the coat of arms of Bohemia, Slovakia, Moravia and Silesia.*

Regiment were authorized to wear a lanyard in the red and green of the Croix de Guerre (Military Cross). The Legion wore standard equipment, although this was predominantly brown rather than blackened leather.

Polish Units

A Polish army was formed in France in 1917, drawing in recruits from Polish prisoners who had been in German service or Poles from the foreign legion. The uniform matched

▶ African American soldiers of the 15th Regiment Infantry, New York National Guard. The US transferred four regiments of black soldiers to French command in 1918.

contemporary French uniforms very closely, most particularly that of the chasseurs, but a cloth cap (the square-topped konfederatka) was permitted and this had a leather peak for officers. A white Polish eagle on a red disc was worn on the shoulder straps of the greatcoat, and the eagle motif was also used on some Adrian helmets.

Infantry had green unit numerals on the collar, along with a horn, while artillery had light blue, cavalry had white

and engineers had scarlet. Infantry and cavalry officers wore silver rank insignia, artillery officers wore gold. Polish troops returned to Poland in 1918 and many fought the Bolsheviks in 1919 dressed in this uniform.

Czechoslovakian Chasseurs

Two regiments of Czech volunteers were raised in December 1917 (they were termed the 21st and 22nd Battalions of Chasseurs) and, like the Polish infantry, were uniformed in the style of French chasseurs. According to a decree of April 1918 they wore a tunic, similar to that of the alpine chasseurs but with shoulder straps, which had blue collar patches (piped red) with the regimental numeral in gold. A cypher (which superimposed an 'S' on a 'C') was worn on the shoulder straps in red. The troops wore an Adrian helmet with the arms of Bohemia, Moravia and Slovakia on the front. A dark blue beret was also worn, again resembling that of the alpine chasseurs, and this had the same badge, in gold, pinned to the front. These troops formed the basis of the new Czechoslovakian Army.

◀ PRIVATE, CZECH LEGION, 1918 The Czechs wore a beret similar to that of Alpine troops but it bore a badge, not the white within blue within red cockade originally envisaged.

▶ CHASSEUR, CHASSEUR REGIMENT, POLISH LEGION, 1917 The Polish Legion wore an Adrian helmet, with eagle and hunting horn device, but a more typically Polish beret, or konfederatka, when off duty.

American Troops

Although uneasy with the idea of front line units composed only of African Americans, the US Army ensured that four American regiments with black personnel (the 369th, 370th, 371st and 372nd) did not fight alongside their white American compatriots. Instead they were transferred to French command in 1918. The regiments formed a French division, which was trained and equipped at French expense; the men wore Adrian helmets (with grenade badges) and carried French weapons and equipment. However, tunics and breeches were generally of standard American manufacture.

COLONIAL TROOPS

During the course of the war, the French Army would make use of Frenchmen residing or serving overseas, or of native inhabitants, whether volunteers or conscripts, in order to boost the number of troops it had available.

The history of units raised in the colonies is complicated but, essentially, there were a number of key units that played an important part in the war. The most famous were perhaps the 31

▲ *French stretcher bearers carry wounded soldiers, including Algerian tirailleurs, away from the battlefields of the Battle of the Marne to a field hospital.*

battalions of zouaves, formed from native Frenchmen resident in Algeria or Tunisia (although eight battalions were actually raised in Paris and Lyon). These, like the Foreign Legion, were formed into composite March Regiments. There were also the 32 battalions of tirailleurs (sharpshooters) raised from volunteers in Tunisia and Algeria, later supplemented by men from Morocco. Morocco was in the process of being pacified in 1914 and few men were available at first; those who were recruited were initially grouped into five battalions of native chasseurs.

Less reliable were the Light Infantry of Africa (Infanterie Légère d'Afrique), composed of those sentenced to penal service in Africa. France also had a number of colonial troops who had originally been the responsibility of the Ministry of the Marine. There were

12 regiments of colonial infantry, Senegalese tirailleurs from West Africa, Tonkinese tirailleurs from Indochina and tirailleurs from Madagascar. A number of other colonies also raised troops for service in the war.

The Zouaves
Zouaves wore a comfortable uniform, much imitated across the globe, which was pseudo North African. They wore a distinctive red cap ('chéchia'), which could be worn with a blue cover, which was a kind of fez with a blue tassel (gold thread for NCOs and officers), and a blue waistcoat edged in red and with red ornamentation. This had been modified in 1893 but was of an even older design. Beneath the waistcoat was a blue shirt, piped in red. The zouaves wore red, baggy trousers which were of heavier cloth for winter wear. These were replaced by white cotton trousers on campaign in the summer. Zouaves assigned to cycle companies needed to wear much less

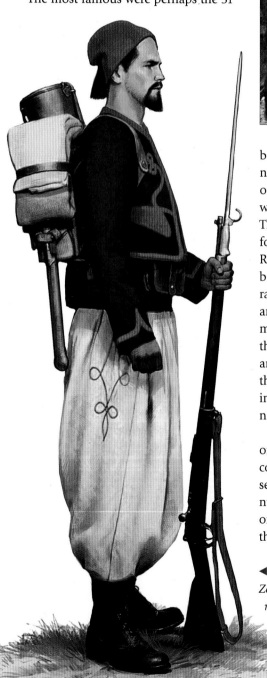

◀ PRIVATE, 1ST ZOUAVES, 1914 *The 1st Zouaves, shown here, had red lace and a solid red roundel on the jacket, while the 2nd Zouaves had a white roundel within the loop. The 3rd had a yellow roundel, the 4th had red lace with a blue roundel.*

▲ PRIVATE, 1ST ZOUAVES, 1914 *Zouave regiments wore blue waistbands and this differentiated them from the tirailleurs, who wore red sashes.*

generous trousers. An indigo waistband, very similar to that worn by the alpine chasseurs was also worn. Shoes were worn with black gaiters embellished with silver buttons, but these rapidly found themselves replaced by ankle boots and puttees.

NCOs wore additional red piping around the cuffs, this was piped with gold for officers. As from 1911, officers could also wear a white or light brown tunic when off duty, and although still

worn in Africa this was largely replaced by dark blue tunics after September 1913.

Equipment was generally the same as the line infantry regiments and included black leather cartridge cases of the M1888 pattern.

Uniform Reforms

The zouaves suffered heavily in August 1914, standing out in their red or white trousers. As early as September, khaki was being considered as a way of subduing the uniform, and by the end of the month the ministry had agreed to clothe the zouaves in a mustard-colour khaki cloth. Trousers were issued, as was a tunic of the same cut as that of the alpine chasseurs and a khaki chéchia cover. There were delays but priority was given to issuing the toned-down trousers and chéchia cover. As winter began the troops were issued with infantry greatcoats (they had originally used hooded capes in bad weather) which were either dark blue or, increasingly, horizon blue. By early 1915 the zouave uniforms in France were looking at best varied, at worst ragged.

France's African troops would largely be clothed in the new khaki colour, despite British complaints that the resulting uniform could be confused with their own uniforms.

Even so it was Britain that supplied the two million metres of cloth needed by the French. Greatcoats of the simplified version of 1915 were being issued in khaki towards the end of 1915 and, apart from the colour, other items, such as the tunic, helmet and trousers (sometimes piped in yellow), were brought into line to reflect the new uniform of the line infantry. The regimental numeral, in red, and two bars of piping were worn on the greatcoat and tunic.

Headgear

Zouaves had also received the metallic skull cap to wear beneath their chéchia. With the advent of the Adrian helmet it was initially envisaged that it would be issued

with a crescent and the letter 'Z'. Although troops initially wore horizon blue helmets with a grenade badge, in August 1915 the crescent (although some later had distinctive insignia: a crescent with the regimental number, for example) was prescribed and these helmets were issued painted in khaki.

▼ CORPORAL, 9TH ZOUAVES, 1918 *The mustard-coloured tunic had red collar piping and the regimental numeral in red. The badge on this man's sleeve shows he is an expert machine gunner. A hunting horn would have denoted an expert marksman and two crossed cannon barrels a machine-gun operator.*

The Tirailleurs

Algerian and Tunisian tirailleurs were also formed into composite regiments, and wore a uniform very similar to that worn by the zouaves, which had actually been designed in 1853. It was, however, in a lighter shade of blue and with yellow piping and ornamentation rather than red. Unlike the zouaves the waistband was red. The chéchia was also in red but had a tassel which was white, red or yellow according to the battalion. The tirailleurs experienced similar changes to that endured by the zouaves, and were issued with mustard-coloured khaki uniforms. This time the

regimental numeral and piping were blue, and those regiments which mixed zouaves and tirailleurs together had numerals in red with one strip of piping in red and one in blue.

Penal Battalions

The Light Infantry of Africa (three battalions) had been formed to reform conscripts by exposing them to harsh service in Africa. They wore a uniform similar to that of the Foreign Legion, complete with blue waistband and red trousers. In 1915 they were also issued khaki greatcoats, tunics and trousers and had battalion numerals and piping in violet.

Colonial Regiments

France had 12 active colonial regiments in 1914 – although the first was dissolved – and 12 reserve battalions. All of these were recruited in France for service overseas, although Morocco also raised a much-decorated mixed colonial regiment. The uniform was similar to that of the line infantry but the troops wore blue trousers, a blue kepi (piped in red) and a double-breasted greatcoat that had two buttons at each cuff. The belt had a large bronze buckle but the main distinction was the use of a red anchor on the kepi and on the buttons.

◀ PRIVATE, 8TH REGIMENT OF MARCH TIRAILLEURS, 1915 *The headgear, which came in endless sizes and shapes from squat to shako-like, was usually covered with a mustard coloured cloth, and the rather lavish light blue jacket has been covered by a similarly drab greatcoat. The French bayonet shown here was often found to be too long for trench warfare, and trench knives and revolvers were usually preferred by assault troops.*

▶ CAPTAIN, 1ST MARCH REGIMENT OF TIRAILLEURS, 1914 *The march regiments were formed of detachments drawn from different parent regiments. Other ranks would wear ornate jackets in light blue in zouave style, with coloured roundels (red for the 1st, white for the 2nd, yellow for the 3rd and light blue for the 4th).*

The troops were issued with horizon blue uniforms in 1915, being distinguished by collar patches which bore regimental numerals in red along with piping and, from 1917, a red anchor (gold anchor alone for officers). The helmet bore a grenade and anchor badge. Khaki uniforms were issued in the summer of 1918.

Troops from Senegal

The tirailleurs from Senegal began the war in dark blue uniforms with a red fez. On arrival in France they also adopted dark blue greatcoats of the style worn by the

◀ **PRIVATE, TIRAILLEUR SENEGALAIS, 1917** *This man wears mustard-coloured puttees but, initially, and due to shortage of stock, troops arriving from the colonies often wore horizon blue puttees. He wears a helmet cover but these were often discarded when it was found that fragments of cloth complicated head wounds and made infections more common. Helmets were painted instead.*

▶ **PRIVATE, 23RD COLONIAL INFANTRY REGIMENT, 1914** *Colonial infantry regiments were raised for service in Africa, the Caribbean and Indochina. They wore badges with anchor insignia, a throwback to the time when the Ministry of Marine was in charge of colonial units.*

wore a similar uniform but with red waistband, red fez (later khaki helmet) and green anchor insignia.

Asian Troops

Tonkinese and Annamite troops from Indochina were sent to serve in Europe (principally in Macedonia). The tirailleurs remaining in Indochina saw service in 1917 in putting down a mutiny of the Garde Indigène (native gendarmerie) in Thai Nguen.

Led by European French officers, these troops wore native footwear, cotton khaki trousers, and khaki tunics bearing a light blue anchor insignia. They also wore a native round hat, known as the salacco, which was traditional wear in Vietnam.

colonial regiments. In 1915 they were issued with horizon blue and only switched to khaki in early 1916 (the decision to do this had been taken in August 1915), and even then greatcoats remained horizon blue until 1918. The tirailleurs wore tunics that had yellow anchor insignia and their fez was covered with a khaki cover.

When the Adrian helmet was issued it also bore the anchor and grenade device. Tirailleurs from Madagascar

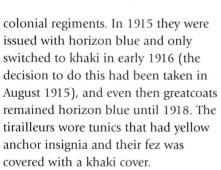

▶ *A group of French troops and French colonial Algerian cavalry congregate after the Battle of the Aisne, September 1914.*

CAVALRY

France's cavalry began the war at full strength and were dressed in resplendent uniforms but soon found themselves reduced in number and issued with more practical dress.

Cavalry was still nominally distinguished as being either heavy (designed to deliver a knockout charge on the battlefield, mounted on bigger horses and carrying heavier equipment, or light (intended to serve as scouts or highly mobile infantry). The former included cuirassiers and dragoons, while the latter included mounted chasseurs ('chasseurs à cheval'), hussars or mounted rifles. France had 12 regiments of cuirassiers in 1914, 32 regiments of dragoons, 21 regiments of chasseurs (plus six regiments of chasseurs d'Afrique) and 14 regiments of hussars. There were also some four regiments of 'spahis', cavalry raised in North Africa but officered by Europeans.

◄ BRIGADIER, 8TH DRAGOONS, 1914
The uniform of the dragoons had changed little since the time of Napoleon III (reigned 1852–70). The helmet was covered by a beige oilcloth on active service.

Cuirassiers

The cuirassiers saw themselves as an elite and in 1914 went proudly into battle much as they had done in 1870.

The officers still technically had to maintain four kinds of uniform (morning dress, weekly dress, full dress and campaign dress). Campaign dress consisted of a dark blue tunic (fastened with nine buttons) which had a red collar and dark blue collar patch with silver bursting grenades), and which was worn with silver epaulettes, red breeches (piped in black), black cavalry boots with spurs and a nickel-plated cuirass. They also wore a leather, silver-plated helmet, adopted in 1874, worn without a plume (this being reserved for staff officers, parades and Sundays). Brown gloves were worn (white for full dress). A beige or brown helmet cover was worn, and sometimes the cuirass was also worn with a cover. Officers carried a pistol, a sabre and a pair of binoculars in a black leather case.

Troopers wore very similar uniforms, although they had red epaulettes, a steel cuirass and a uniform of poorer manufacture. They were armed with carbines.

A number of cuirassier regiments dismounted squadrons in 1915 and these continued to wear their helmets, but minus the comb. By then horizon blue was being introduced for the majority of cavalry units and they began to resemble the infantry in some aspects of their dress. Breeches were piped in blue.

triangular collar patches, again with red numerals and piping, a design established in December 1914. This was silver for NCOs and gold for officers, quickly adjusted to silver for officers as well. In July 1916 six regiments were officially denoted as being dismounted cuirassiers (the 4th, 5th, 8th, 9th, 11th and 12th) and these added a strand of yellow piping to be worn in addition to the two red strands on the collar. They also wore a coloured disc at the point of the collar patch: black for the first battalion, red for the second battalion, yellow for the third and green for the depot company. In January 1917 the triangular-style collar patch was changed to that of a lozenge.

All six of the dismounted cuirassier regiments would be awarded lanyards in the red and green of the Military Cross. These units generally preferred to rely on pistols, knives and hand grenades rather than carbines or rifles. For all regiments, leather gaiters or puttees were now in use.

Dragoons

The uniform of French dragoons was similar to that worn by the cuirassiers. The 1874 helmet, with gilded dome and front plate, and metallic scales, was worn with or without a cover. The officers and men wore a very dark blue tunic (nearly black for officers) with nine silver buttons, a beige collar with dark blue collar patches and the regimental numeral worn in red. Red breeches and the tall leather boots preferred by the heavy cavalry completed the uniform. The men were armed with carbines and the 1913 model lance. Officers used the heavy cavalry sabre of 1880.

Horizon blue was introduced to the dragoons and the uniform was quickly adjusted to resemble the profile of the rest of the Army. The Adrian helmet replaced the cavalry helmet, with or without the comb, and horizon blue tunics, greatcoats and breeches (now piped in blue) were worn. The regimental numeral appeared in white on a dark blue collar patch along with two strands of piping.

Dragoons continued to make use of the lance with triangular blade and steel shaft after 1915 but also carried a carbine. They had brown leather belts and cartridge pouches and frequently carried additional belts of ammunition slung around the horse's neck.

▼ **Brigadier, 12th Cuirassiers, 1917** *A brigadier was the equivalent of an infantry corporal, and rank is indicated on the cuff of this NCO's greatcoat which, in design, conforms to that worn by the infantry. He carries a semi-automatic Ruby pistol, which could fire nine relatively light rounds, attached to his belt.*

▲ **Captain, 1st Cuirassiers, 1914** *Cavalry officers were issued brown leather gloves, which were officially known as dog-skin gloves. The cuirass was usually covered to prevent excessive glare and wear and tear.*

The cuirassiers were distinguished by red regimental numerals and two bands of red strands on the collar tab. The Adrian helmet was now worn. They also wore a cavalry greatcoat that was longer than that for the infantry and was single breasted. It also had

The gendarmes, charged with maintaining order, had a very similar uniform but with white grenades on the collar patches and a carbine that could be fitted with a bayonet. They wore white piping on their breeches.

The Light Cavalry

The vast majority of chasseur à cheval and hussar regiments wore an elegant light blue shako in 1914. However, a helmet, resembling that worn by the dragoons and also made out of steel, was supposed to have been introduced in 1913. This helmet was to have a hunting horn emblem for the chasseurs and a star for the hussars. The number of helmets issued has remained obscure but the 5th Chasseurs, along with the 10th and 15th, probably wore them while the 8th and 14th Hussars were issued helmets by 1914 and five further regiments received them in late 1914. For those regiments which were not issued with helmets, the leather light blue shako with hunting horn for chasseurs and Hungarian knot for hussars had to suffice. The peak was black and had a gilt edge for NCOs and officers. Pompons in squadron colours were also worn (blue, red, green, light blue and yellow).

Chasseurs wore a light blue tunic with red collar and white regimental numeral; instead of epaulettes there were white trefoils. Breeches were red, with light blue piping, and black leather cavalry boots (with spurs). Equipment belts were brown and, as with the dragoons, a carbine was carried without a bayonet. Hussars wore a nearly identical uniform, but with light blue collars piped in red.

The advent of horizon blue uniforms meant that the chasseurs and hussars adopted the practical uniforms adopted by the dragoons in 1915. Chasseurs were distinguished by green regimental numerals and strands of piping, while hussars wore

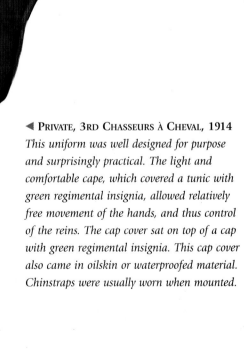

◀ **PRIVATE, 3RD CHASSEURS À CHEVAL, 1914**
This uniform was well designed for purpose and surprisingly practical. The light and comfortable cape, which covered a tunic with green regimental insignia, allowed relatively free movement of the hands, and thus control of the reins. The cap cover sat on top of a cap with green regimental insignia. This cap cover also came in oilskin or waterproofed material. Chinstraps were usually worn when mounted.

light blue numerals and strands. Both were supposed to wear dark blue piping on light blue breeches.

Colonial Cavalry

The Chasseurs d'Afrique began the war in a uniform which resembled that of the other chasseurs but had distinctive narrow-topped shakos (known as 'taconnets') with red crowns and light blue bands. They did however use the traditional hunting horn emblem on the front of their shakos. Their collars were yellow. The spahis wore Arabic-style dress complete with turban and red cloak, red sash and red jacket with dark blue

▲ *French dragoons cover British infantrymen as they erect a temporary barricade near the Somme in 1916.*

ornamentation. They also wore the zouave chéchia. Officers tended to favour a more European appearance with a kepi, red tunic, light blue trousers and cloak. Brown boots or gaiters were worn as footwear.

Whereas the bulk of the cavalry adopted horizon blue, these African units were issued khaki in 1915 and wore a shako or chéchia in a light brown cover. Both units wore yellow regimental numerals and yellow strands of piping on their blue collar patches; they were also supposed to have dark blue piping on their cavalry breeches. Although the chasseurs adopted the khaki tunic, it was not, however, something worn by spahi troopers, they preferred a loose-fitting khaki coat or cloak with equipment worn on the outside.

◀ **CAPTAIN, 5TH HUSSARS, 1917** *By 1916 hussars were wearing standard Adrian helmets with flaming grenades. Only the collar insignia indicated a hussar regiment.*

▶ **CAPTAIN, 4TH SPAHIS, 1914** *The dramatic woolen cape came with a hood and covered the equally dramatic red tunic. The cape was essential wear in the desert when temperatures could plummet overnight. Such a uniform did not last much beyond 1915.*

ARTILLERY

Artillery would be the pre-eminent arm of the French Army in the long years of the war, growing in numbers and potency as the army sought to blast its way through the enemy's trench system. It also developed in other ways, from the number and type of gun, to new ways of transporting guns (motorized transport) and designation of new targets (anti-aircraft artillery made an appearance in serious numbers).

Development

The majority of France's artillerymen served in the field artillery, but there were also foot artillery units (heavy artillery), horse artillery units, mountain artillery, garrison artillery, coastal artillery and colonial artillery units. By the end of the war there would also be anti-aircraft artillery and tank (known as special artillery) units. The latter are dealt with in the next section.

Early Years

France's field artillery wore a uniform, which resembled that in use by the foot chasseurs. The kepi, which had only replaced the artilleryman's shako in 1884, was of the same style, but piped in red and with a red regimental numeral. Some horse artillery batteries had been issued with a helmet which

▲ *A mobile French anti-aircraft gun during the Battle of the Somme.*

resembled that worn by the mounted chasseurs. First designed in 1902, and bearing a crossed cannon emblem, it was little used. A second version, developed in 1905 and manufactured from blackened leather, was issued to the 13th and 54th regiments. These could still be seen in 1915 and were worn with horizon blue covers in the spring of 1915.

◀ CORPORAL, 3RD FIELD ARTILLERY, 1914
This corporal wears a standard artillery uniform with red piping and regimental number on the collar.

▼ ARTILLERY BADGES *1 Field artillery. 2 Heavy artillery. 3 Mountain artillery. 4 Foot artillery. 5 Artillery in Africa. 6 Musician.*

▼ FRENCH ARTILLERY, 1917 *1 A trench mortar, or grenade launcher, was found to be vital. This trench mortar, nicknamed 'little toad', was issued in large numbers from 1917. 2 A mortar round.*

◄ **PRIVATE, 32ND FIELD ARTILLERY, 1914**
A helmet had been issued to some artillery batteries in 1902 and was occasionally seen at the front in 1914. The Adrian helmet finally rendered it obsolete.

belts (1893 model), smaller than those used by the infantry, and were issued with an artillery carbine. Bayonets were carried in black scabbards, suspended from the black waistbelt. Rank insignia consisted of red chevrons on the lower sleeve. Observers wore a special badge showing four lighting bolts exploding off a grenade.

Uniforms for the horse artillery were very similar but they preferred cavalry gaiters or boots. Horse artillery generally wore reinforced breeches (black leather inners), rather than trousers of the infantry cut. They also carried sabres and pistols in preference to the carbines of the field artillery.

Changes

The artillery was issued with horizon blue at around the same time as the infantry. Despite the limited use of the artillery helmet of 1905, and some firemen's helmets that were brought into service in 1914, France quickly found it essential to do more to protect artillerymen from counter-battery fire. The Adrian helmet, bearing a crossed cannon device, was quickly brought into service. In June 1915 some 350,000 Adrian helmets were issued bearing this device.

The field artillery continued to wear scarlet piping on their trousers, as did the horse artillery, while the regimental numeral on the collar was fixed as a light blue numeral with light blue strands of piping for the field artillery and dark blue for the horse artillery. The number was green with green strands of piping for the men of the foot artillery and white for the mountain artillery.

► **PRIVATE, 12TH FIELD ARTILLERY, 1917** *This uniform, with its red collar insignia and Adrian helmet badge was, in all other respects, identical to that worn by the infantry.*

Greatcoats were worn in cold weather, and were generally carried rolled over the shoulder in spring and autumn. Equipment increasingly became standardized, with brown leather belts and infantry-issue items predominating.

Colonial artillery units wore horizon blue uniforms, very similar to those adopted by the European artillery units, only adopting khaki in March 1918. They, however, did make much use of the colonial anchor insignia on buttons and Adrian helmets. The artillery wore red trouser piping and a dark blue anchor device on the collar instead of a regimental number.

The tunic was dark blue, almost black, and was of the style adopted in 1873 (fastened by nine buttons) and with red collar patches with the regimental numeral in dark blue. Trousers were of the same colour but with two bands of red piping. Most gunners wore boots, but puttees became more common in 1914.

Artillerymen generally did without the knapsack, as it was usually carried on the limbers, while personal items were carried in saddlebags, so gunners frequently restricted themselves to a bread bag and a one- or two-litre canteen. They wore black cartridge

TECHNICAL TROOPS

The complexities of digging and defending trenches, developing and countering new forms of warfare and bringing up munitions supplies in ever more massive quantities, called for the development and increase in specialist units. These varied from supply units (often known as train units), to tank drivers. Tank units were actually a branch of the artillery, but are dealt with here as a specialist group.

◄ CORPORAL, ENGINEERS, 1917 *This corporal has his rank chevrons in red on his sleeve, and a collar patch in black and red. His helmet has the distinctive cuirass and helmet badge of the engineers.*

▼ TECHNICAL TROOPS KIT 1917 *1 An officer's whistle with leather attachment strap and chain. 2 Gas mask container. 3 and 4 Equipment used in laying, charging and detonating underground mines.*

▲ *A French Renault tank heads to the front in 1918, watched by British artillerymen.*

Supply Troops

Soldiers and officers of the train wore uniforms based heavily on that of the artillery, but they wore grey kepis and tunics (much as they had done under Napoleon), buttoned with silver or grey buttons, and trousers (sometimes red, sometimes blue overalls). These were supposed to have red piping. Horizon blue uniforms were then adopted, with green piping and a scarlet squadron numeral on the green collar patch.

The train itself was growing – more and more troops needed supplying with more and more ammunition and food – and diversifying into various subgroups, from ambulances to the drivers of meat wagons. The automobile service wore uniforms similar to the train but with the red letter 'A' on the collar of the greatcoat and tunic. Red brassards with 'A' in white were also used. Drivers wore large fur coats and heavy mittens when driving in the windowless cabs of the trucks then in use.

Specialist Troops

French engineers had a tremendous reputation and this was enhanced by the painful duties assigned to them in the war. They performed all kinds of functions and one, the 5th Regiment, was tasked exclusively with work on maintaining and repairing railways.

Engineers wore artillery uniforms with black facings and red piping on the trousers and red regimental numerals on the collar patch. In 1915 they switched to horizon blue with black collar patches (which were made of velvet for officers) and trouser piping, and with red numerals on the collar patch. The Adrian helmet was issued bearing a device that represented a cuirass (body armour worn by French engineers during sieges), stamped with the letters 'RF' and a crested helmet. It sometimes also featured crossed axes beneath the main device, but this could have been a private purchase helmet. In terms of specialist functions, the 5th Regiment bore an insignia on its sleeve showing a locomotive device.

Engineers generally carried standard infantry equipment in addition to any specialist equipment required for digging or laying cables or barbed wire. Some protective equipment was used by engineers and might include a black steel front-and-rear cuirass and peaked steel helmet with cheek protectors. This equipment was the same as that worn by Napoleonic engineers.

Tank Troops

These troops were technically a part of the artillery but were termed 'special' artillery. They wore horizon blue with red collar patches and numerals and strands of piping in iron grey. By the autumn of 1917 they had also developed a special insignia consisting of crossed cannon with a crested helmet and this was worn on the standard artillery tunic.

Leather coats were popular as were additional protective equipment varying from driver's gauntlets and padded protective vests to helmets with visors or leather helmets with chainmail visors. Anything, in short, to protect personnel from ricochets from shell fragments within the actual vehicle. Renault light tanks were the most common tank, Schneiders were also used. Adrian helmets, bearing the standard device worn by other artillerymen, were also issued to tank crews.

◀ CAPTAIN, TANK ASSAULT UNIT, 1918
The black leather jacket was popular among tank crews, drivers and aviation personnel. Tank crews developed their own insignia and, by late 1917, they had a special artillery badge on the Adrian helmet.

▶ SECOND LIEUTENANT, 23RD TRAIN REGIMENT, 1918 *This junior officer wears a bonnet de police, or fatigue cap, his Adrian helmet would have had a crossed cannon badge.*

Tank troops were generally armed with pistols or automatic pistols, rather than rifles or artillery carbines.

Medical Troops

Officers wore infantry officers' tunics and red trousers in 1914. The kepi had a red band and a red crown with gold piping. By 1915 doctors or hospital assistants were wearing an Adrian helmet bearing the traditional serpent and staff, crimson collar patches and grey-blue unit distinctions. Stretcher bearers were indistinguishable from other troops, apart from wearing a white brassard with a red cross.

FLYING TROOPS

France had made use of observation balloons in the 1790s, but the developments in aerial observation and aerial combat led to the establishment of a new and distinctive branch of the armed forces.

Early Years

The troops operating observation balloons, known as the 'Service Aéronautique', had belonged to the

▲ *An autographed photograph of French pilot, Georges Boillot, beside his Nieuport Bébé.*

engineers until 1910, and a subsection of the Ministry of War specifically dealing with aviation was only created in April 1914. In August 1914 there were 159 aeroplanes, assigned to 21 squadrons. Two hundred pilots were trained and available to fly, assisted by 4,000 ground crew. A year later, in August 1915, there were 588 machines, including 193 Farmanns (MF7). By November 1918 there would be 7,620 planes in service, served by 12,000 pilots, and 4,000 observers who flew as spotters and machine gun operators.

Uniforms were initially the same as the engineers but with scarlet unit numbers on blue collar patches, and brassards. Special insignia was quickly introduced to distinguish those flying planes. Pilots often had a winged star on their collars or a winged propeller on their sleeve, but such personnel were prone to wearing their own uniforms. Many pilots came from the cavalry (bored by inaction once trench warfare began), and so hussar

or chasseur uniforms tended to predominate, but with aviation insignia. Brassards were also used to denote flying personnel, and again the winged star or winged wheel were favoured marks.

Uniform Variations

By the end of 1915, flying units were wearing horizon blue. They wore standard greatcoats and tunics which

◄ **Lieutenant, Fighter Squadron, 1915**
There was a degree of flexibility when it came to the uniforms of the aviation service. This uniform is restrained, and the officer has the early winged insignia on his collar.

▶ **Captain, Fighter Squadron, 1916**
This figure wears the winged insignia on red tabs, and the tunic is of the new 1916 model with metallic buttons.

◀ PILOT IN NON-REGULATION UNIFORM
Many of the pilots were drawn from cavalry units – this individual once served in the hussars, and he has retained his regimental cap and breeches.

▶ OBSERVER, 1916 *Observers flew as part of an aircraft crew, acting as spotters and gun operators. Padded, all in one flying suits, such as this, were common to all aviation services, and most of it was privately purchased.*

worn by the British, along with British officers' belts. This tunic had seven metallic buttons, a stand-up collar (known as a de Saxe collar) and folded-back cuffs. It had four pockets, closed by four small buttons, and shoulder straps. Pilots often preferred to wear brown 'aviation' boots, which protected the legs. They were tall and laced all the way along the front. Ground crew wore black ankle boots and horizon blue puttees.

Insignia

Officers wore rank insignia that was the same as the infantry, and they were entitled to carry a sword and pistol. Buttons were generally gold and bore the winged propeller.

Special insignia was introduced in September 1916, replacing the haphazard system in place until that date. Officers wore a winged wheel or winged star on their collars, observers wore a winged star on their right breast and aircraft crews a circle with golden thunderbolts.

Ground crews wore insignia on their left sleeves, mechanics wearing a dark blue cog or a winged grenade and armourers crossed cannon in blue (gold for NCOs) or crossed cannon below a bursting grenade for those assigned to maintaining an aircraft's machine guns.

Electricians wore a badge consisting of two circles and eight golden thunderbolts, while drivers attached to the service wore blue wings. Electricians serving in hangars wore a badge representing a hangar, and this changed from being red in 1915 to being dark blue.

were meant to be identical to those worn by the alpine chasseurs. Breeches had orange piping, while a horizon blue kepi, without piping, or unit numeral, had a black leather visor and chinstrap. If they wore the Adrian helmet, it was of the infantry type. Collar patches on the greatcoat and tunic were orange with black strands of the piping and the corps numeral ('1' or '2'). This was reversed for balloon operators and later changed to red rather than orange.

Some pilots continued to wear the uniforms of their previous units or adopted a tunic that resembled the one

Many personnel also wore special squadron insignia, which varied from a black panther or an axe to a fox wearing a monocle.

Equipment

Flying equipment initially consisted of privately purchased leather jackets and flying helmets with driver's goggles. Those used by military drivers and motorcyclists were also used, as were fur coats (for observers especially). When flying gear began to be manufactured, insignia was sometimes sewn on, but the unofficial badge of the squadron was most often used.

RUSSIA

The Russian empire was enormous but that very size masked a vulnerability. Russian society was incredibly divided between wealthy rulers and the impoverished ruled. The elite, realizing the need to reform, was incapable of reform, despite the sharp warning of the revolution of 1905. In 1914 it embarked on a war in the hope that foreign adventure and patriotism would rally the people and persuade them to forget their grievances. That was not to be; the war exerted even more stress on a brittle society, and another revolution was the result. That revolution, in turn, sparked a series of wars, the effect of which can still be felt today. In the Caucasus, central Asia and the western borderlands of what had once been the Russian empire, nationalists, revolutionaries, anarchists, reactionaries and troops sent to intervene by Western powers all fought a long, protracted and bitter series of wars into the 1920s.

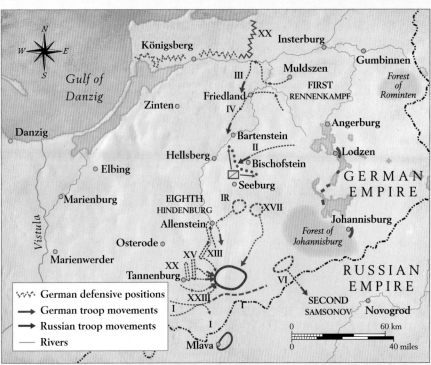

▲ *The Battle of Tannenberg, in August 1914, was a decisive engagement between the Russian and German empires in the first weeks of the war. It did not destroy Russia's armies, but it did blunt Russia's offensive ability until 1916.*

◄ *Somewhere in Poland in the winter of 1914, a long line of Russian prisoners of war stand waiting to be moved on by their German escorts. Russian prisoners faced great hardships in German prison camps especially late in the war, when food was scarce.*

THE RUSSIAN EMPIRE IN 1914

Russia was vast in 1914. Its territories had expanded hugely in the 19th century to cover an incredible one sixth of the Earth's land surface. Having emerged from the Napoleonic Wars holding Finland, much of Poland and Moldova, it then went on to absorb territory in Siberia, central Asia (and even Alaska) as well as seeking to dominate in the Caucasus. This brought it into conflict with the Ottoman empire, and into a rivalry with Britain, while expansion in Asia led to war with Japan in 1905.

The People of Russia

Russia's population was 130 million by the close of the 19th century and 143 million in 1906. By 1914 it was estimated at 167 million. Population

▼ *Czar Nicholas II of Russia inspects troops in the first weeks of the war. The troops wear full dress uniform, complete with plastron lapels and coloured caps.*

growth was concentrated in the cities. St Petersburg (renamed Petrograd at the start of the war) was the capital in 1914, but Moscow was exerting some prominence as an industrial and economic centre. There were 14 other cities each boasting a population of more than 100,000. The national population itself was divided linguistically and ethnically. Great Russians were the majority and attempts at Russification in the late 19th century had spread some ill-will but had also had some success.

A product of this ethnic diversity was that the military swore an oath of personal allegiance to each czar rather than to the Russian nation, a sensible procedure given the complexities of nationalism within the state.

Russia had its own version of the pioneering spirit, and emigration did reduce the population, but only by a fraction. Many Jews had gone to the New World, many Russians had

headed into Siberia and central Asia. Cossack communities were those formed from peoples who had once been on the frontiers of the Russian empire. There were eleven such regions; Don, Kuban, Terek, Astrakhan, Ural, Orenburg, Siberia, Semirechie, Transbaikal, Amur and Asuri.

Religious Divisions

The population was also divided by religion. The majority was Orthodox Christian, but there were a sizeable number of Catholic and Armenian Christians too. Muslims accounted for around 14 million of the population and were concentrated in south-central Asia. The government was relatively tolerant of belief, so long as political loyalty was unquestioned. One religious minority, however, found itself singled out – the Jews. People of Jewish descent were restricted to living only in certain areas (mostly present-day Lithuania and Belarus) and barred from certain professions.

Agriculture and Industry

Russia was rich in agricultural land but was undergoing something of an industrial revolution by 1900. Peasants were emancipated in 1861, but rural life was still very much dominated by the big family estates. Life for the peasant was hard and the work was labour-intensive (there were few steam engines). There was little attempt to reform the ownership of land. Urban growth allowed some respite for those seeking to escape conditions in the fields, but, even so, life in the expanding towns was relatively grim for all those except the aristocracy and the slowly emerging middle class.

The main industries were mining of coal (in the Ukraine and Poland) and ore, textiles, paper (concentrated in Finland), and chemical industries. Food (cereals and flour) was exported as was petrol, wood and cotton. Russia imported machinery and was

▲ *The capacity of the shipyards at Kronstadt, near the Russian capital of St Petersburg, allowed the Russians to rebuild their fleets, which had been destroyed during the Russo-Japanese War.*

dependent on foreign manufacturers for its shipping, railway and arms industries. Russia had experienced the railway boom relatively late, there being an explosion in growth up to 1905. From then on expansion continued at a more sedate pace, financed by hefty French loans. Navigable rivers eased some of Russia's chronic transport problems, but the primary mode of transporting goods revolved around the horse.

The Russian Military

Militarily Russia seemed a formidable power. It had a strong fleet in the Baltic (at Kronstadt, near St Petersburg) in 1914 and had embarked on a naval programme that saw the purchase of a number of ships from Great Britain. The Black Sea fleet (at Sebastopol and Kerch) was less formidable and would find itself bottled up by any Ottoman closure of the Dardanelles. Those straits had been the focus of Russian ambition since the middle of the 19th century, and the Russians saw that free passage (at the very least) was crucial to its economy.

Russia had a number of key strategic positions fortified. Warsaw was an important military centre and railway hub, as was Brest-Litovsk and Kovno. The Caucasus was dotted with military outposts, although the sheer difficulties of passing through that mountainous region protected the empire to some extent from intruders from that direction.

The Ruling Elite

Politically, however, Russia was far from being modern. Frustration at the pace of reform had led to radicalism, but the assassination of Alexander II resulted in conservatism, a stance embodied by Nicholas II when he came to the throne in 1894. Although unsuitable in some ways for ruling such a vast empire, Nicholas had a passion for detail concerning military uniform and equipment. His self-assurance was shaken by defeat against Japan and the revolution of 1905 that followed; a revolution that included more than 400 mutinies among supposedly loyal Russian troops. Nicholas increasingly turned to his wife for moral support and advice, but she herself relied on a small group of advisers, one of whom was the notorious monk Rasputin. The czar agreed to countenance a legislative assembly (the Duma), and embarked

on a series of expensive and chaotic reforms. The country's elites, absorbed by more opportunities for political bickering, meanwhile failed to address underlying problems. While Russia was economically resurgent, wealth was dissipated by ancient social systems and the lack of strong leadership.

Russia's political problems were compounded by an excessively shambolic bureaucracy with an administration that was only partially functioning, and an elite dominated by those who did not see the need to change. This affected every aspect of Russian life, from registering babies to running factories. The dissatisfaction expressed openly in 1905 gave the administration one last chance for far-reaching political reform, but when war came in 1914 it disguised the fact that little had been achieved and, indeed, it provided an opportunity for the government to distract the population and focus energies on defeating the external enemy. Yet few in Russia knew why they were going to war or what was expected to be gained. For so many it would require further sacrifices for little purpose.

▼ *A rare formal portrait of Rasputin, the influential mystic, taken in 1911, together with a member of the Russian royal family (right) and an army captain (left).*

THE RUSSIAN ARMY

Although the 19th century had seen the continued growth of the Russian empire, with the Army basking in reflected glory, the defeat against Japan in 1905 served as a sharp reminder that all was not well in the czar's armed forces.

Military reform, encouraged by social disturbances in the wake of defeat, began at once and vast sums were spent. This, coupled with Russia's potential strength, alarmed the Germans. The situation, however, obscured the underlying problems of Russia's armed forces.

Reforms

The reforms were convulsive. Infrastructure was improved: railways were built westwards (but suitable platforms were not) and roads much improved (but not in the south). Institutional reform was also

attempted, leading to the creation of a functioning General Staff but this now found itself in competition with older, unreformed institutions. Indeed, internal wrangling between various factions of Army officers plagued the military up until 1917 (and beyond). As a result, there was a great deal of chaos. Decision-making, promotion and responsibility was too subject to individual whim. Even when money was spent, Russian industry was not structured to meet the resulting demand. Even by 1915, the Tula arms factory was only producing 350 machine guns a month, despite demands for 2,000.

▼ *Russian troops surrender to Japanese forces at Port Arthur in January 1905. This defeat humiliated the Russians, sparked a revolution and forced the empire into a series of political and military reforms.*

The Navy, humiliated by Japan, was hurriedly rebuilt but still faced the strategic problem that Germany confined Russian ships to the Baltic, while the Ottomans restricted the Russians to the Black Sea.

Funding

The Army too received huge amounts of money, but a large army costs more, and much of the new funding was swallowed up in clothing and feeding the Russian steamroller. Unfortunately for the infantry, much of the rest was used up on fortress artillery. Machine guns were not deemed vital: there were supposed to be 4,990 in 1914, but even this ridiculously inadequate target fell short by 883. Only in October 1915 was an order for 31,170 placed. Ammunition was short – by 600 million bullets in 1914 – and the artillery was making desperate appeals for munitions by the end of August 1914. Artillery itself would be lacking throughout the war, particularly any kind of newly developed artillery (such as trench mortars) that had been unforeseen in 1914.

Army Hierarchy

Socially the Army was largely unchanged. Military service was still regarded as a kind of serfdom by the rank and file. Discipline was harsh, physical punishment was common, strict forms of address were rigidly adhered to. Troops had to follow stringent rules and regulations on and off duty. Conditions in peacetime were poor, and training was neglected; men were deployed as free labour on building sites and fields.

Life for officers was better but was increasingly regarded as second best to life in the civilian world. Many of the officers were, surprisingly, of relatively humble backgrounds (although not in the upper ranks, the cavalry or the guards). Others were of foreign ancestry, for example in the Life

Grenadiers in 1914 there were seven German officers and four Swedes; some 30 per cent of officers in the unit were non-Russian.

Officer Training and Promotion

The performance of Russian officers had been criticized after the war with Japan. Reforms focused on reserve officers in particular and, in 1913, a new educational programme was introduced which stipulated that such officers should have six years of secondary education plus two years of active service training (during which the individual served as a volunteer). Only 21,000 reserve officers were called to the colours in 1914, and other drastic measures were used to make up for the lack of trained personnel. More than a thousand officers were called back from retirement and three thousand soldiers were promoted at once. The expansion of the army only made the situation worse. There were around 41,000 officers in April 1914 and 146,000 by January 1917. Some 63,000 officers were casualties between

▼ A group of Russian Guard officers, and a motorcycle despatch rider (on the left), pose with captured items of German uniform (including a lancer's cap and tunic) in Poland in 1915.

those dates, and by March 1917 there were scarcely any of the pre-war regular officers still left with the colours.

Pay and Conditions

Conditions of service were harsh, with low salaries. Status in the infantry being poor, a situation much worse for the soldiers who were not allowed to

▲ A group of Russian soldiers guard cattle some time in 1914. In peacetime troops were used to assist with agricultural work.

attend the theatre or ride on public transport, and had to address their officers with excessive deference. Influence was correspondingly lacking. Promotion, if it happened, was slow.

Reserve officers were inadequately trained, it being necessary, for reasons of economy, not to call the reserves out too often. There was a great shortage of NCOs, as those with experience and who were qualified were often promoted to junior officers.

Elite Units

The Russian cavalry was still seen as something of an elite but was later wound down with officers drifting into

▲ *Cossacks from a squadron of the Imperial Guard stand to attention in full dress in St Petersburg in 1914. Despite the ferocious appearance, the regiment used Mendelssohn's Wedding March as its regimental march.*

▼ *Russian naval infantry, stand to attention behind a rather corpulent officer in Victory Square, St Petersburg. The Winter Palace can be seen in the background and the square itself was built to celebrate victory over Napoleon in 1812.*

the guards and squadrons being reduced in strength. Artillery was a distinct technical branch but one which had been unevenly supplied. Romania, for example, had a better supply of howitzers than the Russians. Technical officers were lacking, as they were in most armies in 1914, but the state did not have the resources to train officers when the need became apparent. Equipment, such as field telephones, was sparse. Motor vehicles were very scarce. The French would have 90,000 cars in 1918, the Russians just 14,000.

The situation was different in the Guards, and in certain other elite units. The Guards had an extremely strong corps spirit. Officers, who had to be accepted into the regiment, were aristocratic and privileged and with better promotional prospects. Recruitment into the Guards had been incredibly select, and faintly ridiculous, with the Life Guards Moskovsky Regiment selecting recruits with red hair and the Lithuanian Regiment insisting on men with blond hair. The 4th Imperial Family Rifle Regiment even preferred recruits to have snub noses. Such distinctions were swept away by the war.

Cossacks were another branch of service with a strong professional bond. Conscription of Cossacks was separate from the mainstream obligation and was governed by the Cossack Regulations. Despite a poor showing against the Japanese (due to their improved infantry firepower), Cossacks were still deemed useful skirmishers and scouts.

Recruitment

Because of Russia's obsolete conscription laws, the burden of recruits being called up fell unevenly. In peacetime some 48 per cent of men were exempt. However, in wartime

even the exempt (family men, the educated and the unfit) found themselves drawn into the reserves. A high proportion of these, unlike in Germany, were used to provide replacements. Given Russia's appalling casualty rate in 1914 and 1915, many quickly found themselves at the front. The conscripts themselves were drawn

▲ *The czar inspects troops in Poland in 1915. He wears a colonel's uniform, which he generally preferred to wear. The czar was also entitled to wear the uniform of the 4th Guard Rifles, as he was colonel-in-chief of eight Guard regiments. His shoulderboards bore his monogram of Alexander II overlaid with Alexander III, to mark the fact that he had been an aide-de-camp to his father.*

▼ *Pro-czarist forces (the Whites), launched offensives against the Bolsheviks (the Reds) in 1917, 1918 and 1919. Supported and assisted by Allied forces, the anti-Bolsheviks (shown in blue) almost reversed Russia's revolution.*

from the uneducated and, as physical standards were so low in the Russian military, the relatively unfit. Wastage was high, marching rates were poor, and sickness was rife.

Russia had a labour-intensive and inefficient economy, which needed agricultural labourers and, increasingly, industrial workers. The obsolete conscription laws targeted certain groups (peasants) but exempted others (the educated) and the result was that the military and the population as a whole suffered from an early stage of the war. As the conflict wore on, that suffering increased exponentially. This, coupled with the fact that the reasons for being at war were poorly understood, was a recipe for disaster. This was particularly true in 1915 when, after the heavy casualties of 1914, the military had to call up vast numbers of men who had previously been exempted. As in other countries, this proved to be an enormous strain as there were insufficient officers and experienced NCOs to lead the resentful men who found themselves in the apalling conditions of the front line.

GENERALS AND STAFF

Russian high command suffered a decade of reform and upheaval between 1905 and 1914. It was a period of uncertainty, confusion and growing malaise, punctured by far-reaching and modernizing reform. New trends also had an impact on matters of uniform.

Infantry Generals

Setting aside the flamboyant and archaic full dress uniforms of Russia's numerous military elite (there were 2,250 generals on active service in

▲ General of Cavalry Brusilov, Russia's most successful general, was remembered for the development of new offensive tactics used in the 1916. He wears a French tunic, named after the British general.

1916), generals in the field were equipped in a practical and modern manner by 1914. Infantry generals wore a khaki tunic, khaki breeches (slightly greener than the tunic but sometimes replaced by blue trousers with red piping) and a khaki or green cap. A summer version (the 'kittel') was of lighter cloth and was also considerably browner. The tunic itself was fastened with five yellow metal buttons with eagles (sometimes

replaced with brown buttons made of horn), and some tunics had upper and lower pockets. The collar was piped in scarlet, as were the fold-back cuffs and the stiff shoulderboards.

Shoulderboards were often khaki in the field with a cypher or monogram, sometimes of the general's old regiment or sometimes that of a member of the royal family, especially if the general also served as aide-de-camp; for example, Czar Nicholas wore his father's cypher, an 'A' for Alexander III. The shoulderboards could also be

◄ GENERAL OF INFANTRY, 1916 The general has piping on his collar and at his cuff, and only his buttons and his shoulderboards indicate that he is an infantry general. Many Russian generals were aged 60 or more.

► GENERAL OF CAVALRY, 1915 The pointed cuffs on this general's tunic show that he belongs to the cavalry, although he has removed the distinctive aiguillette.

the imperial eagle. It bore an officer's cockade (black within orange within black with a silver surround). In winter generals generally wore a fur cap called a 'papakha' (issued in 1910), and this was usually grey astrakhan with a khaki cloth top and a cockade on the front. Adrian helmets became popular after 1916.

Equipment usually consisted of a map case, binoculars and a pistol, all carried on natural leather crossbelts or braces (Sam Browne belts became popular later in the war), and a sword (usually the M1909 hilt-less Shashka) in a black scabbard with ornamental sword knot (gold and brown ribbon finished with a golden knot). While belts were usually brown leather, a silver sash was sometimes worn.

A simple tunic (more like a shirt), the 'gymnastiorka' (worn by just about all Russian infantry), was authorized for use by officers in September 1914. By 1915 a tunic known as a French tunic (named after the British general) came into vogue. This had large pockets and was longer than the standard tunic.

Artillery generals wore buttons with crossed cannon barrels, and guard artillery generals also had piping along the bottom of the collar. Many generals wore aiguillettes (decorative cords that ran from under the shoulderboard and were attached to the top button of the tunic) on their right shoulders, as did staff officers. These were usually khaki or gold thread. When greatcoats were worn they were of light grey cloth with scarlet lapels.

Cavalry Generals and Staff Officers

The cavalry generals wore tunics which were slightly shorter than those of the infantry and with pointed cuffs (this was also true for horse artillery generals, but those from the guard cuirassiers were the exception, wearing straight cuffs). Cavalry generals

▲ GENERAL OF CAVALRY, 1916 *This figure wears a tunic with horn buttons, and aiguillette to show he is on the imperial staff, and shoulderboards with Nicholas II's cypher.*

of the metallic braid sometimes found in the field (and on which stars designated the exact rank of the general). The shoulderboards had a yellow metal button close by the collar, which was of the standing variety.

The officer's cap was khaki and the peak was usually painted in khaki as well. It was sometimes worn stiff (with wire along the crown) but a popular fashion was to remove the wire and wear it 'soft'. The chinstrap was of brown leather and was attached to the cap with two bronze buttons bearing

preferred breeches. usually worn in blue with red piping. Cavalry boots with spurs were worn.

Staff officers were distinguished by the use of aiguillettes. These were either white or khaki. Various brassards were used to denote special duties. Again, the French tunic with Sam Browne belt was popular from 1916, as was a black tunic of similar cut. Apart from the officers' cap and Adrian helmet, another helmet, which was manufactured in Finland, was worn by some staff and army officers. This was the Sohlberg helmet, first issued in late 1916. A similar helmet was produced at the Izora factory near St Petersburg, but comparatively few examples were produced before the turmoil of 1917.

▶ STAFF CAPTAIN, 1917 *Adrian helmets were worn by officers from 1916. This staff officer has attached his cap's cockade to the helmet.*

IMPERIAL GUARD

Although much of Russia's army struggled with economies imposed from above, the guards were lavished with fine uniforms and choice recruits.

Guard Infantry

Russia's foot guards wore uniforms introduced in 1907. They wore khaki tunics, with piping down the front, on the cuffs and on the pocket flaps, and, in the field, cloth shoulderboards piped in the same colour as the tunic piping and bearing a cypher – usually that of Nicholas II. The reverse of the shoulderboards was scarlet for other ranks (crimson for the rifle regiments). The tunic had a standing collar, and regimental badges were often worn on the breast or on equipment belts. Facings and distinctions are shown in the table.

Officers had shoulderboards in the button colour, and privately tailored tunics. Breeches were khaki. Caps for officers and men were higher in the crown and stiffer than those used in the line. They bore the imperial cockade, but officers sometimes chose to wear the St Andrew's Cross above their cockade. Some Adrian helmets were imported, and some helmets of a Russian design were used in 1917. Boots were preferred.

Equipment consisted of a black knapsack, rolled blanket and brown cartridge belts on a brown belt (or sometimes white: the first three regiments in the division were supposed to have whitened belts) with a guard buckle. The bayonet was kept in the rifle. Officers carried revolvers, map cases and binoculars, along with the hiltless Shashka (the 1909 model). In the winter a papakha fur cap was used in place of the peaked cap. Greatcoats of various designs (the six-buttoned guard model of 1881 was still popular, but the grey-blue peacetime model was also sometimes worn in the field) were also worn in winter; the coat would have collar tabs in the same colour as the tunic piping, and this was piped in various colours.

Guard Cavalry

Russia's guard cavalry was an elite within an elite. Regimental distinctions were jealously guarded, and divergence

◄ **PRIVATE, FINLAND GUARDS REGIMENT, 1914** *Other ranks in this regiment were supposed to be short and slim, a preference which did not continue very long into the war as recruitment became more and more urgent.*

▲ **CAPTAIN, MOSCOW GUARDS REGIMENT, 1916** *This regiment was composed of red-haired soldiers in 1914 but, by 1916, that distinction had lapsed. This officer wears a regimental badge, or jeton. Some preferred to wear a jeton from the school or academy from which they had graduated.*

from regulations often tolerated. Most cavalrymen wore the simple khaki tunic while on campaign. This had pointed cuffs and coloured piping and cloth shoulderboards with cyphers, and the coloured side matched that of

▼ **PRIVATE, GRODNO GUARDS HUSSAR REGIMENT, 1914**
This uniform shows a transitional style – colourful hussar breeches worn together with a sombre jacket. This regiment tried to maintain the distinction of having its men mounted on greys, with the 4th squadron riding white horses.

Distinctions of the Life Guard Regiments

Regiment	Cuffs	Pocket & Tunic	Button	G-coat Piping
Preobrazhenskii	white	red	gold	n/a
Semenovskii	white	blue	gold	scarlet
Izmailovskii	white	white	gold	scarlet
Jäger	white	green	gold	scarlet
Moscow	red	red	gold	green
Grenadier	red	blue	gold	n/a
Pavlovskii	red	white	gold	n/a
Finland	red	green	gold	n/a
Lithuania	yellow	yellow	silver	n/a
Kexholm	yellow	blue	silver	yellow
Saint-Petersburg	yellow	white	silver	yellow
Volhynia	yellow	green	silver	yellow
1st His Majesty's Rifle	crimson	crimson	silver	n/a
2nd Tsarskoe-Selo Rifle	white	crimson	gold	crimson
3rd His Majesty's Rifle	n/a	crimson	silver	crimson
4th Imperial Family Rifle	n/a	crimson	gold	crimson

the trouser stripe. Breeches were generally khaki too, with regimental stripes, but red breeches or blue breeches were often worn in the early stages of the war. Similarly, brown leather equipment was worn on campaign, but it was still possible to see whitened leather belts and straps in 1914.

Cavalry equipment consisted of bandoliers or cartridge belts for carbines with officers carrying Nagant revolvers in brown holsters. Boots with spurs were worn.

Technical troops

The guard also boasted its own artillery (horse and foot), plus a regiment of sappers. The Guard Foot Artillery had three brigades. The first wore white lace on the cuff, the second blue and the third yellow. Horse artillery had black lace on their pointed cuffs. For all units shoulderboards were red on the coloured side. Buttons were gold for the foot artillery and silver for the horse artillery. Greatcoat patches were black piped red.

▶ **CAPTAIN, LIFE GUARD HUSSARS, 1914**
Imperial Guard officers kept their distinctive white belts, even at the front, where they became targets for enemy fire.

ELITE INFANTRY

Apart from the guard infantry, the Russian Army boasted other elite forces. First among these in 1914 were 16 regiments of grenadiers. Four more regiments were raised in 1917 (the 17th to 20th). Other regiments were added, as were some battalions of veterans or decorated infantry.

The Grenadier Regiments

Recruits were initially selected for their height and physique. The 1st and 13th regiments, known as Life-Grenadier regiments, were even more exclusive.

In 1914 the grenadier regiments wore uniforms that resembled those in use by their line infantry counterparts. Their caps were usually peaked and bore the imperial cockade, but peakless variations with coloured cap bands were known and were sometimes worn in the field, as was the peakless side cap (or pilotka). The grenadier regiments wore tunics that were green-khaki. The gymnastiorka was worn by some – and this may have included red piping down the slit in the top of the shirt, particularly for officers – and trousers or breeches in green or light khaki. Grenadiers had a distinctive belt buckle (in either bronze or white

metal, depending on the unit's button colour), which featured a bursting grenade rather than the more usual double-headed eagle. Most men carried rolled blankets and two brown cartridge pouches, each containing 30 cartridges. Officers carried pistols in brown holsters and with a pistol cord (in silver), which was attached to the pistol butt at one end and worn around the neck at the other.

Their chief distinction was that they wore shoulderboards in distinctive colours. The coloured side of the board was a bright yellow for grenadiers, which formed a base for the gold embroidery worn on officers' shoulderboards by the first twelve regiments and silver for the last eight.

▶ SAPPER, 9TH SIBERIA GRENADIERS, 1914
The sapper wears a distinctive badge on the upper sleeve of his shirt, which has been bleached by the sun. As a grenadier he would wear a bursting grenade motif on his belt and buttons.

▼ SHOULDERBOARDS, TOP ROW, FROM LEFT; *1st Yekaterinoslav (Life), 2nd Rostov, 3rd Pernau, 4th Nesvizh, 5th Kiev, 6th Taurica, 7th Samogitia. 8th Moscow.*

The monograms displayed on the shoulderboard were painted in red for other ranks. Officers' shoulderboards were either of gold or silver, according to the button colour, and with yellow as the base colour. Buttons were gold, apart from for the last eight regiments, which had silver. Rank insignia was the same as for the infantry (combinations of stars and stripes). Piping was as shown in the table.

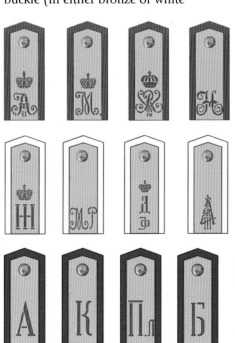

▲ MIDDLE ROW, FROM LEFT: *9th Siberia, 10th Little-Russia, 11th Phanagoria, 12th Astrakhan, 13th Yerevan (Life), 14th Georgi, 15th Tiflis, 16th Mingrelia.*
BOTTOM ROW, FROM LEFT: *17th Aladjun, 18th Kars, 19th Pleven, 20th Bazardjik.*

Grenadier Regiment Distinctions

Regiment	Shoulderboard Piping	G-coat Patch	Monogram (Cyrillic)
1st Yekaterinoslav (Life)	red	red	AII
2nd Rostov	red	blue	M
3rd Pernau	red	white	FWIV (Latin)
4th Nesvizh	red	black	N
5th Kiev	blue	red	Alexis' monogram
6th Taurica	blue	blue	M
7th Samogitia	blue	white	S
8th Moscow	blue	black	FM
9th Siberia	white	red	NN
10th Little-Russia	white	blue	MR
11th Phanagoria	white	white	D/F
12th Astrakhan	white	black	AIII
13th Yerevan (Life)	none	red	NII (white), MF red
14th Georgia	none	blue	A white
15th Tiflis	none	white	K (and T in 1915)
16th Mingrelia	none	black	D
17th Aladjun	green	red	A
18th Kars	green	white	K
19th Pleven	green	blue	PL
20th Bazardjik	green	black	B

Wartime changes included the introduction of the Adrian helmet with eagle badge, or helmet of Russian design, or the peakless side cap (the pilotka) in place of the peaked cap. The 8th Regiment replaced the monogram of the Duke of Mecklenburg in August 1914 with a capital 'M' for Moscow. In the spring of 1917 a number of regiments decided to replace the monogram of royal patrons with insignia relating to the regiment's title. For example, the 12th Astrakhan Regiment chose to use a capital 'A' for Astrakhan. Rank insignia also began to be worn on the sleeve rather than on the shoulderboard.

Grenadier artillery and grenadier engineers wore scarlet shoulderboards rather than the yellow of their infantry colleagues.

▶ GRENADIER KIT, 1916

1 *Cartridge belt with 60 rounds.*

2 *Nagant revolver in holster.*

3 *Bread bag.*

4 *Campaign bag.*

5 *1909 waterbottle.*

6 *Short spade, Model 1894.*

Other Units

The growth of elite units towards the end of the war is sparsely documented. Shock Battalions or Battalions of Death were mostly formed hastily in the summer of 1917, and some continued until after the Bolsheviks seized power. They wore various insignia, mostly the Death's Head.

▼ SERGEANT, 16TH MINGRELIA GRENADIERS, 1916 *This grenadier's backpack would contain spare shirts, underwear and foot cloths as well as a sewing kit and rifle-cleaning materials. The bread bag carried salt, bread and army biscuit.*

INFANTRY

Russia had a massive army and vast numbers of infantrymen. It therefore had to equip its troops in a practical and economic fashion.

Years of Change

Although the equipment and dress of the Russian infantryman went comparatively unchanged between 1914 and 1917, with a few notable exceptions, the same cannot be said of the early years of the 20th century. Thanks partly to the spirit of reform then current in Europe, and partly to the czar's personal interest in military uniform, Russia's infantrymen were subjected to a number of uniform changes well before war began in August 1914.

Defeat at the hands of Japan had necessitated some quick changes. Russian troops had fought in that war dressed in white or dark green (and even black). Although the uniform of enlisted men was relatively plain and economical, it was not always practical. Russia's Ministry of War was quick to test various versions of khaki in 1906, and in 1907 resolved to distribute tunics, trousers and caps in a greenish khaki. Due to supply problems, and the effects of the weather, it was very difficult to fix an exact shade. Most

Russian uniforms appear to be greenish-brown but tunics and trousers could be almost beige after washing and bleaching. The uniform was made across the empire and came in five different sizes.

Initially a tunic was issued in either cotton or wool (for winter) with a standing collar. This tunic was relatively common until 1912, when it was supposed to be phased out, but it could still be found on soldiers during the war.

The tunic was generally replaced by the long shirt or gymnastiorka, which began to make its presence felt in 1910, when it was issued in substantial numbers. The 1910 version had an opening to the left of the shirt front, but this was placed more centrally in a 1912 version, and there were minor adjustments in 1914 (concealed buttons and pockets) and 1916. The most common style in 1914 was the 1912 version with its two collar buttons and shirt opening fastened by three buttons made from horn or wood. So many of these garments were

▶ PRIVATE, 51ST LITOVSKI INFANTRY REGIMENT, 1914 *The gymnastiorka, or shirt, was issued to troops in cotton for summer and in wool for winter.*

◀ SHOULDERBOARDS, TOP ROW, FROM LEFT: *Adjutant, 255th (Akerman) Regiment; Sergeant-Major, 109th (Volzh) Regiment; Sergeant-Major, 6th (Libau) Regiment; Sergeant-Major, 9th Siberian Rifles; Private, 2nd (Sofia) Regiment; Volunteer Corporal, 191st (Larga-Kagul) Regiment; Grenadier, 9th Grenadiers.* BOTTOM ROW, FROM LEFT: *Private, 74th (Stavropol) Regiment; Private, 52nd (Vilna) Regiment; Sergeant-Major, 10th Siberian Rifles; Private, 9th Rifles; Sergeant-Major, 1st Caucasian Rifles; Private, 143rd Dorogobuzh Regiment.*

needed that there were a number of variations: some had pockets, some had rear vents and some had fold-back cuffs.

Officers generally wore privately tailored tunics (the kittel) in a greener shade and with breast pockets. This tunic was made from better quality material, as was the gymnastiorka, should the officer feel the need to dress like the men he commanded. Later in the war so-called French-style tunics were favoured by officers.

Shoulderboards

Attached to the tunic or gymnastiorka by a button were shoulderboards. These were generally rigid but had two

Russian Shoulderboard Colours

1st Infantry Division	Shoulderboards
1st Brigade	
1st His Highness the King of the Hellenes Neva Regiment	red
2nd Emperor Alexander III's Sofia Regiment	red
2nd Brigade	
3rd General-Field Marshal Mikhail Golitsyn's Narva Regiment	blue
4th King of Saxony's Kopore Regiment	blue
2nd Infantry Division	
1st Brigade	
5th Emperor William I's Kaluga Regiment	red
6th Prince Frederick-Leopold of Prussia's Libau Regiment	red
2nd Brigade	
7th General Shukov IV's Reval Infantry Regiment	blue
8th Estonia Infantry Regiment	blue

sides. One side was coloured and the other khaki. Both sides generally bore the regiment's number or a cypher if it had a royal or imperial patron, but the khaki side was sometimes left blank.

The coloured side came in three colours, depending on the regiment's position in a division and brigade. The regiments in the first brigade of a division wore red shoulderboards, those in the second brigade wore blue.

Unit distinctions (numbers or cyphers) were stencilled on to the shoulderboard in yellow for those regiments with red shoulderboards, or in white for those with blue shoulderboards. The stencilling was generally yellow on the khaki-side of the shoulderboard.

◀ PRIVATE 14TH OLONETZKI INFANTRY REGIMENT, 1914 *The cotton or linen cap had a leather peak and was common throughout the army and was issued without a chinstrap. Pre-war piping was removed. Neck cloths were worn in the Caucasus in summer.*

▶ COLONEL, 80TH KABARDINSKI INFANTRY REGIMENT, 1915 *This senior officer wears the gymnastiorka, rather than the regulation tunic. It was more comfortable and also made officers less conspicuous. Officer casualties were very heavy in 1914, and a less pronounced profile for commanders was increasingly common.*

NCOs wore red stripes across the shoulderboards (or a yellow or metallic stripe for a sergeant). For officers the colour of the enlisted men's shoulderboards formed the base colour for their own rigid boards, which were then overlaid with gold or silver braid and officer distinctions (combinations of stars and stripes). On the khaki side the regimental numeral or cypher was worn in bronze. Casualties among officers led to the habit of adopting less conspicuous distinctions, including soft rather than rigid shoulderboards. Volunteer officers wore shoulderboards or shoulder straps that were piped in interwoven black, white and orange cord.

Regiments with Royal Patrons	
Regiment	**Cypher**
1st His Highness the King of the Hellenes Neva Regiment	GI
2nd Emperor Alexander III's Sofia Regiment	AIII
4th King of Saxony's Kopore Regiment	FA (*)
5th Emperor William I's Kaluga Regiment	WI (*)
6th Prince Frederick-Leopold of Prussia's Libau Regiment	FL (*)
9th Emperor Peter the Great's Ingermanland Regiment	PP (*)
14th His Majesty the King of Serbia's Olonets Regiment	PI
18th His Majesty the King of Romania's Vologda Regiment	CC (*)
39th His Imperial Highness Archduke Ludwig of Austria's Tomsk Regiment	LV (*)
48th Emperor Alexander I's Odessa Regiment	AI
51st His Imperial Highness the Heir and Czarevitch's Lithuania Regiment	A
54th His Majesty the Czar of Bulgaria's Minsk Regiment	F
65th His Majesty's Moscow Regiment	NII
67th Grand Duke of Oldenburg's Tarutino Regiment	FA (*)
68th Emperor Alexander III's Borodino Leib-Regiment	AIII
81st Grand Duke George Mikhailovich's Apsheronsk Regiment	EII
84th His Majesty's Shirvan Regiment	NII
85th Emperor of Germany and King of Prussia Wilhelm II's Viborg Regiment	WII(*)
89th His Imperial Highness the Heir and Czarevitch's White-Sea Regiment	A
145th Emperor Alexander III's Novocherkassk Regiment	AIII
206th His Imperial Highness the Heir and Czarevitch's Saliany Regiment	A
Cyphers in Cyrillic unless (*) for Latin script	

◀ **PRIVATE, 13TH BELOZERSKI INFANTRY REGIMENT, WINTER 1914** *This private carries a spade in its canvas cover and a gas mask. The spade is the Linnemann entrenching tool, invented by a Danish officer and patented in 1869. It was versatile and practical, and doubled as a frying pan. The woollen hood, issued during winter with the greatcoat, is shown to good effect here.*

Those regiments that had members of the Austrian or German royal families as patrons in 1914 (such as 6th Prince Frederick-Leopold of Prussia's Libau Regiment) unstitched their cyphers and replaced them with plain numbers.

Other Uniform Distinctions

Greatcoats made from grey or greyish brown wool were worn in winter, and these were generally single breasted (the 1911 version) or with hooks and eyes (the 1881 version), with fold-back cuffs. This was often also used as a blanket and was generally rolled with a tent canvas and worn across the chest (usually both ends were bound and tucked into the mess tin). When the greatcoat was worn, the tent cloth was still worn across the chest. A hood was also worn when the temperature reached minus five, and this had long straps that were usually worn across the chest and tucked into the belt, the hood then hanging down the soldier's back. Shoulderboards, of a slightly bigger dimension than those worn on the tunic, were sometimes worn on the greatcoat, but this was not always the case. Decorations and regimental badges were worn on the tunic or greatcoat breast.

Headgear

Infantrymen wore peaked caps of a style introduced in 1907 and modified in 1910. It was khaki with a black peak (usually painted green or brown) and, after a certain time, became relatively shapeless. Officers wore stiffer caps with chinstraps and NCOs sometimes had these too. Generally, enlisted men did without. Caps bore the imperial cockade on the front, and this was a black within orange (or gold) within black within orange oval. For NCOs the cockade was larger and their

▲ **PRIVATE, 146TH INFANTRY REGIMENT, 1914**
Full dress uniform for infantry included a tunic with plastron lapels. This proved costly and many of these tunics were left in regimental depots, to be used once again during the Revolution.

version had a wider silver edge. That for officers was similar but with a crenellated edge and rounder front. In winter a fur or lambs' wool cap was worn. This was known as the papakha and came in various shapes and colours (mostly grey or brown). The fur cap had a khaki crown and bore the imperial cockade. It also had a band that could be folded down over the neck and ears, giving protection

essential in the Russian winter. It was so successful that it lasted for much of the 20th century.

French Adrian helmets bearing the double-headed eagle badge were used in Russia from 1916, but these were mostly confined to elite units or officers. A steel helmet (the Sohlberg M1917) was designed and manufactured by the Sohlberg and Holmberg company in Helsinki (then in Russian territory). It was issued in limited numbers in 1917. Captured German and Austrian helmets were also used by Russian troops.

Trousers similar in colour to the infantryman's tunic were adopted in 1907, and these were worn loose on the thigh but tight at the knee. Officers sometimes had khaki piping down the outer edge. All trousers were made of cotton or wool and tucked into black leather boots. Strips of cloth, bound around the feet, were used in place of socks. Foot cloths were much cheaper to source than socks, more comfortable (if used correctly) and easier to wash and faster to dry in combat conditions.

▲ **INFANTRY COCKADES** *1 Territorial unit cross. 2 NCOs' cockade. 3 Non-Christian territorial unit cross. 4 Soldiers' cockade. 5 Soldiers' peacetime cockade.*

▶ **PRIVATE, 143RD DOROGOBUYSKI INFANTRY REGIMENT, WINTER 1915** *The wide straps across this figure's chest belong to the hood – these would be tied together when the hood was worn. The belt was usually blackened by this date.*

Equipment and Kit

The Russian infantryman's equipment was relatively simple. Knapsacks were generally not used, being confined to the guards. Soldiers wore a brown or black belt with a double-headed eagle buckle. Two brown cartridge pouches (the M1893) were worn either side, each containing 30 rounds. Bandoliers carrying extra ammunition were also sometimes used. Most troops carried a canteen or aluminium bottle on straps, an entrenching tool (the Linnemann style with leather cover) and some kind of bread bag or haversack (such as the M1910), which was of light brown or white canvas.

This contained additional cartridges and personal effects. Gas masks came into use in late 1915, either imported Allied versions or the Zelinsky mask (the first effective filtering charcoal mask) in an aluminium container.

Officers wore brown belts (often without buckle plates) with or without brown braces as was approved for use in 1912. They generally carried binoculars (of German Zeiss manufacture), pistols in leather holsters and map cases, along with the hiltless and slightly curved Shashka sword (M1909) or, from 1916, a dagger in black sheath.

Rifle Regiments

Russia had numerous regiments of riflemen who were, for all intents and purposes, little different from the regular line infantrymen. There were Rifle regiments, Finnish Rifle regiments, Caucasian Rifle regiments, Turkestan Rifle regiments and Siberian Rifle regiments. Latvian Rifles were raised later in the war.

Rifle regiments were distinguished by raspberry- or crimson-coloured shoulderboards. These bore yellow regimental numerals or cyphers. In addition it was common for the Turkestan regiments to add a 'T' after the numeral, the Latvians a Cyrillic 'L'

◀ SERGEANT, 10TH SIBERIAN RIFLES, 1916
This NCO has acquired an officer's grey-blue greatcoat. Rank is shown by painted yellow or gilt stripes on the shoulderboard. These boards were of fine woollen cloth reinforced with cardboard and they were supposed to be 6.7 cm wide.

▲ *A mounted Russian officer leads his men along a snow-covered road in the bitter cold of a Caucasian winter. They would repeatedly defeat Ottoman troops here in 1915.*

and the Siberians a Cyrillic 'S'. The 13th Rifles had a cyrillic 'NN' and '13', the 15th an 'NI' and '15', while the 16th had 'AIII' and '16' below. The 1st Caucasian Rifles had 'M' and Cyrillic distinctions for the Siberian regiments were as shown in the table below.

Officers used the raspberry colour as the base for their own shoulderboards.

Riflemen wore patches on their greatcoat collars and these were generally black piped in raspberry. NCOs wore a button on this collar patch, as well as stripes (gold or khaki) across the shoulderboards.

Caps were as for the infantry, with a papakha being worn in winter. This again came in various shapes and sizes, the Siberians being distinguished in particular for wearing a rounder,

Siberian Rifles with Cyphers	
Regiment	**Cypher**
1st His Majesty's Siberian Rifles	NII
11th Her Imperial Majesty Empress Maria Theodorovna's Siberian Rifles	MF
12th His Imperial Highness the Heir and Czarevitch's Siberian Rifles	A
21st Her Imperial Highness Alexandra Theodorovna's Siberian Rifles	AF

◄ **CAPTAIN, 4TH CAUCASIAN RIFLES, 1916**
The fatigue cap would become very popular wear among troops of all ranks in the summer but, at this date, it was still relatively rare. The shoulderstrap which is attached to his belt could also carry small pouches for revolver ammunition.

bushier version in black or dark grey. Belts and straps were supposed to be blackened for Rifle regiments.

Russian officers sometimes wore regimental badges on their equipment braces. As in other armies, wound stripes were also instituted in the Russian Army. They were usually yellow or sometimes red, one bar for each wound or gassing.

Regimental scouts wore a green stripe above their cuffs, machine gunners wore a raspberry-coloured stripe and those working on trench artillery wore a scarlet stripe. Sappers wore a crossed spade and axe in red on their sleeves.

Some brassards were also worn by Russian troops. Military Police wore a red brassard and black Cyrillic 'MP'. Those individuals detached to gather supplies or replenish ammunition wore brassards with the blue or black Cyrillic letters 'SO'.

► **SCOUT, 16TH RIFLES, 1915** *Scouts wore green piping on the sleeve but, in all other respects, conformed to the uniforms of their parent regiments. One cartridge pouch was worn in peacetime but two were worn in wartime and while in training camps. The rifle is the Mosin-Nagant and it had a permanent flat-headed bayonet.*

The war brought about a number of changes. The peacetime establishment of four battalions was reduced to three when the number of regiments was increased (from 209 to 336). The militia were used to create regiments 393 to 548. As noted, those regiments which had the cypher of rulers of enemy powers on their shoulderboards replaced it with a number. Some other changes took place – the 89th (Belomorsky) Infantry Regiment received a royal cypher in December 1916 when the Czarevitch Alexis, the hemophiliac heir to the Russian throne, became its honorary colonel. Just two years later the prince would be executed by the Bolsheviks, along with the rest of his family.

▼ **RIFLE BRIGADES KIT, 1915**
1 Haversack. 2 Cartridge pouch. 3 90-round cartridge belt. 4 Entrenching tool. 5 and 6 Mess tins. 7 Zelinsky gas mask container.

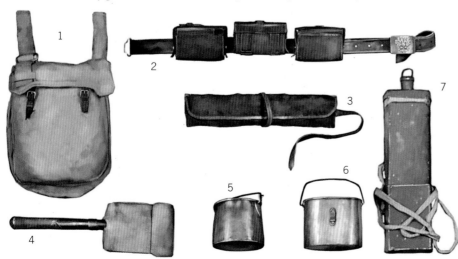

Grenadiers

The Russian grenadier regiments were not the only grenadiers in the Russian Army. In the autumn of 1915 men were being selected to join assault groups armed predominantly with grenades. These grenadiers initially consisted of ten men per company formed into a squad attached to regimental headquarters. By the end of 1915 most infantry and rifle regiments had a grenadier section of 50 men armed with carbines, grenades, daggers and axes. In February 1916 these men were to be distinguished by the wearing of a red (or sometimes blue) grenade badge on the left sleeve of their tunic or greatcoat.

Later, after special grenadier schools had been formed, this simple insignia became more complicated. Troops who had completed a course could wear a grenade with a red or blue flame (depending on shoulderboard colour) and a black base with a white cross. Rifles wore a raspberry-coloured flame, officers and guardsmen had golden or metallic crosses on the base of the grenade.

Special Purpose Regiments

To the Western Allies it seemed as though Russia had a shortage of equipment but a surplus of men. It therefore requested the despatch of troops to other theatres. A brigade was sent to France in the spring of 1916, and it was composed of volunteers formed into the 1st and 2nd Special Purpose Regiments. The 3rd and 5th Brigades followed later, while the 2nd and 4th Brigades were sent to Salonika to fight on the Macedonian front in late 1916.

These regiments wore khaki tunics or shirt-tunics in the Russian style with khaki shoulderboards, sometimes bearing regimental numerals and sometimes piped in white. The shoulderboards bore the regimental number in Roman numerals, but it seems that some of the units switched to using Arabic numerals in a departure from this rule. Volunteers had their shoulderboards piped in orange and black. Loose breeches were commonly worn, and most of the soldiers retained boots made from blackened leather.

Most troops arriving in France had belts and haversacks but were then issued with French khaki helmets (bearing the double-headed eagle or no badge). French canvas knapsacks and ammunition pouches to contain ammunition for Lebel or Berthier rifles were liberally distributed and French equipment braces were common.

◄ PRIVATE, 3RD SPECIAL PURPOSE REGIMENT, 1916 *Formed for service in the Balkans and France, these units wore Russian uniforms with French equipment. The M2 gas mask, for example, seen here carried in a metal case, was supplied to these units when they landed in France.*

► PRIVATE, RUSSIAN LEGION, 1917 *The Russian Legion was built from the remains of the Russian units in France. Many of the personnel had mutinied and been disbanded, with the mutineers being executed or sent to penal units in North Africa. Note the national flag on the sleeve, an insignia that would also be associated with White units in the Civil War.*

blue above red Russian flag on their sleeves and an Estonian flag may have been worn by an Estonian company within the Legion. Officers may have worn dark blue trousers or breeches.

▲ *Russian infantry await the signal to advance, rifles at the ready. There was such a lack of rifles by 1915 that a number of men were selected to form grenadier detachments armed with grenades, axes and wirecutters. These were initially assigned to regimental headquarters and formed the core of future grenadier assault groups.*

Bayonets were worn in sheaths when not in use and these were attached to the belt with straps.

In 1917, following the disastrous Nivelle offensive, and rumours of revolution back home, the Russians in France became restless. Those that mutinied were sent as convicts to Algeria, those that stayed loyal were partly disarmed or were persuaded to join the Russian Legion. It fought in France in late 1917 and 1918 before disbanding and returning to Russia or settling in France.

The Special Purpose regiments in Macedonia were disarmed and disbanded, many choosing to join the Serbs or to return home.

The Russian Legion

This legion wore uniforms very similar to those of the Special Purpose regiments but, as time wore on, they took on an increasingly French appearance. Most troops wore khaki tunics or greatcoats like the Moroccan infantry (the Legion served within a Moroccan division). These bore the legend 'LR' in the corner of the collar, surmounted by two strips of blue braid. French rank distinctions were used, as well as French equipment. The Legion may have been issued with helmets bearing the 'LR', but it is likely that they continued to wear their older helmets, now without imperial badges. Many troops wore the white above

▼ **PRIVATE, GRENADIER, 4TH RIFLE BRIGADE, 1917** *Grenadiers were being formed into assault units. This individual is lightly equipped for trench raiding and wears an Adrian helmet with a Russian badge. Assault troops generally avoided using rifles – pistols were preferred as were sharpened entrenching tools (with short handles) and daggers. Axes and seven or eight grenades were also carried.*

Provisional Government

The abdication of the czar led to far-reaching changes within the Army. The impact on uniforms was more limited. Belt buckles bearing the imperial eagle were filed down, as were Adrian helmets (sometimes just the crown above the eagle was removed). Shoulderboards were largely abolished and rank distinctions were now switched to various stripes in red and

▼ Captain, St George's Regiment, 1917

This elite unit was recruited from those who had won St George medals – and they had shoulderboards in the red and orange of the order. The winter fur cap could also be decorated with an orange and black band.

▶ Sergeant, 7th Shock Battalion, 1917

Shock battalions, raised by the Russian Provisional Government in a desperate attempt to shore up the line, created their own insignia, usually making use of a skull motif. Many officers would also wear a dagger, or kortik, which was worn suspended from the belt with leather straps. This had initially been a naval weapon but trench warfare made it popular with infantry officers.

black worn above the cuff of the tunic or greatcoat for officers and red and black chevrons for NCOs. Cockades on caps were largely replaced by the national colours of white above blue above red.

The Army as a whole, however, started to disintegrate. The Provisional Government tried to raise Shock Battalions, or Battalions of Death, in a vain attempt to shore up the line and concentrate reliable men into units that could take the offensive.

It also seems that individual Army Groups raised a battalion of men decorated with the St George's cross. These were known as St George's battalions and were uniformed as for the line infantry but with distinctive shoulderboards. These were either entirely orange and black or were a base colour heavily edged with interwoven orange and black lace. Officers had orange and black piping down the seams of their breeches or trousers, on their cuffs and, occasionally, down the front of their tunics. Decorations were worn on the chest. Shock Battalions wore distinctive insignia on the sleeves of their tunics and greatcoats, and frequently decorated their caps with a metallic skull badge. Other units wore skulls on their shoulder straps. The Women's Battalion of Death, which ended up defending the Winter Palace against the Bolsheviks, wore a distinctive uniform described in the section on White armies in the Civil War.

Romanian Troops

Russia played host to numbers of foreign volunteers. There were Serbs, Romanians and Poles but the most famous were undoubtedly the Czechs.

The Romanians appear to have worn Russian uniforms but replaced the cockade with a flash of blue, yellow and red cloth. Poles also wore Russian uniforms, but in 1917 began to wear Polish eagle cap badges and, possibly, collar patches and eagle badges on their sleeves.

Polish Troops

The Poles initially formed the Legion Pulawski which had infantry wearing Russian uniforms with shoulderboards bearing the initials '1LP' in yellow. Three lancer squadrons were formed and these had khaki tunics with dark blue breeches. They wore red, blue and yellow facings respectively. A full dress uniform with plastrons on the tunic, stripes on the blue breeches (red for the first regiment, white for the second regiment and yellow for the third), cuffs and cap bands in these colours was also worn. Infantry were later absorbed into a Polish rifle brigade with white Polish eagle cap badges. A smaller Polish Legion was formed in Finland in 1917.

Other nationalist forces were raised in 1917, but most of them quickly became involved in the wars for independence against the Red and the White armies.

◀ **PRIVATE, 2ND CZECH REGIMENT, 1916**
Czech volunteers serving in the Russian Army wore Russian uniforms with flashes in the national colours on the cap (thereby replacing the Russian cockade) or on the sleeve. In
winter, the ubiquitous fur cap also received a flash in the national colours. This soldier has a 1914 model grenade tucked into his belt. This grenade replaced one issued in 1912, which exploded just four seconds after being charged by the thrower.

Czech Troops

The Czechs are more famous still. Many were prisoners of war, taken during fighting with the Austro-Hungarians in Galicia and the Ukraine. Others were already living in Russia or had joined the Serbs and, following Serbian defeat in 1915, fled to Russia. Although the Russians hesitated to form units from prisoners of war (this was against the Geneva Convention), a reserve battalion formed by ethnic Czechs and students existed in 1914, and a second was formed in 1915. A Czech Regiment was formed from these in early 1916. When the Provisional Government came to power it put what force it had into raising a Czech Legion, mostly by making use of volunteers among the prisoners of war.

The Czech Regiment initially seems to have worn Russian uniform but with

▲ *Czech troops on an armoured train in Russia in 1918. These soldiers, Czech volunteers from prisoner-of-war camps, fought in the Revolution and were eventually repatriated to form the nucleus of the new Czechoslovakian Army.*

the cockade being worn on top of a strip of red and white cloth worn diagonally on the cap band. This replaced the cockade altogether in 1917. This was also done on the papakha and on the officers' Adrian helmets. Shoulderboards were eventually replaced by shields worn on the sleeves of the tunic or greatcoat. These did not come into authorized use until early 1918. They showed the wearer's rank by means of coloured chevrons on the right sleeve and the wearer's unit by means of a coloured numeral within a shield on the left arm of the tunic or greatcoat.

In the confusion of late 1917 various oddments of uniform were pressed into use and the Czechs made the best of what they could find. Only in 1918, when they joined with the Allies and turned on the Bolsheviks in their attempt to evacuate Russia, did they receive supplies of clothing and formalize their rank and unit insignia. For that reason more can be found on the Czechs in the section on White armies of the Civil War.

CAVALRY

The Russian cavalry was reorganized in 1910, but heavy casualties in 1914 led to a rapid rethink of the role of the mounted soldier.

Dragoons

Most Russian cavalry regiments had been converted into dragoons, but this caused such a storm of protest that many regiments were converted back into lancers or hussars. In 1914 there were 20 dragoon regiments. They wore tunics that resembled those worn by the infantry but with pointed cuffs. Shoulderboards were piped in blue and bore a numeral followed by a Latin 'D'. The following regiments wore a cypher: 1st Emperor Peter the Great's Moscow Life-Regiment, 2nd Empress Maria Theodorovna's Pskov Leib-Regiment, 3rd Grand Duchess Helen Vladimirovna's New-Russia Regiment, 6th Empress Catherine the Great's Glukhov Regiment, 8th General-Field Marshal Grand Duke Nicholas Nikolaevich's Astrakhan Regiment, 9th Grand Duchess Maria Nikolaevna's Kazan Regiment, 10th King of Württemberg's Novgorod Regiment, 14th The Crown Prince of Germany and Prussia's Little-Russia Regiment, 15th Emperor Alexander III's Pereiaslav Regiment, 17th His Majesty's Nizhni-Novgorod Regiment, and 18th King Christian IX of Denmark's Regiment.

The dragoons' caps were often worn peakless but again followed the pattern used by the infantry. Fur caps were worn in winter. Breeches were initially blue, although khaki ones were often used instead, with scarlet piping except for the 6th, 11th and 12th Regiments (light blue); 5th, 7th, 8th and 20th Regiments (yellow); 14th Regiment (green); and 2nd Regiment (pink). Boots with spurs were worn.

Equipment consisted of a carbine (with strap), cartridge pouch (or bandolier), bayonet and sword. Personal effects were carried on the saddle. Capes with hoods were worn in preference to greatcoats, although there was a cavalry greatcoat that was longer than that of the infantry.

▶ TROOPER, 5TH DRAGOONS, 1915 *Russian cavalry were uniformed in a similar fashion – lettering on the shoulderboards indicated whether a man was a dragoon or a hussar.*

Lancers

There were 17 regiments in 1914 and some independent Polish squadrons were later added (these became a regiment in 1917). Russian lancers wore a uniform that was similar to that worn by the dragoons. The days of wearing a Polish-style czapka were gone, and the more practical peaked cap was almost universal – sometimes with a coloured band piped in the regimental colour. Lancers wore tunics as above and shoulderboards piped in dark blue, the coloured side was as for the piping on the breeches, which bore a regimental numeral followed by a Cyrillic 'U' or, for the regiments below, a cypher: 2nd Emperor Alexander III's Courland Leib-Regiment, 3rd Emperor Alexander III's Smolensk Regiment, 5th King Victor-Emmanuel III's Lithuania Regiment, 7th King Alphonse XIII of Spain's Olviopol Regiment, 8th Grand Duchess Tatiana Nikolaevich's Voznesensk Regiment, 9th Archduke Franz Ferdinand of Austria's Bug Regiment, 10th Grand Duke of Luxemburg's Odessa Regiment, 11th Empress Maria Theodorovna's Tchuguev Regiment, 12th Emperor of Austria Franz Joseph's Belgorod Regiment, and 14th Grand Duchess Maria Alexandrovna's Yamburg Regiment.

Breeches were again blue and were piped in scarlet for all regiments apart from the 2nd, 6th, 12th and 14th Regiments (light blue); the 4th, 8th, 10th and 13th Regiments (yellow); and the 3rd, 7th and 11th Regiments

▶ **SERGEANT, 7TH WHITE RUSSIA HUSSARS, 1915** *The breeches and boots with hussar cut worn by this figure show how elements of the traditional hussar flamboyance were still evident in 1915. Cavalry usually carried the 1891 carbine.*

(white). Equipment was as for the dragoons and lances without pennons were carried by half the regiment.

Polish lancers wore crimson piping and, when the Provisional Government came to power, displayed Polish eagles on their caps and as regimental badges.

Hussars

The hussars followed the style adopted by the dragoons although officers often retained colourful breeches and wore shoulderboards with zigzag lace. The shoulderboards of the troops were piped in light blue and bore the regimental numeral followed by a Cyrillic 'G'. Those regiments with cyphers were: 1st King Frederick of Denmark's Sumy Regiment, 2nd Alexander III's Pavlograd Leib-Regiment, 5th Empress Alexandra Theodorovna's Aleksandriya Regiment, 6th Grand Duke Ernst-Ludwig of Hesse's Klyastitsy Regiment, 8th Archduke Otto of Austria's Lubny Regiment, 9th King Edward VII's Kiev Regiment, 10th Grand Duke of Saxe-Weimar's Ingermanland Regiment, 11th Prince Henry of Prussia's Izyum Regiment, 12th Grand Duchess Olga Aleksandrovna's Akhtyrka Regiment, 13th William II The Emperor of Germany Narva Regiment, 14th Prince Albert of Prussia's Mitau Regiment, and 15th Grand Duchess Ksenia Aleksandrovna's Ukraine Regiment.

Breeches were often red and piped in yellow (gold for officers) except for the 5th, 6th, 7th, 8th, 13th, 14th, 15th and 18th regiments, who wore white (silver for officers). Boots were usually Hessian in style.

COSSACKS AND NATIVE CAVALRY

A key element of Russian armies for 300 years, the Cossacks were regarded as useful scouts and skirmishers.

Cossack Hosts

Some Cossacks served in Russia's Imperial Guard. However, traditionally Cossacks grouped themselves into regiments that were deemed to be from the Caucasus (the Kuban and Terek Hosts) or from the steppe (the Amur, Astrakhan, Don, Orenburg, Semiretschi, Siberian, Trans Baikal, Ural and Usurski Hosts). The Caucasus

also provided Ingush, Daghestan, Chechen and Circassian mounted troops, not designated as Cossacks.

Regiments were formed from the Cossack population, the less able being concentrated into second line units used primarily for escort duties.

The days of colourful Cossack uniforms were largely over, and in 1914 most of them wore uniforms which resembled those of the dragoons. Even so, Cossacks often preferred to wear very baggy blue breeches, fur capes and caps in winter and additional bandoliers or sashes; anything, in short, to restore some Cossack swagger. They wore boots but without spurs. Caucasian Cossacks were a little more distinctive as they shaved their heads (but often grew bushy moustaches) and retained black or grey kaftans or cherkesska coats with bushier astrakhan fur caps. They often wore cartridges around their waist belt.

The different Hosts were to be distinguished by coloured piping on the shoulderboards and by piping on the breeches. The Kuban had red piping on the shoulderboard and breeches (regimental numeral followed by 'Kb'), the Terek opted for light blue (shoulderboards bore a Cyrillic 'V' and 'G'). Lace was silver. For the Steppe Hosts the piping was as shown in the table opposite.

Steppe Cossacks often wore a letter after their regimental numeral to distinguish themselves further. The Orenburg regiments, for example, used 'O', the Don Cossacks a Cyrillic 'D', the Amur Cossacks an 'A', the Siberian Cossacks a Cyrillic 'S' and 'B', and the

Trans Baikal regiments a Cyrillic 'Z' and 'B'. Greatcoats were not generally worn but the 'burka' (a cloak made from sheepskin or goatskin) was preferred or, failing that, a cape or cloak. Greatcoats were supposed to carry collar patches in the same colour as that used on the breeches piping.

Cossack artillery wore red shoulderboard piping, gold lace and no piping on the trousers. Cossack horse artillery wore dark blue shoulderboard piping and gold lace. Greatcoats had black collar patches piped in red. Lace, where worn, was silver.

◀ KUBAN COSSACK, KOUPER REGIMENT, 1915
Note the traditional weaponry and way of carrying cartridges, although by 1914, these were ornamental.

▶ LIEUTENANT, 1ST VOLGA REGIMENT, KUBAN COSSACKS, 1917 *Kuban Cossacks came as cavalry and infantry units.*

Cossack Host Piping

Host	Shoulderboard Piping	Breeches Piping
Amur	green	yellow
Astrakhan	yellow	yellow
Don	blue	red
Orenburg	light blue	light blue
Semiretschi	crimson	crimson
Siberian	red	red
Trans Baikal	yellow	yellow
Ural	crimson	crimson
Usurski	yellow	yellow

The Kuban Host also raised some infantry, and these were equipped as for the cavalry but with khaki trousers and crimson piping to the shoulderboards (and a black collar patch on the greatcoat piped crimson).

Cossacks were generally armed with Cossack carbines, bayonets, swords (the Shiska, or family weapons passed down from one generation to another) and daggers, as well as lances for the other ranks of the steppe Cossacks (half the regiment, those placed in the front rank, carried lances). Cossacks supplied their own horses and much of their own equipment and uniform.

Native Cavalry

Regiments of cavalry raised in the Caucasus were usually volunteers and came dressed in assorted native costumes. Most wore black, grey or light brown cherkesski coats or black kaftans, colourful undershirts and astrakhan caps. Caucasus cavalry units were supposed to be distinguished by shoulderboard piping, and this was probably light blue for the Chechens, red for the Circassians, light blue for the Daghestan Regiment, red for the Ingush, light blue for Kabardia and scarlet for the Tartars.

Hoods piped in white were also worn. These were yellow for the Chechens, white for the Circassians, red for the Daghestan Regiment, light blue for the Ingush, white for Kabardia and red for the Tartars. Blue breeches were sometimes worn, but these were often replaced by native items. Officers wore uniforms similar in appearance to those of the steppe Cossacks.

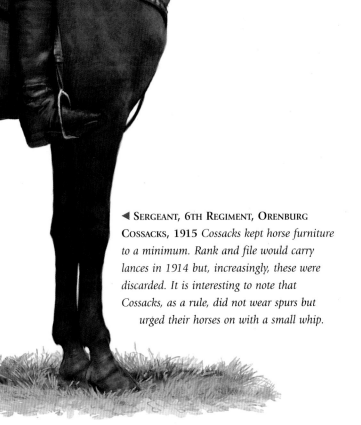

◀ SERGEANT, 6TH REGIMENT, ORENBURG COSSACKS, 1915 *Cossacks kept horse furniture to a minimum. Rank and file would carry lances in 1914 but, increasingly, these were discarded. It is interesting to note that Cossacks, as a rule, did not wear spurs but urged their horses on with a small whip.*

ARTILLERY

Russia's artillery had enjoyed a reputation for bravery and dedication since the 18th century. This past glory, however, could not mask very modern failings with shortages throughout the service and much investment wasted on fortress artillery.

Field Artillery

Russia's field artillery was organized into brigades of six batteries assigned to infantry divisions. The guards were supported by guard artillery and the grenadier regiments by grenadier

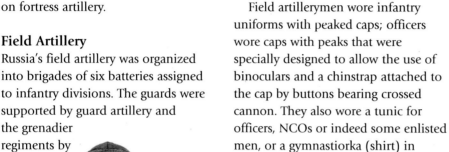

batteries with personnel designated by crossed cannon barrels and a grenade on the shoulderboards. Trench artillery was often served by squads of specially trained infantrymen or artillerymen assigned as cadres to infantry units.

Field artillerymen wore infantry uniforms with peaked caps; officers wore caps with peaks that were specially designed to allow the use of binoculars and a chinstrap attached to the cap by buttons bearing crossed cannon. They also wore a tunic for officers, NCOs or indeed some enlisted men, or a gymnastiorka (shirt) in various styles. Officers wore breeches, men trousers, with puttees or boots.

The distinguishing mark for the field artillery was shown on shoulderboards. These were scarlet on the coloured side with yellow stencils showing the brigade number in Roman numerals and a crossed cannon device above the numeral. For officers this principal was repeated but with gold embroidered shoulderboards (silver stars denoting rank) with metallic numerals and metallic crossed cannons. Officers later

◄ **GUNNER, 12TH FOOT ARTILLERY REGIMENT, 1916** *The 1881 greatcoat was also worn by the artillery – it was fastened by hooks and was thicker than the single-breasted coat issued in 1911.*

adopted cloth shoulder straps and did away with much of the piping in an attempt to reduce personal visibility.

In winter, artillerymen wore the standard greatcoat with collar patches in black (black velvet for officers) piped red. The fur cap was the same as that worn by the infantry.

Equipment was generally very similar to that of the infantry, although black leather belts and braces were preferred and the artilleryman's belt buckle bore crossed cannon as well as the double-headed eagle. Canvas bandoliers came into fashion later in the war, as an economy measure. Officers carried swords (actually worn with the blade reversed, an unusual practice unique to Russia) and pistols (with a red pistol cord).

Fortress Artillery

Stationary artillery units based in such key positions as Kronstadt, Brest Litovsk or Vladivostok, had orange shoulderboards and had the initial of the fortress below crossed cannon

▼ **MAXIM PORTABLE MACHINE GUN ON WHEELS, 1916** *All Russian artillery weapons and ammunition caissons were painted green.*

barrels. Further distinctions were made by insignia worn on the sleeves or brassards, such as crossed red flags on the upper left sleeve, for signallers.

Horse Artillery
Russian horse artillery was traditionally assigned to cavalry divisions and wore uniforms very similar to those of the dragoons. Tunics were of the

same cut and had pointed cuffs. Shoulderboards were light blue (with white stencils) or, on the khaki side, khaki piped light blue with light blue unit numerals and crossed cannon. Breeches followed the style of those worn by the cavalry, either being light blue piped red or, later, simple khaki breeches (sometimes reinforced with leather innards for officers). Men were armed with carbines, officers with pistols (with red pistol cords).

◄ **SERGEANT 15TH HORSE ARTILLERY REGIMENT, 1916** *The canvas pouch, worn across the chest, was introduced in 1892 and carried 30 cartridges. The red lanyard doubles back and is attached to his pistol handle – so that if he drops it when he is firing from the saddle, it does not fall to the ground.*

▲ **SHOULDERBOARDS FOR FORTRESS ARTILLERY, 1916, TOP ROW, FROM LEFT:** *Kronstadt, Kovno, Ust-Dvinsk, Warsaw.* **MIDDLE ROW, FROM LEFT:** *Novgorod, Brest-Litovsk, Ivangorod, Osovets.* **BOTTOM ROW, FROM LEFT:** *Mihailov, Narva, Vladivostok and Nikolaev.*

Mountain Artillery
These wore very similar uniforms to the field artillery, although increasingly taking on characteristics of the troops they were attached to (sharing depots exacerbated this). For example, artillery attached to Siberian rifle divisions would wear the bushier Siberian fur cap. Cossacks raised and equipped their own artillery formations. An unusual distinction for mountain artillery was that they encouraged their men to wear black leather breeches rather than the standard light blue or khaki.

◄ **GUNNER, SEVASTOPOL FORTRESS ARTILLERY, 1916** *The initials of the fortress the gunner was posted to are shown on the shoulderboards: the Cyrillic letters 'SVS' for Sevastopol in this case. Equipment carried by this figure has been reduced down to just the 1909 model canvas bread bag.*

TECHNICAL TROOPS

Although Russia had lagged behind in the early 20th century, the war with Japan had taught the military some lessons about defending and assaulting fixed positions.

Guns, Tanks and Armoured Cars

Russia not only attached machine guns to infantry units, it also raised some independent machine gun units. These autonomous detachments wore shoulderboards that displayed a detachment number and,

▶ CAPTAIN, RAILWAY REGIMENT, 1916 *The Nagant revolver, first issued in 1895, was the preferred weapon for Russian officers, and was recommended by the 1907 regulations. The holster had a little interior pocket which could carry an additional seven rounds.*

above it, a stencil of a machine gun on a tripod. Gunners assigned to the armoured cars wore green shoulderboards showing the platoon number and, above it, a winged wheel below a machine gun. This was changed in 1916 to scarlet shoulderboards. Personnel often wore leather tunics and leggings, leather gauntlets and soft peaked caps with goggles. Tankers would wear an identical uniform, although tanks only played a minor part on the Eastern Front (some were supplied to White forces in 1918 and 1919).

Russia had such a shortage of crews for armoured cars that an appeal was made for foreign volunteers and instructors. A squadron of Belgians with ten armoured cars served with the Russians. Personnel wore Belgian artillery uniforms but with Russian shoulderboards piped in volunteer cords of black, white and orange, and officer distinctions. A British unit also served with the Russians but retained British uniforms and insignia.

Engineers and Sappers

Technically these armoured car units had been a part of the engineering branch. This itself was a highly respected branch of service with an excellent record. Engineers wore brown shoulderboards with yellowish brown numerals and crossed picks and shovels. The khaki side showed brown

◀ CORPORAL, 18TH SAPPER BATTALION, 1915 *This sapper wears the 1911 greatcoat with metallic buttons. It could be tightened at the rear with a belt. He also carries the spade, or kindyal, sometimes used in hand-to-hand fighting.*

numerals and crossed pick and shovel with the addition of a 'K' for fortress engineers. In the winter artillery greatcoats were worn with the universal fur cap. Engineers attached to the grenadier divisions had a grenade added to their shoulderboards.

Specialist branches of the engineers included pontooneers (as for the engineers but with the addition of a

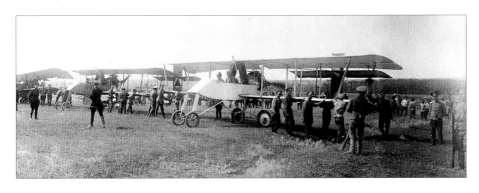

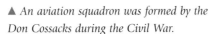

▲ *An aviation squadron was formed by the Don Cossacks during the Civil War.*

▼ CAPTAIN, TELEGRAPHIC BATTALION, 1916 *Two battalions were formed in the war but there were also companies in Siberia, Turkmenistan, St Petersburg and each of the major fortresses. They wore lightning bolts on their shoulderboards as well as any initials denoting their geographic location.*

saw and axe as well as an anchor on the shoulderboards), miners (crossed oars with an anchor) and railway troops (crossed anchors with an axe). Those involved with signals, telegraphs, telephones or laying cables had double lightning bolts on their brown or khaki shoulderboards.

Medical Troops

Russia lacked adequate facilities to cope with the numbers of wounded that were expected, and foreign volunteers helped make up the numbers. Russian medical personnel wore orange shoulderboards with the number of the hospital in white and, above it, a Cyrillic 'L'. This was repeated in orange on the khaki shoulderboard. Doctors wore a variety of civilian and military coats and tunics, stretcher bearers wore red cross brassards.

Aviation

Russian military aviation was relatively young, although observation balloons had been used in the 1870s and against the Japanese. An aviation service established in 1912 was technically a part of the engineers, and was uniformed accordingly. Aviation personnel were to be distinguished by the use of either a winged anchor (balloon troops) or by a winged propeller (for pilots and aeroplane ground crews). The general pattern of the uniform followed that of the

engineers, but ground crew could also wear dark blue tunics. Pilots, inevitably, diverged from the standards of dress adopted by engineer officers. They wore a variety of flying helmets (often imported from France) or, on the ground, a coloured engineer's peaked cap. The pilotka (a peakless side cap) was popular. Pilots wore black leather tunics (often cut in the French style), or tunics of their original regiments, and black leather breeches with aviator or cavalry boots. A pilot's badge was worn on the breast of the tunic or flying coat. It consisted of a winged shield, bearing a double-headed eagle, placed before crossed swords and superimposed on a wreath. A badge for observers was similar with the addition of a telescope.

▶ LIEUTENANT, PILOT, 1916 *Black leather jackets were popular among all pilots, and their flying helmets were usually imported from France.*

THE RUSSIAN CIVIL WAR: RED ARMIES

Russia dissolved into chaos in the autumn of 1917. From that chaos the Bolsheviks would emerge as the rulers of a new Russia. This was thanks, in part, to their mastery of the resources available to them, including what remained of the army.

From the Ashes

Most Russian soldiers simply went home in the autumn of 1917, voting to end the war with their feet. The Bolsheviks,

led by Lenin and inspired by Trotsky, were quick to sue for peace with the Germans and turn to face internal enemies and, particularly after 1918, those raised and sponsored by outside powers (be they German, Polish, French or Turkish).

The Bolsheviks gathered what armed forces they could. In part these were detachments of Red Guards, volunteers mostly drawn from urban workers or sailors. Detachments of Red Guards had in fact been formed during the revolution of 1905. Most had distinguished themselves by wearing armbands with revolutionary slogans. They took on a new life in 1917 and 1918 and began to form regiments (later absorbed into the Red Army). Countless bands were raised across Bolshevik-controlled Russia. Most of those supporting the revolution of 1917 wore red armbands with black or white lettering.

Formation of the Red Army

The Red Army itself stumbled into being. The government made use of those troops who did not initially desert, forming detachments and, eventually, converting all infantry into rifle units grouped into rifle divisions. Initially uniforms consisted of those worn under the Provisional Government (imperial uniforms but minus shoulderboards, cockades and the now entirely obsolete rank distinctions) plus red cockades or brassards. Increasingly badges were worn, such as a shield-shaped badge

◀ COMPANY COMMANDER, 51ST RIFLE REGIMENT, 1918 *The Red Army abandoned the old rank system and introduced a simplified pattern of uniform distinctions for commanders.*

▶ PRIVATE, 53RD RIFLE REGIMENT, 1918 *This practical uniform shows how the winter cap could protect the face and ears from the cold.*

with red piping on the left sleeve. Sometimes these were insignia taken from old imperial uniforms (crossed cannon barrels for artillery, a crossed pick and shovel for sappers). More commonly a hammer and plough (symbolizing unity between worker and peasant), then, sometime after 1922, the hammer and sickle, within a red star began to be used on caps (although simple stars could be worn on caps) or on the tunic breast. In 1918 red chevrons, worn on the

◄ PRIVATE, 10TH RIFLE REGIMENT, 1921
The Red Army uniform had evolved by 1921, and many of the uniform shortages, and shortages of weaponry and equipment, had been overcome. The cap worn here is the famous 'budenovka'.

uniforms (British and French); only by 1919 was some semblance of uniformity being imposed.

The means of distinguishing officers was even more fraught. The system of ranks used in the old army was abolished in November 1917 and commanders were to be elected. These were quite often only distinguished by being equipped with pistols and boots and increasingly by red chevrons or red stars above the cuff.

By 1919 some senior commanders were wearing greatcoats with red breast tabs, insignia on the cuff (red star and tabs) and the famous 'budenovka', a peaked cap with pointed crown. This had ear flaps and a large star stitched to the front. More common was a fur cap with red star badge.

The 1919 uniform was slowly introduced and was only common by 1922. Rifle units had red distinctions (tunic tabs, collar patches and a red star on the cap).

Cavalry

The Red Army cavalry wore breeches (occasionally red, sometimes blue, mostly khaki) and boots, plus tunics adorned with red stars or red brassards on the arm. Fur caps or peaked caps were worn, again with red stars or strips of red cloth. Sometimes the caps worn in action were the coloured versions usually reserved as full dress, but pressed into service.

The new Red Army uniform, released in 1919 but adopted slowly, had blue distinctions for cavalry (a blue star on the cap, blue tunic tabs, blue collar patches on the tunic and greatcoat). Red cavalry docked their horses' tails to distinguish themselves from White units. Cossacks wore their traditional uniforms but with the addition of Bolshevik insignia.

Specialist Troops

Artillery and engineers struggled along in all kinds of uniforms until the 1920s, when the 1919 uniform was almost universally adopted. It called for black distinctions for engineers and artillerymen (sometimes piped red).

▼ *Leon Trotsky, a Bolshevik revolutionary leader, addresses the troops in Moscow, 1919.*

lower sleeve, were also stitched on to tunics. Some regions received their own insignia: troops in Siberia had red stars on black backgrounds.

Distinctions and Commonality

An increase in the number of forces available (conscription was introduced in May 1918) necessitated some further reform, and a military commission was formed in April 1918 to resolve the issue. In October, when all infantry units were designated as rifles, plans were announced to have unit numerals stencilled or stitched on to the collar of the tunic or of the greatcoat. The increase in size inevitably led to shortages and the wearing of captured

THE RUSSIAN CIVIL WAR: WHITE ARMIES

Opponents of the Bolsheviks were often termed 'White' although opposition was actually composed of several factions, many of which operated against each other.

Disparate Forces

Although it was easy to term the Bolsheviks 'Reds', the label 'White' only appeared later. It was linked to monarchist forces (who were branded White following the use of this term during the French Revolution). But opposition to Bolshevik rule was not the preserve of the monarchists. The Revolution also unleashed anarchist forces, and nationalist forces striving to set up an independent Ukraine for example, or the Baltic States, or fiefdoms in central Asia. And then there were the opportunists, who formed bands of partisans and rampaged for their own profit. Nor was it the case that everyone was against the Reds; Whites fought nationalists, anarchists fought Whites and vice versa.

Shock Battalions

Opposition to the Bolsheviks initially centred on isolated bands of troops remaining loyal to particular generals. The Provisional Government had relied on a number of shock or death battalions to bolster the front.

The Women's Battalion of Death remained loyal, unsuccessfully defending the Winter Palace against Bolshevik troops. It wore standard imperial infantry uniforms plus white shoulderboards with a central black and red stripe. Other so-called death battalions had black skulls stencilled on to khaki shoulder straps. Shock battalions, who had worn a Death's Head badge (skull with crossed bones set on a wreath), and red and black chevrons on the lower sleeve, also formed a core of troops who would remain loyal to those usurped by Lenin. So too did St George battalions, with their white shoulderboards piped

◀ **PRIVATE, WOMEN'S BATTALION OF DEATH, 1917** *This battalion had been raised from volunteers in the summer of 1917 by Maria Bochkareva, a female soldier who had gained special permission from Czar Nicholas to join the 25th Tomsk Reserve Battalion of the Imperial Russian Army. They had distinctive shoulderboards and rank insignia, which was now being worn on the sleeve in the form of chevrons.*

▲ **SERGEANT, 42ND YAKUTSK REGIMENT, 1918** *This individual has retained his old rank distinction – by now he should have point down chevrons on his sleeve in white-blue-red, but cloth was scarce and old insignia carried on being used.*

in orange and the Cyrillic 'S' and 'G' above the unit number (officers wore gold piped orange and orange piping on the tunic and breeches).

The Volunteer Army

An army of sorts, soon to be known as the Volunteer Army, formed in southern Russia in late 1918. Other forces concentrated in northern Russia – in the Baltic states and in the far north – gathering around an Allied expedition in Murmansk. Other formations slowly began to form in Siberia, eventually led by Admiral Kolchak, and by the Caspian, led by General Dutov. The Whites were strongest in the summer of 1919,

and red shoulderboards bearing a silver skull and silver 'K' and, on the left sleeve, a light blue shield with a skull and crossbones above crossed swords. This black, red and silver combination was used to distinguish other troops operating under Kornilov.

The situation was so bad that a number of units were raised only to be destroyed. Clothing supplies were short and uniformity impossible. Some units were composed of officers only, such as General Drozdovsky's Rifles and Cavalry Regiment; these wore shoulderboards with a Cyrillic 'O' and 'P' for infantry and 'O' and 'K' for cavalry, as well as a black cross badge

bolstered by arms and equipment (including tanks and gas) from their Western supporters and, indeed, by an Allied military presence. This would include British troops as well as Americans, Greeks, Serbs, French and Japanese soldiers. Poland, which itself mounted an unsuccessful invasion in 1919, would still be sending Whites and Ukrainians against the Soviets into the 1920s. The Japanese stayed on until 1923.

General Alexeyev was the driving force behind the formation of the Volunteer Army and it commenced operations in December 1917. He was later joined by the notorious General Lavr Kornilov and supported by the initially half-hearted Don Cossacks.

Volunteer Uniforms

Most of the Volunteer Army had to make do with whatever uniforms they could find. Cockades were worn in caps and these were either the old imperial cockade or the Russian national colours of white, blue and red. Tunics were generally khaki, as were breeches and caps.

Shoulderboards were reintroduced (and became the chief distinguishing mark between the Reds and the Whites) and these were generally red or yellow for infantry and red piped black for artillery. Cavalry wore

▲ *Members of a women's regiment from Petrograd, loyal to the Provisional Government, who defended the White Palace against the Bolsheviks, at their camp.*

▶ KORNILOV'S SHOCK REGIMENT, 1918
Kornilov's units were initially dressed in quite exotic uniforms but it is not clear how long they lasted in the field. Note the Adrian helmet, a rare sign of good fortune, and the sleeve patch, which is supposed to have been printed on hospital linen for want of available cloth. Some patches were painted on leather, others were sewn from cloth.

coloured caps and blue breeches, if available. A composite guard regiment operated with caps piped in company colours and coloured shoulderboards.

Distinctions

Some other distinguishing insignia was worn. Many troops wore the Russian national colours as a chevron on their sleeves or a badge relating to a particular commander. Some officers in units under Alexeyev chose to wear white tunics (nostalgia for the old-style uniform), as did some of General Markov's men, along with a black Maltese cross badge bearing 'M'.

Kornilov's men wore an even more distinctive uniform based on that worn by the Kornilov Shock Battalion of 1917. They wore black

▲ Lieutenant, 2nd Regiment of Cavalry, Czech Legion, 1918 *The fur cap, modelled on an old Russian design, was worn with a Czech badge and red cloth bag.*

on the sleeve. They also wore caps with white crowns and blue bands.

The Volunteer Army was supported by sizeable numbers of Cossacks, and these generally wore the same uniforms as they had during the war against Germany. A few special units attempted to impose uniformity, such as Kornilov's Kuban Cossacks. Cossacks probably had coloured tops to their fur caps and coloured peaked caps (blue crowns and red bands for Don Cossacks, yellow bands for Kalmucks).

Allied equipment and uniforms were issued in large numbers. Troops made use of British or French uniforms with Russian shoulderboards and distinctive insignia.

Northern Russia

A number of White troops managed to organize themselves in Latvia, initially with German support, and were eventually led by General Yudenich. The situation there was amazingly complicated, with nationalist partisans also operating against both Reds and White Russian forces. Here Russian troops usually wore their old imperial uniforms (yellow shoulderboards for infantry, blue for cavalry) but with the addition of some distinctive insignia. The most common was a white cross, worn as an enamel badge on the breast or sewn on to the left sleeve, and appearing on various dark backgrounds, such as black shields. The Balt, Prince Anatoly Lieven, commanded men in Latvia who wore the white cross with a shield in the centre painted in Russian national colours and shoulderboards with a Cyrillic 'L'.

Troops around Murmansk benefited from being able to use British and American stores and equipment. They generally wore British tunics and caps with Russian insignia (including shoulderboards), belts and rifles.

Eastern Armies

Troops operating in Siberia were also supplied with British uniforms in 1919. Siberian rifles, for example, had green shoulderboards with white piping. Kolchak's troops wore a variety of uniforms from standard imperial dress to cavalry with khaki French-style tunics, red breeches and caps with red crowns and black bands.

Also caught up in the war in the east was the Czech Legion, trying to head home via Vladivostok. Russian-style uniforms gradually gave way in 1919 to

▶ Ukraine, Corporal, 1st Regiment, 1919 *Ukrainian infantry were distinguished by blue insignia and rank was shown by pips on the collar.*

a more distinctive appearance. A peaked khaki cap was common among the infantry, and this bore a shield badge with rampant lion, set beneath a white and red flash of cloth. Cavalry seem to have preferred a white or grey fur cap with red bag and black plume. Tunics were khaki (made from Japanese cloth) with crimson collar tabs for the infantry and yellow or beige for the cavalry.

Unit numerals were worn on a shield on the left sleeve, and this also later showed rank insignia. Shields were khaki piped red for the infantry and artillery and white piped red for the cavalry. Chevrons within the shield indicated rank (three for a

lieutenant, for example) and these were yellow for the infantry and white for the cavalry and artillery. Greatcoats had collar tabs and the rank insignia shields on the left sleeve. Service stripe chevrons were worn on the right sleeve. There was great variation in dress given the constraints of serving in the far east of Russia during a civil war.

Nationalist Armies

Troops fighting for the independence of Estonia and Latvia wore dark grey uniforms, German helmets, peaked caps or fur caps. Most of the headgear bore a cockade in national colours (for example, blue, black and white for Estonia). Armbands further distinguished such troops. In 1919 more standardized uniforms were issued. For the Estonians it was grey tunic, black trousers and grey peaked caps. Collars on the tunic were black and bore rank insignia (silver pips). Finnish soldiers began by wearing white armbands and lion badges on their sleeves. A number combined this

▼ **Captain, Kuban Cossack Regiment, 1919**
This officer has silver, black and red shoulderboards. Rank and file wore red boards with black edging and 'K'. The rest of the costume is in traditional Kuban Cossack style.

with German uniforms and helmets, others wore civilian greatcoats and fur caps.

The most complicated, but in some ways most significant, fighting took place in the Ukraine. Apart from various bands fighting Whites and Reds, and each other, there were also troops loyal to the independence movement (an assembly formed in March 1917).

Russian-style uniforms were worn at first with blue shoulderboards piped in yellow and with the national badge (the trident or tryzub).

Reforms in early 1918 led to the adoption of new uniforms. These were based on a khaki tunic cut in a style like that worn by the Austro-Hungarian Ukrainian troops, with rank insignia displayed on the collar patch. The collar patch was in branch of service colour: blue for infantry, yellow for cavalry and red for artillery. Cossack-style or peaked caps were popular.

AMERICA AND OTHER ALLIES

Great Britain, France and Russia were supported by a host of allies. Some, Belgium and Serbia, for example, were involved from the start, while others came in at a later date. The USA brought vast resources in terms of manpower and industrial capacity, while others made a more modest, but still important, contribution. The peace dividend was also divided for the Allied nations – some, such as Belgium, emerged ruined and bloodied from the war, while Japan made considerable gains and took huge geopolitical advantage for comparatively little cost. In some sense it was the sheer scale of the forces ranged against the Central Powers that was overwhelming. The German, Austro-Hungarian and Ottoman empires were surrounded by hostile armies, outnumbered and forced to divide their forces between one front and another. An additional, and perhaps decisive, factor was the disparity between the resources the Central Powers could make use of and those which could be mobilized by the Allied powers.

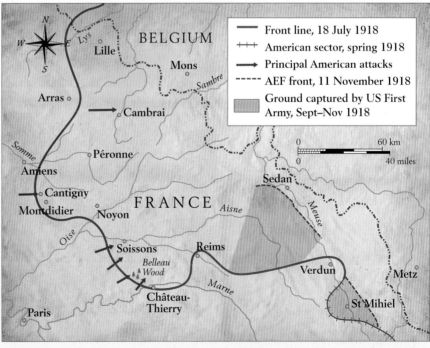

▲ *Operations by the American Expeditonary Force (AEF) in the autumn of 1918 took place in the much-contested ground around Verdun.*

◄ *A convoy of Belgian cavalry, with carbines slung over their shoulders, advances towards the Western Front in the area around Ypres in 1916.*

THE USA ENTERS THE WAR

The United States had watched Europe go to war in 1914, and its politicians had promised the people to preserve neutrality. However, war found a way of crossing the Atlantic.

Neutrality

The United States was governed by President Woodrow Wilson, an idealist who initially distanced himself, and his country, from the war being fought in Europe. Public opinion was divided, with traditional allegiances being split into either a pro-German camp or a pro-Allied force. There was something of an ethnic divide with Irish, Polish and German sympathies often attaching themselves to the opponents of Britain and Russia, and others feeling that German aggression had been the root cause of all the trouble in the first place.

Although British policies towards neutral shipping initially upset the Americans, the United States

▼ *A poster declaring 'Take Up the Sword of Justice' advocates that Americans take revenge for the sinking of the* Lusitania.

eventually accepted the idea of a blockade of Germany. British heavy handedness could be overlooked; German submarine warfare, on the other hand, could not. Germany had declared the eastern Atlantic a war zone in February 1915 and sank a luxury cruise ship, the *Lusitania*, in May. World outrage made the Germans back down and promise restraint. German interference in Central America was also resented, especially when it took place in Mexico, a troubling development for the Americans who had seen much turbulence on their southern border.

America Declares War

President Wilson attempted to act as a means of bringing both sides towards a negotiated settlemen,t but was frustrated by the inability of the Europeans to commit to a process that many saw as an indication of weakness. The return of unrestricted submarine warfare in 1917, and the collapse of Russia, prompted the Americans to take up arms.

The Americans were quickly followed by a large number of South and Central American countries. Peru, Uruguay, Ecuador and Brazil, among

▲ *On 2 April 1917, President Woodrow Wilson addresses the US Congress to request that the country declare war on Germany.*

others, all declared war and seized German assets and shipping. Even the Ononddago Indian nation declared war on Germany in August 1918.

Army Recruitment

Although attempts had been made to increase the size of the US Army (the Navy had benefited from considerable improvements and had been needed to police the waters around Central America, Cuba and the Philippines), it was still a ridiculously small force for the task it had been assigned. It was expanded by use of the National Guard and the quick adoption of a series of conscription laws, which ensured that the ranks were swollen by drafts of conscripts (initially aged between 21 and 30). Social conditions were such that the majority of those inducted into the Army would come from the urban centres of the north-east, many of the men being recent immigrants themselves or from immigrant families. A good number of conscripts were illiterate or poorly educated (something which led to the adoption

▲ *A soldier of the 71st Infantry Regiment, New York National Guard, says goodbye to his sweetheart as his regiment leaves for training at Camp Wadsworth, Spartanburg, South Carolina, 1917.*

of multiple choice questions), and many of them spoke languages other than English.

The United States faced particular political issues when drafting black recruits. The prewar US armed forces were racially segregated and this was maintained during the war. Army and Navy leaders also wanted black troops kept out of combat units. Most therefore found themselves in supply formations or working as labourers in pioneer corps. A few black regiments were raised, but even these were kept apart from white units, and were mostly assigned to French command.

Social Impact

The American economy may have benefited from the war but the social strains brought other tensions to the fore. There were strikes and bitter disputes about the employment of women. There were racial tensions, as black workers were brought in to staff northern factories. Further, casualties

were heavy in the fighting in the last months of the war. Although American intervention in the war ended without any American territorial gains, peace itself would bring benefits (the exhaustion of all European rivals). It would also bring challenges, some of which stemmed from that very exhaustion in the heart of Europe, but another of which was the rise of Japan in the Pacific that would trouble those who cared to look beyond the frontiers of the United States.

▲ *A limited number of women were recruited to the US Marines during the war. Here a group of them take the oath of loyalty in 1918. It was not until World War II that female Marines were trained to use firearms, and in both wars their role was supportive.*

▼ *The few black-only regiments raised by the USA served with the French. Here General Eli Helmick, Commander of the US 5th Division, pins African-American soldiers with the Distinguished Service Cross. Admiral Moreau of the French Navy stands by.*

ALLIED ARMIES

In addition to the main protagonists, the war brought a varied collection of other nations together into one (occasionally) unified alliance. Such collaboration between the small and the large finally led to a successful outcome for the Allies.

Portugal and Belgium

The progression of the war eventually led to the participation of such far-flung countries as Liberia and Siam, but two European states were quickly involved in a war in Africa, as well as on the European mainland. Portugal had probably gone to war to preserve its extensive colonies in Africa, and to make gains on that continent at Germany's expense. It also despatched an expeditionary force to northern Europe, which ended up fighting on the Western Front. There it suffered appalling casualties in the German Spring Offensive of 1918.

Belgium too had a sizeable territory in Africa, but it hardly volunteered its participation in the war, being largely

▲ *A shallow trench is defended by a unit of Romanians against the Austro-Hungarians on the Romanian front in the Carpathian Mountains in October 1915.*

▼ *Belgian cavalry and civilian refugees evacuate from a lost town in Belgium, in October 1914.*

overrun by a German invasion in August 1914. The Belgian Army was reduced to holding a slim strip of territory in western Belgium, fighting alongside British and French allies. Belgium itself suffered in the war, being placed on starvation rations,

having its workforce conscripted, and with raw materials being seized and carried away. Belgium preserved its colonies in Africa and also fielded some troops on that continent, although these were more in the nature of militarized police.

Italy and the Slavs

Because of their garrisons in Libya, which had remained there to pacify the territory following war with the Ottomans in 1911, Italy also had troops in Africa. Most of Italy's effort was, however, very much focused on Europe, particularly on its main rival Austria-Hungary. Italy fought a bitter war in the mountains against the Hapsburgs, seeking to destroy the Austro-Hungarian Navy in the Adriatic and win a hold on Albania in order to stop Austro-Hungarian annexation of more of the Balkans. It mobilized large forces and placed a tremendous strain on an Austria-Hungary already depleted by war with Russia (and severely challenged by Serbia), a situation which yet again led to Germany propping up its ally. Italy had joined the Allies with specific hopes and detailed claims to particular territories along its borders and along the Adriatic coast and in Ottoman territory. It was to be largely disappointed at the peace table, losing out to the new Yugoslavia, a fact that led to heartfelt internal debate as to why Italy had been engaged at all.

The kingdom of Serbia was involved right from the very beginning. Montenegro, a loyal ally of the Serbs, also found itself sucked into the conflict, fielding some 35,000 troops in 1914. The Serbs, whose armed forces had been augmented by territorial gains in the Balkan Wars, mobilized a much more impressive force but one with severe shortages. Both kingdoms were overrun in 1915 and the Serb Army (with many Montenegrins) was evacuated to Greek islands. These troops, reformed and refitted, were sent back into the Balkans and played a major part in the offensives against the Germans and Bulgarians in September 1918. Serbian victory over the Austro-Hungarians led to the establishment of the kingdom of the Serbs, Croats and Slovenes, which was given the name Yugoslavia.

Latecomers

Romania also benefited in 1918, snatching Transylvania, which had been overrun by 1917. The Romanian king, although of German descent, had sided with the Allies in order to increase the country's territory at the

expense of the Hapsburgs and Bulgaria, a rival of Romania from the time of the Balkan wars. A swift reaction from the Austro-Hungarians, Germans and Bulgarians quickly defeated the country and led to a short occupation and brief peace before the Romanians quickly took to the field again in late 1918.

Greece was also ruled by a monarchy with German roots, and this was one of the reasons why the king

▼ *British and French forces arrive in Salonika in 1915, but were too late to prevent Serbia's conquest by the Central Powers. A large Allied force was built up at Salonika in 1916–17 but achieved little until the final weeks of the war.*

▲ *Japan and the United States sent forces to Siberia in 1918 to bolster the armies of the White Army leader Admiral Aleksandr Kolchak against the Bolshevik Red Army. Here the US and Japanese generals and staff are photographed in Vladivostok, Siberia, 1919. US Major General Graves, is seated third from the left, next to Japan's General Otani.*

and his supporters preferred neutrality. There was strong opposition to this from politicians who saw the war as an opportunity. A messy civil war, punctuated by coups and confusion, was the result before Greece finally sided with the Allies. It provided men and equipment for the campaign in the Balkans in 1918 and, thereafter, found itself sucked into a bloody war with the Ottomans in Asia Minor.

An Asian Power

Japan was also drawn into the conflict by requests from the Allies to help in the Far Eastern territories. Japan had cleared the Germans from Chinese territory and some Pacific islands in 1914, and had enjoyed a boost to its economy. In 1917, encouraged by its allies, Japan provided troops to oppose the Bolsheviks in Russia. An expedition of four infantry regiments and one cavalry regiment, together with American forces, took Vladivostok in the summer of 1918. Japanese troops would stay in the region until 1923 and would later return to Manchuria in greater numbers.

US INFANTRY

▲ *America's 4th Infantry marches through the streets of Brownsville, Texas, while townspeople watch.*

Infantry units wore a woollen khaki tunic (M1912), which was fastened with five bronze buttons bearing an eagle device. The khaki was olive drab but could vary in tone, depending on the age of the cloth, the place of manufacture and the conditions in which the material was being worn. It initially had four pockets (a modified

▼ **Major General, 1918** *British trenchcoats and Brodie helmets were popular among senior American officers.*

When the United States declared war on Germany, in April 1917, the US Army was an extremely small force. In addition, it had relatively little experience of modern combat.

Call to Arms

In April 1917 the Americans had some 6,000 officers and 122,000 men under arms in the regulars and an additional 80,000 National Guardsmen. These would be hurriedly supplemented with conscripts called to the colours under the Selective Service Law. An initial division was dispatched under General Pershing, and this was to be followed by the bulk of the American Expeditionary Force in the coming months, substantial numbers being deployed in France in April and May 1918.

By the time of the armistice there were some 7 regular divisions, 17 National Guard divisions and 16 conscript divisions in France (and some further troops in Italy).

Originally, it had been President Wilson's wish to keep the Americans apart, and maintain a distinct identity, but divisions were loaned to the Allies. They underwent a steep learning curve. American forces had been engaged in Mexico, Nicaragua or the Philippines, and some officers had seen action in the invasion of Cuba. However, experience of warfare on a grand scale and against an experienced enemy, would be a novelty for most American officers and men. Training, provided by the French and British, helped overcome this problem. In addition, being so far from home and sizeable depots, many American troops found themselves dependent on Allied supplies of equipment and weapons.

Infantry Uniforms

American troops began to wear a shade of khaki (a kind of mustard brown, known as olive drab) in 1903, after experience in the war against Spain in Cuba. The uniform supplied to the infantry was largely introduced in or around 1912.

▲ *US forces arrived in France in 1917. General Pershing, left, was commander of the American Expeditionary Forces.*

version in 1918 had hidden pockets) and shoulder straps, and had a standing collar. There were bronze disks (an idea dating from 1902) on each side of the collar, although these were sometimes made of painted leather rather than metal. The insignia on the right-hand side bore the initials 'US' for regular units, 'USNG' for National Guardsmen and 'USNA' for the draft or conscript units. These distinctions were gradually phased out in 1918, but before then some regiments managed to issue their own particular versions (mostly with regimental numerals). The disk on the left showed the branch of service of the wearer and, for the infantry, this was crossed rifles (sometimes with a regimental number or company letter below, sometimes with other letters, such as 'MG', for machine-gunner, stamped above). An army shirt was worn under the tunic, and a neck cloth or cravat was a common addition.

Breeches were made from the same material and had two side pockets and two rear pockets. They were buttoned below the knee, and not particularly comfortable for marching troops. For winter the troops were issued with a double-breasted greatcoat with two

rows of four buttons of the same type as the tunic. This was very long and troops found it quickly became heavy when wet or when encrusted with mud. It was made shorter in 1918. Canvas waterproofed raincoats were sometimes issued, officers often providing their own or purchasing trenchcoats locally, and hooded capes also put in an appearance. In the summer troops could make use of a cotton uniform that was of a similar design to the woollen uniform.

▼ **Private, 9th Infantry, 1917** *The 1912 uniform was worn by the first troops arriving in France in 1917. Note the roundhat, or Montana (also known as the lemon squeezer).*

The Americans were distinguished upon their arrival in France by the use of the roundhat, or Montana. This offered poor protection against the weather or anything else, and quickly became relegated to use behind the front line only. Infantry wore the Montana with blue cords, gold and black for officers. Adrian helmets were issued to some units arriving in France, and to the divisions of black Americans assigned to the French, and British helmets were also used.

▼ **Captain, 167th Infantry, Spring 1918** *Although many American officers wore riding boots, puttees and ankle boots were more common at the front.*

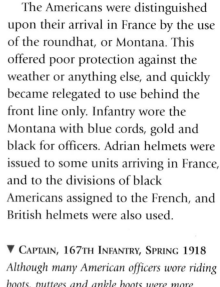

Pershing boot, and was brown and studded with hobnails. It was generally worn with puttees although some canvas gaiters continued to be worn into 1918.

Privilege of rank

While NCOs initially wore rank insignia on both sleeves (brown cloth chevrons), it was later ruled that such marks should be worn on the right. Officers wore metal bars on

▼ PRIVATE, 54TH INFANTRY, AUTUMN 1918 *Divisional symbols began to appear in early 1918, following a British trend, and this man sports that of the 6th Division.*

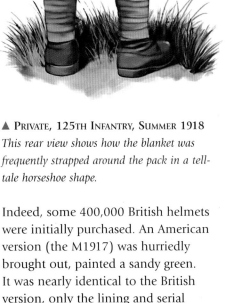

▲ PRIVATE, 125TH INFANTRY, SUMMER 1918
This rear view shows how the blanket was frequently strapped around the pack in a tell-tale horseshoe shape.

Indeed, some 400,000 British helmets were initially purchased. An American version (the M1917) was hurriedly brought out, painted a sandy green. It was nearly identical to the British version, only the lining and serial numbers revealing a difference. Side caps were very common both in and out of the trenches and were often piped in blue for officers and gold for generals. Boots quickly wore out, and in 1917 a new kind of footwear was issued. It was the

▲ PRIVATE, 370TH INFANTRY, SUMMER 1918
One of four black regiments transferred to French command, this regiment was supplied with French helmets and equipment.

their shoulder straps (often sewn from metallic thread) or on the cuffs of coats (black knotted ornamentation). They also had lace on their tunic cuffs. Uniforms, generally, were better made than those of enlisted men and were frequently of a green hue. Collar disks were not worn but the relevant initials ('US', 'USNG', 'USNA') were worn alongside the branch of service insignia (crossed rifles for infantry).

Officers wore leather boots and puttees or high, laced brown boots, known as aviators' boots.

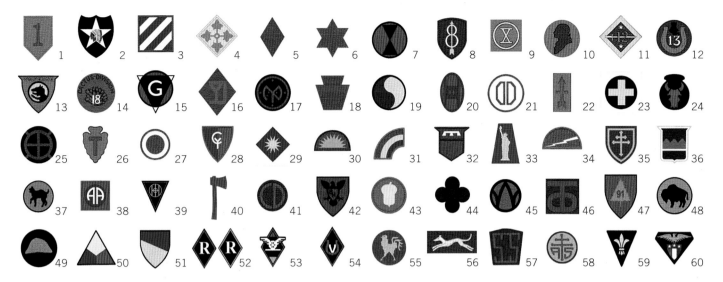

▲ **US Infantry Division and Other Unit Shoulder Patches and Names** *1 1st The Big Red One. 2 2nd Indian Head Division. 3 3rd Mame Division. 4 4th Ivy Division. 5 5th Red Diamond Division. 6 6th Sight-Seeing Sixth. 7 7th Hourglass Division. 8 8th Pathfinder Division. 9 10th X. 10 11th Lafayette Division. 11 12th Plymouth Division. 12 13th Lucky 13th Division. 13 14th Wolverine Division. 14 18th Cactus Division. 15 19th xix. 16 26th (NG) Yankee Division. 17 27th (NG) New York Division. 18 28th (NG) Keystone Division. 19 29th (NG) Blue and Gray Division. 20 30th (NG) Old Hickory Division. 21 31st (NG) Dixie Division. 22 32nd (NG) Red Arrow Division. 23 33rd (NG) Prairie Division. 24 34th (NG) Red Bull Division. 25 35th (NG) Santa Fe Division. 26 36th (NG) Texas Division. 27 37th (NG) Buckeye Division. 28 38th (NG) Cyclone Division.*

29 40th (NG) Sunshine Division. 30 41st (NG) Sunset Division. 31 42nd (NG) Rainbow Division. 32 76th (NA). 33 77th (NA) Statue of Liberty Division. 34 78th (NA) Lightning Division. 35 79th (NA) Lorraine Division. 36 80th (NA) Blue Ridge Division. 37 81st (NA). 38 82nd (NA). 39 83rd. 40 84th. 41 85th (NA). 42 86th. 43 87th (NA) Acorn Division. 44 88th (NA). 45 89th (NA) Middle West Division. 46 90th (NA) Tough Ombres. 47 91st (NA) Wild West Division. 48 92nd (NA) Buffalo Division. 49 93rd (NA). 50 Tank Corps. 51 Chemical Warfare Division. 52 Quartermaster Corps. 53 Rail Transport/ Rolling Kitchens Quartermaster Corps. 54 Quartermaster Corps. 55 Ambulance Corps. 56 Postal Express & Courier Service. 57 Service of Supply. 58 Advanced Section, Service of Supply. 59 District of Paris. 60 Central Records Office.

Distinctions

As with other armies, special insignia were worn by American specialist troops. There were skill badges and marksmanship awards, often worn on the breast. Mechanics, for example, wore a crossed hammer device on the sleeve, buglers a hunting horn.

Overseas chevrons were also adopted. They were worn above the left cuff, one chevron marking six months in the field. Wound badges also came into use, one chevron marking each wound, and these were worn above the right cuff. These were mostly embroidered with gold thread. A number of brassards were also worn by American infantry personnel, scouts,

for example, wore a black armband while signallers wore blue.

Although divisional insignia was very popular with the British and dominion forces, they were not really approved of by the American authorities, receiving grudging acceptance only in the summer of 1918 (and were made a requirement on 15 October 1918).

Generally known as shoulder patches, they were decorated with a huge variety of insignia (shown in the table above) and they were generally worn on the left sleeve and also sometimes painted on to helmets. They were relatively rare during the war but were worn by some of the troops

remaining in Europe. The insignia themselves were made of cloth, and officers sometimes edged their insignia with gold or silver thread.

Some regiments were entitled to wear French lanyards, issued to them for distinguished service while attached to the French Army.

Equipment

Many officers wore Sam Browne belts, map cases and binoculars. They often carried pistols and gas masks, and bread bags of the kind popular in the French Army.

Infantry were issued with the M1910 belt holding a series of canvas cartridge pouches or pockets. They also made use of an extremely uncomfortable canvas knapsack, or pack, which was worn with canvas belts and was sometimes topped with a rolled blanket. This pack carried a great deal of equipment from a razor to four pairs of spare socks and tent pegs. The belts and pack were coloured a yellowish-green.

Bayonets were suspended from the belt in wooden scabbards, and entrenching tools were generally attached to the pack. Canteens, often of French design, were used, as were a number of bread bags or grenade pouches. Gas masks, which had not been part of the American soldier's equipment when in the United States, were also quickly issued, mostly the French M2 carried in a canvas bag slung over the shoulder or worn with the bag on the chest.

US MARINES

Marines had served as naval infantry for more than a century and in many countries gradually evolved into a force (a corps in the United States) tasked with mounting small-scale expeditions or as pathfinders for larger expeditions.

The United States Marine Corps was the responsibility of the United States Navy and was seen, certainly by itself, as a crack force specializing in raids and overseas expeditions. It had valuable combat experience and was among the first to be despatched to Europe in 1917 – the 5th and 6th Marines leading the way.

Marine Distinctions

The uniform worn by the Marines resembled that worn by the Army's infantry, but there were some key distinguishing features. The overall profile was similar, and towards the end of the war, even the colouring became similar, but Marine officers sought to distinguish themselves and their men from Army units.

The Marines' tunic dated from 1912 (it was slightly modified in 1917) and was in a shade known as forest green. Initially there were no identifying discs on the collar, but the tunic itself was fastened by five buttons bearing the eagle, globe and anchor insignia of the Marine Corps. The tunic had pointed cuffs, and rank insignia was initially worn on both sleeves. Marine NCOs wore a combination of red and green rank insignia that differed from Army markings. Shirts with pointed pocket flaps were worn beneath the

▲ *United States Marines drill wearing gas masks in 1918. The first experience of gas was a shock for most troops, and drilling was essential not only in terms of putting the mask on quickly, but also in getting familiar with wearing it.*

tunic, and the collar of the shirt was sometimes used to protect the neck from rubbing by the rougher tunic collar. Marksmanship badges were common on the tunic, as were overseas stripes and wound stripes by 1918.

A lighter tropical uniform could be worn in hot weather, but was not issued in France, and an overcoat (with larger buttons than those used on the tunic) was worn in winter. Trousers were usually straight trousers in forest green rather than the uncomfortable Army breeches. NCOs had stripes on the outer leg. Puttees and boots (usually brown in preference to black) quickly replaced the impractical gaiters in the trenches.

Marines arrived in France in 1917 wearing the Montana, or lemon squeezer hat, which bore the Marines' insignia but no distinguishing cords (although officers could wear red and gold intertwined cord). It was quickly abandoned in favour of the British helmet (sometimes painted green with a stencilled badge) or, off duty, a side cap in olive drab with Marine badge.

◄ CORPORAL, 6TH MARINES, 1917 *The Montana hat was quickly replaced by the steel helmet or, off duty, the overseas cap. The hat was traditionally made of rabbitskin felt and had four ventilation holes punctured into it to reduce sweating. The leather chinstrap was usually worn on the back of the head, as the leather was uncomfortable and rubbed on the chin and neck when the soldier was marching.*

Equipment

Marine equipment was very similar to that worn by the infantry, although the studs on the cartridge belt again bore the Marines' badge, and was in a slightly greener hue than that used by the Army. The huge, cumbersome backpack was worn, however; only being discarded in the front lines in favour of grenade bags and bread bags of various kinds. The Marines' canvas equipment was sometimes stamped 'USMC' or showed that it had been supplied by the Navy. Most Marines carried the 1903 Springfield rifle, the 1905 bayonet, carried in a fabric and leather scabbard, and either a French or British gas mask worn around the neck. NCOs and officers usually carried pistols.

Most Marines wore the M1917 gas

▲ *The Marine Corps emblem of the eagle, globe and anchor, is sometimes abbreviated as 'EGA'. The eagle stands for a proud country, the globe for worldwide service, and the anchor signifies naval tradition.*

mask which was carried in a canvas pack, usually in the ready position on the chest. The gas mask was based on the British small box respirator with a face mask and a tube which connected it to a filter held within the pack. The Marines, as with the rest of the AEF, made some use of Allied equipment, particularly heavier pieces such as machine guns, grenade throwers and trench mortars. Officers were distinguished much as they were in the infantry, second lieutenants initially had no distinguishing bar on the shoulder (this only came into use in

◀ **PRIVATE, 6TH MARINES, 1918** *The 1918 overcoat was made from wool and became heavy in muddy conditions – rain ponchos kept the rain off more effectively. This soldier has also wrapped his Springfield rifle in cloth – a canvas weatherproof version was also issued and this was fastened by studs. The helmet is the 1917 model in manganese steel and it was often painted in forest green in an attempt to match the colour of the Marines' tunics.*

▶ **PRIVATE, 5TH MARINES, 1918** *The cartridge belt was greener than that worn by the infantry regiments and had USMC insignia on the studs. This cartridge belt consisted of ten pouches which could each carry two clips of five rounds for the Springfield rifle. Additional ammunition was often carried in a cotton bandolier.*

1918) but wore a belt with the Marine insignia on the buckle or Sam Browne belts, leggings and a cap with the Marine insignia.

Evolution

In early 1918, Marines were being told to use Army olive drab, but most could still be seen in forest green by the summer, officers making great efforts to retain the distinctive colour. Strangely, the forest green cloth was in use again after the war. In August 1918, Marines were also being instructed to wear eagle, globe and anchor collar discs to replace the US Army disc. Divisional insignia also made an appearance on the sleeve or helmet.

US TECHNICAL TROOPS

Although the American Expeditionary Force was largely made up of infantry units, other branches of service provided essential support and a boost to the numbers – and firepower – of the expedition.

Cavalry

Some US cavalry served in France, although few mounted actions were fought. US cavalry wore crossed sabres on their collar discs, breeches with reinforced inners, riding boots and carried pistols and carbines rather than the Springfield. When the round Montana hat was worn it had yellow cords, although helmets quickly replaced it. The horse carried most of the troopers' personal effects; the 1904 saddle was surrounded by equipment including saddle bags and spare ammunition belts, so cavalrymen were unencumbered by packs. They still, however, wore cartridge belts and carried gas masks.

Arm insignia that showed rank and badge of service came into use, in limited numbers, for many non-infantry units. Divisional insignia also made an appearance in the autumn months of 1918.

Artillery and engineers

American artillerymen arrived in France wearing the Montana hat with scarlet cords, a uniform very much resembling that of the infantry but with artillery insignia on the collar disc. This was generally crossed cannon for the field artillery and crossed cannon with two 'A's above them for anti-aircraft artillery or 'TM' above them for trench mortar units.

Artillerymen generally wore less equipment than their infantry colleagues. Engineers wore a collar disk showing a barbican and scarlet and white cords if they wore the lemon squeezer hat (the Signals Corps used orange and white cords and had crossed flags on the collar disk; personnel often wore blue brassards in the field). Collar disks often showed a company letter above or below the insignia.

◄ PRIVATE, MILITARY POLICE, 1917 *The lettering on the MP brassard could be white or red. A Military Police Corps was created in France in July 1918 and a company was allotted to each division. Divisional insignia was then often worn on the sleeve. The MPC had numerous duties, including traffic policing and processing prisoners of war.*

► PRIVATE, ENGINEER CORPS, 1918 *This engineer is lightly equipped but carries a British Small Box Respirator slung around his neck and available for quick access. Note the dog tag around the soldier's neck – usually a round aluminium disc stamped with the soldier's name, unit and enlistment date.*

There were a number of other specialist branches or distinguishing marks for specialists. Military police, responsible to the Provost Marshal General, for example, wore blue or black brassards with 'MP' in red or white ('PG', for Provost Guards, and 'PM' for Provost Marshal, also existed). A Military Police Corps was formed in July 1918 (120 men) and this is supposed to have worn a collar disc bearing 'MP'. MPs were expected to pay considerable attention to regulations, and wear uniforms accordingly. They became part of the occupation forces and remained in Europe until 1922.

▲ *Pilot Eddie Rickenbacker (centre), the most decorated American pilot during World War I, with other members of the 94th Squadron. Note the insignia painted on to the side of the biplane, which led to the squadron's informal name of the 'Hat-in-the-Ring' squadron.*

Train personnel were largely the responsibility of the Quartermaster Corps and the Motor Transport Corps. Branch of service colours were buff and purple respectively, and both organizations made liberal use of brassards to denote specific kinds of transportation. Divisional train personnel also wore a 'T' on their collar disk.

A US Tank Corps was formed early in 1918, using grey as its arm of service colour. The Tank Corps used a variety of insignia (including a collar disc showing a Mark IV tank) and showed a preference for leather jackets and protective leather caps.

Army Air Service

The Americans had been slow to grasp the potential of military aviation, despite their enthusiasm for powered flight in the early 1900s. As with most armies, flying personnel originally formed a branch of the engineers, specifically the Signals Corps. Uniforms were initially based on those worn by the Signals Corps (with crossed flags on the collar disc for enlisted men, and on the collar itself for officers), although officers were inspired by French and British styles, and made use of aviator boots and Sam Browne belts. Wings were also worn and were officially sanctioned (a wings and propeller device coming into use) in 1918. Side caps, often privately tailored, were very popular. Flying gear was largely borrowed from the Royal Flying Corps or the French service. Squadron badges were worn on flying gear and occasionally on tunics, and most flying officers carried a pistol as a weapon of choice.

Health and Law

Most medical personnel wore the red cross brassard in the field along with a pouch bearing a first aid kit. Medical officers wore the winged staff and serpents, long established as a symbol of the medical profession.

▶ Captain, 148th Aero Squadron, 1918
The aviation service was a part of the Signal Corps, and insignia from that branch of service was retained until 1918.

PORTUGAL

Portugal was emerging from a decade of political chaos at the start of the war, and managed to stay neutral until 1916. In Feburary of that year, at Britain's request, Portugal interned German ships anchored in Portuguese ports, and in retaliation Germany declared war on the country in March 1916. A Portuguese expeditionary force (Corpo Expedicionário Português, or CEP) was established, and in 1917 30,000 soldiers were sent to Flanders.

Infantry

The whole Portuguese military had been reformed in 1911, following the abolition of the monarchy and the establishment of the republic. New uniforms were introduced, slowly, and the Portuguese sent to northern Europe had to be speedily brought up to date and prepared to face the cold northern climate. They would be equipped with woollen (rather than cotton) uniforms in a colour similar to horizon blue (it was slightly greyer).

Tunics had standing collars and breeches were worn with puttees. Light brown boots were common initially, but these were often replaced by French or British boots, and officers generally preferred riding boots or aviators' boots. Privates and NCOs initially wore a peaked cap but then switched to a steel helmet that was either of the British model or of a Portuguese design with a fluted top for additional strength. This helmet was actually produced in Britain and it was painted the same shade of the uniform. Officers wore a peaked cap with leather chinstrap, a tunic that was very similar to the British pattern (with horizon blue shirts and black or blue ties) and Sam Browne belts.

▶ **Captain, 10th Cavalry Regiment, 1917** *The cavalry wore crossed sabre insignia on their collars. In winter, all manner of civilian items were worn by Portuguese troops as supplies from home proved problematic. This officer has acquired a driver's fur coat.*

◀ **Private, 21st Infantry Battalion, 1916** *Portuguese troops in Africa suffered from enormous shortages of equipment – this man's tunic has been bleached almost white in the sun and is showing its age. The helmet sometimes bore a green and red Portuguese cockade.*

Infantrymen wore crossed rifles in black on their standing collars (officers wore the same insignia in gold) and on the peaked cap, if this was worn. Rank insignia was worn on the shoulder (bars of cord on the shoulder straps) with NCOs having one to four stripes in light blue edged with dark blue and officers adopting a similar system but in gold thread. Generals wore three silver stars on their cuffs and a five-pointed star on peaked caps. Most infantry regiments sent to Flanders wore a unit identifier (usually the regimental number) on the upper sleeve on a square of fabric.

Equipment had originally been purchased from the Germans but khaki webbing had been developed in 1911 for use with the blue-grey uniform. However, those Portuguese sent to the Western Front were usually issued with British equipment and weapons. Greatcoats were double-breasted for privates and NCOs and single-breasted for officers, both types having falling collars. Various other coats were quickly brought into service to keep out the penetrating cold of Flanders.

Some divisional insignia came into use in 1918, mostly variations of geometric shapes in green and red.

Other Arms

Uniforms for other branches of service very much resembled that of the infantrymen. The collar insignia differed, with the crossed rifles being replaced by crossed swords (or lances) for the cavalry, crossed cannon barrels for the artillery (this varied on the collar according to the type of artillery), crossed machine gun barrels for machine gunners and a tower for engineers. Regimental numerals were often worn above the insignia on the peaked cap. Pilots wore a crossed wheel and, again, equipped themselves in a style similar to that of British and French pilots.

Colonial Troops

Most Portuguese troops in the colonies wore khaki but troops sent out from Portugal itself often found themselves issued with a light grey cotton uniform which very quickly faded to white. The regimental numeral was worn on the collar on this uniform, but rank insignia was again restricted to the shoulder straps. Soldiers sent from Portugal were often equipped with a white or grey tropical helmet, although slouch hats or peaked caps were more comfortable and quickly adopted, and this helmet was sometimes worn with

a spike and sometimes with a red and green Portuguese cockade. Native troops wore khaki uniforms with a red fez or khaki pillbox cap. They often fought and marched barefoot,

▼ **PORTUGUESE INFANTRY INSIGNIA, 1917** *1 Crossed rifles for infantry. 2 Crossed swords for the cavalry. 3 Cannon barrels for the artillery. 4 Lances for the Lancers. 5 A single tower for the engineers. 6 The crossed barrels of machine guns for the machine gunners.*

▶ **SERGEANT, 20TH INFANTRY BATTALION, 1917** *The Portuguese wore a peculiar ribbed helmet, but British Brodies, painted or in green, were also common. The ribbed helmet had been of a design initially tested for British troops, but the Brodie had proved more resilient in testing. The stock of ribbed helmets was then donated to the Portuguese.*

Portuguese Troops Sent to the Western Front

First Division
1st, 2nd and 3rd Brigades
Second Division
4th, 5th and 6th Brigades
Cyclist Battalion
Mining Battalion
Railway Battalion
Heavy Artillery Corps

although puttees were sometimes worn with boots in areas of dense bush or thorns, and carried equipment and weapons predating 1911.

BELGIUM

Forced into war in August 1914 by a German invasion, Belgium maintained the struggle right through until the armistice of 1918. Belgium's troops fought not only in Europe (a small strip of Belgian territory escaped occupation), but also in Africa. The Belgian Congo was a substantial territory, which held huge natural resources that the Belgians were determined to retain.

Unprepared

The Belgian Army was in the throes of reform when Germany invaded. Uniforms were being overhauled in 1914 but the Belgian soldier often found himself sent to the front in a distinctly 19th-century uniform. Reforms in 1913 had improved the situation a little, by enforcing the adoption of more practical colours for facings, or by phasing out dolmans in favour of practical tunics, but the situation in 1914 was chaotic, and older items still predominated.

Infantrymen

The 1913 tunic resembled that worn by French chasseurs. It was very dark blue, single breasted, had a standing collar, pointed cuffs, side pockets and was fastened with nine gold buttons. An earlier version, first adopted in 1897, was also seen. Facings were displayed as piping on the collar, down the front of the tunic and on the pointed cuffs. In 1911 the infantry had switched from scarlet facings to blue-grey. Trousers were also supposed to have piping down the seams but this was usually not worn. Equipment was in black leather. Belts and cartridge pouches (a single one, the M1896, worn on the very front of the belt) were black, and the knapsack was also of black leather reinforced by a cane skeleton. A blanket was worn rolled over the top and a mess tin was strapped on the back. Canteens and haversacks were also worn.

Infantrymen were initially issued with a shako (M1893), which had a red band and golden royal crest on the front. This was covered by black oilskin bearing a red or white regimental numeral on the outline of a red shield.

◀ PRIVATE, 9TH REGIMENT, 1914
The shako shown here had a brass shield insignia with the regimental number. It is protected by black oilcloth here.

▶ PRIVATE, 14TH REGIMENT, 1915
Belgian troops did adopt a more practical uniform, but this individual still carries the heavy knapsack.

A cap, in the style of the French chasseurs, was also sometimes worn.

Most troops went to war dressed in the dark blue double-breasted greatcoat (M1906), which was fastened by bronze buttons bearing the regimental numeral. NCOs wore silver chevrons piped red. Officers wore stars on their collars and additional piping on their caps.

Belgium's regiment of grenadiers initially wore a bearskin but quickly switched to a kepi. They wore red piping. The light infantry (carabiniers) wore a Tyrolean hunting hat,

▲ *The Belgian Army used strong-muscled dogs to haul heavy machine guns to the front. Dogs were also used by other forces to deliver vital messages between the trenches.*

with turned up brim, green tunics and yellow facings. The cyclist battalion wore the same uniform but with a kepi in French chasseur style (which again had yellow piping).

Adaptation

Uniform changes were dramatic as depots were overrun, supplies fell short and modern warfare jeopardized the use of colourful facings. Brown corduroy trousers were used, shakos were replaced by French-style kepis with arm of service piping (all usually covered with black oilskin) and metallic buttons were painted grey or black. The dark blue greatcoat continued to be worn. In the spring of 1915 khaki cloth began to be issued to surviving Belgian units in sufficient quantities for the uniform to be overhauled again. Double-breasted

▼ DOG-PULLED CART, 1917 *The distinctive Belgian Army uniform in the war extended to their unique use of dogs to pull machine guns.*

khaki greatcoats were issued with shoulder straps piped in grey-blue for the infantry, red for the grenadiers and yellow for the carabiniers. Tunics of the same cloth were also worn with collar patches in red piped blue for the infantry, scarlet piped blue for the grenadiers and green with yellow piping for the carabiniers, and regimental numerals on the shoulder straps (a grenade for grenadiers). Steel helmets were also being introduced: the Belgians adopted the Adrian helmet, generally issued with a Belgian lion insignia (an insignia also worn on the infantry's buttons). Many officers adopted a peaked cap with this badge or with a regimental numeral below the black-yellow-red cockade.

Cotton webbing was also introduced, although the black leather belts continued to be worn into 1916. The 1915 webbing resembled the British pattern webbing but had four cartridge pouches on either side of the belt buckle. A new, lighter, canvas knapsack was also issued. Trousers were also in khaki and were sometimes – at least by officers – worn with piping as for the greatcoat.

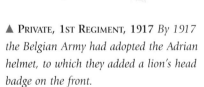

▲ PRIVATE, 1ST REGIMENT, 1917 *By 1917 the Belgian Army had adopted the Adrian helmet, to which they added a lion's head badge on the front.*

◄ **PRIVATE, 1ST GUIDES, 1914** *The coat being carried here was green and stretched down to the guide's hussar boots. He carries a Mauser carbine and would also have a curved sword and a lance.*

fortress artillery, which wore the number of the fortress. Grey blue or dark blue breeches were worn with red piping, although black overalls or brown corduroy trousers began to replace this colourful combination in early 1915. Inevitably, the uniform of 1914 was quickly swept away by events and khaki quickly replaced the blue uniform for field and horse artillery. Both types of artillery wore blue collar patches piped red with divisional (Roman) numerals on the shoulder straps. Engineers had worn shakos bearing insignia representing a helmet, blue tunics (piped red) and trousers as for the artillery. By 1915 they wore a very similar uniform to that of the artillery but with black collar patches piped red. Train troops wore light blue collar patches piped dark blue.

Mounted Troops

Belgium began the war with varied regiments of colourfully uniformed cavalry. There were two regiments of guides wearing green tunics with scarlet facings (collars, cuff piping and piping down the front of the tunic), scarlet trousers (piped yellow) and brown fur colpacks (with red bags). These troops, like all cavalry, carried lances, with pennons in the national colours, and carbines - generally Mausers. Most also wore cavalry boots with spurs or ankle boots with spurs and leather gaiters. There

were five regiments of lancers with blue tunics; faced crimson for the first two regiments, white for the third, blue for the fourth and white for the fifth, with grey-blue trousers. The lancers also wore a very 19th-century Polish lancer cap, the square-topped czapka, with a regimental number painted on the black oilskin cover.

Belgium's other arms of service had the same need for change as that felt by the infantry. Progress was rapid, if uneven, as the army switched from greens, reds and blues to the safe, but drab, khaki manufactured in Britain.

Artillery

Artillerymen wore a tunic and breeches similar in design to that worn by French artillerymen. They wore a distinctive colpack (a fur shako without a peak) bearing crossed cannon barrels as an insignia. The dark blue tunics were worn with scarlet piping, and regimental numerals were worn on the shoulder straps; except for

► **PRIVATE, 1ST LANCERS, 1914** *The square-topped cap, or czapka, was common to all of Europe's lancer regiments. It was usually worn in an oilskin cover, but offered almost no protection to the head.*

▲ *Belgian cavalry riding down a street in the centre of Brussels.*

elite guides) and had varied collar patches on the standing collars. This was crimson piped green for the guides, white piped blue for the lancers and yellow piped blue for the mounted chasseurs. Officers, as for the infantry, wore stars on the collars of their tunics or on their riding capes. They generally wore brown leather belts and pistol holsters, as well as brown riding boots with spurs. Cavalry continued to distinguish themselves by wearing breeches and cavalry boots

▼ 2ND LIEUTENANT, 2ND LANCERS, 1918
The lion's head shown on the helmet was also used on the buttons of Belgian infantry and cavalry.

rather than trousers and puttees and by carrying considerably less equipment than the average infantryman.

African Service

Belgian troops in Africa adopted khaki long before their counterparts in Europe. Tropical helmets were worn, as were slouch hats and peaked caps, most of which bore the Belgian cockade and/or the Belgian lion badge in a wreathed and crowned shield – which was the official insignia of colonial troops.

Most European troops wore khaki shirts, officers preferring tunics that were similar to those worn by the British. Native troops wore khaki but also made use of older light blue tunics and trousers or khaki shorts. They generally wore a red fez with a light blue cover. Red waistbands were also sometimes worn. Equipment was generally out of date or had been purchased from British or South African suppliers.

Belgium's mounted chasseurs wore shakos, very similar to those of the French chasseurs and hussars, but, again, usually covered with a black cover. They also wore dark blue tunics with yellow facings for the 1st Regiment and red for the 2nd and 4th Regiments, as well as grey-blue trousers with white piping. There were supposed to be four regiments, but the third had still not been raised in 1914. Gendarmes wore bearskins and dark blue tunics piped red, with grenades on the collar.

All these distinctions quickly faded away as khaki was adopted in 1915 and the Adrian helmet spelled an end to colpacks and czapkas. The cavalry all wore regimental numerals on their shoulder straps (supplemented by a crown for the

ITALY

Italy was unprepared for large-scale warfare and had spent much of its military budget in a recent war with the Ottoman empire. Despite severe limitations, it eventually fielded a sizeable army in May 1915, which survived – but only just – mutiny and dissolution in the dark days of 1917.

▼ GENERAL OF BRIGADE, 1917 *The 1909 uniform was of finer cloth for senior officers and of a more fashionable cut. The cap was well made with a leather peak and a rounded top which kept it from getting too wet.*

On the Cusp of War

Italian infantry had been equipped with dark blue greatcoats and black shakos in 1909, but in that year a greyish green (more green than grey) had been adopted and was worn throughout the Army. Experience in Libya in 1911 and 1912 proved that such a decision had been a wise one, although shortages meant that second line units often went to the front in older blue uniforms.

Italy's infantry was divided into line regiments (146 at the outbreak), 12 regiments of light infantry (the famous Bersaglieri), mountain troops (8 regiments of Alpini) and territorial militias. The line units included a regiment of grenadiers.

Line Infantry

Tunics were issued in 1909 with a standing collar, no exterior pockets and concealed buttons. It was smart and practical. The tunic had rolled shoulder straps (preventing slings and belts from slipping) and, on each collar, a collar patch in brigade colours. The grenadier regiment had red patches with silver lace; most line regiments had a simpler coloured version with a Savoy star where the collar closes, and a button at the back. The colour patch was a single colour for some brigades, or a variety of stripes. Regiments were distinguished by buttons and by regimental numerals on caps.

The Italian infantryman wore a cap with a leather peak and with a regimental numeral beneath a royal crown. The M1909 kepi was stiffer and rounder, the M1915 had a baggier top. Officers wore a more rigid version. Generals wore an eagle badge and red and silver ornamentation. Adrian helmets began to arrive in October 1915, initially stamped with French insignia. They were soon manufactured without an embossed badge. Italians painted on unit insignia or stencilled numerals on to a brown-green helmet cover. The Italian helmet, which was manufactured as a single piece rather than riveted, was an improvement on the French model.

A greatcoat was worn with Savoy stars on the falling collar, and a lighter cape – with a star of Savoy on the collar – was also issued to some infantrymen. The war with Austria-Hungary was largely fought in mountainous, and very cold, terrain. Infantrymen wore grey-green breeches, which fastened beneath the knee. Puttees and ankle boots were preferred.

▼ *A group of Italian scouts gathers on a mountain trail with their bicycles.*

▲ *Italian Bersaglieri, with their distinctive round hats, at camp.*

◄ SERGEANT, 33RD INFANTRY REGIMENT, 1917 *The 1912 cape was a popular item – the collar could be worn up and the cape fastened at the front.*

▼ CORPORAL, 115TH INFANTRY REGIMENT, 1915 *The tunic had rolls of cloth at the end of the shoulder to prevent equipment sliding off.*

bugle and crossed rifle badge surmounted by an eagle. Taller mountain boots, for ankle support, were worn with puttees or high socks.

Later in the war special assault units (called 'arditi') were formed. They wore a tunic with an open collar, and usually a black or khaki polo-neck, with black swallow-tailed patches on each side (again with the Savoy star). A sword within wreaths (silver on black cloth) badge was worn on the left sleeve. Officers wore a flaming grenade badge on their headgear.

Bersaglieri
Italy's elite unit, the Bersaglieri, wore a distinctive round hat of waterproofed felt and a blackened cockerel-feather plume (which hung down over the right side). It had an Italian red-white-green cockade and a bugle horn and crossed rifles badge, but the hat was normally worn with a cover and stencilled insignia. A red fez was also sometimes worn. The tunic was as for the line, but had a swallow-tailed collar patch in reddish brown. An M1912 cape was preferred to the greatcoat.

Equipment dated back to 1907 and was in leather, often painted green. It consisted of a belt and four cartridge pouches carrying a total of 96 cartridges. A grey-green knapsack carried 12 further cartridges as well as personal effects. Gas masks, canteens and haversacks were also carried.

Alpine Infantry
Known as the Alpini, Italy's Alpine troops wore a similar uniform, but with green collar patches. They wore a distinctive felt hunting hat with a domed crown and wide brim (usually upturned around the sides and at the back) with a feather. Alpini wore a

Cavalry

Italy began the war with 30 regiments of cavalry, all of which bore regional titles (as did infantry regiments).

Italian cavalrymen wore a grey-green tunic similar in design to that of the infantry. It too bore collar patches that distinguished individual regiments. Line cavalry, light cavalry and lancers were numbered together. The first four regiments were line cavalry and had pink, red black and yellow facings (collars, piping to caps, cuffs and shoulder straps). The 5th to 10th Regiments plus the 25th and 26th were lancers. The 5th had white facings, the 6th red, the 7th pink, the 8th light green, the 9th orange and the 10th yellow. The 25th had black and the 26th light blue. Line cavalry wore a flaming grenade badge on their caps, lancers wore crossed lances beneath a crown and behind the regimental numeral in a circle. Light cavalry had hunting horns on their caps and swallow-tailed piping of one colour superimposed on a collar of another colour. The details were: 11th black/red; 12th yellow/black; 13th pink/black; 14th orange/black; 15th black/red; 16th black/white; 17th red/black; 18th black/light green; 19th white/light blue; 20th white/black; 21st black/pink; 22nd orange/black; 23rd and 24th red/white; 27th white/pink; 28th red/light blue; 29th light green/white and 30th red/yellow.

Mounted policemen (carabinieri) wore black collars with white lace bars. They also preserved the black bicorne.

Trumpeters wore a hunting horn device on their sleeve, marksmen a hunting rifle.

Cavalrymen wore breeches with riding boots and spurs, or black leather gaiters with ankle boots. They also wore cartridge pouches swung diagonally across the body (the 1897 bandolier). Additional ammunition for the soldier's carbine was often slung around the horse's neck.

Crowned helmets had put in an appearance for the line cavalry early on in the war (sometimes worn with covers), but these were replaced by a grey-green cap, pointed fore and aft, which was itself abolished in 1916 and was eventually replaced by the Adrian-style helmet (with stencilled devices). Infantry kepis with cavalry stencils were sometimes worn. Capes, rather than coats, were worn. Black chevrons on the tunic denoted NCOs, while embroidered stars on the cuff and silver metallic lace on the cap denoted officers, as did collars in a single facing colour.

Most cavalry were dismounted in 1916, either serving as infantry or, following the reduction in squadrons, providing spare personnel.

Artillery and Technical Troops

Italian artillery wore uniforms of a similar design to that of the infantry, but their collar patches were tailed

▼ Italian lancers on parade in full dress in 1915. Note the cross of Savoy on the front of the helmet.

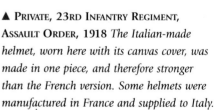

▲ PRIVATE, 23RD INFANTRY REGIMENT, ASSAULT ORDER, 1918 The Italian-made helmet, worn here with its canvas cover, was made in one piece, and therefore stronger than the French version. Some helmets were manufactured in France and supplied to Italy.

rather than rectangular (they curved down to a point at the rear). For field artillery the collar patch was black piped yellow, and black piped red for engineers (there were six regiments in 1915). Bridging companies played an important role in a theatre dominated by wide rivers, and they were distinguished by black collar patches piped pink and a cap badge that had a flaming grenade bearing the company numeral above crossed anchors. Mountain artillery wore this style collar patch on the uniform of the Alpini. Cap badges also differed with field artillery wearing a grenade over crossed cannon barrels, engineers wearing a grenade over crossed axes and mountain artillery having an eagle over a bugle horn resting on crossed cannon barrels. Officers wore stiffer

▼ **PRIVATE, 3RD ALPINI REGIMENT, 1916** *The felt hat was a distinctive feature of these units – it bore a black bugle badge on the front – but the equipment carried here is of the standard kind first issued in 1907.*

caps with eagle badges, extra lace, and stars on the cuffs, as for other arms.

Some autonomous machine gun regiments were also formed and these were distinguished by the following; 1st Regiment, white collar patches with a red vertical stripe; 2nd Regiment, red with a white stripe; 3rd, green with a blue stripe; 4th, blue with a green stripe. Some independent groups also served and they had red (Fiat), blue

(St Etienne) and green (Maxim), all with three white vertical stripes. They also wore machine gun badges in silver on their sleeves. Pilots usually wore the uniform of their original regiment, but with wing insignia on their sleeves.

▼ **PRIVATE, 17TH CAVALRY REGIMENT 1915** *The cap shown here had a leather peak and piping in light cavalry colours. Ammunition for the trooper's carbine is carried in a leather bandolier.*

SERBIA AND MONTENEGRO

The first country to be invaded, Serbia suffered heavily in the war. Montenegro, a neighbouring kingdom, supported the Serbs and paid with occupation by the Austro-Hungarians.

Serbia's Army

Although it had gained in the Balkan wars, Serbia's army was exhausted by the years of struggle. There were shortages of all kind, from uniforms to ammunition. The result was that the Serbian Army took to the field in a variety of uniforms and carrying various types of rifles (the Mauser or the Mosin-Nagant supplied by Russia in the summer of 1914). Officers could purchase revolvers privately from an approved list of makers. There were few machine guns. Most soldiers were issued with a tunic and a cap, every other man receiving a greatcoat. There was a severe shortage of leather equipment (pouches and bandoliers) and knapsacks. Most men rolled personal effects in a blanket.

Theoretically a new uniform had been adopted in 1908. The cloth was grey-green but the actual shade of cloth differed even within regiments. Infantrymen wore a soft cap, with a v-shape cut into the crown at the front and rear, and for officers this had a leather peak and royal cypher (a Cyrillic 'P' beneath a crown) cockade. Some officers wore caps similar to those worn by Russian officers. The tunic had a standing collar with coloured patches denoting the branch of service. Shoulder straps were rolled to support strapping. Greatcoats were double-breasted with coloured patches on the collar and fold-back cuffs. Officers wore shoulderboards in the Russian style in silver or gold, piped in branch of service colour and with metal stars bearing a regimental number denoting rank. Their collar patches were in velvet. Some officers wore a silver sash with red and blue strands on duty. NCOs wore stars on their shoulder straps but it was extremely difficult to tell NCO uniforms from those worn by the men.

A grey uniform had been issued to some troops for summer service. Some blue coats and trousers, worn before the 1908 reforms, continued to be worn. This was particularly the case in second-line divisions.

◀ SERBIA, PRIVATE, 12TH INFANTRY REGIMENT, 1914 *The classic Serb cap (known as the shikatch) tops a uniform introduced in 1912 during the Balkan Wars but which itself was based on regulations introduced in October 1908.*

▶ SERBIA, PRIVATE, 2ND INFANTRY REGIMENT, 1916 *Serb troops fighting alongside the French around Salonika were equipped with French helmets and equipment.*

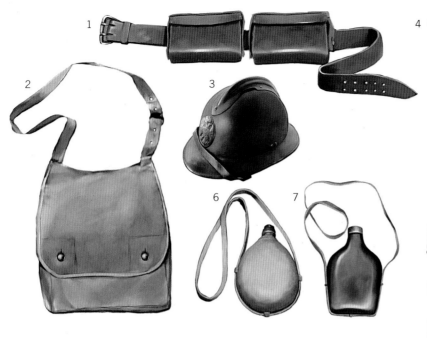

▲ **SERBIAN KIT** *1 Cartridge pouches based on the Russian model. 2 Canvas haversack. 3 Serbian Adrian helmet. 4 Mauser rifle from 1910. 5 Trench knife. 6 Early model canteen. 7 Canteen issued in 1916.*

▶ **MONTENEGRO, CORPORAL, 4TH INFANTRY REGIMENT, 1915** *The uniform was simple and the rifle, which was supplied by Russia, was supplemented by private items.*

Militiamen were usually just issued a single-shot rifle and officers were given a tunic and cap.

After evacuation from Albania in late 1915, the remnants of the Serbian Army were re-equipped with French or British supplies. An Adrian helmet with Serbian eagle was issued to officers and some NCOs. Some khaki greatcoats were issued, along with horizon blue or khaki tunics and trousers. Equipment conformed to French or British standards. Puttees or leggings

▼ *Serbian troops defending Belgrade in 1915.*

(white cloth bound with brown straps, known as 'navoii') were worn, although officers preferred boots. The leggings lasted for around three months in campaign conditions, and many Serbs went barefoot.

Infantry were distinguished by crimson collar patches, cavalry by dark blue, artillery by black, engineers by pink and administration by grey. Officers wore piping to their caps, shoulderboards and trousers. Gendarmes wore blue tunics with red facings, shoulder straps, and dark blue breeches. Cavalry could also be distinguished by the occasional use of dark red breeches.

Montenegro

Serbia's ally, Montenegro, fielded some 35,000 men (provided with 25,000 Mosin-Nagant rifles). The infantry wore a green uniform introduced in 1910. Officers were uniformed and equipped in a style almost identical to that of Russian officers, the royal coat of arms being worn on the cap and on the buttons. Officers' shoulderboards were also in the Russian style with piping in branch of service colours: red for infantry, light blue for machine

gunners, green for engineers, and yellow for the artillery) and gold or silver thread with stars and a strip of branch of service colour. NCOs and privates wore a simple tunic with no unit or branch of service distinctions. They also wore a pillbox cap in green and a cockade that varied according to rank. Officers carried Russian swords (which did not have a hand guard) on a black leather belt, and a revolver. Infantrymen carried very little in the way of equipment, usually only the rolled blanket, a canteen and a haversack. Cartridge belts were usually of the Russian model.

ROMANIA

The Romanian decision to enter the war in the summer of 1916 was opportunistic, designed to take advantage of a successful Russian offensive and the apparent weakness of Austria-Hungary. Romania's military was, however, dreadfully unprepared for combat and short of money and equipment. Defeat in 1916 and then occupation of most of the country in 1917 was inevitable.

Early Uniforms

Romanian troops wore a grey-green uniform that had been adopted in early 1912 and replaced dark blue tunics for the infantry, brown tunics for the artillery and red or blue dolmans for the cavalry. Such was the state of the country that these older uniforms could still be seen as late as 1916. In design the new uniform resembled that worn by the Austro-Hungarians, as did the design of the cap (although the front of the crown was pointed). Officers wore a version with a black leather peak. Caps bore a regimental numeral or a national cockade, and were piped in branch of service colours.

Tunics had standing collars with branch of service collar patches and piping on the shoulder straps (which also bore regimental numerals). Piping was also repeated on the breeches for the infantry. Romanian cavalry and artillerymen generally wore black breeches and cavalry boots. The infantry wore puttees in a variety of colours and boots of military or civilian design.

Officers initially wore a stiffer cap with Romanian cockade (blue, yellow, red), leather peak and chinscales. They also had metallic stripes on their shoulder straps. When Romania

entered the war, rank distinctions in the form of rows of gold lace were also worn at the corners of the collar. A gold sash with red and blue interwoven threads was sometimes worn on duty. NCOs were distinguished by bars of lace across the shoulder straps.

Infantry wore a grey greatcoat and cavalry wore a much longer version. Both had falling collars with

◄ LIEUTENANT, 6TH INFANTRY REGIMENT, 1916 *Many Romanian officers would be uniformed in French horizon blue by 1918 although supply of this cloth was haphazard, and this uniform shows the greenish-blue style worn in 1916. Khaki was also often used and this was supplied by the British. Generals wore a similar uniform but with black breeches. The cockade is in the national colours of blue, yellow and red.*

► PRIVATE, 10TH CAVALRY REGIMENT, 1916 *Cavalry wore a long greatcoat in winter with the arrowhead device on the collar. The boots had notches in them, in hussar style; a gilt rosette and spurs were usually worn.*

◀ PRIVATE, 4TH ARTILLERY REGIMENT, 1917
The Austro-Hungarian style cap was piped in black but no unit number was worn there. Artillery, as well as some cavalry, were supposed to wear black breeches.

Romania's cavalry was mobile, highly trained and very motivated both on horseback and as dismounted infantry, the cavalry were elite troops that bolstered the Romanian forces wherever they went. Cavalry were divided into rosiori (named after one of the oldest cities in Romania) and calarasi (a city near the border of Bulgaria). The rosiori, some ten regiments strong, formerly wore red tunics; the calarasi, consisting of eight regiments, used to wear blue. The rosiori wore black patches and piping, the calarasi red (with black piping on the collar patch). The rosiori carried lances (made of steel in the German pattern), as well as sabres and carbines like the calarasi. Cavalry officers sometimes wore Hessian boots and black cloaks with gold shoulder cords.

Artillerymen still continued to wear brown jackets although the grey-green version with black patches (piped red for engineers) and piping replaced these. Crossed cannon were worn on the cap beneath the regimental numeral. Officers wore black greatcoats and golden sashes. Aviators wore engineers' uniforms but with wings on the arm or 'Av' on the shoulder straps and on the caps.

Developments

Romania had been isolated and starved of resources between 1914 and 1916, but some French equipment made its way into the country in late 1916. The Adrian helmet, bearing a royal cypher ('F' for Ferdinand), was supplied by France via Russia and saw service in

1917 and 1918. Uniforms were also supplied by Russia and France, and cloth was sent by Italy.

Inevitably, great variations in colours could be seen, especially in 1918 when materials captured from Russian supplies were pressed into service. Horizon blue uniforms were relatively common among officers in 1917 and 1918, and horizon blue greatcoats were also issued to the troops in 1918 (as were British khaki coats and trousers). French equipment also predominated in the later months of the war. In 1919 Romanian troops in Hungary could be seen with Adrian helmets, French greatcoats and British webbing equipment.

coloured branch of service patches. Infantry equipment was relatively sparse and most troops carried rolled blankets, haversacks and canteens. Some knapsacks (of the German model) were also used. Most infantrymen carried the Mannlicher rifle with ammunition carried in brown cartridge pouches (one on each side of the belt buckle) dating mostly from the 1890s.

Infantrymen were distinguished by red patches and piping, riflemen by green with battalion numbers on the shoulder straps and, beneath a hunting horn, on the cap.

▶ PRIVATE, 5TH INFANTRY REGIMENT, 1917
The pointed cap (known as a capela cap) was a distinctive mark of Romanian troops and was worn by infantry, cavalry and artillery. It bore the regimental number in red. This soldier is lucky to have the regulation 1891 cartridge pouches for his 1893 Mannlicher rifle.

GREECE

The Greek military sided with the Allies and participated in the campaign in the Balkans in 1917 and 1918. It then went on to fight a vicious war with the Turks in Anatolia.

Chaotic Beginnings

Greece had gained significantly from the Balkan Wars, being rewarded at the Treaty of London in early 1914 with 55,000km² (21,2300 square miles) of

◀ COLONEL, 5TH INFANTRY REGIMENT, 1917
The cap shown here replaced a tall French-style kepi, although the latter could still be seen in the early stages of the war. This colonel has three stars on his shoulder straps, a lieutenant colonel would have two and a major would have one.

▲ *Greek cavalry, wearing soft caps and carmine-piped uniforms, in Salonika, 1915.*

additional territory. Now a regional power, opportunities were lost when political rivalries plunged the country into civil strife. The camp opposed to the Central Powers emerged victorious in 1917 and war was declared in June.

The confused years between 1913 and 1917 affected the military on many levels. Some units were loyal to the prime minister, Eleftherios Venizelos, and assisted his pro-Allied policies. Most troops remained loyal to the monarchy, and maintained a neutral, if not hostile stance. Only in 1917, with Allied assistance and equipment, were sizeable Greek forces mobilized.

The royal army had uniforms that were inspired by contemporary Danish fashions (King George, who had died in 1913, was of Danish origin). A greenish khaki uniform had been introduced in 1908. Most troops wore tunics cut very similarly to British tunics, but officers adopted tunics

resembling those of their Austro-Hungarian equivalents. Tunics were single breasted with piping around the collar and coloured shoulder straps. These had metallic lace for officers with branch of service piping and six-pointed stars to denote rank. NCOs wore chevrons below the elbow (for infantry these were gold stripes piped in red).

In summer a cotton uniform was worn but without shoulder straps and with much lighter trousers. In winter troops wore a brownish greatcoat, which was single breasted and had piping on the cuffs and collar and coloured shoulder straps. Peasant leggings, such as those worn in the Serbian Army, were also found on Greek troops.

The Greek Army wore a peaked cap inspired by Danish styles. This had a cloth peak for NCOs and enlisted men and a leather peak and chinstrap for officers. Branch of service piping ran around the crown of the cap and a Greek cockade (blue and white) beneath a crown was worn on the front. Officers had bands of khaki lace around the hat band (up to three

◀ PRIVATE, 2ND EVZONES BATTALION, 1918
These elite soldiers started the war wearing white breeches, and the cloth headgear known as the 'farizan', but in the field this was replaced with the much more practical and protective Adrian helmet when in action.

▶ SERGEANT, 2ND INFANTRY REGIMENT, 1916
Greek infantry carried the 1908 leather belt with cartridge pouches with ammunition for the 1903 Mannlicher.

generally also of natural leather. The infantry had red shoulder straps and piping, and gold metal buttons.

There was an elite corps of rifles called Evzones who had adopted distinctive dress by 1917. They wore a longer tunic (with folding collar), piped in red and with red facings, but replaced the usual cap with a soft green fez (the 'farizan') which drooped over the left ear and had a long black tassel. They wore their traditional white breeches and leggings (tied below the knee with black or blue garters) with a white kilt (later replaced by standard khaki breeches and puttees). The Evzones had black or natural leather shoes with pompoms but, again, these were replaced for service in the field.

Some militia units continued to wear the older-style blue tunics and white trousers. Towards the end of the war, Greece was flooded with large quantities of French equipment and French Adrian helmets (bearing a cross in a shield beneath a crown) which were painted khaki. British khaki cloth (of a browner hue) was also worn.

Cavalry and Technical Troops

Greek cavalry wore breeches and riding boots and discarded most infantry equipment in favour of ammunition bandoliers and haversacks. Piping and shoulder straps were purple and buttons (and rank chevrons) were silver. Artillerymen had black shoulder straps and piping and infantry uniforms. They wore silver buttons and chevrons, as did the engineers (with blue facings and piping). Train troops had green facings and piping.

bands for company officers, one wide band with one to three narrower bands above for field officers). Generals wore ornamental gold lace on their caps.

Infantry

Infantrymen wore tunics with standing collars and caps as above. They also had long trousers and ankle boots, but these were often replaced by trousers with puttees. Infantry equipment was based on the German 1895 model with three cartridge pouches in natural (brown) leather and a knapsack, canteen and haversack. Straps were

Equipment

Greek army equipment was similar to that in use with European armies. There were two cartridge pouches in brown leather with a further reserve pouch (containing 60 rounds) worn at the rear. The bayonet was suspended with brown frogging from the belt and protected by a black scabbard. The Arisaka rifle, adopted in 1905 (and known as the 38 model), was the most common infantry weapon, cavalry and artillery making use of a carbine of similar design. The Arisaka was produced in great quantities and was sold to Russia and to Britain.

JAPAN

Japan fought a successful war and emerged as a regional power, taking over territory in the Pacific, dominating China and intervening in eastern Russia.

Other Areas of Conflict

Japan had finished the 19th century with a successful war against China (the Sino-Japanese War of 1894–95) and began the 20th century with victory against Russia (which concluded in 1905). These triumphs were the culmination of years of military reform in which French and German advisers had played a role.

Japan would send a relatively large expedition against the German enclave at Tsingtao in China and into various German Pacific islands. It also despatched a naval force to the

Mediterranean. Following the Russian Revolution, the Allies hoped for Japanese intervention along the Trans-Siberian railway and, indeed, Japanese troops were to be involved in eastern Russia until 1923. Japanese troops therefore fought in a number of varied conditions, from the cold of Siberia to the heat of the Marshall Islands.

Uniforms

Some reforms followed the Russo-Japanese war, and the dark blue tunics and trousers were phased out in favour of a much more practical uniform. In 1913 the 45 model, so called because it was adopted in the 45th year of the emperor's reign, was brought into service. It consisted of a yellowish-green tunic (of cotton and yellower in the summer, of wool and a darker

▼ *Japanese soldiers stand alongside a partially camouflaged field gun outside Tsingtao in 1914. This action, which took place very soon after the opening of hostilities in Europe, saw the Japanese (supported by a small Allied force) besiege and force the surrender of an important German enclave in China.*

▶ PRIVATE, 2ND INFANTRY REGIMENT, 1914
The long coat disguises the regimental insignia on the standing collar. The cap had red piping but, on campaign, colourful distinctions were removed and the red band covered with a khaki or brown cloth band. This made for a simple and plain uniform.

colour in the winter) with standing collar, fastened by five yellow metal buttons with no insignia.

The tunic had two breast pockets and piping on the cuff, and, instead of shoulder straps, there were two coloured tabs at the extremity of the shoulder (these were buttoned on to the fabric). This was in branch of service colour and bore stars as rank indicators. A central stripe in the button colour was worn by NCOs and officers and this was supplemented by a stripe on either edge for officers up to the rank of major. Majors and colonels wore tabs, which were striped gold and red and had one or three golden stars respectively. Officers also had branch of service piping down the sides of their breeches, favoured swords and pistols and wore long boots rather than the puttees worn by the troops.

A white or khaki shirt was worn beneath the tunic or alone in summer. A greatcoat (which also had shoulder tabs) was used in winter, although a simpler raincoat was much favoured.

Japanese Expeditionary Force Sent to the Russian Far East in 1918

14th, 24th, 47th, 72nd Infantry
   Regiments
12th Cavalry Regiment
12th Field Artillery Regiment
Medium Artillery Battalion
12th Engineering Battalion
1st Field Signals Unit
1st Radio Unit
1st Air Unit (with nine aeroplanes)
1st Railway Unit
Mapping detachment
Medical detachment

This latter item had a hood and was popular despite being shorter than the greatcoat and useless in cold weather. Greatcoats were often worn rolled in the field or strapped to the top of the knapsack along with a brown field blanket.

Collars had collar patches (in the shape of a pennon) and these also bore regimental numerals in gold thread, khaki or yellow oils.

Headgear

Japanese troops wore a peaked cap with black leather peak and chinstrap. It had a coloured band, denoting branch of service, and piping around the crown. A golden star was worn in

the centre of the coloured band. The cap was usually worn with a plain cloth cover, which showed no distinguishing marks.

Distinctions

Infantry had red collar patches, shoulder tabs, cuff piping and cap piping. Cavalry had green distinctions, artillery wore yellow patches, tabs and piping, and engineers (including a small aviation service) initially had crimson but switched to dark brown as the crimson was too similar to the red of the infantry. Train troops wore light blue distinctions.

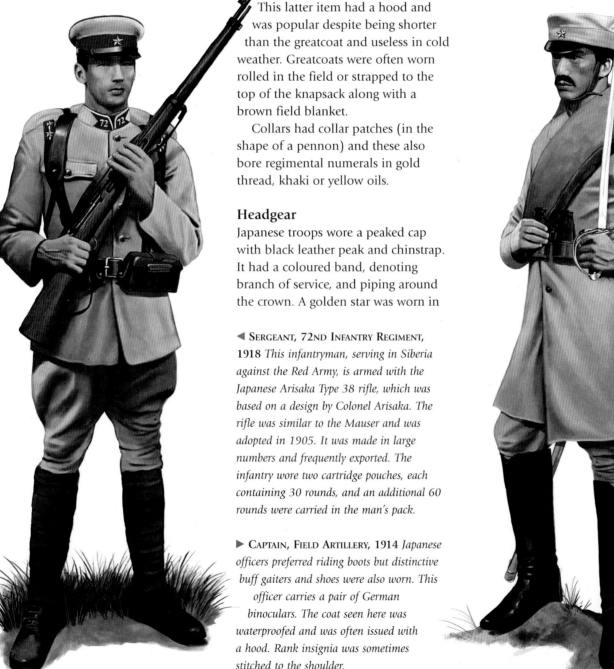

◀ SERGEANT, 72ND INFANTRY REGIMENT, 1918 *This infantryman, serving in Siberia against the Red Army, is armed with the Japanese Arisaka Type 38 rifle, which was based on a design by Colonel Arisaka. The rifle was similar to the Mauser and was adopted in 1905. It was made in large numbers and frequently exported. The infantry wore two cartridge pouches, each containing 30 rounds, and an additional 60 rounds were carried in the man's pack.*

▶ CAPTAIN, FIELD ARTILLERY, 1914 *Japanese officers preferred riding boots but distinctive buff gaiters and shoes were also worn. This officer carries a pair of German binoculars. The coat seen here was waterproofed and was often issued with a hood. Rank insignia was sometimes stitched to the shoulder.*

GERMANY

Like many a European power, German at the beginning of the 20th century was forged in war. Even so, the Germany of 1914 took a special pride in its armed forces, and the military held considerable power in the German Reich. German expansion in Europe in the 19th century, and in colonies across the world, added to this. Yet Germany was not a homogenous state, it had only recently been united and was too young for that. There were distinctive local customs and privileges throughout the country, and these could occasionally surface as tension and hostility within the ruling elite.

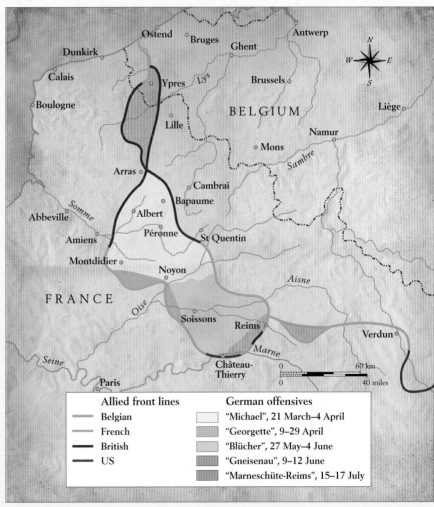

Allied front lines	German offensives
Belgian	"Michael", 21 March–4 April
French	"Georgette", 9–29 April
British	"Blücher", 27 May–4 June
US	"Gneisenau", 9–12 June
	"Marneschüte-Reims", 15–17 July

▲ *Germany's final offensive in the spring of 1918 was a determined effort to break the impasse on the Western Front. Using innovative tactics, and fresh troops from the Russian Front, this final push almost succeeded.*

◀ *This 3.7cm M-Flak gun prepares to open up on Allied aircraft. It fired an impressive 300 rounds per minute as ammunition was fed in from the drum on the left. Guns of this type were usually used to guard observation balloons. Heavier artillery, such as the 8.8cm K-Flak gun, was also developed by a German military keen to keep Allied aircraft at bay.*

A MILITARY STATE

Analysis of pre-war Germany is retrospectively determined by post-war thinking. Germany is judged to have been aggressive and militaristic at the beginning of the 20th century, dominated by conservative aristocrats keen to develop a culture of war. The true picture is rather more complex, and Germany as a whole had so many issues with militarism that it would be wrong to force a simplistic label upon it.

Prussian Habits

The impression that Germany was a militaristic society largely stems from an image of Prussia that Frederick the Great was keen to foist on Europe. Prussia, it was said, was not a state with an army, but an army with a state. Concepts of Prussia having no national industry, save that of war, were bandied about after Prussia's victories against

▼ *German soldiers were rigorously trained in all aspects of military life even before the war began. Here, in 1910, officers of the 2nd Guard Infantry Brigade stand at attention at a swimming contest, spoons clenched in their teeth, in preparation for an egg race.*

Napoleon in the Wars of Liberation and again when it defeated Austria, Denmark, and France in the 19th century. But Germany in 1914 was not Prussia, and Prussia itself was not what it had been in the 1750s.

Germany had triumphed in Europe not because it was a society dedicated to war, but because Prussia, and then Germany, had found a war-winning

▲ *Kaiser Wilhelm II (centre, on horseback) returns from a military review in Berlin in 1912. He is surrounded by privates of the Imperial Footguards, whose uniforms reflect the styles of a previous era.*

formula: modernity. Those who accused Germany of militarism overlooked the fact that modern war required a degree of militarism to persuade conscripts to go forward against machine guns, barbed wire and accurate rifles. France relied on patriotism to do the trick, Germany invested in training.

Tradition Gives way to Modernity

The fact that the German military showed considerable interest in new technology, developing new tactics and mastering the relationship between war and industry, was not unique. But a climate of new ideas flourished in Germany more so than elsewhere. There were few internal voices raised against the idea that Germany should benefit from the modern, even while France was defending the right of its soldiers to retain their red trousers.

Of course there were elements in German society that could be called

militaristic but they seldom worked together, with a united policy. There was a hard-working general staff, a flourishing debate on military theory and Kaiser Wilhlem II, a leader who saw himself as a soldier-emperor. His rhetoric was powerful, and he poured funds into the Navy, but he was not Germany. The large numbers of volunteers who swelled the ranks of the German Army have also been noted, but many of these were students who were technically exempt from conscription and large numbers of volunteers were raised as readily in other countries (Italians in France, or Australians for example).

Many opponents saw the Army as a way of preserving the status quo; a force for conservatism, which could put the brakes on liberalizing elements. This alone reveals that there was a rather fluid political scene in Germany. There were Social Democrats in parliament and their reforms had improved the health and wealth of considerable bands of the population, including the Army. German society was advancing at a fast rate.

▼ *Frederick Wilhelm Victor Albert was the last German emperor and king of Prussia, ruling from 15 June 1888 to 9 November 1918. Among the Allies he was known as The Kaiser, or Kaiser Bill.*

▲ *German reservists are driven to battle in 1914. In Germany, as across Europe, enthusiastic volunteers found themselves quickly transported to the front.*

Making Germans

The Army added to the process of advancement. It was a modernizing force, which exposed its recruits or employees to education, new ideas and new technologies. Military service brought conscripts together from across Germany, and demolished some of the regional insularity typical of much of the country. Conscription also affected a considerable number of men. In the small town of Freiburg in Baden, for example, some 249 men marched off to join the Army in 1913. After serving as conscripts the men would serve in the reserve and then various militias. The situation would be different in wartime, of course. During the war some 20,000 men of Freiburg would wear German uniform.

Nor was Germany's military without its flaws. Germany suffered from a shortage of NCOs, for whom pay was poor and prospects bleak. In addition, the officer class itself was diversifying.

Further, in 1918, German society itself turned against the war. It was a defeat that allowed Germany to be blamed for a culture that was common to most European nations in 1914, one which saw a short war as a means to an end, and which had no concept of what a world war would entail.

Public Opinion

Although Germany might have seemed militarized, German public opinion was divided on the issue of going to war in 1914. Many rural communities were very much against the war even if their disdain was overshadowed by crowds of young middle-class men cheering the news of war in German towns through the summer of 1914.

Germany had its own peace movement, political parties were by no means uniformly pro-war (and the war split the German Socialist party) and individual pacifists were just as common in Germany as they were in Britain, France or Russia. The spirit of 1914 was different for different people. Some took to the streets to join the crowds, others stayed, sullen and fretful, at home.

PRUSSIA AND THE GERMAN STATES

The idea of a unified state was one that many Germans were still getting used to. Loyalty, dialect, custom and tradition all still stemmed from regional concepts. At around the time of the Peace of Westphalia (1648), Germany consisted of some 300 states and territories. The Napoleonic Wars considerably reduced the number and assured the rise of Prussia, a state which dominated northern Germany and established itself on the Rhine.

Unity

Germany was united after the Franco-Prussian War but acted as a federal empire and maintained some independence for its 26 states (which included three Free Towns and the newly-acquired imperial territory of Alsace (Elsass) and Lorraine (Lothringen). The states were

▼ In 1914, Germany had only recently been united and, inevitably, German states still retained some autonomy in the running of local affairs and in finance. Royal and aristocratic families held sway in various territories across the German empire.

represented in legislative bodies, while imperial bodies controlled the armed forces and foreign policy, along with imperial finances and also (in times of crisis) the railways. Some states still had the right to send ambassadors abroad, but appointments were vetted by Berlin.

Germany was also divided according to language, not surprising when its territories included northern Poland and the Baltic coast as far as Memel (modern Kalipeda), as well as parts of France. The empire included three million Poles, mostly in Silesia and around Posen (modern Poznan), 120,000 Lithuanians and 140,000 Danes. Germany's colonies were administered by a department of the foreign office, apart from territory in China, handled by the Navy.

German Armies

Germany's armed forces were largely centralized and dominated by Prussian conventions. But, even here, there were limits. Prussia had gradually been absorbing the armies of smaller German states into its own system,

▲ King Frederick Augustus III of Saxony reviews Saxon troops in Romania, c.1917. Frederick Augustus served in the Royal Saxon Army before becoming king, and later was promoted to field marshal. He abdicated on 13 November 1918.

with a numbering system for regiments based on the older Prussian model. Saxony relinquished its independent army in 1866, and Baden, Württemberg and Hesse followed suit in 1871. The inclusion of regiments from other states meant that some German regiments had two numbers.

Bavaria, being a little more self assured, maintained a level of independence, although it, too, harmonized its hierarchy and badges of rank to conform to the Prussian model by 1873. It continued to retain its own uniforms and some semblance of independent command (including an air force). The king of Bavaria oversaw the Bavarian system, but appointments had to be agreed with the emperor.

Other contingents, such as those of the former kingdoms of Saxony or Baden, were often concentrated in specific corps to reflect the 'nationality' of the troops.

▲ *Ludwig III (1845–1921) was the last king of Bavaria. Here he reviews the troops in 1917. Ludwig was the first of the monarchs in the German empire to be deposed.*

Regiments in the German Army were given names that indicated either the region in which the regiment was recruited (although recruitment could spill over into neighbouring areas, as was the case with Alsace), or some honorary name awarded for historic reasons. Some regiments were named after a region but had shifted recruitment elsewhere without a name change. The influx of volunteers in 1914 also affected this general picture.

Landwehr (militia) regiments also drew their personnel from specific areas. The 77th Landwehr Regiment, for example, recruited in Osnabrück. It did not necessarily follow that the 77th Infantry Regiment also recruited there.

This had the advantage of giving a sense of regional identity to a regiment (much as was the case with the British Pals, men who were encouraged to enlist in the same regiment as their family members and friends), but the disadvantage was that when the regiment suffered heavily, an entire local community was devastated.

Regional Differences

Apart from the name, the German Army also maintained a few distinctive signs that could indicate where the regiment was from. This was most obvious for Bavarian units, which proclaimed their identity in a number of ways. The infantryman's distinctive spiked helmet (the pickelhaube) frequently bore a front plate (the wappen) featuring a state coat of arms. For Prussia this was the eagle, Baden had a griffin, Bavaria and Württemberg used royal coats of arms, Saxony used a star badge and Hesse had the rampant

lion. In addition some 17 states used cockades on the spiked helmet and on the caps used when helmets were not being worn. Buttons too had distinctive elements.

It was inevitable that particular characteristics attached themselves to certain contingents. East Prussians and Brandenburgers were said to be hardy, determined soldiers, while Saxons were said to be less disciplined.

▼ *Soldiers and recruits in the Bavarian Army are called to present themselves at their barracks, during the early months of the war.*

WARTIME DEVELOPMENTS

Germany put an impressive military force into the field in 1914, but it was one that was quickly compelled to face the reality of a long and drawn out conflict.

Germany's pre-war Army was quickly overwhelmed by the enforced growth of the summer of 1914. There were problems coping with armed forces that quickly achieved wartime strength. The influx of volunteers posed a strain on training and, generally, there were not enough NCOs or officers (particularly in the reserve units) to cope. Equipment was short too, although front-line units made the best of the situation. Landwehr would be sent marching out in the blue tunics of the 1890s, shakos were used instead of helmets, and some helmets were even borrowed from the fire brigade. Maintaining supplies was also a problem and substitute materials (particularly alloys, used in preference to bronze or steel) made an early appearance.

▼ *German wives and mothers say goodbye to their husbands and sons as they head off to the battlefronts of the war. These recruits of 1914 wear brand-new uniforms.*

Later Pressures

The Allied blockade would exacerbate the problem, even though Germany made careful use of its resources and showed great enterprise in producing synthetic replacements. Even so, shortages had an impact on the appearance of the troops and the quality of the equipment and weapons they handled. Increasing shortages in everything from dyes to petrol gave the commissariat a permanent headache,

▲ *A convoy of largely horse-drawn vehicles carrying supplies is sent off to the German front line. Lines of supply were vital, and huge amounts were sent out from Germany with characteristic efficiency.*

and stripping raw materials from occupied territory did not solve the problem. But the true problem was with the home front, and when families started to go hungry, morale in the trenches began to slide.

There was also an increasing shortage of manpower. This was brought about not only through casualties, but because of increasing demands for industrial labour. Recourse to conscripted labour (800,000 workers from Poland) or prisoners (Russian PoWs) did not prevent the Army from having to assign men to agricultural or industrial work. By 1918 striking workers were being sent to the front, something that did not improve the morale of either the workers or the soldiers.

Strained Alliances

Demands on men and material came from other quarters as well. Germany had supported allies and potential partners with military assistance (selected personnel, training facilities and instructors) and loans for military equipment prior to 1914. It had also, rather belatedly, sought to support its closest ally, Austria-Hungary, offering troops and collaboration, or timing offensives to coincide with Hapsburg needs. But, as the war continued, these responsibilities became more pressing.

Germany was soon responsible for directing Austro-Hungarian armies in the field, something it had done when invading Serbia in 1915, and at this point they completely took over responsibility for the war on the Eastern Front. More and more advisers were sent to support the Ottomans, and ever-increasing numbers of technical troops were sent to their assistance (many fighting in Palestine and Syria). Supplies were also delivered in vast quantities. When battle was successful, more troops were required to occupy and hold the new territories (the Ukraine tied up a vast number of troops in 1918). This became an additional strain on German strength.

▼ *Owing to the great shortage of men in Germany, women were employed in practically all the government departments in Berlin. This photograph shows the section of the war department in Berlin which compiled and updated lists of the German troops who had been captured by the Allies.*

Streamlining

Despite these limitations, the German Army proved a well-organized and effective force, particularly so in defensive positions. The Army was quick to adapt to new conditions and develop new tactics. Its defensive lines were established with exacting precision, and it quickly excelled at developing the concept of using elite troops on raids and as an initial wave to prepare the ground for larger

▲ *German troops entrenched on the newly established Salonika, or Macedonian, front in 1915, which remained relatively stable until the end of the war.*

offensives. These stormtroopers would prove their worth in 1918. As with other armies, artillery, technical and supply troops were all massively increased, while the cavalry was stripped of men and horses.

Germany made full use of air power, before succumbing to Allied superiority in numbers of machines and pilots. Anti-aircraft guns were improvised, adapted and developed, and the situation changed from an initial 18 anti-balloon guns in 1914 to a more complex (and much larger) arsenal of specialist guns and gunners.

The Germans were initially slow to adopt the tank, but their use of submarines almost brought the Allied economies to their knees. However, when the war at sea became total, German ruthlessness triggered American participation. Just as ruthlessness in Russia in 1918 would show what a German-imposed peace might mean, so ruthlessness at sea provoked a devastating reaction. Total war was not without consequence.

GENERALS AND STAFF

German generals wore uniforms that were privately tailored. Although smart, they were nevertheless designed to be practical, particularly after 1914. They wore a tunic (called the Waffenrock) for service dress (full dress was much more flamboyant) that had been introduced in 1910. Although it conformed to a general pattern, there were subtle variations between generals holding commissions from Baden, Bavaria, Hesse, Mecklenburg, Prussia,

Generals' Shoulderboard

Region	Thread Colour
Baden	yellow and red
Bavaria	light blue
Hesse	red
Mecklenburg	blue and red
Prussia	black
Saxony	green
Württemberg	black and red

Saxony and Württemberg. The tunic had falling collars piped in red and an oblong collar patch that was also red.

Prussian officers wore a gold embroidered motif based on that traditionally worn by the Alt-Larisch Regiment, Mecklenburg had silver oak leaves, and Bavaria had silver laurel leaves. The tunic had two breast pockets with flaps and was piped red down the opening and on the cuffs.

Generals wore field grey trousers, which bore three red stripes (called 'lampassen'), although these were often reserved for more formal occasions. Boots in black or brown were preferred.

Shoulderboards

The kings of Bavaria, Saxony and Württemberg still had a nominal say in the uniforms of their troops. The chief

distinction was the lace worn on the red collar patch and the threads interwoven on the metallic lace shoulderboards. Shoulderboards had scarlet bases, rounded ends and were held in place by a gold or silver button. They were embroidered in gold and silver and a thread in the colours shown in the table, left.

Field marshals (of whom there were six in the army) wore crossed battons on their shoulderboards, colonel

◀ FIELD MARSHAL, 1917 *Paul von Hindenburg wears a generals' greatcoat with scarlet facings and piping at the cuff. Hindenburg had been promoted to general in 1905 and retired in 1911 but was called out of retirement in 1914. As a field marshal he wore the uniform of the 3rd Foot Guards with the appropriate distinctions.*

▶ MAJOR ON THE GENERAL STAFF, 1915 *Although this staff officer wears a light grey peaked cap, normal attire included a dragoon helmet. The cap had a silk or artificial silk lining, and an internal band of leather to provide some shape and absorb sweat. The piping on the breeches is crimson.*

▲ *General Alexander Von Kluck (centre), and his staff. Kluck's First Army was defeated at the Marne in 1914. Moustaches were common but not regulation throughout the officer classes of European armies at this time.*

generals (generaloberst) wore three stars, generals two stars, lieutenant generals one and major generals went unadorned. Buttons were in gold, except for Bavaria and Mecklenburg, which used silver. Grey buttons were later adopted.

General officers wore the 1910 officer's field cap with double cockade (imperial cockade and state cockade), red piping, red band and leather peak. Spiked helmets, usually with covers, were also worn and these were usually of the dragoon variety, although infantry versions were not unknown.

Greatcoats were of the 1903 version in light grey. They had shoulderboards, dark blue folding collars (light blue for Bavaria, just blue piping for Saxony), red piping down the front and on the cuff and red fold-back lapels.

A number of generals preferred to wear the uniforms of their original regiments with the addition of rank distinctions. General Paul von Hindenburg preferred the uniform of the 3rd Foot Guards. Prussia's Crown Prince varied his dress, making use of the uniforms of regiments of which he was patron. In addition, a number of

officers were brought out of retirement in 1914 and were often obliged to take up their positions wearing slightly dated items, including blue tunics and frock coats. Off-duty generals wore a different cut of tunic, double breasted and known as the litewka.

Equipment

Generals carried pistols (the standard 1908 Luger) in brown holsters, map cases and binoculars. An 1889 officers' sword might also be worn, or a cavalry sabre, with the appropriate sword knot. Later, bayonets were worn instead. Orders and decorations were often worn at the collar or ribbons pinned to the opening of the tunic.

The only real changes for generals were the introduction of the steel helmet, the use of gas masks and the reduction in coloured piping.

General Staff Officers

Officers on the general staff had an important function and were dressed in uniforms similar to those worn by general officers. The collar patches

▶ **LIEUTENANT GENERAL, 1915** *The decoration on the collar was known as 'alt-larisch', a device worn by a regiment of this name in the Prussian Army, and it is here fixed to the collar of the newly issued 1915 tunic. The belt buckle bears the cypher of Kaiser Wilhelm II.*

were in crimson (without motifs) as was the piping and stripes on the trousers. Rank distinctions were worn on the shoulderboards and these were backed in crimson. Headgear consisted of an officer's peaked cap piped in scarlet and with a scarlet band. Helmets, if worn, would be as worn by the dragoons (Bavarians chose the infantry version).

General staff officers also wore a coloured sash with silver thread over the right shoulder. This was usually in state colours, as for the thread on the shoulderboards. It was often replaced by a brassard on active duty. These uniforms were modified in accordance with changes introduced for infantry officers.

GUARDS

The uniform of Germany's Imperial Guard was based on that of their Prussian antecedents. These were concentrated in divisions. Guard units from other German states were numbered into the line.

Guard Infantry

The German Guard wore spiked helmets in 1914 and these were worn with a plain brown or khaki cover. Tunics were field grey with falling collars (stiffer and more upright for officers) and gold

or silver buttons (brass or nickel for guardsmen). Cuffs were Swedish or Brandenburg (the Garde-Schützen had French cuffs), and red piping was worn down the front of the tunic, around the collar and down the outside of the field grey trousers. The collar had a decoration in the form of lace on a background colour; this colour was also used to pipe the shoulder straps of the enlisted men and as an underlay for the officers' shoulderboards. The collar decorations were in white (yellow for the 3. Königin Elisabeth Garde-Grenadier) or silver for officers and mostly consisted of double bars (litzen) with red centre lines (old Prussian litzen were used by 5. Garde-Regiment zu Fuß and 5. Garde-Grenadier-Regiment). Shoulder straps were piped in the appropriate colour but carried no distinguishing device for the foot guards. The Grenadier Guards wore monograms in red.

Guards retained shoulder strap colouring in 1915, wearing them on the newly introduced loose tunic (the 'bluse') with reduced collar litzen.

Guard light infantry consisted of a regiment of jäger and one of schützen. These wore uniforms similar to that of the Guard infantry but in grey green and with litzen on the collars. Piping was in green for the jägers and black for the schützen. Shoulder straps were just piped and had no distinctive monogram. Black leather shakos were worn with a star-shaped badge, although plain shako covers were also worn. Officers wore peaked caps with either green or black bands.

Technical Troops

Guard engineers followed the uniforms worn by their line equivalents but with litzen on black velvet collar patches

◀ CAPTAIN, 1ST FOOT GUARDS REGIMENT, 1914 *Guards units wore plain helmet covers and their spiked helmets bore a distinctive Prussian eagle and star device.*

▲ PRIVATE, 4TH FOOT GUARDS REGIMENT, 1914 *This guardsman's helmet would be lined with leather and have air vents at the base of the spike to keep the head cool.*

piped red. They wore spiked helmets. Shoulder straps bore grenades for the four Guard field artillery regiments and one of foot artillery, and piping was scarlet, except for the third regiment, which had yellow, and the foot artillery, which had white. Cuffs were Swedish for the field artillery and

Guard Cavalry Distinctions

Regiment	Colour	Buttons
Gardes du Corps	scarlet	silver
Garde-Kürassier	blue	silver
1. Garde-Dragoner Königin Viktoria von Groß Britannien	red	gold
2. Garde-Dragoner Kaiserin Alexandra von Rußland	red	silver
Leib-Garde-Husaren-Regiment	scarlet	grey
1. Garde-Ulanen	white	silver
2. Garde-Ulanen	red	gold
3. Garde-Ulanen	yellow	silver

Brandenburg for the foot artillery. Machine gun detachments (of which there were two) dressed as for the jägers but with yellow collar litzen and red collar patches and piping.

Guard Cavalry

Very much an elite within an elite, the Guard cavalry were superbly equipped. Tunics were worn by all regiments, except the hussars and lancers ('ulans') who wore a dolman (the attila) and ulanka respectively. Tunics had standing collars (with litzen on coloured backgrounds), Swedish cuffs

▼ LIEUTENANT, 3RD GUARD ULAN REGIMENT, 1914 *Ulans were unique in that they wore their medals on the right side of their tunic.*

and piping in the regimental colour. For the Gardes du Corps and Garde-Kürassier a white line ran around the inside of the shoulder strap piping, but these were otherwise blank; dragoons wore monograms in red.

The Guard hussars wore a grey attila with grey decorative loops down the front and coloured knotted shoulder straps (red in this case). They wore grey fur caps (busbies), breeches and boots. The Guard lancers wore ulanka tunics which had standing collars (with litzen on coloured patches; the litzen were yellow for the 2nd regiment) and plastron lapels. The tunic was piped in the regimental colour. The lancers wore the square-topped tschapka cap although officers often wore the peaked cap with a band in the regimental colour.

INFANTRY

Field grey was introduced for German infantry in 1910, and it gave the infantryman a practical, hard-wearing uniform that was not radically altered before 1918.

Rank and File

Germany's infantry regiments were all issued with a standard tunic (the feldrock), which was loose fitting and comfortable. It was closed by eight nickel buttons and with sealable pockets on the tunic skirts. The tunic had a falling collar

(which bore double litzen for those line units which had once been Guard regiments of particular German states: 89, 100, 101, 109, 115, 119 and 123; grenadier regiments had single litzen), piped in red, and red piping down the front opening. Cuffs varied according to regiment (either Swedish, Saxon or Brandenburg), as did shoulder straps. These were coloured initially so as to indicate the Army Corps the regiment was serving in: white except for the III, IV, XI, XIII, XV XIX, II Bavarian (which had red), the V, VI, XVI, XVII and III Bavarian (which had yellow), the VII, VIII, XVIII and XX (which had light blue) and the XXI (which had light green). Units had red (with yellow for a few exceptions) numerals or monograms on their shoulder straps.

Shoulder straps were attached to the tunic by a button bearing the number of the company or an 'L' for any Leib regiment. (Leib means 'life', as in Life Guard, and is a designation associated with an elite unit or a unit which had or once had Guard status.) NCOs had golden thread embellishments to their collars and to their sleeves, as well as a larger button worn on the collar. This bore the relevant state's arms (a lion for Bavaria, variations of

◀ SERGEANT, 113TH INFANTRY REGIMENT (BADEN), 1914 *The tunic was made from wool and had red wool piping. The collar was rounded and the shoulder straps removable. The belt bore the motto 'GOTT MIT UNS' (God with us) for Prussian units and those of the smaller states, which prompted British troops to shout 'We've got mittens too!' at confused German front lines.*

▶ SERGEANT, 93RD INFANTRY REGIMENT (ANHALT), 1914 *The heavy pack, which weighed so many German troops down in 1914, was made from cowhide and was issued in 1895.*

crowns for other states). Regiments 73 and 79 wore the word Gibraltar in yellow on a light blue strip of cloth above their right cuff. Officers and NCOs of the 92nd Regiment wore a silver skull between the cockades on their caps.

Trousers were field grey in 1914 with red piping (M1907) and worn with natural leather boots or, from December 1914, laced ankle boots and puttees. Greatcoats were worn in winter and were grey with red collar patches

▲ Private, 135th Infantry Regiment
(Lorraine), September 1914 *The stencilled
or stitched unit number on the helmet cover
was now in green rather than red and it was
removed altogether in 1916. Regiments with
cyphers on their straps had the regimental
number on their helmets. Helmet covers had
been introduced in 1892 and were hooked to
the back and front of the helmet.*

(although the 150th Regiment had
yellow, the 151st had light blue and
the following had white: 146th, 148th,
152nd, 154th, 156th, 158th, 160th,
162nd, 164th, 166th, 171st, 173rd,
175th). These coloured patches were
discontinued in 1915.

Infantry Regiment Distinctions

Regiment (*number or monogram)	Cuffs	*n/m	Strap Piping
(the first 12 regiments were Grenadier regiments)			
1 Kronprinz (1 East Prussian)	B	m	white
2 König Friedrich Wilhelm IV (1 Pomeranian)	B	m	white
3 König Friedrich Wilhelm I (2 East Prussian)	B	m	white
4 König Friedrich der Grosse (3 East Prussian)	B	m	white
5 König Friedrich I (4 East Prussian)	B	m	yellow
6 Graf Kleist von Nollendorf (1 West Prussian)	B	n	yellow
7 König Wilhelm I (2 West Prussian)	B	m	yellow
8 (Leib) König Friedrich Wilhelm III (1 Brandenburg)	B	m	red
9 (Colberg) Graf Gneisenau (2 Pommeranian)	B	n	white
10 König Friedrich Wilhelm II (1 Silesian)	B	m	yellow
11 König Friedrich III (2 Silesian)	B	m	yellow
12 Prinz Karl von Preußen (2 Brandenburg)	B	n	red
13 Herwarth von Bittenfeld (1 Westphalian)	B	n	light blue
14 Graf Schwerin (3 Pommeranian)	B	n	white
15 Prinz Friedrich der Niederlande (2 Westphalian)	B	n	light blue
16 Freiherr von Sparr (3 Westphalian)	B	n	light blue
17 Graf Barfuß (4 Westphalian)	B	n	light green
18 von Grolmann (1 Posen)	B	n	light blue
19 von Coubière (2 Posen)	B	n	yellow
20 Graf Tauentzien von Wittenburg (3 Brandenburg)	B	n	red
21 von Borcke (4 Pommeranian)	B	n	yellow
22 Keith (1 Upper Silesian)	B	n	yellow
23 von Winterfeldt (2 Upper Silesian)	B	n	yellow
24 Mecklenburg-Schwerin (4 Brandenburg)	B	n	red
25 von Lützow (1 Rhineland)	B	n	light blue
26 Fürst Leopold von Anhalt-Desau (1 Magdeburg)	B	n	red
27 Prinz Louis Ferdinand von Preußen (2 Magdeburg)	B	n	red
28 von Goeben (2 Rhineland)	B	n	light blue
29 von Horn (3 Rhineland)	B	n	light blue
30 Graf Werder (4 Rhineland)	B	n	yellow
31 Graf Bose (1 Thuringian)	B	n	white
32 (2 Thuringian)	B	n	red
33 to 40 were Fusilier regiments			
33 Graf Roon (1 East Prussian)	B	n	white
34 Königin Viktoria von Schweden (1 Pommeranian)	B	m	white
35 Prinz Heinrich von Preußen (1 Brandenburg)	B	n	red
36 General-Feldmarschall Graf Blumenthal (1 Magdeburg)	B	n	red
37 von Steinmetz (1 West Prussian)	B	n	yellow
38 Graf Moltke (1 Silesian)	B	n	yellow
39 Upper Rhine	B	n	blue
40 Fürst Karl-Anton von Hohenzollern (1 Hohenzollern)	B	n	light blue
41 von Boyen (5 East Prussian)	B	n	white
42 Prinz Moritz von Anhalt-Dessau (5 Pommeranian)	B	n	white
43 Herzog Karl von Mecklenburg (6 East Prussian)	B	n	white
44 Graf Dönhoff (7 East Prussian)	B	n	white
45 (8 East Prussian)	B	n	white
46 Graf Kirchbach (1 Lower Silesian)	B	n	yellow
47 König Ludwig III von Bayern (2 Lower Silesian)	B	m	yellow
48 von Stülpnagel (5 Brandenburg)	B	n	red
49 (6 Pommeranian)	B	n	white
50 (3 Lower Silesian)	B	n	yellow	▶

Regiment	Cuffs n/m	Strap Piping
51 (4 Lower Silesian)	B	n	yellow
52 von Alvensleben (6 Brandenburg)	B	n	red
53 (5 Westphalian)	B	m	blue
54 von der Goltz (7 Pommeranian)	B	n	white
55 Graf Bülow von Dennewitz (6 Westphalian)	B	n	light blue
56 Vogel von Falkenstein (7 Westphalian)	B	n	blue
57 Herzog Ferdinand von Braunschweig (8 Westphalian)	B	n	light blue
58 (3 Posen)	B	n	yellow
59 Freiherr Hiller von Gaertringen (4 Posen)	B	n	light blue
60 Markgraf Carl (7 Brandenburg)	B	n	light green
61 von der Marwitz (8 Pommeranian)	B	n	yellow
62 (3 Upper Silesian)	B	n	yellow
63 (4 Upper Silesian)	B	n	yellow
64 Friedrich Karl von Preußen (8 Brandenburg)	B	n	red
65 (5 Rhineland)	B	n	light blue
66 (3 Magdeburg)	B	n	red
67 (4 Magdeburg)	B	n	yellow
68 (6 Rhineland)	B	n	light blue
69 (7 Rhineland)	B	n	light blue
70 (8 Rhineland)	B	n	light green
71 (3 Thuringian)	B	n	red
72 (4 Thuringian)	B	m	red
73 (Fusilier) Albrecht von Preußen (1 Hanoverian)	B	n	white
74 (1 Hanoverian)	B	n	white
75 Bremen (1 Hanseatic)	B	n	white
76 Hamburg (2 Hanseatic)	B	n	white
77 (2 Hanoverian)	B	n	white
78 Friedrich Wilhelm von Braunschweig (1 East Friesian)	B	n	white
79 von Voigts-Rhetz (3 Hanoverian)	B	n	white
80 (Fusilier) von Gerdsdorff (1 Kur Hessian)	B	m	light blue
81 Friedrich I von Hessen-Cassel (1 Kur Hessian)	B	n	light blue
82 (2 Kur Hessian)	B	n	red
83 von Wittich (3 Kur Hessian)	B	n	red
84 von Manstein (1 Schleswig)	B	n	white
85 Herzog von Holstein (1 Holstein)	B	n	white
86 (Füsilier) Königin (1 Schleswig-Holstein)	B	m	white
87 (1 Nassau)	B	n	light blue
88 (2 Nassau)	B	m	light blue
89 1 Mecklenburgisches (Grenadier)	B	m	white
90 1 Mecklenburgisches (Fusilier)	B	m	white
91 Oldenburg	B	m	white
92 Brunswick	B	m	white
93 Anhalt	B	m	red
94 Großherzog von Sachsen (5 Thuringian)	B	m	red
95 (6 Thuringian)	B	m	red
96 (7 Thuringian)	B	n	red
97 (1 Upper Rhine)	B	n	light green
98 Metz	B	n	yellow
99 (2 Upper Rhine)	B	n	red
100 Leib-Grenadier (1 Saxon)	Sa	m	white
101 Grenadier Kaiser Wilhelm (2 Saxon)	Sa	m	white
102 König Ludwig III von Bayern (3 Saxon)	Sa	n	white
103 (4 Saxon)	Sa	n	white ▶

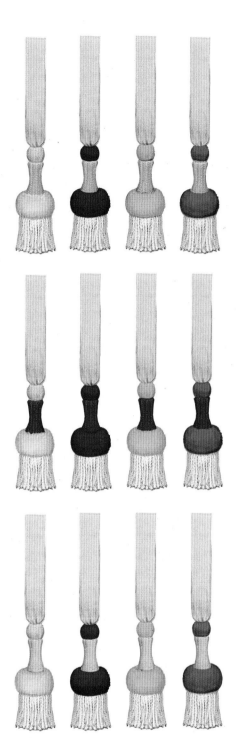

▲ Infantry Regiment Bayonet Knots, 1915
Top row, from left: *First battalion, companies one to four.* Middle row, from left: *Second battalion companies one to four.* Bottom row, from left: *Third battalion, companies one to four.*

Officers

The officers' tunic was of finer material and had a high collar, golden buttons (quickly painted black or grey), silver bullion shoulderboards with backings coloured above and with unit numbers or monograms. They wore golden stars to denote rank.

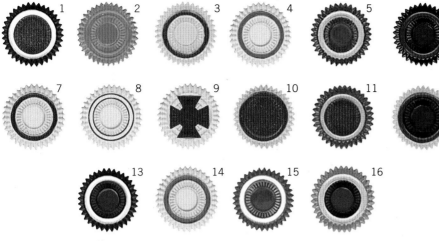

Calfskin backpacks with support straps were worn, although a brown cotton version had been introduced in 1913. Greatcoats were rolled and strapped to the pack, and mess tins were attached to the backpack flap. These were usually painted black. Canteens, padded in felt or cotton, were worn behind, as were bread bags. Entrenching tools were carried. NCOs carried pistols and swords. Officers were initially entitled to wear waist sashes in silver with state coloured threads. They carried swords, pistols, binocular cases and map cases.

Headgear and Equipment

The infantry wore the famous spiked helmet (pickelhaube) for the infantry (M1895, Bavaria M1896) with front and rear visor. This was made from blackened leather and a metallic badge bearing the relevant state's coat of arms. The helmet was worn with a cover (grey cotton) with the regimental numeral stencilled on in red and, from September 1914, in green (with an 'R' for reserve regiments). Officers wore a superior version or a peaked cap. This was grey, piped red with a red band, and had a black visor and black

▼ *A view of a well-constructed German trench avenue on the Western Front, which shows the elaborate constructions that were carved out of the earth, February 1917.*

▲ STATE COCKADES. **1915** *1 Reich's (post 1897). 2 Anhalt. 3 Baden. 4 Bayern. 5 Braunschweig. 6 Württemburg 7 Bremen (Hessen caps). 8 Hessen (helmets only). 9 Hamburg and Lübeck. 10 Lippe. 11 Mecklenburg. 12 Waldeck and Reuss. 13 Prussia. 14 Saxony. 15 Schwarzburg-Rudolstadt. 16 Saxe-Weimar.*

chinstrap. It bore an imperial cockade on the crown (black outside, white, red) and a state cockade on the band. It could be worn with a grey cover.

Equipment consisted of a natural leather waist belt with state badge buckle, this bore a crown and 'GOTT MIT UNS' (God with us) for Prussian troops or plain for NCOs. Three natural leather cartridge pouches were worn on the waist belt and the bayonet suspended from it. This had a bayonet sword which was predominantly white but had coloured knots and stems according to company or battalion. NCOs' swords had white knots with state coloured threads.

▶ SERGEANT, BAVARIAN LEIB-REGIMENT, 1915 *This standard bearer wears a gorget with the Royal Bavarian coat of arms in gilt. The same coat of arms would appear on the front of the helmet.*

Trench Warfare

Measures were quickly taken to dull down the uniform for the new trench-based conditions. Buttons were overpainted, waist sashes were replaced with natural leather belts, belt buckles were blackened. A spiked helmet with removable spike and darkened front plate was issued and covers were now not to have unit numerals stencilled on. In September 1915 troops were ordered not to wear the spike in action. Trousers were now stone grey, and no longer had the red piping. Greatcoats without the coloured patches began to be issued in

1915, as did simplified tunics with grey buttons. But the most significant change was the introduction of a loose jacket or bluse. This was issued to officers, enlisted men and NCOs alike. It was slightly darker in tone and had a fold down collar. This showed a green lining (the Bavarians had field grey collars edged by a distinctive grey and blue matt, silver and blue for officers, border, something reduced to two small strips in 1917). Litzen

▼ **PRIVATE, 128TH INFANTRY REGIMENT (DANZIG), 1916** *The white brassard worn here was used by assault troops to differentiate them from the enemy.*

▲ **PRIVATE, 24TH INFANTRY REGIMENT (4TH BRANDENBURG), 1915** *This individual wears a helmet with removable spike. The spike had made the German soldier's profile too visible and it was seen as a liability by early 1915. Metal fittings, which had reflected light, were chemically oxidized to reduce glare.*

◄ **SERGEANT, 17TH INFANTRY REGIMENT (4TH WESTPHALIAN), 1915** *The soft cap (or 'krätzchen') worn by this figure originally had a coloured band but camouflage bands in grey were later issued. The cockade would not, however, be covered over.*

continued to be worn. Shoulder straps became smaller and simplified, being piped in white for the majority of infantry (the 114th had light green, the 7th, 11th and 118th yellow, the 117th had violet, the 145th had light blue and the 8th, 115th and 168th had red), with red numerals or monograms as before. The jacket closed with six zinc buttons and had two exterior pockets and five interior ones.

▼ CAPTAIN, 94TH INFANTRY REGIMENT (5TH THURINGIAN), 1916 *This officer wears leather gaiters rather than the standard Model 1866 infantry boot. He is armed with a P08 Luger and leather holster.*

Regiment	Cuffs n/m	Strap	Piping
104 (5 Saxon) Kronprinz	Sa	m	red
105 (6 Saxon) König Wilhelm II von Württemberg	Sa	n	red
106 (7 Saxon) König Georg	Sa	m	red
107 (8 Saxon) Prinz Johann Georg	Sa	n	red
108 Saxon Schützen (Füsilier) Prinz Georg (jäger uniform)	S	n	green
109 (1 Baden) (Leib-Grenadier)	S	m	white
110 (2 Baden) (Grenadier) Kaiser Wilhelm I	B	m	white
111 (3 Baden) Margraf Ludwig Wilhelm	B	m	red
112 (4 Baden) Prinz Wilhelm	B	n	light green
113 (5 Baden)	B	n	blue
114 (6 Baden) Kaiser Friedrich III	B	m	light green
115 Leibgarde (1 GD of Hesse)	B	m	red
116 Kaiser Wilhelm (2 GD of Hesse)	B	m	white
117 Leibregiment Großherzogin (3 GD of Hesse)	B	m	blue
118 Prinz Carl (4 GD of Hesse)	B	n	yellow
119 (1 Württemberg) (Grenadier) Königin Olga	S	m	red
120 Kaiser Wilhelm (2 Württemberg)	B	m	red
121 Alt-Württemberg (3 Württemberg)	B	n	red
122 (4 Württemberg) (Füsilier) Kaiser Franz Josef	B	n	red
123 (5 Württemberg) (Grenadier) König Karl	S	m	red
124 König Wilhelm I (6 Württemberg)	B	m	red
125 Kaiser Friedrich, König von Preußen (7 Württemberg)	B	m	red
126 Großherzog Friedrich von Baden (8 Württemberg)	B	n	red
127 (9 Württemberg)	B	n	red
128 Danzig	B	n	yellow
129 (3 West Prussian)	B	n	yellow
130 (1 Lorraine)	B	n	yellow
131 (2 Lorraine)	B	n	light green
132 (1 Lower Alsace)	B	n	red
133 (9 Saxon)	Sa	n	red
134 (10 Saxon)	Sa	n	red
135 (3 Lorraine)	B	n	yellow
136 (4 Lorraine)	B	n	red
137 (2 Lower Alsace)	B	n	light green
138 (3 Lower Alsace)	B	n	light green
139 (11 Saxon)	Sa	n	white
140 (4 West Prussian)	B	n	yellow
141 Kulmer	B	n	yellow
142 (7 Baden)	B	n	red
143 (4 Lower Alsace)	B	n	yellow
144 (5 Lorraine)	B	m	yellow
145 Königs (6 Lorraine)	B	n	light blue
146 (1 Masurian)	B	n	light blue
147 (2 Masurian)	B	n	light blue
148 (5 West Prussian)	B	n	light blue
149 (6 West Prussian)	B	n	white
150 (1 Ermland)	B	n	light blue
151 (2 Ermland)	B	n	light blue
152 Deutsch Ordens (1 Alsace)	B	n	red
153 (8 Thuringian)	B	m	red
154 (5 Lower Silesian)	B	n	yellow
155 (7 West Prussian)	B	n	yellow
156 (3 Silesian)	B	n	yellow ▶

Regiment	Cuffs n/m	Strap	Piping
157 (4 Silesian)	B	n	yellow
158 (7 Lorraine)	B	n	light blue
159 (8 Lorraine)	B	n	light blue
160 (9 Rhineland)	B	n	light blue
161 (10 Rhineland)	B	n	light blue
162 Lübeck (3 Hanseatic)	B	n	white
163 Schleswig-Holstein	B	n	white
164 (4 Hanoverian)	B	n	white
165 (5 Hanoverian)	B	n	red
166 Hessen-Homburg	B	n	light green
167 (1 Upper Alsace)	B	n	red
168 (5 GD of Hesse)	B	n	red
169 (8 Baden)	B	n	red
170 (9 Baden)	B	n	light blue
171 (2 Upper Alsace)	B	n	red
172 (3 Upper Alsace)	B	n	red
173 (9 Lorraine)	B	n	yellow
174 (10 Lorraine)	B	n	red
175 (8 West Prussian)	B	n	white
176 (9 West Prussian)	B	n	white
177 (12 Saxon)	Sa	n	white
178 (13 Saxon)	Sa	n	white
179 (14 Saxon)	Sa	n	red
180 (10 Württemberg)	B	n	red
181 (15 Saxon)	Sa	n	red
182 (16 Saxon)	Sa	n	white

Bavarian

Regiment	Cuffs n/m	Strap	Piping
Leibregiment	S	m	white
1 König	B	m	white
2 Kronprinz	B	m	white
3 Prinz Karl von Bayern	B	m	white
4 König Wilhelm von Württemberg	B	n	red
5 Großherzog Ernst Ludwig von Hessen	B	n	red
6 Kaiser Wilhelm, König von Preußen	B	m	yellow
7 Prinz Leopold	B	n	yellow
8 Großherzog Friedrich II von Baden	B	n	red
9 Wrede	B	n	red
10 König	B	m	yellow
11 von der Tann	B	n	yellow
12 Prinz Arnulf	B	n	white
13 Franz Josef I, Kaiser von Österreich	B	n	yellow
14 Hartmann	B	n	yellow
15 König Friedrich August von Sachsen	B	n	white
16 Großherzog Ferdinand von Toskana	B	n	red
17	B	n	yellow
18 Prinz Ludwig Ferdinand	B	n	red
19 König Viktor Emanuel III von Italien	B	m	yellow
20 Prinz Franz Lindau	B	n	white
21 Großherzog Friedrich Franz IV von Mecklenburg	B	n	yellow
22 Fürst Wilhelm von Hohenzollern	B	n	red
23 König Ferdinand der Bulgaren	B	m	red

*Number or Monogram

▲ PRIVATE, 22ND INFANTRY REGIMENT (1ST UPPER SILESIAN), 1918 *Dyes used in the manufacture of German uniforms were unstable – there were many variations from green through to grey – and this private's tunic, a left-over from the early years of the war, has been re-dyed and repaired.*

NCOs no longer had the decorative edging to their collars and were now reduced to simple chevrons on the points of the collar. Feldwebels (a rank similar to sergeant) wore chevrons (yellow or white) on their upper sleeve. Officers wore the jacket with stiffer and higher collars.

Grey trousers were reintroduced in 1917 but all shades of grey, black or brown trousers were seen in the field. German troops now mostly wore ankle boots but the quality of the leather was very poor and captured boots were often preferred. Puttees, again often captured and dyed grey, were also worn in the late war period. Officers wore breeches (called stiefelhose) and boots.

Greatcoats were manufactured in the same cloth as that of the jacket and with the light green collar (grey with border for Bavarians). This was worn without litzen but with NCO distinctions.

▶ **PRIVATE, 79TH INFANTRY REGIMENT (3RD HANOVER), 1918** *The greatcoat collar could be turned up and closed using buttoned tabs sewn under the collar. This regiment had the word 'Gibraltar' stitched in blue thread on the right arm of its tunic, a battle honour from the time the regiment had been in Hanoverian, and hence also British, service in the 18th century.*

Equipment now included a gas mask initially worn in a bag around the neck, and then carried in a cylindrical container. Officers no longer carried swords, many preferring the bayonet or dagger.

Headgear Developments

Officers had worn peaked caps when not wearing spiked helmets. These were now covered in grey cloth. NCOs wore a peakless version (the feldmütze) as did enlisted men. On 21 September 1915 a helmet with detachable spike was introduced. The new steel helmet soon replaced these. An earlier steel helmet (known as the von Gäde) had been tried in 1915 but had limited circulation.

In December 1915 a small number of pressed felt helmets were issued for troops heading to the Balkans (some also found their way to troops in France). Instead of a helmet plate it had a number on a metallic scroll and is therefore known as a scroll helmet. In the Balkans they were often worn with a neck guard (called a nackenshutz) to protect the wearer in hot weather.

The more famous stahlhelm helmet was produced in 1916 (invented by Schwerd and Bier) after tests in November 1915. It came in five sizes and was mostly manufactured without a chinstrap (these were taken off the spiked helmet and riveted to the

◀ **LIEUTENANT, 79TH INFANTRY REGIMENT (3RD HANOVER), 1917** *The 1916 steel helmet was manufactured with lugs on each side to support a steel visor and to provide some ventilation. The helmet had been tested in the winter of 1915 and was first issued in January 1916.*

helmet at the depots). It was later attached to the lining rather than the helmet, and it seems that some chinstraps were made from cloth in 1917. A slightly altered version of the helmet came out in 1918 with indents above the ear (apparently to stop a ringing effect produced by the old helmet during artillery bombardment). It was not widely issued and was only really used after the war. Most troops had to make do with the 1916 model, which was usually painted dark grey although camouflage paint was sometimes applied. Helmet covers were in light brown, white or khaki.

COLONIAL UNIFORMS

The foreign force, known as the Schutztruppe, was the African force of Imperial Germany from the late 1800s to 1918. Similar to other colonial forces, the Schutztruppe consisted of volunteer European commissioned and non-commissioned officers, medical and veterinary officers. Most enlisted ranks were recruited locally. Colonial uniforms were also sometimes worn by troops assisting the Ottomans or fighting in the Balkans.

German East Africa

Germany's defence in east Africa mainly consisted of companies of Schutztruppe comprising German officers and NCOs and local enlisted men. Officers and NCOs generally wore khaki tunics and trousers, piped blue, with rank being displayed on shoulderboards for officers and by means of chevrons on the arm for NCOs (these were from one to four inverted chevrons, white on blue for Europeans, red for native NCOs).

Most of these men wore colonial helmets; domed helmets made of cork and covered in khaki cloth, although sometimes white helmets were worn. Helmets bore the imperial cockade (no state cockades were worn by troops in the colonies) and a twisted cord around the base; this was black, white (silver for officers) and red, the imperial colours. Boots were worn, although puttees and ankle boots were also popular. Native troops (askaris) wore a khaki fez, usually with an imperial eagle badge removed, khaki tunics, trousers and puttees. Captured equipment was used, as were captured weapons and clothing. Buttons bore the imperial eagle.

South-west Africa

Germany's colony in south-west Africa was protected by European Schutztruppe consisting of

◀ PRIVATE, SOUTH-WEST AFRICA SHUTZTRUPPE, 1914 *The shoulder strap was in imperial colours of red, black and white. The hat, which resembled the slouch hat, doubled up as a pillow.*

▶ ASKARI, EAST AFRICA, 1914 *The fez was sometimes worn with the decorative badge or with feathers. As the conflict wore on, civilian items replaced the neat, uniform appearance shown here.*

European officers, NCOs and men. They wore the standard cotton khaki tunic piped in blue on the collar, cuffs and down the tunic front. Officers piped their trousers (made from cotton or more durable cord) in the same colour and leather boots were worn. Shoulder straps were in the imperial colours (silver replacing white for the officers), although NCOs had chevrons denoting their ranks (apart from a lance corporal who wore a

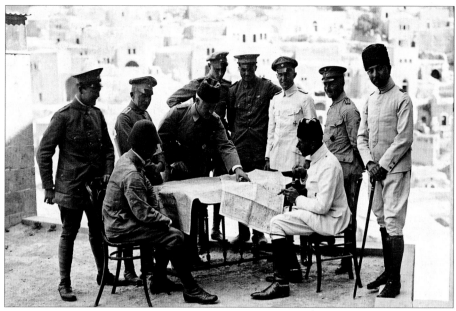

▲ *A group of German advisers attached to the Ottoman Army in Jerusalem, pore over maps with their Ottoman colleagues. Standard uniforms were worn by German officers, although some chose to wear Ottoman colpacks. One officer (probably pilot Gerhardt Felmy), standing third from the right, wears a privately purchased white tropical tunic.*

button on the collar). In contrast to the tropical helmets used in East Africa, troops here preferred the famous slouch hat. This was in grey with blue piping around the brim and the right side turned up and pinned to the crown by an imperial cockade. Peaked caps were sometimes worn by officers. These were in grey with blue bands and piping with one cockade.

Mounted equipment was used, the troops using cartridge pouches or bandoliers of ammunition, the officers often using captured Sam Browne belts. Troopers wore bayonets and had bayonet knots with particular colours denoting their company.

A small number of Boers volunteered to fight for the Germans and these were formed into a Freikorps with civilian clothes and some items of German equipment (slouch hats with South African cockades).

West Africa

As with East African forces, the core of Germany's forces in West Africa consisted of native troops led by

German officers and NCOs. The khaki tunic, piped in blue, was worn as were slouch hats, peaked caps and tropical helmets. The slouch hat was piped in red, and peaked caps had red bands and red piping. Some troops were mounted, some fought on foot. Native Schutztruppe wore khaki tunics piped in red and with plain shoulder straps. They wore a red fez (often with khaki cover and neck guard) with an eagle badge and black tassel.

The Middle Eastern Front

German troops serving with the Ottomans initially wore German field grey uniforms, with some slight modifications (tropical helmets, for example), although those sent out in 1917 were issued with some cotton khaki items (brown shirts manufactured for this purpose are supposed to have been bought and used by the Nazis in the 1920s). Tunics were with falling collars, buttons with eagles, and khaki shoulder straps (piped in white for infantry, red for cavalry and black piped red for artillery). Caps were khaki with a single cockade. Helmets had a cockade on the right and cords as for the piping on the shoulder straps. Rank insignia conformed to that worn

by the German Army in Europe. Trousers were khaki and puttees were preferred. European uniforms were worn in cold weather. Some troops in Macedonia wore khaki tunics and breeches, as well as colonial helmets, straw round hats and scroll helmets (pressed felt rounded helmets issued in 1915). Troops serving in China were mostly formed from naval battalions.

▼ PRIVATE, 701ST BATTALION OF INFANTRY, ASIENKORPS, 1917 *These units were uniformed in brown, and when deployed to Palestine this led to them being confused with British infantry. They therefore took to wearing items of field grey.*

JÄGERS AND MOUNTAIN TROOPS

German light infantry had, by and large, traditionally worn green. This custom was maintained even after most of the Army switched to field grey. The Bavarians were the exception; their two battalions wore field grey.

Jägers and Schützen

In 1914 there were 14 numbered battalions of jägers in addition to the Guard Jägers, plus a regiment of schützen and a battalion of Guard Schützen. For historical reasons the Schützen regiment was numbered in amongst the line regiments, being the 108th Regiment. Bavaria had two battalions of jägers. Jäger battalions wore a grey-green tunic with green piping around the collar and on the Swedish cuffs. Shoulder straps showed the battalion number in red; the 12th and 13th had red hunting horns above, as did the schützen who, had black piping rather than green. The 14th Battalion wore collar and cuff litzen, the 10th had a Gibraltar cuff title (as well as historical battle honours shown on the shako plate). The Saxons had silver buttons, the rest had yellow metal. Grey-green breeches were also worn. Equipment was in natural leather and belt plates reflected the state of origin of the battalion.

Jäger battalions wore a leather shako (the M1895) with front and rear peaks, a blackened chinstrap and imperial cockades where the chinstrap was riveted to the shako. Most jäger battalions had a white cockade with black centre on the shako crown, although the 14th had the Mecklenburg cockade, the 7th had Schaumburg-Lippe's cockade and the 12th and 13th had the Saxon arms. Bavarians wore their traditional light blue and white. Shako covers were worn, but the central cockade was worn on the outside of the cover, and these sometimes bore battalion numbers stencilled on in green. Saxon shakos had no rear peak.

◀ PRIVATE, 4TH JÄGER BATTALION (MAGDEBURG), 1914 *The leather shako had a rear peak and cockade on either side of the chinstrap and was standard issue to most jäger troops. Only the Saxons introduced a more squat version that resembled a cap rather than a shako. Only the top and rim of the Saxon shako was made of leather, the rest was of compressed felt.*

▲ PRIVATE, WÜRTTEMBURG MOUNTAIN RIFLE BATTALION, 1915 *The ingenious ski cap had flaps which covered the neck and ears. The tunic had distinctive green wings, and this design was a throwback to the style of tunic issued to Württemburg Jägers in 1859. NCOs would wear a similar uniform but with gold threading around the collar patch.*

In 1915, with the introduction of the bluse, the jägers retained their green piping on their shoulder straps. Steel helmets quickly replaced the shakos in 1916.

Jäger Battalion Shako Plate Distinctions

Battalion	Device
1 Graf Yorck von Wartenburg (East Prussian)	eagle and FWR
2 Fürst Bismarck (Pommeranian)	eagle and FWR
3 Brandenburg	eagle
4 Magdeburg	eagle
5 von Neumann (1 Silesian)	eagle and FWR
6 (2 Silesian)	eagle and FWR
7 Westphalian	Schaumburg arms on the Prussian eagle
8 Rhineland	eagle
9 Lauenburg	eagle
10 Hanoverian	eagle, Waterloo, Peninsula and Venta del Pozo battle honour
11 Kur Hessian	eagle
12 (1 Saxon)	Saxon arms
13 (2 Saxon)	Saxon arms
14 GD Mecklenburg	starburst
Jäger-Bataillon Prinz Ludwig (1 Bavarian)	Bavarian arms
Jäger-Bataillon (2 Bavarian)	Bavarian arms

Mountain Troops

The use of ski-equipped troops in war, was first recorded in the 13th century. and the speed and distance that ski troops were able to cover during the war was comparable to that of light cavalry. Bavaria fielded four ski battalions, with Württemberg raising an additional company. This latter became the Württemberg Mountain Battalion in October 1915. These fought in the Vosges against the French and in the Carpathians on the Eastern Front. They would also serve in Romania and Italy.

The Bavarians and Württembergers wore green jackets (known as skilitewkas), and grey breeches with puttees and studded ankle boots (alpine socks were also sometimes worn). The Bavarians' jackets did not have shoulder straps but the Württembergers had green wings to prevent equipment sliding off.

The Württembergers had green collar patches with a button showing their company number (this was later replaced by a button with the state arms), the Bavarians had a dark green 'S' sewn on to their green patches. NCOs had silver embroidered ends to their collars.

All ski troops wore the famous peaked skimütze. This green cap had light green piping and a fold-down flap that covered the neck and ears; in this respect it was similar to the Austro-Hungarian infantry cap. Caps often bore an edelweiss badge and imperial and state cockades, one on each side. Goggles were

▶ **LIEUTENANT 5TH JÄGER BATTALION (SILESIA), 1916**
The newly issued chromium-nickel steel helmet was produced in a green finish. The chinstrap was taken off the old spiked helmet and attached to the new helmet by means of a loop through a metal pillar. This officer wears the bluse tunic issued in 1915 and designed to be a more practical garment than that of 1914. Jägers wore straps piped in light green and, as a lieutenant, this officer would be entitled to wear a single star on his strap. He would carry a revolver and, on parade, an 1889 officer's sword. This would be left behind on campaign, and probably replaced with a bayonet or dagger.

a popular addition. Steel helmets were sometimes worn in action. Greatcoats were not generally worn, various capes and waterproof jackets being used instead. White or grey waterproof overalls were also worn. Mountain troops carried their own skis, coils of rope, ammunition and personal effects, carried in a rucksack.

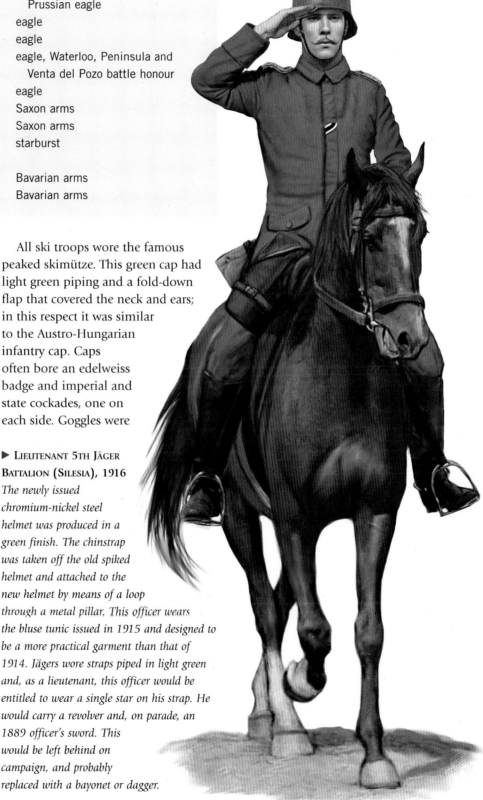

STORMTROOPERS

Germany's attempt to break the deadlock of trench warfare revolved around preceding general assaults with elite bands of trained volunteers. These stormtroops earned themselves a tremendous reputation and spearheaded Germany's great gamble in the spring of 1918.

Origins

When it was apparent that trench warfare was a permanent fixture on the Western Front, Germany began to train assault groups and form them into specialist parties in 1915, a trend which also showed itself in most armies. The concept of sending select volunteers forward to enable a breakthrough was not a new idea, and had been used as a military tactic from Roman times. Major Willy Rohr, a leading advocate of these tactics, took over command of a detachment (Sturmabteilung) in 1915, and other similarly minded officers were also forming special detachments. By 1916 Storm battalions were being formed for each of the 17 German armies in the west (there were 17 created in 1916 and 1917, Rohr's detachment becoming number 5). Increasing uniformity was being imposed on stormtroopers' dress by 1917.

Stormtroop Battalion number 5 was largely composed of pioneers and engineers, the 3rd was drawn from jäger personnel. Battalions numbers 6 and 15 were Bavarian. Most battalions had a company of flame throwers, and these were generally drawn from the Guard reserve pioneers. These men had black collar patches, piped red, with litzen. They also, from the summer of 1918, had a skull and crossed bones insignia sewn to their left sleeves (the skull had rather macabre white teeth).

Uniform Distinctions

Initially, stormtroopers wore the uniform of their original unit. They went forward in assault order, that is

▲ *German stormtroopers, urged on by an officer, emerge from a thick cloud of phosgene poison gas as they attack British trench lines.*

▼ **PROTECTIVE ARMOUR 1916** *1 A cuirass and set of body armour, joined by webbing and lined with felt, of a kind produced in large numbers. 2 A sniper's mantlet. 3 A 1916 steel helmet fitted with the special visor, or sniper's plate. This was supported by lugs on either side of the steel helmet and was supposed to protect the wearer from being shot in the head by small arms fire (the standard helmet could not deflect a direct hit).*

without packs (greatcoats were wrapped in trench canvases and worn around the body) but with additional grenades carried in grenade bags, daggers, clubs and axes, wire cutters and pistols. Assault groups often preferred the shorter carbine to the infantryman's rifle and carried engineers' tools rather than the standard entrenching tool issued to the infantry.

▶ **PRIVATE, STORMTROOP COMPANY, 17TH DIVISION, 1918** *The canvas cartridge bandolier held an additional 70 rounds.*

Buttons and belt buckles were blackened. Trousers were often replaced by breeches or climbing breeches (reinforced with leather and buttoned below the knee) or had leather patches on the knees (tunics also had reinforced elbow patches). Field grey, steel grey or green trousers were worn with alpine socks or puttees and boots (the studded boots used by mountain troops were very popular in storm battalions). Puttees allowed the wearer to climb and run much more comfortably than the boots worn by most infantrymen.

Equipment

Stormtroops sometimes carried Madsen light machine guns, the Bergmann automatic rifle and the Bergmann machine pistol. The latter was an effective sub-machine gun, but it only made an appearance relatively late in the war. Most German grenades were stick grenades, a weapon which first made its appearance in 1915. In its most common guise it had a cylindrical head and wooden stick handle. Some were developed to explode on impact, most detonated after a six-second pause.

Reforms

In February 1917 some attempt was made to impose a sense of order on troops dressed in various styles. Most troops were wearing their original uniform with perhaps the addition of a small metal badge on the tunic breast or unofficial insignia worn on the tunic sleeve. From 1917 stormtroops were supposed to wear infantry uniforms with white shoulder strap piping and a battalion number in red. The pioneers, working the flame throwers, had black shoulder straps piped red (no numeral, as these were guard pioneers); those manning the trench mortars were to have the same but with 'MW' in red, while those serving the battalion's artillery were to have red shoulder straps, a battalion number and flaming grenade in yellow. Machine gunners wore a machine gun badge on the upper

sleeve, and some specialist grenadiers appear to have worn a stick grenade badge on their upper sleeve. Major Rohr's men continued to be the exceptions, trying to retain uniforms that resembled assault engineers.

In addition to the stormtroop battalions, many German divisions had independent assault groups, raiding detachments and hunting companies. These sometimes adopted unofficial insignia of their own devising, but most of them wore standard assault equipment and regimental uniforms.

 ◄ PRIVATE, STORMBATTALION, 1917 *The 1822 Model spade carried by this stormtrooper had its own case and was strapped on to the shoulder strap. It was a practical weapon that allowed assault troops to dig in quickly and take cover in open ground.*

► PRIVATE, STORMBATTALION, 1918 *Additional grenades were stored in the bags carried under the shoulder. Most grenades would have been the type of stick grenade first introduced in 1915. This detonated six seconds after a cord was pulled and largely replaced a grenade which, after a pin was removed, exploded upon impact.*

LANDWEHR

Germany's militia, the Landwehr (the translation is 'defence of the country') constituted a reserve to the front line units, providing garrisons, escorts and, occasionally, being brought into the line as fighting troops. Those who were too old or too unfit served in the Landsturm, a secondary militia very much assigned to support roles.

Reserve of the Reserve

German reservists were usually gathered into reserve regiments, each with a parent unit in the front line. Shortages meant they were poorly equipped but they were used to fill gaps as casualties mounted. Reserve regiments generally wore the uniform of their equivalent parent unit but with an 'R' on the shako or spiked helmet cover, as well as the unit number (the young Austrian Adolf Hitler served in the 16th Bavarian Reserve Infantry Regiment). Behind them stood the Landwehr. This organization evolved from the War of Liberation against Napoleon, and harked back to the idea of a nation in arms. Those too old for service in front line units were assigned to the Landwehr (if they were younger than 39).

Landwehr Uniforms

The 96 regiments of Landwehr were poorly equipped in 1914 but Landwehr infantry generally followed the uniform of front-line infantry units. The most remarkable feature of their uniforms was the leather shako (most frequently the 1895 model used by the light infantry). This had a cross within an oval, all usually painted grey by 1915, a state cockade above the cross and an imperial cockade on each side of the shako where the chinstraps were held in place. Officers often had spiked

helmets with covers bearing an 'L' and the unit number (the helmet itself would have an eagle and Landwehr cross front plate). Sometimes helmets were painted grey to save on cloth. Shortages were such that some units used adapted firemen's helmets. Only later were steel helmets brought into use, most units having them by 1917. Some Landwehr units wore soft peaked

◀ PRIVATE, 82ND LANDWEHR REGIMENT, 1914
The tunic could be tightened by means of buttoning a cloth belt at the rear.

▶ SERGEANT, 5TH BATTALION BAVARIAN LANDSTURM, 1914 *Landsturm headgear came in many guises from the 1813 oilcloth cap to the equally obsolete 1860 leather shako. Underneath the shako cover it bore the traditional Landsturm cross. Most Landsturm received outdated headgear, such as cast-off shakos from the jäger depots, before being issued with the spiked helmet in 1916.*

Landwehr troops often carried obsolete rifles and inferior equipment. Many units were issued with old models of knapsack and ammunition pouches, such as the 1895 pouches in black leather, or the 1889 cartridge boxes, which could only hold 30 rounds of ammunition.

Landsturm Units

These units formed a kind of Home Guard and were composed of the too young or too old. They were generally assigned to guard prisoners, garrison forts (away from the front line) and as occupation troops in Belgium and the Ukraine. Lansturm infantry battalions wore the 1813 peaked cap (usually black and covered in oilskin, sometimes of grey cloth) or the leather shako with a large cross in a white (or silver) oval beneath a state cockade. Officers preferred to use spiked helmets with eagle plates bearing a Landsturm cross in the centre.

The Landsturm wore field grey tunics (generally with buttons bearing crowns) with blue shoulder straps (light blue for the Bavarians, scarlet for artillery and yellow for foot artillery) devoid of piping or of numerals. Blue tunics with standing collars could still be seen throughout the war. Saxons wore shoulder straps with pointed ends. The relevant Army Corps number in roman numerals was actually worn on the collar alongside the battalion number in Arabic numerals. These distinctions (although sometimes absent or only partially used) were retained when the Landsturm switched from the feldrock to the bluse in 1916. Trousers came in all shapes from the black trousers with red piping worn by the Landwehr to brown civilian breeches or field grey infantry issue.

Landsturm men were again poorly off when it came to equipment and weaponry, being very much at the back of the queue. Obsolete bolt-action rifles or captured guns were used, along with whatever else could be collected, by way of personal equipment (civilian knapsacks, dated ammunition pouches and privately purchased boots and belts). Cavalry squadrons were also formed and wore uniforms of their particular branch of service, and with Landstrum crosses on their headgear.

▼ PRIVATE, 18TH LANDSTURM BATTALION, 1917 *The collar shows the Army Corps number (XIII), then the battalion number (18) in dull brass. This individual is deployed as an assault trooper – the Landsturm formed assault platoons in imitation of the stormtroopers. A large number of personnel in these units were issued with the Gewehr 88 rifle.*

▲ PRIVATE, WÜRTTEMBERG, 5TH LANDSTURM BATTALION, 1916 *This soldier has a superb civilian fur-lined coat and, underneath, is lucky enough to have a 1910 field grey tunic with Saxon cuffs. Some Landsturm units were still wearing the pre-1910 dark blue uniforms as late as 1916.*

caps of a type first seen in 1813. Shortages were such that a number of Landwehr units marched to the front in obsolete blue tunics and black breeches piped red. Black greatcoats were also seen in 1914.

CAVALRY

German cavalry played an important role in 1914, but their role and presence was steadily diminished as the war continued. By 1918 they had become a marginal force.

The old distinction between heavy cavalry (used to deliver knockout blows on the field of battle, a role still performed by German cavalry in the 1870s) and light cavalry still existed in 1914. The difference between dragoons and cuirassiers – usually kept in reserve – and hussars, lancers, mounted jägers and light horse was an important one. The latter were primarily used for probing and scouting, The Germans who advanced into Belgium were preceded by such cavalry, just as they were in Poland in 1914 and 1915. The ulans were seen as ubiquitous, restless and ever active, a concept stemming from the fact that plenty of German cavalry carried the lance and were thus mistaken for lancers.

The Heavy Cavalry

The cuirassiers wore field grey tunics with standing collars, Swedish cuffs and shoulder straps. Regimental colours were shown on the piping along the shoulder straps (bordered by white lace on the inside), down the front of the tunic and along its edges, as well as on the cuffs (officers went without piping on the collar and cuffs, and Saxon regiments did without the piping on the collar). Regimental lace was worn on the collars and cuffs. Some regiments had red regimental numerals on their shoulder straps,

▲ PRIVATE, 20TH ULAN REGIMENT, 1914
When the square top of the helmet was removed, the helmet resembled that of the infantry in shape. Here the helmet is covered with a protective cloth cover.

Dragoon Distinctions

Regiment	Piping Colour	Button
1 Prinz Albrecht von Preußen (Lithuanian)	red	gold
2 (1 Brandenburg)	black	gold
3 Grenadier-zu-Pferd von Derfflinger (Neumark)	pink	silver
4 von Bredow (1 Silesian)	sand	silver
5 Freiherr von Manteuffel (Rhineland)	red	silver
6 Magdeburg	black	silver
7 Westphalia	pink	gold
8 König Friedrich III (2 Silesian)	yellow	gold
9 König Karl I von Rumänien (1 Hanoverian)	white	gold
10 König Albert von Sachsen (East Prussian)	white	silver
11 von Wedel (Pomeranian)	crimson	gold
12 von Arnim (2 Brandenburg)	crimson	silver
13 Schleswig-Holstein	red	gold
14 Kurmark	black	gold
15 (3 Silesian)	pink	silver
16 (2 Hanoverian)	yellow	silver
17 (1 Mecklenburg)	red	gold
18 (2 Mecklenburg)	black	silver
19 Oldenburg	white	silver
20 Leib-Dragoner (1 Baden)	red	silver
21 (2 Baden)	yellow	silver
22 Prinz Karl (3 Baden)	black	silver
23 Leib-Dragoner (1 Hessisches)	red	silver
24 Leib-Dragoner(2 Hessisches)	white	silver
25 Königin Olga (1 Württemberg)	white	gold
26 König (2 Württemberg)	yellow	silver

Cuirassier and Heavy Cavalry Distinctions

Regiment	Piping	Buttons
1 (Leib) Großer Kurfürst (Silesian)	black	gold
2 Königin (Pomeranian)	crimson	silver
3 Graf Wrangel (East Prussian)	light blue	silver
4 von Driesen (Westphalian)	scarlet	silver
5 Eugen von Württemberg (West Prussian)	pink	gold
6 Kaiser Nikolas I. von Rußland (Brandenburg)	blue	gold
7 von Seydlitz (4. Magdeburg)	yellow	silver
8 Graf Geßler (Rhineland)	light green	gold
9 Saxon Garde-Reiter-Regiment	cornflower blue	gold
10 Saxon Karabiner-Regiment	cornflower blue	gold
Bavarian Heavy Cavalry		
1 Prinz Karl von Bayern	scarlet	silver
2 Erzherzog Franz Ferdinand	scarlet	gold

a star). The helmet was worn with a light green cover and, from September 1914, this bore a green regimental numeral. The Bavarians wore a helmet similar to that worn by Bavarian infantry. Peaked caps were worn with bands in the regimental colour. Breeches were grey, often reinforced with black leather, without piping. Long jackboots (with knee protection) were worn, although these were sometimes replaced by natural leather boots. A simplified tunic was adopted in late 1914, and the bluse introduced in 1915 with white shoulder straps and regimental piping. Steel helmets were also introduced in 1916.

▼ PRIVATE, 17TH HUSSAR REGIMENT (BRUNSWICK), 1915 *This hussar cap was made from seal skin on a bamboo frame.*

although the 1st, 2nd, 6th, 8th and 9th had cyphers and the Bavarians had plain straps piped red.

Heavy cavalry wore a black spiked helmet (M1889), which had a long neck guard and state cockades, as well as a plate with the relevant state's symbol (for the Saxons this was

▶ PRIVATE, HORSE GUARD REGIMENT (SAXON), 1915 *The steel helmet worn by the heavy cavalry had a longer neck guard.*

Hussar Distinctions

Regiment	Rgt. Colour	Cord Colour
1 (1 Leib)	black	white
2 (2 Leib) Königin Viktoria von Preußen	black	white
3 von Zieten (Brandenburg)	scarlet	white
4 von Schill (1 Silesian)	brown	yellow
5 Fürst Blücher (Pommeranian)	red	white
6 Graf Goetzen (2 Silesian)	green	yellow
7 König Wilhelm I (1 Rhineland)	grey-blue	yellow
8 Kaiser Nikolaus II von Rußland (1 Westphalian)	blue	white
9 (2 Rhineland)	cornflower	yellow
10 Magdeburg	green	yellow ▶

Dragoons

Originally dragoons were mounted infantry but, by the late 19th century were, to all intents and purposes, heavy cavalry. German dragoons wore field grey tunics with standing collars (piped as appropriate) and regimental piping on the Swedish cuffs. Shoulder straps were piped in the regimental colour (officers had this colour as the base of their shoulderboards) and bore a number in red or a cypher for regiments numbered 3, 8, 9, 10, 17, 18, 23, 24, 25 and 26.

Regiments 23 and 25 had litzen in white on their collars and cuffs. All regiments wore spiked infantry-style helmets in 1914 with state plates (Guard eagles for regiments 1 and 3) and cockades. Regiments 9 and 16 had Waterloo battle honours on their helmets, the 9th also adding Peninsula and Göhrde. Peaked caps wore regimental coloured bands, and the 2nd Regimentals had an eagle between the two cockades. The bluse replaced the tunic in 1915 and shoulder straps

▶ PRIVATE, 1ST BAVARIAN ULAN REGIMENT (KAISER WILHELM II), 1917 *The black belt supports the cartridge pouches, which were introduced in 1909.*

were to be light blue with regimental piping. Steel helmets were worn from 1916.

Hussars

The hussars retained a distinctive uniform in 1914, influenced by traditional hussar dress. They wore an attila tunic (M1909), based on the traditional dolman and with black (green for Saxon) and grey cords decorating the front and embroidering the rear. Shoulder cords were twisted braid of regimental and the unit's historical cord colours, as in the table (officers had straps with regimental colours piped with cord colours).

Hussars wore black fur busbies with state cockades worn outside the cover, and chinstraps. Grey covers with green regimental numerals were worn. Peaked caps had regimental-coloured bands (with a skull between the cockades for the 1st, 2nd and 17th). Breeches with braid and cords were worn with boots. The bluse was partially introduced in 1915, many regiments retaining the attila.

Hussar Distinctions con't

Regiment	Rgt. Colour	Cord Colour
11 (2 Westphalian)	green	white
12 Thuringia	cornflower	white
13 König Umberto von Italien (1 Kur Hessian)	cornflower	white
14 Hessen-Homburg (2 Kur Hessian)	blue	white
15 Königin Wilhelmena der Niederlande (Hanoverian)	blue	white
16 Franz Josef von Österreich (Schleswig-Holstein)	cornflower	white
17 Brunswick	black	yellow
18 (1 Saxon) König Albert	cornflower	yellow
19 (2 Saxon)	cornflower	white
20 (3 Saxon)	cornflower	white

Bavarian Chevauxleger Distinctions

Regiment	Piping
1 Kaiser Nikolaus von Rußland	crimson
2 Taxis	crimson
3 Herzog Karl Theodor	orange
4 König	red
5 Erzherzog Friedrich von Österreich	red
6 Prinz Albrecht von Preußen	orange
7 Prinz Alfons	white
8	white

Bavarian Chevauxlegers

There were eight regiments of Bavarian light horse uniformed in field grey ulankas with Swedish cuffs and falling collars. Piping was as in the table, and spiked helmets with Bavarian coats of arms were worn until 1916, when the steel helmet was introduced.

Mounted Jägers

The 13 jäger cavalry regiments wore greenish-grey tunics with standing collars and Swedish cuffs. Piping was white for the 1st and 8th, red for the 2nd and 9th, yellow for the 3rd and 10th, light blue for the 4th and 11th, black for the 5th and 12th, blue for the 6th and 13th and pink for the 7th. Shoulder straps had red numerals, only the 1st Regiment had a cypher. Spiked helmets were worn until 1916.

Ulans

Germany's lancers wore a modified version of the traditional Polish uniform. They had a rather squat square-topped cap, a tunic called an ulanka (inspired by the Polish kurtka jacket) with plastron lapels and rounded shoulder straps (red numbers for regiments 2, 4, 5, 8, 9, 10, 11, 12, 14, 15, 17, 18 and 21). Piping was worn around the jacket and at the cuffs and shoulder straps. The tunic had standing collars, except for the Bavarians, and Polish (pointed) cuffs. Simplified tunics were worn from March 1915, with scarlet shoulder straps piped in regimental colours.

▶ SERGEANT, 2ND BAVARIAN CHEVAUXLEGER REGIMENT (TAXIS), 1918 *The lance pennon was in Bavarian colours, Saxon units had green and white and the rest black and white.*

ARTILLERY

German artillery was highly regarded, proficient and professional. It provided effective and enduring support all along the Western Front, in the east and, on loan, in the Ottoman empire.

Field Artillery

The field artillery wore the standard field grey tunic (the feldrock) with black piping around the collar, cuffs and rear, and red (it actually varied from pink to burgundy) piping down the tunic front. Cuffs were generally Saxon, although some regiments'

were Swedish (the 12th, 28th, 32nd, 48th, 64th, 68th, 77th, 78th, 115th, 245th and 246th). Buttons were yellow metal (there were eight down the front, one on each shoulder strap and one on the pocket flaps plus six on the rear tails and three on each cuff). Shoulder straps were piped in red for Saxon (regiments 12, 28, 32, 48, 64, 68, 77 and 78) and Bavarian (12 regiments) units and were piped according to the relevant corps for all other regiments: The III, IV, XI, XIII, XIV, XV and XIX had scarlet piping; the I, II, IX, X had white; the V, VI, XVI, and XVII had yellow; the VII, VIII, XVIII and XX had blue; and the XXI had green.

Regiments 25 and 61 had red piping and 25 was a special case. This was the Grand Duchy of Hesse Regiment and it had silver litzen on the collar and cuffs, yellow with central white lace for enlisted men. Shoulder straps generally had the regimental number in red with a flaming grenade above it.

Field artillery wore field grey trousers piped in red (this piping was quickly abolished). Artillery drivers wore cavalry-style breeches with leather inners.

◀ SERGEANT, 30TH FIELD ARTILLERY REGIMENT (1ST BADEN), 1914 *The artillery helmet, seen here with its cover on, had a ball on top, and a much less rounded front than the infantry helmet.*

▲ *German troops pull trench artillery over heavily shelled fields. 23 March 1918.*

Field artillery wore infantry helmets but with the spike replaced by a ball (except for the Bavarians who retained the spikes). State cockades and helmet plates were worn. A grey or light brown cover with regimental number was worn in the early months of the war. Peaked caps had black bands with red piping on the crown.

In 1915 the bluse was introduced for field artillery and this had red shoulder straps. Steel helmets were introduced in 1916.

Artillery serving in the Ottoman Empire and in the Balkans sometimes wore khaki cotton tunics and trousers, with German distinctions and shoulder straps. Tropical helmets or peaked khaki caps often replaced headgear worn in Europe.

Foot Artillery

There were some 20 foot artillery regiments and they wore very similar uniforms to the field artillery. All had Brandenburg cuffs and white shoulder strap piping (only the 12th and 19th had red). There were three regiments of Bavarian foot artillery. When the bluse was worn it had yellow shoulder straps for foot artillery regiments with crossed shells above the regimental number (except the Bavarians). Foot artillery

▲ *German troops examine a gigantic cannon, abandoned by retreating Italians, near Udine in northern Italy.*

served heavier guns, mostly heavy howitzers, but also some substantial pieces powerful enough to shell Paris from behind the German lines. Trench artillery was generally served by infantry or engineer personnel.

Equipment

Field and foot artillery were issued artillery backpacks and were armed with long barrelled pistols (the P08 or the Mauser), carried in a brown leather holster attached to the waist belt. Officers initially wore swords with sword knots but later bayonets were preferred (although sword knots were often retained). Officers also carried map cases, binoculars and gas mask canisters. Greatcoats had blue (green for Saxons) collars piped red for officers and black collar patches (piped red for the 25th Regiment) or, for the Saxons, grey piped black.

Mountain Artillery

There were some five battalions of mountain artillery by the end of 1914 deployed in the Vosges and Italy. The batteries from Württemberg and Bavaria quickly adopted uniforms in the style of ski troops with peaked caps and litewkas. The caps and tunics were piped in black and grenade badges were worn on the shoulder straps, as well as on the side of the caps.

Artillery Train

Troops of the artillery train wore field artillery uniforms but with Swedish cuffs and light blue piping. Caps had light blue bands and crown piping and battalion numbers on their blue-piped shoulder straps. When the bluse was introduced in 1915 they wore blue shoulder straps with yellow battalion numbers.

▼ LIGHT FIELD HOWITZER 1914 *Developed in the early 1900s, this gun was issued to the artillery from 1909. Known as the 10.5cm field howitzer, it was an essential component in*

▲ LIEUTENANT, 27TH FIELD ARTILLERY REGIMENT (NASSAU), 1916 *Artillery wore black cap bands with red piping. The binoculars are the standard 1908 issue and the case is attached to the officer's belt. Instructions on how to use the binoculars were attached to the inside of the case lid.*

German artillery tactics. It had a short barrel, an ingenious recoil mechanism and tremendous elevation, making it ideal for producing indirect fire over the Allied trenches.

TECHNICAL TROOPS

Germany was well supported by competent technical troops, varying from field engineers to aviators. The only new development relatively neglected by the Germans was the introduction of large numbers of tanks.

Machine Gunners and Tankers

There were eight independent machine gun detachments in 1914 plus an additional Bavarian detachment.

▲ *An early tank, a German A7V, captured at Villers-Bretonneux, France, by the Allies.*

They wore grey-green jäger uniforms but with scarlet piping around the collar, down the front and around the cuffs, and a leather shako with brown leather peaks and a green cloth cylindrical crown. They had the detachment number in red on the shoulder strap and yellow metal buttons. Later, large numbers of independent machine gun detachments were formed, including some elite detachments with yellow or gold sleeve insignia with a Maxim gun in an oval.

Tankers generally chose to wear field grey overalls or leather tunics and leather caps with goggles or visors. They were formed into heavy vehicle detachments, later heavy assault

vehicle detachments. Motor transport detachments generally wore a 'K' on their shoulder straps, black leather overalls, coats and leggings.

Engineers

There were 35 battalions of pioneers, including four Bavarian battalions and two Saxon. Numerous independent companies were formed during the war. The troops wore artillery uniforms but with silver or white metal buttons, Swedish cuffs

◀ **PRIVATE, 16TH PIONEERS, 1915** *The engineer corps consisted of officers, and the manual work of digging and constructing (or demolishing) was done by pioneers. These, unlike their artillery counterparts, wore spiked helmets before 1916. This battalion was recruited in Lorraine.*

▶ **CAPTAIN, 2ND FLYING BATTALION, 1914** *The brocade belt, woven from black and grey bullion, was rare. The flying helmet was of civilian manufacture. A number of pilots added a tube of horsehair around the crown of the helmet to give some additional protection against bumps and bangs.*

◀ THE RED BARON, 1917 *The famous fighter pilot, Manfred von Richthofen, was the most successful ace of the war. Here he wears the tunic of an officer in his former unit, the Von Rußland Ulans.*

▶ PILOT, II BOMBER GROUP, 1916 *Pilots often wore their own civilian coats or adapted greatcoats from their parent regiments. This pilot has aluminium frames with fur lining to prevent the skin freezing to the metal.*

number and 'SMW', 'MMW' or 'LMW', for heavy, medium and light, were introduced in 1915. Guard pioneers were famous for operating flame thrower equipment. Troops entrusted with developing and testing new equipment, including gas shells and cylinders, wore a 'V' on their shoulder straps along with engineer uniforms.

Signals troops generally wore engineer uniforms but with a 'T' and battalion number on the shoulder strap. In 1917 the bluse was worn with light green shoulder straps piped red.

Labour battalions wore field grey tunics with armbands bearing the battalion number in red. Mining companies were dressed as engineers but with crossed hammer devices (worn in blue by Bavarian units).

Aviation Personnel

Initially the air service was based on airship and observation balloon crews. Personnel wore officer's tunics or enlisted men's feldrocks with light grey shoulder strap piping and shoulderboard underlay and black collar and cuff piping. Shakos were worn. Officers bore gold propeller devices on their shoulderboards, enlisted men had the same in red. Officers had guard lace on their collars, enlisted men a simpler lace bar. Ground crewmen often wore battalion numbers on brassards. Pilots had considerable licence in dress. Many wore the uniform of their original units but with flying personnel shoulderboards; Manfred von Richthofen, the famous Red Baron, for example, wore his 1st Ulan uniform.

Devices were generally transferred to the bluse in 1915 with light grey

and red piping or base colour to the shoulder straps. These straps bore a crossed pick and shovel for Saxon units. They wore spiked helmets with cloth covers and battalion numbers in red. When the bluse was introduced it had black shoulder straps piped red and with red devices. Officers had additional lace on their collars. Railway engineers added an 'E' to their shoulder straps. Additional equipment was carried by engineer troops.

Engineers also operated mortars. Officers had 'MW' added to their shoulderboards; men had this along with the engineer's battalion number. Oval arm patches giving the company

shoulderstraps and red propellers and battalion numbers for enlisted men or an 'L' for balloon personnel. The straps were piped in white, red, yellow or blue for the 1st to 4th Battalions respectively. Oval arm patches were worn with battalion or group numbers.

Equipment consisted of leather helmet, goggles, various leather or fur overcoats, leggings, gloves and scarves. Pistols were carried. Flying badges, worn on the left breast, consisted of a wreath and crown surrounding an aeroplane or, for the Bavarians, a wreath and Bavarian crown with a quartered square (alternate blue and white) in the centre.

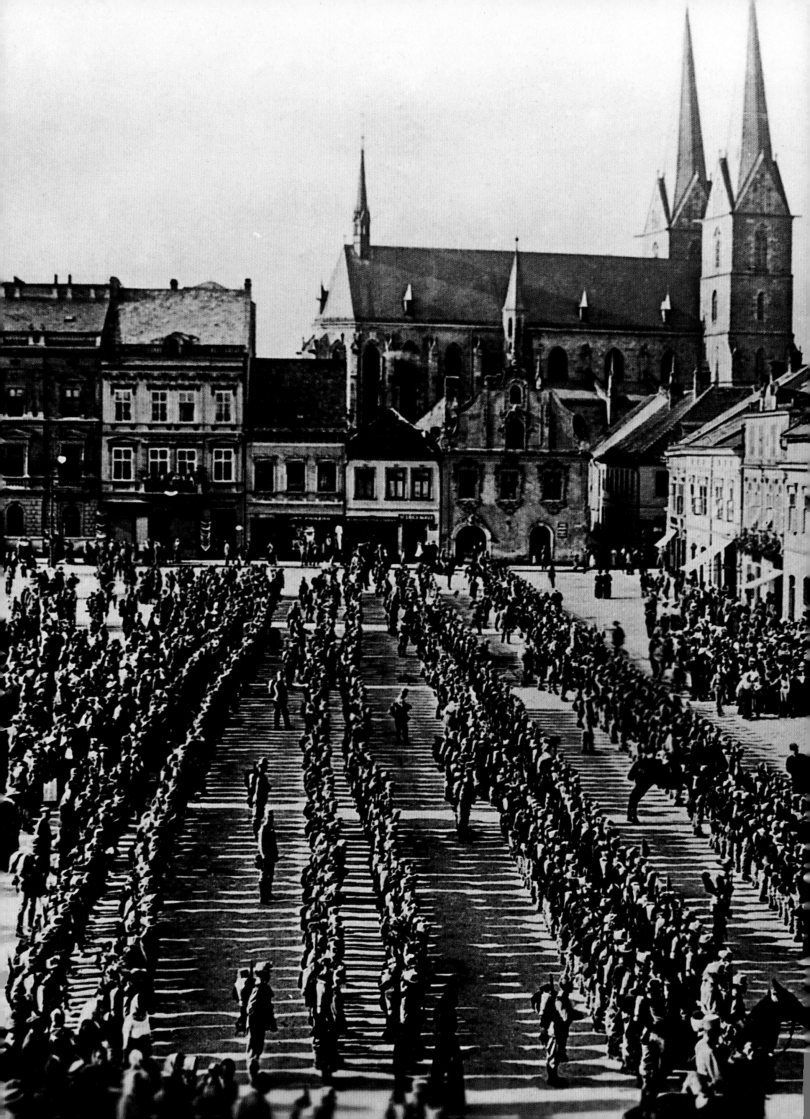

AUSTRIA-HUNGARY AND GERMANY'S OTHER ALLIES

The Austro-Hungarian empire felt itself to be the dominant power in central Europe and yet it was already on the wane by 1914. Rivals, and even allies, were challenging its influence, the imperial budget was insufficient, and agencies within the government were squabbling over what money was available. The empire was to field what was, on paper, a very respectable force with enviable traditions and reputation. Yet it was obliged to field it in the east against Russia, to the south against Serbia and, in 1915, to the south-west against Italy. Such demands were perhaps too great for a power that had resisted modernization. Yet, with German support, the empire's armies performed valiantly. The same could be said of Bulgaria, exhausted by Balkan wars and the Ottoman Empire, regarded as the sick man of Europe.

▲ *Austria-Hungary waged a three-year war against Italy, often in mountainous conditions and brutal weather. An amazing victory at Caporetto in the autumn of 1917 was overshadowed by ultimate defeat at Vittorio Veneto.*

◄ *The 98th Infantry Regiment was largely composed of Czechs. It can be seen here in the summer of 1914 parading at Vysoke Myto, in Bohemia, before leaving for the front.*

THE HAPSBURG MONARCHY

In an age of centralized nation states or federated empires, the Austro-Hungarian empire was a strange anachronism. The state was held together by the monarch, who personally united a diverse collection of lands and territories. In 1914 the emperor could boast the official title of Emperor of Austria, King of Hungary, King of Bohemia, Grand Prince of Transylvania, Duke of Salzburg, Margrave of Moravia and Grand Voivode of Serbia.

After defeat at the hands of Prussia in 1866, reform had made an unwelcome appearance in Vienna's corridors of power. The resulting Compromise of 1867 had enshrined a basic division of the territory into the empire of Austria and the kingdom of Hungary. The emperor of Austria governed the predominantly German and western territories; as king of Hungary he ruled over the vast territories of Hungary, Galicia (southern Poland), Transylvania and Croatia. Of the resulting ethnic mix of his subjects, 24 per cent were German

in 1910, 20 per cent were Hungarian, 17 per cent Czech or Slovak, 18 per cent Polish or Ukrainian, 11% Serbo-Croat and 6 per cent Romanian.

Political control (rather than representation) came through parliaments in Vienna and Budapest; these had considerable autonomy, but a common government could supposedly claim control over foreign policy and armed forces (but not always over finance). Bosnia Herzegovina, as a recently acquired territory, had a separate administration having a Governor General in Sarajevo.

Internal Unrest

Czech attempts to create a Triple Monarchy, recognizing Czech autonomy, had failed in the 1870s, and south Slav resentment against Hungarian rule, which was restrictive for anyone who was not a Hungarian

▼ *The Austro-Hungarian empire in 1914 was a patchwork of ethnicity and language that did not conform to boundaries and was held together by the resolute grip of tradition.*

▲ *By the time he died, in 1916, Emperor Franz Josef had ruled for 68 years, the third longest reign in the recorded history of Europe.*

landowner, and attempts to win greater freedoms, had also been stifled. Antagonizing minorities led to increasing frustration, particularly in territories bordering states composed of similar ethnic groups. Thus, Transylvania contained numbers of Romanians, the Tyrol had a large Italian minority and Slavonia (and Bosnia) contained large numbers of Serbs. A situation such as this could provoke suspicion, or conflict with neighbours, as could, for example, Austro-Hungarian meddling in the Ukraine, Poland and Albania. Such tensions, it was hoped, would become irrelevant at the end of a successful war. Certainly, problems with the south Slavs were seen in this light: a settling of accounts with Serbia would pacify the empire's restless minorities in Bosnia, Croatia and Slavonia.

Map legend

	Germans
	Hungarians
	Romanians
	Slavs
	Poles
	Italians
▬▬▬	Kingdom of Hungary
··········	Division of Slav ethnicity

Map labels: RUSSIA, Czechs, GERMANY, Danube, Ruthenians, Slovaks, AUSTRIA, HUNGARY, Slovenes, Croats and Serbians, ITALY, Adriatic Sea, BOSNIA, 150 km, 100 miles

Military Structure

The Army was itself structured to reflect the political situation. There was a Common Army, which was designated Imperial and Royal (Kaiserlich und Königlich, or KuK), which was the responsibility of the joint minister of war, but there was also an Austrian landwehr (not to be confused with the militia), responsible to an Austrian minister, and a Hungarian equivalent called the honvéd. Regiments belonging to the landwehr were termed Imperial Royal (Kaiserlich Königlich, or KK) and honvéd regiments were called Royal Hungarian (Königlich Ungarisch, or KU). There was also the domobran, a Croatian force created under the auspices of the Hungarian-Croat agreement of 1868.

Language and Communication

It was inevitable that the Army would reflect the multi-ethnic composition of the empire itself. In 1910 the situation in the Common Army (when it numbered 183,000 infantry, 57,000 cavalry and 79,000 artillery) was as shown in the table below

It could be a sensitive issue and certainly complicated an already slow administration (the mobilization order in 1914 was issued in 15 languages). However, the majority of the officer corps was German, and theirs was a vital language for anyone wanting to be commissioned, as it was the language of command and the service language (technical terms), although the language of the recruits was used within the regiment. Professional officers, therefore, were supposed to know the language of their men, but this was not always possible in wartime. Some ethnic groups were also viewed with suspicion by the upper echelons of the Army (who were wont to blame ethnicity for problems that were often caused by poor supply or bad leadership). Czechs and Ruthenians were quickly labelled unreliable, Romanians were thought to be unsuitable for use on the Eastern Front, and Italians would have to serve in the east or in the Balkans.

Budget Constraints

Of more serious concern was the lack of investment in the common army. Spending did not match that of the empire's rivals or neighbours. Russian military expenditure tripled between 1871 and 1914, in the empire it was less than doubled. In 1911 the defence expenditure reached 650 million crowns, compared to Germany's outlay of 1.8 billion. Much of this was then diverted to the navy (which was modern but largely geographically restricted to the Adriatic). The result was that the Austro-Hungarian Army had a serious shortage of equipment for its front line divisions. It had fewer machine guns per division than the Russians and only 42 field guns per infantry division compared to 48 in the Russian equivalent. Much of the artillery was obsolete and shortages even made themselves felt in a lack of uniforms and standard equipment. German generosity and captured Russian equipment would help in 1914 and 1915 but, long term, such a situation was not sustainable.

Recruitment

The Army was also small, having been restricted by a Hungarian parliament composed of powerful landowners who did not wish to see the strengthening of common institutions. Laws restricted the army to a levy of 103,100 men per year and this was not increased in line with the population. The empire was training just 0.29 per cent of its population per year, compared to 0.75 per cent for France and 0.37 per cent for Italy. Fewer troops could be brought into the field, and fewer trained replacements were available should the war go badly or be on a greater scale than predicted. Reform was only really on the agenda by 1912 but, by then, it was too late.

▼ *Recruits for the Austro-Hungarian Army in Przemysl, a city in the region of Galicia, in what is now Poland, in 1904.*

Army Ethnicity	
Nationality	**Per cent**
German	25.2
Hungarian	23.5
Czech or Slovak	16.5
Polish	7.9
Ruthenian	7.6
Serbian or Croat	9.0
Slovenian	2.4
Romanian	7.0
Italian	1.3

AUSTRO-HUNGARIAN GENERALS AND STAFF

The Austro-Hungarian Army reflected the political organization of the country. The empire, sometimes known as the Dual Monarchy, agreed on a Common Army as its primary arm, but the two distinct parts of the empire additionally maintained their own forces. Even within the Common Army there were differences between those regiments uniformed in the German style and those which wore traditional Hungarian uniforms.

◄ EMPEROR KARL IN AUSTRO-HUNGARIAN GENERAL'S UNIFORM, 1914 *The stiff kepi with cockade and loop was worn by generals and emperors. Karl was the grand nephew of Franz Josef and became heir after the assassination of Franz Ferdinand. His Italian wife's connections opened up channels which Karl used to communicate his desire for peace in 1918. His uniform shows field marshals' distinctions on the collar. This rank had been introduced in September 1915. The elaborate medal around his neck is the Order of the Golden Fleece.*

The Commanders

Austria-Hungary had introduced a pike-grey (hechtgrau) uniform in 1908 after prolonged discussion. The shade of the new material varied from a grey to a colour resembling French horizon blue. General officers wore tunics in this colour, complete with concealed buttons and scalloped pocket flaps. These tunics were privately tailored and of superior quality to those worn by junior staff.

General officers usually wore breeches, black cavalry boots or boots plus leather gaiters, as the intention was that they should be mounted. Piping was not worn on the breeches, although Hungarian generals wore Hungarian knots in yellow and black to reflect national identity. General officers wore a gold and black field sash, although this was quickly discarded when losses mounted, and a gold and black sword knot attached to the hilt of their sabre.

One of the key distinguishing features of Austro-Hungarian officers was the stiff kepi (a shortened shako), which had been introduced in 1871 and was frequently seen in either its black version or in a pike-grey equivalent. This had a leather visor and a black or pike-grey chinstrap. This cap, known as an artificial brain, had an imperial monogram ('FJI' for Franz Josef or 'IFJ' for Hungarian generals, and, after 1916, a 'K' for Karl) on the

▲ *General Franz Conrad von Hotzendorf, chief of staff of the Austro-Hungarian Army, supported the initiation of war in 1914 and advocated an aggressive policy towards Serbia. He was considered a great general, but was often faced with mediocre resources and reluctant German allies.*

front with a golden loop. The other key distinguishing feature was the collar patch, which was worn on the front of the stiff collar.

Field marshals had a gold oak leaf on golden embroidery on a scarlet patch, colonel-generals had golden zig-zag lace on a scarlet patch with a silver wreath and three stars, while infantry and cavalry generals retained the stars without the laurel wreath. The number of stars fell to two for lieutenant generals and one for major generals.

Staff Officers

Austro-Hungarian staff officers wore uniforms that were very similar to those of field rank. They wore tunics with stand-up collars and these bore a black silk collar patch with a red edge, gold zigzag lace and silver stars. They also wore the sword knot and sash, later reduced to a knot attached to a bayonet.

AUSTRO-HUNGARIAN INFANTRY

Apart from light infantry, elite specialist and assorted foreign volunteers, Austria-Hungary's Common Army had three kinds of infantry regiments. There were those which were termed German (but were composed of many nationalities) and uniformed accordingly, those designated Hungarian and, in 1914, four Bosnia-Herzogovinia regiments.

New Uniforms

The introduction of pike-grey in 1908 transformed the appearance of Austria-Hungary's infantry, but was not a radical innovation. A number of Austro-Hungarian troops had worn grey in the 19th century, including light infantry and technical troops. The traditional white coats (which even then had been very light grey) had been ruled obsolete, and before 1908 infantrymen wore dark blue tunics, caps and greatcoats. Some of these items continued to be worn in the war, mostly by militia units.

▼ *A Tyrolean jäger regiment in 1915. The southern Tyrol had a long tradition of raising units of volunteer marksmen.*

The new tunic for all three kinds of infantry was pike-grey with concealed buttons. The winter version was of thicker cloth and had six zinc buttons and a standing collar (the neck being protected by a pike-grey neck band or neckerchief). The summer version was similar but made from linen and had a stand and fall collar. It was generally only worn along the Adriatic coast and

▲ *Austrian soldiers from an infantry regiment of the Common Army say goodbye to their sweethearts in Vienna in August 1914.*

by specialists serving with the Ottomans. The tunic had shoulder straps, and sometimes included a distinctive roll to support the rifle sling or equipment straps. Officers did not wear shoulder straps.

Infantrymen in the German regiments wore straight trousers buttoned at the ankle, Bosnian troops wore pantaloons that were loose above the knee and tight below it, while Hungarian regiments wore distinctive trousers that were tight and bore yellow and black Hungarian knots and piping down the seams. Most troops eventually adopted puttees and loose-fitting trousers. Boots were mostly in brown, natural leather but shortages meant that most kinds and colours of footwear could be seen.

Uniform Distinctions

Regiments were distinguished by having coloured collar patches and buttons in either yellow or white metal. The variety of colours used in the facing colours of the 102 regiments

▲ **FULL EQUIPMENT FOR AUSTRO-HUNGARIAN INFANTRYMAN 1914–17** *1 Backpack, made from horse skin, with cartridge belt and rolled tent canvas. 2 Canvas provisions bag, also manufactured in grey. 3 Entrenching tool. 4 Barbed wire cutters. 5 Gas mask or Gummimask. 6 Individual flask for soup.*

◀ **PRIVATE, 14TH INFANTRY REGIMENT, 1914** *This uniform, introduced in 1908, included buttoned gaiters for German infantry.*

patches by folding down their neck bands so that only a sliver of coloured cloth could be seen.

Greatcoats were double breasted and bore coloured collar patches in a distinctive arrow-head shape (known as paroli). Red lanyards were worn by those with marksman qualifications.

Headgear

Another distinction was the soldiers' cap. The German and Hungarian units wore cloth caps in pike-grey and with

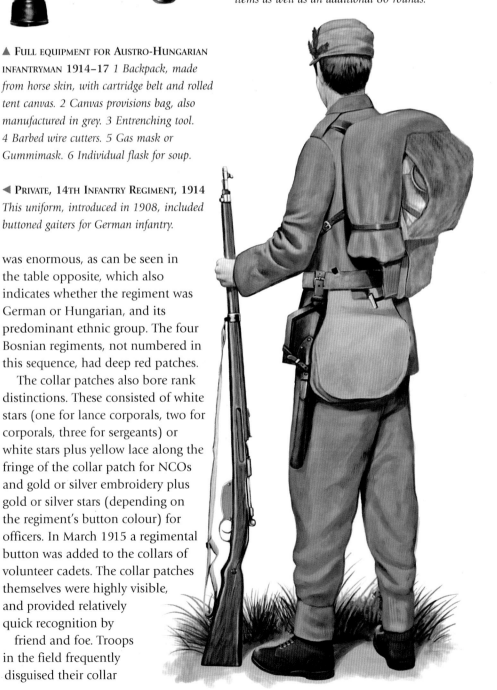

▼ **PRIVATE, 92ND INFANTRY REGIMENT, LATE 1914** *The heavy knapsack carried personal items as well as an additional 80 rounds.*

was enormous, as can be seen in the table opposite, which also indicates whether the regiment was German or Hungarian, and its predominant ethnic group. The four Bosnian regiments, not numbered in this sequence, had deep red patches.

The collar patches also bore rank distinctions. These consisted of white stars (one for lance corporals, two for corporals, three for sergeants) or white stars plus yellow lace along the fringe of the collar patch for NCOs and gold or silver embroidery plus gold or silver stars (depending on the regiment's button colour) for officers. In March 1915 a regimental button was added to the collars of volunteer cadets. The collar patches themselves were highly visible, and provided relatively quick recognition by friend and foe. Troops in the field frequently disguised their collar black peaks (sometimes leather). These had an ingenious flap that buttoned at the front with two regimental buttons but which could be let down to cover the neck and ears in winter. Above the regimental buttons was a cockade bearing the imperial cypher ('K' after 1916, 'IFJ' before then for the Hungarian units, 'FJI' for the German).

The Bosnians were distinguished by the use of a lambswool fez, which was originally deep red but usually grey

▼ PRIVATE, 29TH INFANTRY REGIMENT, 1914
The Hungarian knots on the trousers were a distinctive feature of the Hungarian regiments.

Infantry Uniform Distinctions

Rgt. No.	Name/Ethnicity	Type*	Facings	Buttons
*German or Hungarian				(gold or silver)
1	Kaiser/German	G	burgundy	G
2	Alexander I. Kaiser von Rußland/Hung	H	yellow	G
3	Erzherzog Carls/Czech	G	blue	S
4	Hoch- und Deutschmeister/German	G	blue	G
5	Freiherr von Klobuãar/Hungarian	H	rose	G
6	Carl I. König von Rumänien/German	H	rose	S
7	Graf von Khevenhüller/German	G	brown	S
8	Erzherzog Carl Stephan/Czech	G	grass green	G
9	Graf Clerfayt/Ruthenian	G	apple green	G
10	Gustav V. König von Schweden/Polish	G	green	S
11	Johann Georg Prinz von Sachsen/Czech	G	ash	G
12	Parmann/Hungarian	H	brown	G
13	Jung-Starhemburg/Polish	G	rose	G
14	Ernst Ludwig Gh. von Hessen/German	G	black	G
15	Freiherr von Georgi/Ruthenian	G	madder	G
16	Freiherr von Giesl/Croatian	H	sulphur	G
17	Ritter von Milde/Slovenian	G	rust	S
18	Erzherzog Leopold Salvator/Czech	G	burgundy	S
19	Erherzog Franz Ferdinand/Hungarian	H	blue	S
20	Heinrich Prinz von Preußen/Polish	G	lobster	S
21	Graf von Abensperg und Traun/Czech	G	sea green	G
22	Graf von Lacy/Croatian	G	yellow	S
23	Markgraf von Baden/Hungarian	H	cherry	S
24	Ritter von Kummer/Ruthenian	G	ash	S
25	Edler von Pokorny/Hungarian	H	sea green	S
26	Schreiber/Hungarian	H	black	G
27	Albert I. König von Belgien/German	G	yellow	G
28	Viktor Emanuel III. K. von Italien/Czech	G	grass green	S
29	Freiherr von Loudon/Croatian	H	light blue	S
30	Schödler/Ruthenian	G	pike grey	G
31	Pucherna/Romanian	H	yellow	S
32	Kaiserin Maria Theresa/Hungarian	H	blue	G
33	Kaiser Leopold II./Romanian	H	ash	S
34	Wilhelm I. Deutscher Kaiser/Hungarian	H	madder	S
35	Freiherr von Sterneck/Czech	G	lobster	G
36	Reichsgraf Browne/Czech	G	pink	S
37	Erzherzog Joseph/Hungarian/Rom	H	scarlet	G
38	Alfons XIII. König von Spanien/Hungarian	H	black	S
39	Freiherr von Conrad/Hungarian	H	scarlet	G
40	Ritter von Pino/Polish	G	light blue	G
41	Erzherzog Eugen/Romanian	G	sulphur	S
42	Ernst August H. von Cumberland/German	G	orange	S
43	Rupprecht Kronprinz von Bayern/Rom	H	cherry	G
44	Erzherzog Albrecht/Hungarian	H	madder	G
45	Erzherzog Joseph Ferdinand/PolishRuth	G	scarlet	G
46	Freiherr von Fejérváry/Hungarian	H	green	g
47	Graf von Beck-Rzikowsky/German	G	blue green	S
48	Rohr/Hungarian	H	blue green	G
49	Freiherr von Hess/German	G	pike grey	S
50	Friedrich Großherzog von Baden/Rom	H	green	S
51	von Boroeviç/Romanian	H	ash	G	▶

Rgt. No.	Name/Ethnicity	Type*	Facings	Buttons
52	Erzherzog Friedrich/Hungarian	H	burgundy	G
53	Dankl/Croatian	H	burgundy	S
54	Alt-Starhemberg/Czech	G	apple green	S
55	Nikolaus I. König von Montenegro/Ruth	G	rust	G
56	Graf Daun/Polish	G	blue green	G
57	Prinz zu Sachsen-Coburg-Saalfeld/Polish	G	pink	G
58	Erzherzog Ludwig Salvator/Ruthenian	G	black	S
59	Erzherzog Rainer/German	G	orange	G
60	Ritter von Ziegler/Hungarian	H	blue green	S
61	Ritter von Frank/German/Rom	H	grass green	G
62	Ludwig III. König von Bayern/Hung/Rom	H	grass green	S
63	Freiherr von Pitreich/Romanian	H	orange	S
64	Ritter von Auffenberg/Romanian	H	orange	G
65	Erzherzog Ludwig Viktor/Hungarian	H	pink	G
66	Erzherzog Peter Ferdinand/Slovak	H	pink	S
67	Freiherr Kray/Slovak	H	lobster	S
68	Freiherr von Reicher/Hungarian	H	rust	G
69	Freiherr von Leithner/Hungarian	H	pike grey	S
70	Regiment Edler von Appel/Croatian	H	sea green	G
71	Galgótzy/Slovak	H	lobster	G
72	Freiherr von David/Slovak	H	light blue	G
73	Albrecht Herzog von Württemberg/German	G	cherry	G
74	Freiherr von Schönaich/Czech	G	madder	S
75	-/Czech	G	light blue	G
76	Freiherr von Salis-Soglio/German	H	pike grey	G
77	Philipp Herzog von Württemberg/Ruth	G	cherry	S
78	Gerba/Croatian	H	rust	S
79	Graf Jellaèiç/Croatian	H	apple green	S
80	Herzog zu Sachsen/Ruthenian	G	scarlet	S
81	Freiherr von Waldstätten/Czech	G	crimson	S
82	Freiherr von Schwitzer/Hungarian	H	crimson	S
83	Schikofsky/Hungarian	H	brown	S
84	Freiherr von Bolfras/German	G	crimson	G
85	von Gaudernak/Ruthenian/Rom	H	apple green	G
86	Freiherr von Steininger/Hungarian	H	amaranth	G
87	Freiherr von Succovaty/Slovenian	G	sea green	S
88	-/Czech	G	claret	S
89	Freiherr von Albori/Ruthenian	G	claret	G
90	Edler von Horsetzky/Polish	G	amaranth	G
91	Freiherr von Czibulka/German	G	green	S
92	Edler von Hortstein/German	G	white	S
93	Mährisch-Schönberg/German	G	brown	G
94	Freiherr von Koller/German	G	white	G
95	von Kövess/Ruthenian	G	amaranth	S
96	Ferdinand Kp. von Rumänien/Croatian	H	crimson	G
97	von Waldstätten/Slovenian	G	rose	G
98	von Rummer/Czech	G	hazel	S
99	-/German	G	sulphur	G
100	von Steinsberg/Polish	G	hazel	G
101	Freiherr von Drathschmidt/Hungarian	H	sulphur	S
102	Potiorek/Czech	G	dark green	G

Regiments subsequently added wore light blue and silver buttons.

The newly raised infantry regiments were No. 103–139

28th disbanded in April 1915, re-raised March 1916.

36th disbanded in July 1915.

Croatian includes Serbs.

when worn in the field. The fez had a black or grey tassel attached to it with a rosette. The tassel was silk for officers, although these could opt to wear caps should they prefer. A number of unofficial badges and items were also worn on caps, the most significant was the traditional sprig of oak leaves worn in 1914.

▼ PRIVATE, 4TH BOSNIAN REGIMENT, 1914
Bosnian infantry wore a red fez – which could be grey on campaign. Bosnia, which had been the front line between the Austro-Hungarians and the Ottomans for centuries, provided the empire with a number of formidable units. The majority of the personnel were Muslims.

Weapons and Equipment

The infantryman's load was heavy. Austro-Hungarian infantry wore brown belts with a brass (later grey alloy) buckle bearing a double-headed eagle for NCOs and privates and an imperial cypher for officers. Cartridge pouches were attached to the belt, each infantryman carrying four brown pouches containing 40 rounds, as was a bayonet for the 1895 Mannlicher rifle. Entrenching tools were also suspended from the belt. Personal equipment was carried in a rigid and heavy pack made from horsehide, and this was usually topped with a pike-grey or brown blanket and rolled greatcoat or tent canvas. An additional ammunition pouch was also carried beneath the knapsack. Canteens, bread bags and, after 1915, gas mask cases completed the equipment.

The knapsack was particularly resented and was often replaced by a canvas rucksack initially reserved for

▼ PRIVATE, 20TH INFANTRY REGIMENT, 1916
Gone were the colourful collar tabs of 1914 (this regiment would have had lobster red facings in that year), although rank distinctions stayed on the collar. The rifle carried here is the standard Steyr-Mannlicher.

▲ PRIVATE, 45TH INFANTRY REGIMENT, WINTER 1914 *The infantryman's cap folded down to keep the neck and ears warm, and could be buttoned back up in good weather. It was common for the cap to be decorated with distinctive badges or commemorative insignia.*

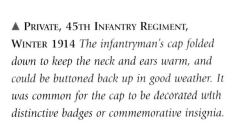

▶ PIONEER, 8TH INFANTRY REGIMENT, ASSAULT EQUIPMENT, 1918 *The simplified tunic, sometimes dyed green, was introduced in 1917. The helmet is the Austrian Berndorfer, which was manufactured by the Berndorfer Krupp Works from 1916. It had a fabric chinstrap and underneath the canvas cover it was painted brown.*

Officers, as in other armies, restricted themselves to minimum equipment in the field, making use of map cases, canteens, binoculars and pistol holsters.

Changes

The pike-grey uniform was supposed to be replaced by a field grey version in the autumn of 1915, tunics being issued with stand and fall collars bearing a thin strip of cloth in the regimental colour. Nettle green uniforms were later adopted and some 4,000 khaki uniforms were produced and may have been worn (captured Italian uniforms were certainly utilized). By 1917 the facings had given way entirely to blue regimental

numerals on grey patches (Bosnian regiments had 'bh' before the numeral) and these were sewn to shoulder straps and the side of caps.

The other major innovation for the infantry was the introduction of the steel helmet. Initially this was the German model but a locally made version was quickly introduced (the Berndorfer) which was wider than the German helmet and usually painted in brown or buff.

▼ PRIVATE, ALBANIAN LEGION, 1916 *This infantryman wears traditional Balkan sheepskin leggings and, in a nod towards nationalist sentiment, soldiers were also permitted to wear a black and red Albanian cockade.*

▲ LIEUTENANT, 3RD JÄGER, LATE 1914 *Oak leaves worn in the hat were a traditional emblem of Austro-Hungarian troops.*

▶ PRIVATE, GALICIAN RIFLES, 1917 *Ukrainian infantry were often referred to as the Sich Rifles. They were volunteers and the legion accepted male and female recruits. Personnel were transferred to Ukrainian service in 1918*

mountain troops. The rucksack came in many forms and colours and had canvas straps. Indeed, as shortages continued, canvas seems to have replaced leather for most Austro-Hungarian equipment.

were abolished in 1917 and patches with a blue 'TJ' (kaiserjäger), 'BHJ' (Bosnian jäger), or 'J', and the battalion numerals were used instead.

Foreign Units

Austria-Hungary was quick to raise Polish and Ukrainian units to aid them in the fight against Russia. The Polish Legion was ready by November 1914. Infantry wore pike-grey tunics (later field grey was worn) with stand and fall collars and a distinctive square cap with Polish eagle badge (a flatter, rounder cap was also used). The 1st Legion wore red collar patches, if patches were worn at all, and the 2nd Legion used green. Officers and NCOs were distinguished by zigzag lace and rosettes (changed to stars after protests in 1916 before being abolished altogether in favour of silver or gold braid). The legions were disbanded in 1917, although personnel were often transferred to the newly formed Royal Polish Army.

The Ukrainian equivalent (Ukrainian Legion or Sich Rifles) were raised from Ruthenian and Ukrainian volunteers. The legion initially wore pike-grey uniforms with a light blue collar patch on a standing collar, then field grey tunics with a falling collar and then nettle green uniforms with a light blue and yellow collar stripe. Troops wore a peaked cap with a 'v' cut into the front of the crown, a cockade badge and a yellow and blue rosette on the side of the cap (replaced by a metal version bearing a lion in 1917). Officers wore lace on the collar and silver rosettes to denote rank. Helmets were introduced for officers in 1917.

An Albanian Legion was also formed in 1916 to police Albania and keep the Allies from the Adriatic. They wore field grey uniforms and a white or red lambswool fez with Albanian (red and black) cockade. Most troops wore peasant leggings and carried obsolete equipment.

Storm Battalions

As in Germany, these battalions of elite specialist infantry were initially formed in an ad hoc manner. There would be 65 such battalions by the end of the war (10 were formed from landwehr units, 11 from the honvéd). They generally wore infantry uniform, usually without knapsack or much equipment (although grenade bags, trench knives and wire cutters replaced some of the more usual items), and wore steel helmets. They were distinguished by the addition of metal badges, usually worn on the breast, or insignia stitched to the arm. Most such insignia featured the death's head.

▼ PRIVATE, STORM BATTALION 11, 1918 *The badge on this individual's breast shows a skull with steel helmet above two crossed grenades.*

▲ SERGEANT, 92ND INFANTRY REGIMENT, ACTING AS STORMTROOPER, 1917 *This individual carries extra grenades, slung in bags around his neck, as well as wire cutters attached to his belt.*

Light Infantry

There were four regiments of kaiserjäger recruited in the Tyrol as well as 29 battalions of feld-jäger (and an additional regiment of Bosnian Jägers). The jägers wore grass green facings with gold buttons (silver for the Bosnians). Officers also wore a bronze hunting horn beneath the imperial cockade, and for troops this also bore the battalion number.

Troops wore Alpine knee-length socks and studded boots, and a variety of insignia from feathers to sprigs of oak in their caps. The green facings

AUSTRO-HUNGARIAN CAVALRY

The cavalry took longer to be persuaded of the new uniform's merits. In 1914, Hapsburg cavalrymen were still very colourfully dressed troops.

Dragoons

These troops wore an elaborate crested helmet (with double-headed badge, but usually covered in a grey cloth), a light blue tunic with collar and cuffs in regimental colour, a light blue pelisse with black fur collar and red breeches. This uniform was inevitably modified, with pike-grey uniforms and collar patches and, eventually, grey patches on shoulder straps and cap, a peakless version of the infantry cap, with a blue 'D' and regimental number.

Hussars

The Austro-Hungarian hussars wore a coloured shako and dark or light blue attilas with yellow lace. Breeches were red with Hungarian lace. White shako covers were worn in the field. In 1915 field grey uniforms were introduced. These later had grey patches with a blue 'H' and regimental number.

▼ MASTER SERGEANT, 13TH DRAGOON REGIMENT, 1914 *The jacket was lined with lambswool and usually worn slung over the shoulder.*

▼ PRIVATE, 9TH HUSSAR REGIMENT, 1914 *The beautifully decorated hussar shako was usually worn with a protective grey cloth cover over it.*

▼ LIEUTENANT, 1ST POLISH LANCERS, 1915 *The high cap is Polish but the sabre is standard for Austro-Hungarian cavalry.*

Ulans Uniform Distinctions

No.	Regiment	Nationality	Shako/collar (1915)	*Buttons
1	Ritter von Brudermann	Polish	yellow	G
2	Fürst zu Schwarzenberg	Polish	green	G
3	Erzherzog Carl	Polish	madder	G
4	Kaiser	Ruthenian	white	G
5	Nikolaus II von Rußland	Croatian	light blue	G
6	Ritter von Brudermann	Polish	yellow	S
7	Erzherzog Franz Ferdinand	Ruthene	green	S
8	Graf Auersperg	Polish	madder	S
11	Alexander II. von Rußland	Czech	cherry	S
12	Ritter von Brudermann	Croatian	dark blue	G
13	von Böhm-Ermolli	Ruthenian	dark blue	S

Dragoon uniform distinctions

No.	Name	Nationality	Facings	*Buttons
1	Kaiser Franz	Czech	red	S
2	Graf Paar	Czech	black	S
3	Friedrich August König von Sachsen	German	red	G
4	Kaiser Ferdinand	German	green	S
5	Nikolaus I. Kaiser von Rußland	Slovenian	orange	S
6	GH von Mecklenburg-Schwerin	Czech	black	G
7	Herzog von Lothringen	Ger/Czech	sulphur	S
8	Graf Montecuccoli	Czech	scarlet	G
9	Erzherzog Albrecht	Romanian	green	G
10	Fürst von Liechtenstein	Czech	sulphur	G
11	Kaiser Nr.11	Czech	scarlet	S
12	Nikolaus Großfürst von Rußland	Czech	orange	G
13	Eugen Prinz von Savoyen	Czech	madder	S
14	Fürst zu Windisch-Graetz	Czech	madder	G
15	Erzherzog Joseph	Czech	white	G

*Gold or Silver

Hussar Uniform Distinctions

No.	Regiment	Shako	Dolman/pelisse	*Buttons
1	Kaiser	dark blue	dark blue	G
2	Friedrich Leopold von Preußen	white	light blue	G
3	Graf von Hadik	white	dark blue	G
4	Artur Herzog von Connaught	red	light blue	S
5	Graf Radetzky	red	dark blue	S
6	Wilhelm II. König von Württemberg	grey	light blue	G
7	Wilhelm II. Deutscher Kaiser	light blue	light blue	S
8	von Tersztyánszky	red	dark blue	G
9	Graf Nádasdy	white	dark blue	S
10	Friedrich Wilhelm III	light blue	light blue	G
11	Ferdinand I. König der Bulgaren	grey	dark blue	S
12	-	white	light blue	S
13	Wilhelm Kronprinz	dark blue	dark blue	S
14	von Kolossváry	red	light blue	G
15	Erzherzog Franz Salvator	grey	dark blue	G
16	Graf Üxküll-Gyllenband	grey	light blue	S

*Gold or Silver

Lancers

Austro-Hungarian lancers wore the Polish-inspired, square-topped czapka with horsehair plumes. The czapka had a coloured top, according to regiment, a light blue tunic (ulanka) with a light blue pelisse (pelzulanka). Breeches were red, becoming field grey (followed by the rest of the uniform, bar the collar, which now showed the coloured facings). The complete transformation to field grey was completed, with regimental distinctions being reduced to a blue 'U' and regimental number.

▼ LIEUTENANT, 9TH HUSSAR REGIMENT, 1918
The steel Berndorfer helmet has replaced the elegant hussar shako.

AUSTRO-HUNGARIAN LANDWEHR AND HONVÉD

Aside from the Common Army, both Austria and Hungary fielded sizeable forces, paid for and equipped by each political entity and comprising infantry, cavalry and artillery.

The Landwehr

Although Landwehr denoted some kind of second-class division with second-class personnel in the German Army, this was not the case with the Austrian Landwehr or the Hungarian Honvéd. These were of the same standard in terms of men and equipment as the Common Army's units. The Landstrum was composed of the older and less suitable recruits.

Landwehr infantrymen were formed into 37 infantry regiments in 1914 (the majority were Czech and German, but there were also Poles and Croatians). They were dressed in uniforms that were very similar to those worn by the line infantry but had distinguishing light green facings and white metal or silver buttons.

Changes implemented in the Common Army were followed in the Landwehr, and when the majority of these regiments became Schützen regiments in April 1917 they wore field-grey uniforms with strips of green on the collar or grey patches bearing green regimental numerals.

Two of the Landwehr infantry regiments were trained as mountain troops (the 4th and 27th) and became Gebirgsschützen regiments in 1917. They wore tunics with falling collars, which bore an edelweiss insignia. They wore breeches buttoned below the knee and had studded boots. Their caps had black feathers, and they carried mountain equipment, including goggles.

The three regiments of Landes schützen (later Kaiser schützen) had similar uniforms, but their officers, uniquely, had shoulder straps (usually green edged in silver with an imperial cypher). These troops often had marksmanship lanyards of gold thread and green woollen pompoms. Some volunteer light infantry (standschützen) were also raised and these initially

◀ CORPORAL, LANDWEHR INFANTRY REGIMENT No. 6, 1918 *This corporal's sword would quickly be discarded once he reached the front, as it was almost useless in trench conditions. Most of the empire's officers replaced it with the 1886 bayonet from the Steyr-Mannlicher rifle. The sword knot is in the imperial colours of yellow and black.*

▶ PRIVATE, LANDWEHR INFANTRY REGIMENT No. 21, 1918 *This infantryman carries a home-made trench club in addition to his regulation weapons. On his back he would have the new rucksack which was issued to replace the standard leather pack from 1916 onwards.*

◄ SERGEANT LANDWEHR INFANTRY REGIMENT No. 21, 1917 *This NCO wears a half coat with fur collar, a practical garment which did not impede the legs but kept the upper body very warm. This infantry unit was converted to Schützen in April 1917.*

Regiment and 'RDS' for the Dalmatian Cavalry Regiment. Artillerymen had green crossed cannon barrels followed by a regimental numeral.

The Honvéd

There were 32 regiments of Hungarian infantry in the honvéd in 1914, and they had infantry uniforms with grey facings and yellow buttons. These uniforms became field grey in 1915 and nettle green by 1917. Collar stripes for the remaining regiments (four regiments had surrendered to the Russians in 1915 and were not reformed: 2nd, 5th, 7th and 8th) became pink at that point, being quickly converted to shoulder strap and cap patches in grey with pink regimental numerals. In April 1917 all the regiments became honvéd infantry regiments and, by that time, most wore steel helmets.

The honvéd cavalry consisted of ten hussar regiments dressed in uniforms very similar to those of the line, but with red lace on the attila and pelisse and red peakless caps with the 'IFJ' cypher. These uniforms were soon obsolete and by 1915 field-grey predominated. The introduction of grey patches with a pink regimental numeral followed by an 'H' made the toning down of the hussar uniform complete.

Artillerymen's patches had pink regimental numerals followed by crossed cannon barrels.

▶ PRIVATE, HONVÉD INFANTRY, 1914 *The marksmanship lanyard was red and worn at the left shoulder. Green lanyards were issued to jägers. Lanyards were sometimes pinned to the chest with a qualifications badge (a metal disc, with, for snipers, for example, a picture of a marksman).*

Landsturm

The landsturm, or territorial militia, was made up of recruits thought to be less able or fit for the landwehr. Troops were originally dressed in out of date blue tunics and greatcoats and carried obsolete rifles and leather equipment. Dark blue caps were also common. By the war's end, however, the landsturm resembled the rest of the infantry, but with white numerals on their shoulder straps and caps. Other units turned out sporting brassards and civilian clothes, equipped with nothing more than rifles.

went to war wearing brassards or infantry greatcoats. By 1916 the uniform was a little more standardized and they had green facings with an eagle badge. Officers, being part of a voluntary unit, were entitled to wear rosettes on the collar rather than stars and, unusually, these were in gold.

Landwehr cavalry finished the war in uniforms similar to those worn by their Common Army counterparts. They bore shoulder strap and cap patches in grey with a green 'U' (for the lancers) and regimental number green 'RTS' for the Tyrolean Cavalry

AUSTRO-HUNGARIAN TECHNICAL TROOPS

Austria-Hungary had gained a reputation for competence in the technical branches, and the artillery in particular had a long tradition of exemplary service (especially during the war against Prussia).

The Artillery

Austria-Hungary's artillery was formed into field artillery (which included foot and horse), mountain artillery and fortress artillery. Foot artillery usually wore uniforms similar to the infantry but with red facings and yellow buttons. Horse artillery showed a preference for cavalry equipment, including bandoliers rather than cartridge pouches. In 1917 the artillery switched to wearing patches on their shoulder straps and cap. These had blue crossed cannon and a regimental numeral for field artillery, and the numeral was in a circle for mountain artillery. The fortress artillery had crossed cannon followed by 'FsR' and the regimental number. Train companies began the war with light blue collar patches and silver buttons, they ended with a blue 'T', or 'T' and the company number, on the standard designation patches.

Those troops sent to assist the Ottomans generally wore khaki uniforms in cotton or linen, with officers and NCOs often adopting a sun helmet (with cockade or without cockade for NCOs) and troops wearing the peaked cap in the same colour as their uniform. Some sun helmets were also worn, however. Many of these troops were sent to Gallipoli and there they wore winter greatcoats and tunics in field grey.

Engineers

The engineers wore cherry red collar patches and gold buttons while the pioneers had grey facings and gold buttons, and carried shovels and pickaxes. The pioneers were often used to build bridges, the sappers were used for digging earthworks and trenches, and for preparing defences. Both generally wore boots and dark trousers. By 1917 sappers wore a blue 'S' by the battalion number and pioneers a blue 'P' by the battalion number on their shoulder straps and caps. A special bridging train battalion bore a 'Br' and a number one. Various insignia were worn by

◀ PRIVATE, HORSE ARTILLERY, 1914 *This soldier is armed with the 1904 cavalry sabre.*

telegraphic units, signals units and railway units (the latter had green facings and gold buttons)

Air Force

Austro-Hungarian aviation troops generally wore the uniform of the artillery (the balloon detachment had been a branch of the fortress artillery) with a balloon insignia on the collar. They could also continue to wear the uniform of their original parent unit, with the addition of this insignia.

Uniforms for pilots were as varied as those in the armies of the other powers. Privately tailored tunics and caps were very common, as were breeches and aviator boots. Cavalry officers liked to retain the colour and dash of the 1914 uniform in

▲ *Austrian soldiers in the mountains of the Italian front.*

a theatre where camouflage was not particularly necessary. Leather jackets and private flying helmets and goggles were worn in the air. A pilot's badge had been introduced in 1913 and this was supposed to be pinned on to the right breast by qualified personnel. It consisted of a green enamel wreath and a bronze eagle (frequently blackened). From 1915 this badge was awarded to pilots who had completed ten sorties rather than just to qualified pilots, and in 1916 the badge became valid for one year (the pilot having to make at least 10 sorties to retain the badge). Some squadron insignia appears to have been worn, stitched to the arms of tunics or worn on greatcoats and jackets.

Medical Troops

Those working in the medical corps wore madder-red collar patches and gold buttons in 1914. Most used the red cross emblem and company number in blue by 1917 (when such distinctions were worn on the shoulder straps and caps). Surgeons dressed as officers, stretcher bearers wore red cross brassards (and were sometimes drawn from local infantry units) and carried first aid kits.

▼ Lieutenant-Colonel, Field Artillery, 1914 *Brown leather belts usually replaced the officers' elegant yellow and black belts at the front.*

◄ Master Sergeant, Field Artillery, 1917 *The breeches are privately-tailored and cut in the style worn by cavalry officers.*

THE OTTOMAN EMPIRE

The Ottoman empire was a vast but poorly organized structure and one which produced an army that had been modernized since 1909 but demoralized by defeat in the Balkans in 1912 and 1913.

Infantry

The loss of the Balkan territory (Ottoman control being reduced to a rump around Constantinople) deprived the empire of one of its richest areas and also a source of some of its best infantry. Defeat posed a real problem for the empire's finances, and loss of guns and equipment severely damaged the armed forces.

The Balkan Wars had been preceded by a period of dramatic reform. The government that swept into power in 1908, generally known by the name of Young Turks, was backed by the military and repaid that support with large injections of money into the army and navy. The reforms never really tackled the fundamentals, however. Most officers were poorly trained, there was a severe shortage of suitable NCOs, and equipment (except in some choice units) was generally

▲ *A Bulgarian, German and Ottoman soldier on patrol in Constanza, Romania, 1915*

lacking. There were few machine guns and only a small number of technical officers who knew how to put modern equipment to good use.

In 1909 the navy blue uniform was abolished for the infantry and a khaki uniform was introduced, which resembled that adopted by Balkan powers at around the same time. The brownish green cloth was used to manufacture large numbers of tunics and trousers. The tunics themselves were single breasted with falling collars, interior pockets and six

buttons. Trousers were loose to the knee and then held tight by khaki puttees. Ankle boots were worn but there was a general shortage of footwear, something that led to troops serving barefoot or in sandals. Greatcoats were greenish-brown and were double breasted (six buttons on each side). The collar was stand and fall and often came with a hood (particularly useful in the Caucasus) and a belt at the rear for tightening the coat.

▶ PRIVATE, NISHAM RIFLES, 1916 *The fez, shown here without a tassel, was still common in the early years of the war as the empire was beset by problems supplying its troops with replacement items, especially helmets, backpacks and cartridge belts. The old red fez, abolished in 1908, often served as an off-duty cap for want of a side cap.*

(for example a captain wore two stars). NCOs had chevrons on the bottom of the sleeve. A number of rifle regiments were formed and these wore green tabs on their collars and on the collars of their greatcoats.

Officers

Turkish officers wore uniforms that were of better quality and were usually greener than those worn by the troops (although all uniforms faded in the harsh sunlight). Generals at headquarters often continued to wear the blue tunic with red collar and cuffs worn by most officers in full dress. The cuffs were piped in gold bullion thread and the astrakhan colpack had a red crown with gold lace. Most generals wore black trousers with red piping. Staff officers wore a green army uniform but with red collars, red crown to the colpack and red piping on the breeches.

Headgear

Ottoman troops had long been distinguished by the use of a fez, and a short khaki fez (without tassel) was indeed worn in some theatres. Its use diminished as the war continued. Red fezzes had been obsolete since 1908.

Arab units wore turbans. By 1915 most troops had adopted a fabric helmet called a kabalak or Enverieh (named after Enver Pasha, its supposed inventor). It consisted of a turban attached to a straw framework. Officers had a stiffer model. Officers often wore a black or grey astrakhan colpack (wider and bushier than a fez) with a red and gold crown. It was sometimes covered in a khaki or green cloth.

A helmet specifically for Ottoman troops was manufactured in Germany late in the war with a notch in the metal rim above each ear. Few examples made it to the Ottomans, but it could be seen on Freikorps troops in 1919.

Equipment

Ottoman reforms had led to an influx of money and a great deal of that had been spent in Germany. Much of the

Ottoman empire's equipment came from the Germans. Leather belts (sometimes with a buckle bearing a crescent) were worn along with six cartridge belts (either in black or in natural leather) and the knapsack (with tent canvas or greatcoat strapped to it) and entrenching tool were often of the German pattern.

▼ **Captain, 35th Infantry Regiment, 1915**
This officer carries a revolver of German manufacture and an infantry model sabre first issued in 1889. The lambswool colpack has a red crown with piping – cavalry officers would have had a steel blue crown to the headgear, while engineers had light blue and artillery had dark blue.

▲ **Turkish General, 1915** *Full dress was a black lambswool colpack and a dark blue tunic with red piping – uniforms in the field were more austere and included a distinctive helmet. The Young Turks' revolution of 1908 had abolished the red fez previously worn by generals in an attempt to make the Army appear more more modern. The ribbon of the Turkish War Medal is discreetly tucked into this general's tunic front.*

Infantry Distinctions

Ottoman infantry units generally did not wear regiment or branch of service distinctions. Officers displayed their rank on their shoulder straps. These were of cloth, backed in red material and with bullion embroidery and a number of stars according to rank

The infantryman's Mauser was also German, although some were manufactured in Germany, as was the bayonet hanging from the waist belt. Bread bags and canteens (many of them of wood or of local designs) were worn, and an iron dish for washing was tied to the back of the knapsack. Officers usually carried a sword, pistol, German map case and binocular case. Their belts were of yellow metal and bore a crescent insignia.

▼ PRIVATE, STORMTROOP, PALESTINE, 1917
A few units were raised on the German model and equipped with German steel helmets and German Mausers. They were deployed in Palestine and, to a limited extent, in the Caucasus in 1918. The bag under his arm contains grenades.

Specialist Troops

A few Ottoman troops were trained as ski troops by the Germans and Austro-Hungarians in Galicia in 1916, but they played a limited role. By 1917 a number of troops had been selected to act as Stormtroopers, along German lines. These were formed into companies and most were issued with steel helmets of German design and painted either light brown or green. They also wore brassards bearing a divisional symbol. They were armed with grenades, knives and rifles and fought in Palestine and Syria in 1917 and 1918, suffering heavy casualties.

Non-Islamic Troops

Most Christian and Jewish troops were kept away from the regular infantry regiments and concentrated into pioneer or labour companies. These wore tunics and trousers, assorted hats, and were generally very poorly equipped. Large numbers or irregulars served in Arabia and in Palestine. Most of them wore native dress with the addition of cartridge belts and a Mauser.

Cavalry

Cavalrymen wore a tunic very similar to that worn by the infantry, but they generally wore bandoliers and a distinctive type of hat. This was similar to a kabalak but had loose bands of cloth that were wrapped under the chin. Officers wore green tunics with grey-blue collars and greatcoats or capes with grey-blue collars. The astrakhan colpack had a grey-blue and gold

▶ PRIVATE, CAVALRY, 1917 *The helmet had cloth bound around it which could be let down and fastened under the chin. The carbine slung over his shoulder is the 1905 Mauser. He would also be armed with a 1909 sabre. Kurdish and Arab auxiliary cavalry served alongside such Ottoman line cavalry.*

crown for cavalry officers. Shoulder straps were predominantly silver with gold stars, backed in grey-blue, and breeches were piped in the same colour (and often had leather inners). A unit of lancers served as guards in Constantinople and they appear to have worn a blue lancer uniform with red facings. Gendarmes wore a very similar uniform to that of the line cavalry but with scarlet facings and yellow buttons. Irregular Kurdish cavalry wore a variety of costumes, including khaki tunics and white or beige trousers. Boots and spurs were worn by officers, NCOs and troopers.

Other Arms

Ottoman artillery were uniformed in a style very similar to that of the infantry. Officers had dark blue collars and piping, colpacks with blue and gold crowns and greatcoats with dark blue collars. The rank and file had dark blue tabs on their greatcoat collars and some wore shoulder straps in blue on their tunics. Engineers wore an identical uniform but with light blue distinctions. Many officers wore gold buttons, some preferred blackened versions.

▲ *Turkish artillery, wearing the soon to be obsolete fezzes, on parade in Constantinople (now Istanbul), 30 October 1914.*

The Ottoman artillery had been lavishly equipped with Krupp field guns and Schneider mountain guns, but other aspects of modern warfare were sadly lacking. There was a real shortage of machine guns and of transport vehicles (there were only 300 vehicles in the whole empire in 1912, including diplomats' cars). Train

◄ CAPTAIN, TURKISH ARTILLERY, 1916 *Dark blue was shown on the bag of the colpack, on the tunic collar and on the greatcoat collar.*

troops were uniformed like the artillery but with red facings. German technical assistance included motor transport (mostly driven by Austro-Hungarian or German personnel).

There was a small aviation corps, trained in Germany and equipped with some rather obsolete German machines. Troops raised by Azerbaijan in 1918 and 1919 were equipped with Ottoman uniforms.

▼ GERMAN 7.7CM FIELD GUN, 1916 *This gun was supplied to the Ottomans in large numbers by the Germans. The Ottomans produced some of their own artillery, modified versions of this standard and efficient piece.*

BULGARIA

Bulgaria had lost the Second Balkan War in 1913. As a result, it decided to join the Germans in 1915.

Infantry

Bulgarian infantry wore predominantly brown (tunics and trousers). Most regiments had red shoulder straps (bearing a regimental number in yellow thread or paint), red standing collars and red cuffs and piping to the trousers, but some ten royal regiments had distinctive cuff and shoulder strap facings, cap crowns and piping:

1st scarlet, 4th yellow, Ferdinand's regiment or the 6th white, 8th light blue, 9th blue, 17th bright red, 18th white, 20th royal blue, 22nd light green and 24th orange. These regiments also wore royal cyphers on their shoulder straps and lace on the red standing collar. Peaked caps initially had blue crowns and red (or with colours as above) bands. Most of these were covered with brown covers.

Officers wore green uniforms with distinctive piping to the Russian-style cap and to the backing of the shoulder straps, which had woven metallic lace and regimental numerals or cyphers, along with metallic diamonds to denote rank. The cap itself had a green peak and a Bulgarian cockade (green, red and white) within a white metal oval. Sashes were sometimes worn; most commonly a black and silver belt was preferred. The officers' greatcoat was light grey with a dark blue collar and red tabs. NCOs wore gold or yellow bars across the shoulder straps.

◀ CAPTAIN, 1ST INFANTRY REGIMENT, 1915
Bulgarian infantry officers wore olive green – elite units had their patron's cypher on the shoulder strap.

▲ *A group of Bulgarian irregular troops, known as Comitadjis, Macedonia, 1915.*

Many infantrymen were issued a field grey uniform in 1915 piped in red to the collar and shoulder straps, and sometimes down the tunic front; regimental numerals were also now in red, the distinctive colours of the royal regiments largely falling by the wayside. In summer most troops wore a light blue shirt and brown trousers.

Equipment was in brown natural leather and consisted of a waist belt and cartridge pouches, and a German-style knapsack and canteen. There was a severe shortage of greatcoats in the Army before the war, and so the military placed an order for 300,000 greatcoats with Russia in 1913 and 250,000 pairs of boots.

German helmets were introduced in limited quantities in 1916 and 1917. These were often painted brown or iron grey. No insignia was worn on them. By the end of the war, all kinds of uniforms were being worn, especially by militias and units composed of Macedonian irregulars. Even troops at the front suffered severe shortages of all kinds and were reduced to fighting barefoot and in rags.

▲ PRIVATE, 14TH INFANTRY REGIMENT, 1917
*Leather boots were rare and the Balkan
sheepskin leggings were used by Bulgarian
troops throughout the war.*

▲ PRIVATE, 27TH INFANTRY REGIMENT, 1916
*The knapsack was first introduced in 1898,
but there were tremendous shortages and
Austrian and German models were utilized.*

Cavalry and Artillery

The cavalry wore green coats (although
blue and brown were also seen) and
blue breeches. The tunics were faced in
red and troopers and officers had silver
buttons. There were four royal
regiments with red cap bands and
shoulder straps (bearing various royal
cyphers) but piped in the following
colour: 1st (Ferdinand's) white, 2nd
scarlet, 3rd yellow and 4th white.
Greatcoats, when worn, had coloured
tabs on the collar and were usually
grey for officers and other ranks. A
regiment of Life Guards was kept in

Sofia. They wore blue uniforms with
white shoulder knots, blue breeches
and red caps. Cavalrymen generally
wore white leather equipment.

Artillerymen wore brown tunics
with black collars with red piping and
a black band to the cap with red
piping. Shoulder straps were usually
black piped red and these bore the
regimental numeral (or in the case of
the 3rd and 4th Regiments, royal
cyphers: a Cyrillic 'B' for the 3rd and a
Cyrillic 'F' for the 4th) in yellow.
Fortress regiments wore a 'K' on the
shoulder strap, mountain artillery a

Cyrillic 'P' and coastal artillery a 'B'.
Officers wore green tunics and
breeches and green caps with a black-
piped red band.

Engineers wore the same uniform
but with silver buttons. Breeches were
generally blue for officers and brown
for other ranks. Buttons bore crossed
cannons for all artillerymen. Specialist
troops generally wore the engineer
uniform but with an anchor on the
shoulder straps for bridging units
and a thunderbolt for signals units.

▼ SERGEANT, 2ND ARTILLERY, WINTER
DRESS, 1915 *The Smith and
Wesson revolver, here shown in
its holster with a red lanyard,
was popular.*

GLOSSARY

Adrian helmet: French-style helmet named after its inventor.

Aide de Camp: an officer of the general staff, assisting a general. Often used to convey messages or despatches.

Aiguillette: a cord worn on the left or right shoulder, to denote a special status or duties (or a battle honour).

Ammunition boots: term for studded ankle boots.

ANZAC: acronym for Australian and New Zealand Army Corps.

Askari: troops recruited from native Africans, usually used for local defence.

Attila: Name given to a close fitting tunic worn by hussars in German-speaking countries, derived from the dolman worn by Hungarian hussars.

Bandolier: leather belting worn over the shoulder and usually containing ammunition.

Bantam: a name applied to British units raised from men who were below regulation height.

Barrage: concentrated artillery fire on a specific point for a specific period.

Bashlyk: hood with strips of cloth, worn by Russian troops in winter.

Battalion: a unit consisting of companies, usually 600 men strong.

Blighty: The Hindu word for 'another land', adopted by the British in India to denote the British Isles or homeland.

Bluse: The German term for loose-fitting tunic.

Boche: French slang for German. Originated from Parisian slang word caboche, meaning thick-headed.

Breeches: a kind of shaped trouser worn by mounted troop or officers

Brodie helmet: classic British round helmet, named after its inventor.

Canteen: water bottle made from wood or metal.

Carbine: a rifle of reduced length, used by cavalry and mounted artillery.

Chasseur: French light cavalry or infantry –troops originally used for skirmishing.

Chevauxleger: French term for light horse, used by some German states to denote light cavalry.

Chinscales: chin straps making use of metal plates; used to secure the helmet on the head. Cockade: a rosette or badge worn on the hat, usually in national colours.

Comb: a solid vertical piece on top of a helmet, usually topped by a crest.

Cossack: Kind of light cavalry volunteers. Recruited from peoples along Russian imperial borders,

▲ *The ruins and bombed out buildings of an East Prussian town destroyed during the war.*

often settlers established there for local security. By 1914 used as mobile additional light cavalry and light artillery for skirmishing and scouting.

Crest: a badge or coat of arms; a piece of fur or horsehair on top of a helmet.

Cuirassier: originally an armoured cavalrymen on a heavy horse; by 1914 a heavy cavalryman (usually with elite status) wearing a helmet and breastplate (if that).

Cypher: ornamental lettering, usually the initials of a member of a royal family. Used on crests and badges, also being embroidered on shoulder straps.

Czapka: Polish square-topped cap.

Dolman: close-fitting jacket originally worn by hussars, decorated with lace.

Dragoon: originally a mounted infantryman, by 1914 standard, line cavalry.

Engineer: the troops involved in the construction of defensive structures, bridge building, and maintenance of communications.

Epaulettes: fringed shoulder straps.

Ersatz: German for replacement; might be used for troops or for equipment and materials.

Farrier: a specialist who shod horses.

▼ *Women and children cheering the arrival of the men of the 57th Division at Lille.*

Feldgrau: German for the many shades of field grey.

Feldrock: term used for German infantryman's tunic.

Fez: round cap without peak, worn by Bosnian troops and some Ottoman troops (usually red with a tassle).

Free Corps: Units raised by volunteers, and often composed of volunteers.

Frog: a combination of straps used to secure a scabbard.

Full dress: uniforms worn for parades and on ceremonial occasions; usually much more opulent and colourful than campaign or service dress.

Fusiliers: originally infantry armed with a light musket; by 1914 standard infantry but with a suggestion of elite status.

Gaiters: cloth or canvas covers for the lower leg, used to fit over the shoe to keep out mud and grit.

Gebirgsschützen: Mountain troops.

Grenadier: originally a man trained to throw grenades; then an elite soldier.

Grenzer: Border guards.

Greyback: slang for the British soldiers grey-blue flannel shirt.

Gymnastiorka: Russian shirt-tunic, made of cotton and either with or without pockets.

Honvéd: Troops raised and maintained by the kingdom of Hungary.

Hussar: originally Hungarian light cavalrymen but used for a generic kind

▲ *American troops march into Perth, Scotland, for a victory parade.*

of light cavalry dressed in the traditional Hungarian style.

Jägers: the German word for hunter, denoting light infantrymen for skirmishing duties.

Khaki: brownish green colour used by a number of armies as the main colour for army uniforms. Derived from the Hindu word for dust.

Kiwi: slang for a New Zealander.

Landsturm: kind of militia, or forces raised as a Home Guard in German-speaking lands.

Landwehr: in the Austro-Hungarian empire, these were troops maintained

by Austria and not part of the common army; in Germany these troops were reserve units, often providing escorts and maintaining garrisons.

Lanyard: coloured cords used to denote marksmen in Austro-Hungarian units, or used by mounted troops in the British Army.

Limber: the vehicle to which a field gun trail was attached to enable the gun to be moved by a team of horses. It came with space for the storage of effects and ammunition.

Light infantry: originally lightly-equipped infantry, trained to fight as skirmishers.

Line infantry: originally infantry trained to fight in lines. By 1914 a generic name for standard, regular infantry.

Major: a rank of field officer, usually commanding a battalion.

Maxim: kind of machinegun, named after its inventor.

MG: acronym for machinegun.

Minnies: slang for a shot from a German trench mine-thrower.

Pals: units of volunteers raised from specific local communities.

Papakha: Russian fur cap, sometimes with neck and ear flaps.

Pickelhaube: spiked helmet, made of leather (mostly) with (later) a detachable spike. Common in many armies in the 19th Century it became synonymous with the Germans.

▼ *Members of the famous 369th Colored Infantry, return to New York City, 1919.*

Pioneers: as with sappers, a kind of soldier tasked with constructing defences or digging trenches and maintaining roads.

Piping: a narrow band of cord or braid cloth which edged a collar, cuff, cuff flap, lapel, or shoulder strap, usually in a contrasting colour to the main uniform fabric.

Plastron: a specific kind of lapel on a lancer's jacket: the front of the jacket has braided piping forming the outline of lapels, the material within is sometimes of a contrasting colour to the rest of the uniform.

Pagoni: Russian for rigid shoulderboards. These showed regiment numerals, branch of service and rank of wearer. They were unpopular and were withdrawn by the Provisional Government in 1917; subsequently worn by some White units in the Russian Civil War.

Poliu: French for infantry veteran. It literally meant hairy one, and was used as shorthand for army veteran as early as the 1830s.

Puttees: strips of cloth (from Hindu for bandages) bound around the lower leg to protect trousers and make running more comfortable.

Reds: term used for Bolshevik troops from 1917(socialists had traditionally used red for their emblems, the

▲ *The Unknown Soldier being transferred in Boulogne to a British ship bound for England.*

Bolsheviks had red banners, armbands and a Red Army).

Sapper: troops equipped and trained to dig field defences.

Sammie: French nickname for an American soldier, derived from 'Uncle Sam', the national personification of the United States.

Schützen: German term for sharpshooter, used as light infantry skirmishers.

Service dress: the uniform to be worn on campaign, in the field and on active duty.

Shako: cylindrical cap, usually made of black leather, with a peak (rear peak was optional)

Shoulder titles: insignia worn on or just below the shoulder straps, usually denoting the regimental name. Metallic for most British regiments, cloth for the Guards.

Spahi: French North African cavalrymen.

Stahlhelm: German steel helmet.

Stormtroopers: Assault infantry, armed and equipped for trench raiding and limited offensives. Used to denote specialist units of such troops by the Austro-Hungarians and Germans.

Territorial Force: Britain's response to enlarging armies: a second army, raised from volunteers, and originally intended for protection of mainland Britain.

Tirailleur: French for sharpshooter. Mostly used to denote regiments recruited from colonial subjects.

Topi: Name for Wolseley tropical helmet.

Ulan: German term for a lancer, usually dress in a Polish-style uniform and armed with a lance in addition to other weapons.

Wappen: decorative metallic plate on the front of the spiked helmet.

Whites: A term which should strictly be reserved for monarchist forces in the Russian Civil War; often loosely used for any anti-Bolshevik troops.

Zouave: Type of French infantry, raised from French citizens in North Africa and dressed in uniforms inspired by North African dress.

▼ *Trees grow among the old trenches in a park that surrounds the Canadian Memorial, marking the site of the Battle of Vimy Ridge.*

INDEX

Page numbers in *italics* refer to
illustrations and captions.

accoutrements, British 43, 62–3
African troops 76–7, 175, 208–9
Allies 7, 30–1
America *see* USA
armistice 32–3
  Armistice Day 35
artillery 7, 20
  American 168–9
  Austro-Hungarian 240
  Belgian 174
  British 68–9
  Bulgarian 247
  French 112–13
  German 220–1
  Italian 178–9
  Ottoman 245
  Russian 146–7
artillery badges, French *112*
Australian Imperial Force 74–5
  1st Australian Light Horse *74*
  23rd Battalion *75*
Austro-Hungarian Empire 7, 9, 225
  conscription 17
  Hapsburg monarchy 226–7
Austro-Hungarian Army 227
  1st Polish Lancers *236*
  3rd Jäger *234*
  4th Bosnian Regiment *232*
  8th Infantry Regiment, equipment *233*
  9th Hussar Regiment *236*, *237*
  14th Infantry Regiment *230*
  13th Dragoon Regiment *236*
  20th Infantry Regiment *233*
  29th Infantry Regiment *231*
  45th Infantry regiment *233*
  92nd Infantry Regiment *230*, *235*
  Albanian Legion *234*
  Emperor Karl *228*
  engineers 240–1
  Field Artillery *241*
  Galician Rifles *234*
  generals and staff *228*
  Honvéd *239*
  Honvéd Infantry *239*
  Horse Artillery *240*
  Landwehr 238–9
  Landwehr Infantry Regiment No. 21
    238, *239*

Landwehr Infantry Regiment No. 6 *238*
  medical troops *241*
  Storm Battalion II *235*
aviation 21
  American *169*
  Austro-Hungarian *241*
  British *67*
  French 116–17
  German *223*
  Russian *149*

Balkans 10–11, 12–13
bayonet knots, German *202*
Belgium 160
  1st Guides *174*
  1st Lancers *174*
  1st Regiment *173*
  2nd Lancers *175*
  9th Regiment *172*
  14th Regiment *172*
  dog-pulled cart *173*
brassards, British 43
breeches, British 43
Bulgaria 6, 7, 19, 225
  1st Infantry Regiment *246*
  14th Infantry Regiment *247*
  2nd Artillery *247*
  27th Infantry Regiment *247*

Canadian Expeditionary Force 72–3
  Fort Garry Horse *73*
  Newfoundland Regiment *73*
  Princess Patricia's Canadian Light
    Infantry *72*

▲ *French infantryman's kit.*

cap badges, British 44, 45, 47, 50, 52, 62,
  65–6
casualties 35
cavalry
  American *168*
  Austro-Hungarian 236–7
  Belgian 174–5
  British 45, 60–3, 64–6
  Bulgarian 247
  French 108–11
  German 199, 216–19
  Greek *185*
  Indian 78, 79
  Italian *178*
  Ottoman 244–5
  Russian 128–9, 142–3, 144–5, 151
  South African 77
Central Powers 7, 32
cockades, German *203*
  cockades, Russian *135*
  colonies 14–15, 25
  conscription 16–19, 40–1, 158–9
  Cossacks 7, 144–5

  Dardanelles 26–7
  death toll 35

▼ *British howitzer.*

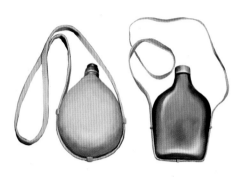

▲ *Serbian canteens.*

distinctions
  American 165, 166
  Austro-Hungarian 229–30, 231–2, 237
  British 47–8, 71
  French 94–5, 99–100, 102
  German 199, 201–2, 205–6, 211, 212, 216, 217, 218–19
  Japanese 187
  Ottoman 243
  Russian 129, 131, 134, 151, 153–4

Eastern Fronts 25
equipment
  American 165, 167
  Austro-Hungarian *230, 233,* 233–4
  British 53–4
  French 83, 91, 100–1, 117
  German 197, 203, 213, 221
  Greek 185
  Ottoman 243–4
  Russian 135–6
Europe 6, 7, 8–9
  Balkan Problem 10–11, 12–13
  colonial involvement 14–15
  manpower 16–19
  political pressures 10

field guns *68, 221, 245*
flare gun *100*
flight *see* aviation
France 6, 7, 8, 81

▼ *Portuguese insignia: cavalry (top), and infantry (bottom).*

conscription 16–17
  Germany 24–5
French Army 82–3
  1st Cuirassiers *109*
  1st March Regiment, Foreign Legion *102*
  1st March Regiment, Tirailleurs *106*
  1st Zouaves *104, 105*
  2nd Infantry Regiment *88*
  2nd Lancers *6*
  3rd Battalion Chasseurs À Pied *99*
  3rd Chasseurs À Cheval *110*
  3rd Field Artillery *112*
  4th Infantry regiment *96*
  4th Spahis *111*
  5th Battalion Chasseurs À Pied *98*
  5th Hussars *111*
  7th Battalion Chasseurs À Pied *99*
  7th Battalion of Chasseurs Alpins *101*
  8th March Regiment, Tirailleurs *106*
  9th Zouaves *105*
  12th Battalion of Chasseurs Alpins *100*
  12th Cuirassiers *109*
  12th Field Artillery *113*
  13th Infantry Regiment *91*
  19th Infantry Regiment *90*
  20th Dragoons *108*
  22nd Infantry Regiment *89, 95*
  23rd Colonial Infantry Regiment *107*
  23rd Train Regiment *115*
  32nd Field Artillery *113*
  35th Infantry Regiment *94, 96*
  43rd Infantry Regiment *94*
  58th Territorial Regiment *90*
  82nd Infantry Regiment *95*
  95th Infantry Regiment *92*
  96th Infantry Regiment *92*
  105th Regiment *89*
  112th Infantry Regiment *91*
  115th Infantry Regiment *93*
  175th Infantry Regiment *97*
  alpine chasseurs *99*
  American troops *103*
  Asian troops *107*
  assault order 96–7
  bicycle and ski companies *101*
  Chasseur from a ski company *101*
  Chasseur, Polish Legion *103*
  colonial troops 104–7
  Czech Legion *102, 103*
  Czechoslovakian Chasseurs *102*
  Engineers *114,* 114–15
  Fighter Squadron *116*
  foot chasseurs 98–9
  Foreign Legion *102*
  General of Division *87*
  generals and staff 86–7
  horizon blue 93
  Marshal *86*
  medical troops 115
  Observer *117*
  officers 88–9
  patriotic uniforms 88
  penal battalions 106
  Pilot *117*
  Polish units 102–3
  rank and file uniform 90–1
  Senegalese troops 106–7
  soldiers of 1917 94
  staff officer *87*
  strategy and tactics 82
  supply troops 114
  Tank Assault Unit *115*
  tank troops 115
  tirailleurs 106
  Tirailleurs Senegalais *107*
  uniform reforms 92–3, 105
  uniforms 83, 85
  variations in uniform 97, 116–17
  wartime developments 84–5
  Zouaves 104–5
Franz Ferdinand, Archduke 10, 11

gas 21
Germany 7, 8, 12, 189, 190–1
  1918 campaigns 32
  conscription 17
  France 24–5
  Prussia 190, 192–3
  wartime developments 194–5
German Army 192–3
  1st Bavarian Ulan Regiment (Kaiser Wilhelm II) *218*
  1st Foot Guards Regiment *198*
  2nd Bavarian Chevauxleger Regiment (Taxis) *219*
  2nd Flying Battalion *222*
  3rd Guard Ulan Regiment *199*
  4th Foot Guards Regiment *198*

▼ *French Hotchkiss machine gun with tripod.*

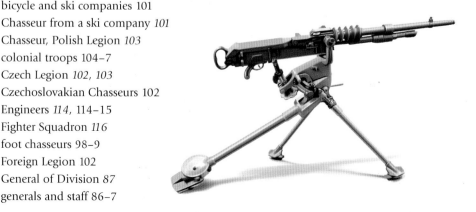

▲ *German infantry regimental bayonet knots.*

4th Jäger Battalion (Magdeburg) *210*

5th Battalion Bavarian Landsturm *214*

5th Jäger Battalion (Silesia) *211*

16th Pioneers *222*

17th Hussar Regiment (Brunswick) *217*

17th Infantry Regiment (4th Westphalian) *6, 204*

18th Landsturm Battalion *215*

20th Ulan Regiment *216*

22nd Infantry Regiment (1st Upper Silesian) *206*

24th Infantry Regiment (4th Brandenburg) *204*

27th Field Artillery Regiment (Nassau) *221*

30th Field Artillery Regiment (1st Baden) *220*

79th Infantry Regiment (3rd Hanover) *207*

82nd Landwehr Regiment *214*

93rd Infantry Regiment *200*

94th Infantry Regiment (5th Thuringian) *205*

113th Infantry Regiment *200*

128th Infantry Regiment (Danzig) *204*

135th Infantry Regiment *201*

701st Battalion of Infantry, Asienkorps *209*

armour *212*

Askari *208*

Bavarian Leib-Regiment *203*

colonial troops *208–9*

engineers *222–3*

Field Marshal *196*

generals and staff *196–7*

Guards *198–9*

Horse Guard Regiment (Saxon) *217*

Jägers *210, 219*

Landwehr *214–15*

Lieutenant General *197*

machine gunners and tankers *222*

Major on the General Staff *196*

mountain troops *211*

Pilot, II Bomber Group *223*

Red Baron *223*

South West Africa Schutztruppe *208*

Stormbattalion *213*

Stormtroop Company *212*

stormtroopers *212–13*

Württemburg 5th Landsturm Battalion *215*

Württemburg Mountain Rifle Battalion *210*

Great Britain *7, 8, 13*

conscription *18*

British Army *37*

1st Life Guards *45*

2nd Dragoons (Royal Scots Greys) *63*

2nd Hussars *6*

5th (Royal Irish) Lancers *60*

12th (Prince of Wales Royal) Lancers *61*

13th Hussars *60*

20th Hussars *62*

1902 Model Tunic *46–7*

African troops *76–7*

Alexandra, Princess of Wales's Own Yorkshire Regiment (Green Howards) *51*

auxiliaries *38–9*

Brigadier General *42*

British Expeditionary Force (BEF) *37*

Cambridgeshire Regiment *51*

conscripts *18, 40–1*

East Yorkshire Regiment *51*

East Yorkshire Yeomanry *64*

field adaptations *54–5*

Field Marshal *43*

footwear *48–9*

generals and staff *42–3*

Grenadier Guards *44*

Guards *44–5*

Highland Light Infantry *57*

Highland Regiments *51–3*

King's African Rifles *77, 77*

King's Own Scottish Borderers *52*

King's Royal Rifle Corps *49*

Lancashire Fusiliers *59*

Lieutenant General *42*

London Regiment *56, 57*

Machine Gun Corps *70*

Manchester Regiment *54*

Middlesex Regiment *47*

NCOs' rank chevrons *47*

North Staffordshire Regiment *55*

Northumberland Fusiliers *48*

Oxfordshire Yeomanry *65*

▲ *German infantry regimental bayonet knots.*

Prince Albert's (Somerset Light Infantry) *59*

Queen's (Royal West Surrey Regiment) *46*

regulars *38*

Royal Engineers *70, 71, 71*

Royal Field Artillery *68–9, 69*

Royal Flying Corps *67*

Royal Garrison Artillery *69*

Royal Horse Artillery *68, 69*

Royal Sussex Regiment *46*

Scots Guards *45*

Seaforth Highlanders *52*

Staff Captain *43*

Tank Corps *70, 71*

Territorials *53, 64–6, 69*

variations in uniform *54*

volunteers *18, 40*

West Yorkshire Regiment *48*

Western Front *46–55*

Westminster Dragoons *66*

yeomanry *64–6*

Greece *161, 184–5*

2nd Evzones Battalion *185*

2nd Infantry Regiment *185*

5th Infantry Regiment *184*

grenades *20*

headgear

Austro-Hungarian *230–2*

British *42–3, 49–51, 55, 57–9*

French *105*

German *203, 207*

Japanese *187*

Ottoman *243*

Russian *134–5*

helmet flashes, British *58–9*

helmets

British *55*

French *93*

▲ *The 7.7cm field gun, supplied by Germany to their Ottoman allies.*

horse furniture, British 63
howitzers *68, 221*

Indian Army 78–9
  29th Punjab Regiment *79*
  90th Punjab Regiment *78*
  Deccan Horse *79*
infantry
  American 162–5
  Austro-Hungarian 229–35
  Belgian 172–3
  British *45*, 46–55, 56–7
  Bulgarian 246
  French 88–97
  German 198, 200–7
  Greek 185
  Italian 176–7
  Ottoman 242–3
  Portuguese 170–1
  Russian 128, 130–1, 132–41
  South African 76–7
  weapons 20, 91, 233–4
insignia
  American 164–5
  British *49*, 55, 63
  French 89, *89*, 117
  Portuguese *171*
Italy 7, 8–9, 160–1
  1915 campaigns 27
  conscription 17
Italian Army 176–9
  3rd Alpini Regiment *179*
  17th Cavalry Regiment *179*
  23rd Infantry Regiment *178*
  33rd Infantry Regiment *177*
  115th Infantry Regiment *177*

Bersaglieri 177
General of Brigade *176*

jackets, British 43, 56–7
Japan 7, 161, 186–7
  2nd Infantry Regiment *186*
  72nd Infantry Regiment *187*
  Field Artillery *187*
  Jerusalem 31

Kenya 77
kit
  British *53*
  French *92, 114*
  Russian *131, 135–6, 137*
Serbian *181*
South African *77*

land transportation 21
lanterns *49*
leg wear, British 48, 56–7, 61

machine guns 20, *100*
Maxim 7, *146*
Middle East 29, 209
Montenegro 181
  4th Infantry Regiment *181*
mortar round *112*

naval warfare 7, 37
neutral states 15
New Zealand 75
  4th Waikato Mounted Rifles *75*
  17th Ruahine Regiment *75*

Ottoman Empire 7, 9, 225
  conscription 17–18
Ottoman Army 242–5
  35th Infantry Regiment *243*
  cavalry *244*
  Nisham Rifles *242*

Stormtroop, Palestine *244*
Turkish Artillery *245*
Turkish General *243*

Portugal 7, 8–9, 160
  10th Cavalry Regiment *170*
  20th Infantry Battalion *171*
  21st Infantry Battalion *170*
  colonial troops *171*
  other arms *171*
Princip, Gavrilo 11

von Richthofen, Manfred 223, *223*
Romania 161, 140, 182–3
  4th Artillery Regiment *183*
  5th Infantry Regiment *183*
  6th Infantry Regiment *182*
  10th Cavalry Regiment *182*
Russia 9, 12–13, 119, 120–1, 225
  1915 campaigns 27
  1916 campaigns 28–9
  1917 Revolution 31
  conscription 16
Russian Army 122–3
  1st Regiment *154*
  1st Volga Regiment *144*
  2nd Czech Regiment *141*
  2nd Regiment of Cavalry *154*
  3rd Special Purpose Regiment *138*
  4th Caucasian Rifles *137*
  5th Dragoons *142*
  6th Regiment, Orenburg *145*
  7th Shock Battalion *140*
  7th White Russia Hussars *143*
  9th Siberia Grenadiers *130*
  10th Rifle Regiment *151*
  10th Siberian Rifles *136*
  12th Foot Artillery Regiment *146*
  13th Belozerski Infantry Regiment *134*
  14th Olonetzki Infantry Regiment *133*
  15th Horse Artillery Regiment *147*
  16th Mingrelia Grenadiers *131*
  16th Rifles *137*
  18th Sapper Battalion *148*

▲ *A light field howitzer issued to the German artillery in 1909.*

▲ *German state cockades.*

42nd Yakutsk Regiment 152
51st Litovski Infantry Regiment 132
51st Rifle Regiment 150
53rd Rifle Regiment 150
80th Kabardinski Infantry Regiment 133
143rd Dorogobuyski Infantry Regiment 135
146th Infantry Regiment 135
Cossacks 144–5
Czech troops 141
elite units 124–5
engineers and sappers 148–9
Finland Guards Regiment 128
General of Cavalry 126, 127
General of Infantry 126
generals and staff 126–7
Grenadier regiments 130–1
Grenadier, 4th Rifle Brigade 139
grenadiers 138
Grodno Guards Hussar Regiment 129
guns, tanks and armoured cars 148
Imperial Guard 128–9
Kornilov's Shock Regiment 153
Kouper Regiment 144
Kuban Cossack Regiment 155
Life Guards Hussars 129
medical troops 149
Moscow Guards Regiment 128
officer training and promotion 123
pay and conditions 123–4
Pilot 149
Polish troops 140–1
Provisional Government 140
Railway Regiment 148
recruitment 125
Red Armies 150–1
regiments with royal patrons 134
rifle regiments 136–7
Romanian troops 140
Russian Legion 138, 139
Sevastopol Fortress Artillery 147
special purpose regiments 138–9
specialist troops 151

St George's Regiment 140
Staff Captain 127
Telegraphic Battalion 149
Volunteer Army 152–3
White Armies 152–3–5
Women's Battalion of Death 152

Serbia 180–1, 225
Austrian offensive 24
12th Infantry Regiment 180
2nd Infantry Regiment 180
shirts, British 48
shoulder details
American 165
British 47
German 196–7
Russian 130, 132, 133–4, 136, 147
Somme 28
South Africa
2nd South African Infantry Battalion 76
9th South African Battalion 76
technical troops
American 168–9
Austro-Hungarian 240–1
British 70–1
French 114–15
German 198–9, 222–3
Greek 185
Italian 178–9
Russian 129, 148–9
technological developments 7, 20–1
Treaty of Versailles 34–5
trench mortar 112

Uganda 77
uniforms 6–7
colour 22
evolution in the field 23
maintaining

regulations 22–3
modification 22
Unknown Soldier 35
USA 7, 157
conscription 19, 158–9
declaration of war 158
neutrality 158
social impact of war 159
USA Expeditionary Force
5th Marines 167
6th Marines 166, 167
9th Infantry 163
54th Infantry 164
125th Infantry 164
148th Aero Squadron 169
167th Infantry 163
370th Infantry 164
artillery and engineers 168–9
Engineer Corps 168
health and law 169
Major General 162
Marines 166–7
Military Police 168

Verdun 28, 81

weapons 20–1
Western Front 27
wound stripes
British 55
French 95

Yugoslavia 161

▼ *The Russian M1910 machine gun.*

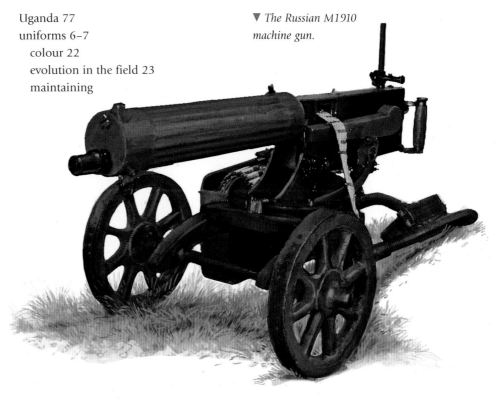

ACKNOWLEDGEMENTS

Thanks are due to the very professional team at Anness, particularly to Joanne Rippin (the patient and supportive project editor), Helen Sudell, Joy Wotton and Joanna Lorenz.

I would also like to thank Digby Smith, Kevin Kiley, and Alexander Mikaberidze, and Jeremy Black and Donald Sommerville for their helpful comments and sharp eyes. The staff at the London Library were tremendously helpful in sourcing and supplying obscure texts and a number of magazines and online forums have also proved of immense help. I am grateful to the editorial team at the French-language Militaria Magazine for providing astute and original articles on all aspects of this vast subject and to those in Russia responsible for Zeughaus Magazine. The artists who illustrated this volume: Peter Bull, Tom Croft, Jim Mitchell, Carlo Molinari, Simon Smith, Sailesh Thakrar, and Matthew Vince, deserve special praise for working with difficult sources and instructions. I thank them along with the diligent editors and proofreader.

Gratitude is also due to my family, especially to my wife, Evgenia, and son, Alexander. My father-in-law, Vasil Kirov, provided material, and my parents were a huge support. It has been a long, but educational, road.

▲ *Private, 6th Marines, 1918,*

Picture Acknowledgements
All figure and kit illustrations are the property of Anness Publishing.

The author and Publishers would like to thank the following picture agencies for permission to reproduce additional images:
Corbis: pp2, 8t, 10t, 11t, 11b, 12t, 12b, 13t, 13br, 14t, 14b, 15t, 15b, 16b, 16t, 17tl, 17tr, 17b, 18b, 18t, 19tl, 19tr, 19b, 20t, 20b, 21t, 21b, 23tl, 23tr, 24t, 25, 26b, 27t, 27b, 28b, 29t, 30b, 31tl, 31tr, 31b, 32b, 32t, 33b, 34t, 34b, 36, 39t, 40b, 41t, 41b, 47b, 49br, 54b, 56b, 80, 82b, 82t, 83t, 83b, 84t, 84b, 85t, 85b, 86t, 88t, 91t, 93t, 96t, 97b, 98b, 100t, 103t, 104t, 107b, 111t, 112t, 114t, 116t, 118, 120, 121t, 123b, 122, 123t, 123b, 124t, 124b, 125t, 126t, 136t, 139t, 141t, 149t, 151b, 153t, 156, 158b, 158t, 159tl, 159tr, 159b, 160t, 160b, 161t, 161b, 162t, 163t, 166t, 167t, 169t, 173t, 175t, 176br, 177t, 178b, 181b, 184t, 186b, 188, 190t, 190b, 191t, 191b, 192t, 193t, 193b, 194t, 194b, 195t, 195b, 197t, 203b, 209t, 212t, 220t, 221t, 222t, 224, 226t, 227, 228t, 229t, 229b, 241t, 242t, 245t, 246t, 248t, 248b, 249t, 249b, 250t, 250b.
Bridgeman Art Libary: 8b, 9t, 9b, 10b, 13bl, 22b, 22t, 23b, 28t, 38t, 38b, 39b, 40t, 57t.

▼ *The Gräf and Stift automobile was a popular staff car in the early years of the war. It was the vehicle of choice for the German and Austro-Hungarian imperial families, and Archduke Franz Ferdinand and his wife were assassinated in one as they drove through the streets of Sarajevo.*

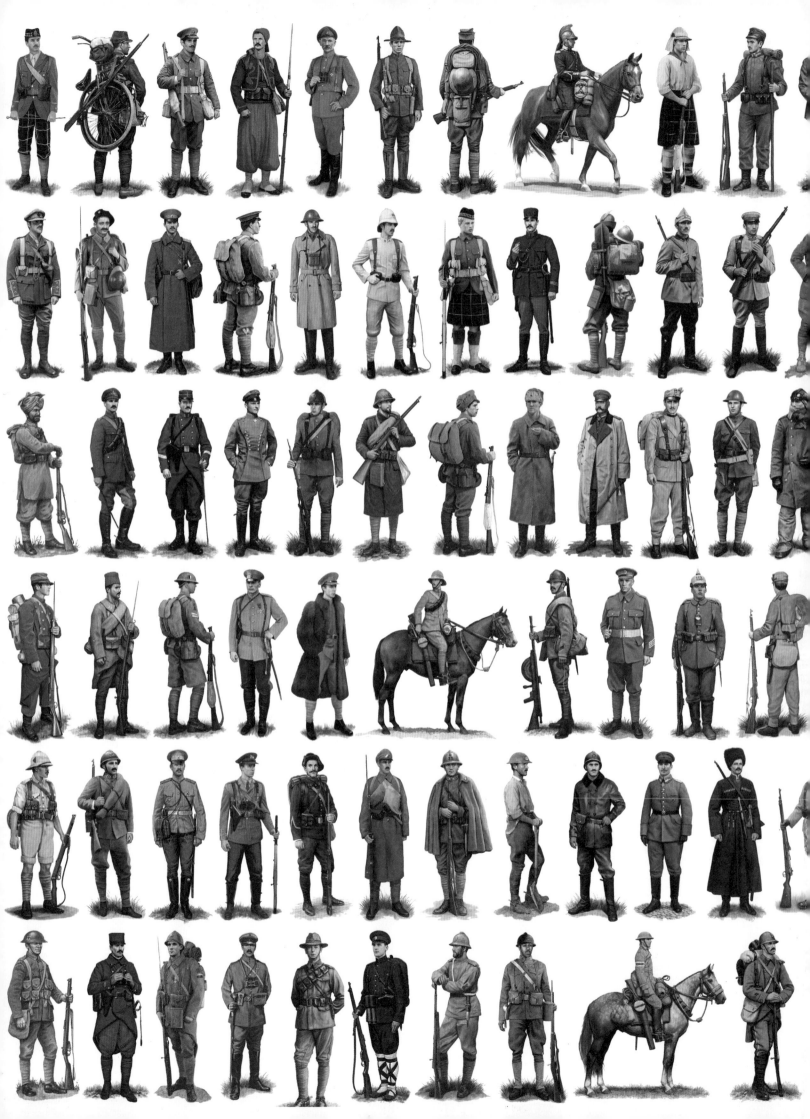